An Introduction to Field Phonetics

Managing Editor
Eric Kindberg

Technical Advisor
Mike Cahill

Volume Editor
Dirk Kievit

Copy Editors
Newton Frank
Barbara Shannon

Production Staff
Lois Gourley, Production Director
Judy Benjamin, Typesetter
Margaret González, Compositor
Randy Hasty, Compositor
Andy Keener, Graphic Artist
Barb Alber, Graphic Artist

Cover Image
"The vocal tract," adapted from Wikipedia, CC BY-SA 3.0
https://en.wikipedia.org/wiki/respiratory_tract

An Introduction to Field Phonetics

Norris P. McKinney and Carol V. McKinney

We regret that Norris McKinney passed away before he could review the final form of this book. We hope the final version is as he would have wanted it.

SIL International®
Dallas, Texas

© 2016 by SIL International®
Library of Congress Catalog Number: 2016960265
ISBN: 978-1-55671-400-9

Printed in the United States of America

All Rights Reserved

No part of this publication may be reproduced, stored in a retrieval system, or transmitted in any form or by any means—electronic, mechanical, photocopy, recording, or otherwise—without the express permission of SIL International, with the exception of brief excerpts in journal articles or reviews.

All sound waveform and spectogram images are © Norris P. McKinney. Used by permission.

All Wikipedia images are public domain, CC BY-SA 3.0.

All other images are adapted by Andy Keener from Wikipedia, "Pharynx," https://en.wikipedia.org/wiki/Pharynx, "Larynx," https://en.wikipedia.org/wiki/Larynx, and "Vocal folds," https://en.wikipedia.org/wiki/Vocal folds.

Copies of this and other publications of SIL International® may be obtained through distributors such as Amazon, Barnes & Noble, other worldwide distributors and, for select volumes, www.sil.org/resources/publications:

SIL International Publications
7500 W. Camp Wisdom Road
Dallas, Texas 75236-5629 USA

General inquiry: publications_intl@sil.org
Pending order inquiry: sales_intl@sil.org
www.sil.org/resources/publications

Contents

List of Figures..vii
List of Tables..ix
Dedication...xi
Preface..xiii
Acknowledgements..xv
1 Introduction..1
2 Anatomy of the Vocal Tract and Phonetic Features of Sounds.......7
3 Sagittal Diagrams..17
4 Fricatives...21
5 Stops..27
6 Vowels...35
7 Flaps, Taps, and Trills..47
8 Stress...51
9 Pitch and Intonation...55
10 Tone..59
11 Nasals..65
12 Nasalized Vowels..69
13 Sibilants...73
14 Palatal, Velar, and Uvular Consonants.........................77
15 Laterals..83
16 Length..87
17 Affricates..91
18 Voiceless Vowels and Glottal Consonants.......................95
19 Central Approximants and Labial Flaps.........................99
20 Double Stop and Double Nasal Articulations...................105
21 Secondary Articulations......................................109
22 Syllabic Consonants, Prenasalization, Preplosion of Nasals, and Apical Vowels .117
23 Phonation and Supralaryngeal Activity........................121
24 Ejectives and Implosives.....................................133

25 Releases, Transitions, Clusters, Glides, Gemination, and Juncture. 141
26 Fronted and Retroflex Consonants; Comprehensive Framework for Places
    of Articulation 149
27 Pharyngeal and Epiglottal Consonants 157
28 Advanced and Retracted Tongue Root Vowels. 161
29 Clicks 165
30 Fortis and Lenis Consonants; Controlled and Ballistic Syllables. 171
31 Speech Variants, Accents, Dialects, and Sociophonetics. 177
32 Palatography 187
33 Acoustic Phonetics 193
34 Phonetic Fieldwork 209
Appendices. 221
    Appendix A: International Phonetic Alphabet (IPA) 221
    Appendix B: Americanist Phonetic Alphabet (APA). 223
    Appendix C: Review Exercises for Chapters 1–20 .229
    Appendix D: Review Exercises for Chapters 21–34 233
Glossary. 239
References 271
Subject Index 275
Language Index 285

Figures

2.1	The vocal tract.	8
2.2	The head and neck.	9
2.3	Parts of the vocal apparatus.	10
2.4	Sagittal diagrams illustrating the nasal port open and closed.	12
2.5	Places of articulation	14
3.1	Airstream mechanism and velic closure.	17
3.2	States of the vocal folds	18
3.3	Placement of velum	18
3.4	Place and manner of articulation	19
4.1	Sagittal diagrams of voiced fricatives [β] and [ɣ]	23
5.1	Sagittal diagrams illustrating the contrast between a stop [g] and a fricative [ɣ] produced at the same place of articulation	28
5.2	Sagittal diagram of a glottal stop	29
5.3	Voice Onset Time (VOT).	30
6.1	Relative tongue positions in production of [i] and [u].	35
6.2	English vowel chart	36
6.3	Tongue height positions for [i] and [æ].	37
6.4	Partial classification of speech sounds	38
6.5	Cardinal vowels.	39
6.6	IPA vowel diagram.	40
11.1	Sagittal diagrams illustrating the difference between a stop and a nasal	66
13.1	Typical tongue shapes for flat fricatives and sibilants	73
14.1	Three voiceless fricatives: palatal [ç], velar [x], and uvular [χ] consonants	78
14.2	Sounds with palatal, velar, and uvular places of articulation	79
15.1	Tongue shapes for fricatives and laterals	83
20.1	Stops [p], [k], and labial-velar double stop [k͡p]	107
21.1	Sagittal diagrams of [p] and [pⱼ] or [pʲ]	110
21.2	Sagittal diagrams of [d] and [d̞] or [dˠ]	111
21.3	Sagittal diagrams of [d] and [d̞] or [dˤ]	112

23.1	Antero-lateral view of the larynx	122
23.2	Posterior view of the larynx	122
23.3	The larynx	123
23.4	The vocal folds	123
23.5	The vocal folds in breathing and speaking	125
24.1	Sagittal diagrams of [k], [k'], and [ʔ]	134
24.2	Sagittal diagrams of [k̠] and [ɡ̠]	136
26.1	Sagittal diagrams of dental, alveolar, and retroflex stops	150
26.2	Sagittal diagrams of fronted postalveolar and postalveolar stops	151
27.1	Sagittal diagram of a voiceless pharyngeal fricative [ħ]	157
29.1	Sagittal diagrams of voiced and voiceless bilabial clicks	167
33.1	The waveform during a brief interval in N. McKinney's pronunciation of the vowel [ɔ] in [ɔɹe͡ɪntʃɨs] 'oranges'	195
33.2	The waveform during a brief interval in N. McKinney's pronunciation of the voiceless sibilant [s] in [ɔɹe͡ɪntʃɨs] 'oranges'	195
33.3	The waveform of the phrase, 'oranges, apples, and pears'	196
33.4	Sound spectrogram of 'he, hay, high, how'	197
33.5	Sound spectrogram of 'ha!, hoe, who'	197
33.6	Sound spectrogram of 'way'	200
33.7	Sound spectrogram of 'bay'	201
33.8	Sound spectrogram of 'may'	201
33.9	Sound spectrogram of 'rack'	202
33.10	Sound spectrogram of 'ray'	202
33.11	Sound spectrogram of 'say sea'	203
33.12	Sound spectrogram of 'she's where?'	203
33.13	Sound spectrogram of 'say gnaw'	204
33.14	Sound spectrogram of 'lease'	204
34.1	Throat microphone in use	216

Tables

1.1	Phonetics versus phonics	2
2.1	Airstream mechanisms	10
2.2	Articulators and places of articulation	13
4.1	Fricatives	21
5.1	Stops	27
5.2	Kiowa stops	28
6.1	Phonetic features of vowels	38
6.2	Diacritics representing slight differences in vowel quality	42
7.1	Flaps, taps, and trills	48
7.2	Tongue movements in taps and flaps	48
10.1	Tone notation	61
11.1	Nasal consonants	65
12.1	Passageways and manners of articulation	70
13.1	Sibilants	73
14.1	Palatal, velar, and uvular consonants	77
14.2	Effect of place of articulation on chamber size and sound quality	79
15.1	Laterals (printed style)	84
15.2	Laterals (handwritten style)	84
16.1	Symbols and names for length	87
17.1	Homorganic central affricates	92
17.2	Lateral affricates	92
18.1	Glottal stop, glottal fricative, and breathy glottal fricative	96
19.1	Central approximants	99
19.2	Examples of approximants in English	100
19.3	Correspondence between vowels and approximants/semivowels	101
20.1	Double stops and double nasals	106
21.1	Summary of symbols for secondary articulations	113
22.1	English syllabic consonants	118
23.1	Breathy stops and affricates	126

23.2	Types of phonation in terms of airflow	130
24.1	Ejectives	134
24.2	Implosives	136
25.1	Release of consonants	142
25.2	Consonant clusters in English words	143
26.1	Dental, alveolar, and postalveolar consonants; fronted and retroflex consonants	151
26.2	Articulator modifications	152
26.3	Terminology summarizing the place of articulatory gestures	153
28.1	Possible phonetic features for advanced and retracted tongue root vowels	162
28.2	Akan vowel harmony sets	163
29.1	Clicks	165
30.1	Etic tendencies for fortis-lenis consonants	172
30.2	Phonetic contrasts of Jju fortis and lenis consonants	173
30.3	Summary of fortis-lenis consonants in Jju	173
30.4	Examples of three-way Korean consonant contrast	174
31.1	Dialect differences in automobile vocabulary for British and American English	178
33.1	Formant frequencies of midwestern American English vowels	198
33.2	Vowel formant chart, with formant frequencies F1 *versus* F2-F1 plotted for averages of American English vowel data	199
33.3	Acoustic correlates of consonantal features	205
33.4	Summary of concepts and methods for acoustic analysis of speech	206

This book is dedicated to the memory of
Dr. Kenneth L. Pike and Dr. Peter Ladefoged:
excellent phoneticians, mentors, colleagues,
friends, and sources of inspiration.

Dr. Kenneth L. Pike

© 1998, Christy McKinney Westerman. Used by permission.

Dr. Peter Ladefoged

© 2004, Christy McKinney Westerman. Used by permission.

Preface

The goal of this book is to introduce phonetics to those who plan to do linguistic and cross-cultural fieldwork. Many fieldworkers study languages for which little help is available to assist in learning and analyzing the languages of the people with whom they work. Progress in fulfilling these goals often depends upon learning to identify, transcribe, and produce speech sounds drawn from the wide variety of sounds that the human vocal apparatus is capable of making, including some that are not found in the fieldworker's own language. To help fieldworkers prepare for these challenges, they need an introduction to articulatory and instrumental phonetics, including acoustic phonetics.

We wrote this book primarily for those planning to do linguistic and anthropological fieldwork. However, we believe that it will also be useful to many who are preparing for other professions, such as dialectographers, speech pathologists, speech therapists, singers, language surveyors, teachers of English as a second language, and those who are teaching or learning another language.

Some people study phonetics as an aid to learning to speak and understand a particular language. They need to master only a few of the amazing variety of distinctions that exist between speech sounds in a stream of speech. Other people need to study most of the possible distinctions between speech sounds. These include phoneticians, students of more than one language, and linguistic consultants.

The phonetic data that field linguists collect are the physical basis for their phonological analyses of the languages they study; therefore, any phonological analysis is only as good as the phonetic data upon which it is based. Most linguists routinely use articulatory phonetics. Articulation refers to the physiological movements and positions of those parts of the body (in the chest, larynx, pharynx, mouth, and nose) that contribute to the production of speech sounds. All of these work together to produce the sequences of vowels and consonants, syllables and stresses, tones and intonation in a stream of speech. In order to collect accurate field data and produce well reasoned analyses of phonetic data, linguists need to understand, and have the ability to apply articulatory phonetics. This subject is essential both for language learning and for linguistic analysis.

Articulatory phonetics forms the core of this book. The model introduced here should appear quite familiar to instructors using the text who have used the traditional SIL phonetics curriculum. At the same time it includes several changes in concepts and terminology that have entered the field of phonetics in recent years. It incorporates knowledge that has been gained through quantitative research, using scientific methods of measurement, especially acoustic phonetics, and it includes exercises using instrumentation as sophisticated as signal analysis on a laptop computer. In the final chapter we discuss the place of phonetics in fieldwork.

This text introduces sounds by individual categories, such as consonants (e.g., fricatives, nasals, stops, sibilants, laterals, approximants) and vowels, the use of pitch as tone and intonation, and much more. Of particular potential help to field linguists are the sections on ways of studying sounds instrumentally, such as through palatography and acoustic phonetics. There are also useful computer programs that enable a field linguist to study individual sounds, as well as the pitch of the voice.

Although this text provides symbols to write most of the known speech sounds and modifications of these sounds, when working on any particular language the field linguist will be studying a small subset of sounds, namely those present in that language. And if you are one of those fortunate fieldworkers who encounters a new sound, the phonetic knowledge in this textbook will provide the framework such that you can write that new sound. Further, it is important to let the wider linguistic world know about your discovery so that others may learn of the new sound(s) you discovered. This book will provide a framework for your phonetic description of those sounds.

In the text the first mention of a key term (or sometimes where it is defined) is in SMALL UPPER CASE TYPE; at the end of each chapter there is a list of the concepts introduced in that chapter. Each of these key terms is defined both in the text and in the glossary.

In this book the International Phonetic Alphabet (IPA) is used in place of the Americanist Phonetic Alphabet (APA), an alphabet that Pike taught and contributed to. The APA was designed to be viable as a "font" for use on a typewriter with only minor adaptations. The APA is still the phonetic "lingua franca" for many linguists doing research on languages of the Americas, and it is included in Appendix B. The IPA, which is introduced in this book, has far more adherents than the APA.

Acknowledgements

We owe a debt of deep gratitude to those who have contributed significantly to the field of linguistics in general and to phonetics in particular. The late Kenneth L. Pike (1912–2000) early contributed to phonetic theory by writing his 1943 monograph *Phonetics* and teaching from it. William C. Townsend, founder of the Summer Institute of Linguistics (SIL), had asked Pike to write such a book, and he eventually wrote it as his doctoral dissertation after he broke his leg and was unable to continue his fieldwork among the Mixteco for a while. Pike taught many students the practical art of recognizing, transcribing, classifying, and reproducing most of the sounds of the world's languages.

Kenneth Pike and William Smalley introduced face diagrams, which are also called *sagittal diagrams*. They are an aid to visualize various contrasts in place of articulation, manner of articulation, and the airstream mechanism used to produce particular sounds. Smalley made an important contribution in his two-volume textbook *Manual of Articulatory Phonetics* (1963; reprinted 1989) by including in each lesson lists of words (many of them artificial) to give students practice in saying sounds in various contexts.

Eunice V. Pike taught phonetics for many years and compiled *Dictation Exercises in Phonetics* (1963). Her book provides exercises for teachers to dictate to their students. We have included a number of language examples from this book and have acknowledged their source when we do so. The examples from Eunice Pike's book have been transliterated from the Americanist Phonetic Alphabet, in which it was originally written, to the International Phonetic Alphabet. We gratefully acknowledge her contribution to this book.

Rick Floyd compiled *A Manual for Articulatory Phonetics* (1981) from lesson plans used in SIL phonetics courses. We sat with Floyd at our kitchen table as we worked with him, helping him edit his compilation. We originally thought this book would be a revision of Floyd's *Manual*. However, Anita Bickford and Rick Floyd have since revised Floyd's manual extensively (Bickford and Floyd 2006). Our book follows the same general outline that SIL schools have used since their earliest days, but with significant changes and additions that update the course according to more current phonetic concepts. Both in remote field locations and in the laboratory, computer technology now makes it both practical and useful to analyze speech sounds in a way that formerly was possible only in specialized laboratories.

Other contributors to the theory and practice of phonetics include Ian Catford, Daniel Jones, Peter Ladefoged, John Laver, Ilse Lehiste, and Ian Maddieson. Ladefoged (1925–2006) was, no doubt, the most broadly knowledgeable and well-known phonetician in the world. He contributed greatly to the study of phonetics in languages throughout the world and certainly influenced our understanding of speech sounds, especially through his writings and through personal contact. We were privileged to work with him briefly. Norris McKinney's mentor was the late Gordon E. Peterson, who co-wrote with

Barney (1952) the enduring classic on the acoustic properties of English vowels, among other subjects. He was a speech scientist par excellence.

We are grateful to many for their help with this manuscript in a variety of ways. The following listing is merely representative and certainly fails to include some who should be recognized, but whose contribution we may have inadvertently forgotten.

We are indebted to Ruth Mary Alexander, Kathryn Keller, William Sischo, Rick Floyd, and May Morrison. We wish to acknowledge Anita Bickford's many valuable contributions to this book. Most of Norris McKinney's teaching assistants have also contributed significantly to this book: Gene Burnham, the late Betsy Edwards, David Whisler, Geoffrey Smotherman, Rita Carter Blake, Laura Nelson de Dios, Darryl Wilson, Darrell Fisher, Mike Cahill, Coleen Anderson Starwalt, Mary Pearce, and others who made suggestions for improving the manuscript as they taught from various trial editions of this book. We thank Pete Unseth for providing many valuable examples from Ethiopian languages as well as encouragement as we wrote this book.

We thank Ken Olsen for his editorial comments that have improved the quality of this manuscript. We are indebted to Lou Hohulin, an experienced field linguist, who reviewed the first few chapters and contributed her suggestions, to Kalon Kelley who made valuable suggestions through reviewing the entire manuscript, and to Christy Glick who provided a student's view for a few chapters. We wish to express our thanks to Joy Sanders who brought to our attention various things that needed correction, and who added written exercises to many chapters. Peter Backstrom contributed significantly by providing phonetic data to use as exercises. We are also grateful to Eric Albright who developed the markup system for formatting this book, the figures, and the tables. Andy Keener drew the sagittal diagrams. We are especially grateful to the many linguists whose field data have been cited in this work. Thanks to all who have contributed so significantly to the book and to our understanding of phonetics. We are deeply indebted to you.

We would also like to express our deep gratitude to the Bajju people in Nigeria, with whom we lived for eight and one-half years. We have continued to study their language and culture and have kept in touch with some of our many Bajju friends. We have cited their language, Jju, numerous times. Our time with the Bajju was the highlight of our lives. They adopted us as their own and often referred to us as *Bashong*, the 'red Bajju'. We would like to acknowledge the contributions of the late M. Zacharia Gaiya, the late Rev. Karick Mikai, the Rev. Iliya Ahuwan, Dr. Abashiya Ahuwan, the late M. Elisha Sambo, the late M. Simon Waziri, M. Haruna Karick, the late M. Yabo Bayei, M. Yabo Yashim, the Rev. Chidawa Kabruck, the Rev. Dr. Musa Asake, Dr. Samuela Waje, and the late M. Daniel Hyuwa, a Bajju linguist with whom we were privileged to work. We express our deepest gratitude to His Excellency Chief Nuhu M. Bature, Agwam Bajju (the chief of the Bajju) with whom we spent many hours in insightful conversation about the Bajju culture, history, and language. May his wise reign long continue. We are also grateful to the late Bulus Tauna for the Atyap data.

Finally, we thank our children, Mark, Eric, Susan, and Christine, who have encouraged us in so many ways. In particular, we want to express our thanks to Christine, who took the phonetics course and made significant suggestions for improvements to this book. She also took the photos of Kenneth Pike and Peter Ladefoged.

Norris and Carol McKinney

1
Introduction

PHONETICS, in its most general form, is the study of sounds that people regularly make in speaking any of the over 6,000 languages spoken in the world. *Phonetic* science studies the characteristics of speech sounds, distinguishing each sound from all the others. It also classifies speech sounds. Phonetic science examines the physiology of speech production, speech perception, and acoustic parameters of human speech sounds.

The student preparing to do phonetic fieldwork must learn the art of recognizing each of the phonetic characteristics of speech sounds, pronouncing sounds clearly in context, and transcribing speech sounds using a standard phonetic writing system, usually the International Phonetic Alphabet (IPA).

Everyone has valuable knowledge and skills gained in learning their first language which help greatly in learning a second language. Speakers of every language develop amazing skills in both hearing and reproducing the subtle contrasts between similar sounds in their language. These skills begin early in life.

No one manages to acquire the phonetic skill of a native speaker for all languages. Yet competent speakers have learned both to recognize and to produce acceptably all of the sounds of their own language, often called their MOTHER TONGUE. Many people also learn one or more other languages besides their mother tongue, often called LANGUAGES OF WIDER COMMUNICATION (LWC), or TRADE LANGUAGES. Everyone brings these hidden skills to the task of learning phonetics.

We can learn phonetic pointers by observing how babies acquire their language skills, and then apply that knowledge to adult language learning. Babies begin life with the ability to differentiate all possible speech sounds; this ability lasts until approximately six months of age. Next they begin to categorize sounds into those that are specific to the language spoken by those around them. They learn acceptable sound combinations in that language, and they also focus on pitch and stress patterns. When they begin to speak at approximately twelve months of age, they mimic individual utterances multiple times. Thus, the sound patterns become ingrained in their brains such that they can readily produce them. The sounds they initially produce they gradually modify to be more in line with the standard pronunciation of speakers of the language. (See Gopnik, Meltzoff, and Kuhl 1999 for further information on infant language acquisition.) As adults we can learn to mimic and gradually modify our pronunciation until it is more in line with that of native speakers of the language we are studying.

Phonetics vs. phonics

Many people who have studied PHONICS in primary school may ask, "Why must I study phonetics again?" Table 1.1 summarizes the differences between phonetics and phonics.

Table 1.1. Phonetics versus phonics

Phonetics	Phonics
A method of studying speech sounds including their production, perception, transcription, acoustic characteristics, and physiology.	A method of teaching reading, writing, and spelling using a system of simple phonetic symbols and rules (Stein and Su 1978:673) so that the learner may pronounce a sequence of graphic symbols.
It is applicable to any language.	Its application is usually limited to one language.
It includes all possible speech sounds.	It includes a limited subset of speech sounds for one language only.

Whereas a good course in phonetics teaches how to recognize, pronounce, and transcribe a large number of speech sounds, phonics teaches speech sounds and their symbols for reading one's own language. This limited subset likely fails to include all the sounds needed for an accurate and complete study of the phonetics of any language other than the one for which phonics was applied.

Articulatory phonetics vs. instrumental phonetics

ARTICULATION refers to the physiological movements and positions of those parts of the body that contribute to the production of speech sounds. Thus, ARTICULATORY PHONETICS is the branch of phonetics that studies the ways in which sounds are produced by movements and positions (articulations) of various parts of the vocal apparatus in the chest, larynx, pharynx, mouth, and nose, all of which work together to produce the sequences of vowels and consonants, syllables and stresses, and tones and intonation in a stream of speech.

While much of the focus in this book is on traditional articulatory phonetics, two chapters deal with other branches. INSTRUMENTAL PHONETICS is the study of speech sounds using various instruments, such as airflow measurement devices, pressure transducers, palatography, fiber-optic laryngoscopes, sound spectrographs, etc. Most of the methods of instrumental phonetics are not appropriate for an introductory textbook. The two topics we have included are PALATOGRAPHY, a means of ascertaining where a sound is articulated on the palate, and acoustic phonetics. ACOUSTIC PHONETICS is the study of the physical properties of the sound wave as it moves from one person's vocal apparatus to another person's ears. The sound wave may be viewed graphically on a display, as from a speech analyzer computer program or a sound spectrograph.

Language interference

When a native speaker of a language is learning to speak another language, the sound patterns of the learner's mother tongue often interfere with identifying and producing unfamiliar sounds. Phoneticians call this LANGUAGE INTERFERENCE. For example, when the Bajju people in Nigeria pronounced the name of our son, Eric, they said "Ori." In Jju, the language of the Bajju people, [ɛ] never occurs at the beginning of a syllable, so the closest they came to it was 'o'.[1] Further, there is no final 'c' [k], so they simply left it off.

A second example from Kenneth Pike (as cited in Pike et al. 1996:44) follows:

> Kenneth Pike had been studying the Mixtec language of Mexico (an Indian group in the highlands of Oaxaca) for some time. One day, however, his Mixtec language teacher decided to try to hear and pronounce an American word. So he asked Pike: "How do you say *cuchi* in your language?" Pike replied: "pig". The native speaker of Mixtec replied, mimicking it as best he could: "wheel". Pike repeated: "pig!!"; the other replied, again: "wheel", and never did much better than that. Why not? The reasons included the following: (1) He had no final consonants

---
[1] Jju is a Benue-Congo language spoken by over 400,000 people in the Middle Belt in Kaduna State, Nigeria.

in his language, so he could not find one to use for /-g/; but he used, even in Mixtec, a few words from Spanish. One Spanish word he used was *sal* for "salt"—so he used the /-l/ from that, instead of the /-g/. (2) He also had no difference between words such as "beat" and "bit" that English has; so he used the closest sound which he does have, which was the vowel of "wheel". (3) Finally, he had no initial consonants with a puff of breath (as aspiration) after it, as English /p-/ does in "pig"; but he reacted (unconsciously) to the fact that it was made with both lips involved—and he knew a Spanish word which had an aspiration related to (but preceding) a labial sound, as in *juez* (for "judge"—where the "ju-" is pronounced as /hw/); so he used the /hw-/ for that. What incredibly elegant action, with such cross-culturally unintelligible results!

The fact that language interference occurs provides good motivation for learning phonetics. The goal is to help you produce sounds that occur in whatever language you may study. Then, when you begin to learn a particular language with sounds that are not in your mother tongue, you will likely be able to pronounce them.

Idiophones and ideophones in idiolects

While this text focuses on sounds produced in human languages, there are some sounds in languages that are not part of the regular sound systems. These are idiophones occurring in idiolects, and ideophones.

An IDIOPHONE is "a speech sound identifiable with reference to a single idiolect" (Crystal 2003:226).[2] Since an idiophone is described with reference to an idiolect, what is an idiolect? An IDIOLECT is "the linguistic system of an individual speaker—one's personal dialect" (Crystal 2003:225). Some people have their own idiolect in which they substitute sounds in their version of the language that are not standard. For example, one of our relatives regularly used a *glottalized* 'k' in final positions in English words, such as in 'pick,' even though glottalized 'k' [k'] does not occur in standard English (more on glottalized consonants later).

An IDEOPHONE is a word that gives a vivid representation of an idea in sound. Ideophones are a special class of expressive words that are used to describe sounds, smells, colors, shapes, manners, etc. They are often interjections, picture words, and words that have onomatopoeia (Welmers 1973:461). Barley (1986:114–115) relates his encounter with such sounds when the Dowayo in Cameroon described to him the sounds associated with smells, particularly *his* smells, which they were afraid would interfere with their hunting expedition:

> It was hoped, remarked one old man, that the smell of the White Man would not frighten away the game. Smell, what did they mean? I washed every day. Had they not seen? Indeed, this was part of the problem, like as not. Possibly part of the smell was soap. White men all smelled. What was it like? Dowayos have a rich series of odd sounds to describe smells, conventionalized but not strictly part of the language, rather like our 'ouch' or 'bang'. A hot debate arose as to whether I was *sok, sok, sok* (like rotten meat, Matthieu helpfully explained) or *virr* (stale milk), to which all lustily contributed…this conversation came as something of a revelation. I promised to keep downwind.

Often ideophones conform to the sound system of a language, as in 'bang' and 'ouch.' However, some sounds occur only in ideophones. For example, in English the click sounds occur only as ideophones and interjections; they are not part of the regular sound system. In cartoons and other writings for English-speaking non-linguists, the click expressing disapproval is written as 'Tsk! Tsk!' This use of clicks contrasts with clicks functioning as full consonants, as in Khoisan languages of southern Africa.

The goal in discussing idiophones, ideophones, and idiolects at this point is to encourage you to be willing to produce sounds that do not occur in your native language, to be willing to sound different, to play with sounds, and to enjoy the creativity of sound.

---

[2] An idiophone is also a type of musical instrument.

Studying sounds

When you listen to audio recordings of phonetic sounds, listen to multiple repetitions of particular sounds. This can be very beneficial in learning them. It is also helpful to have a teacher who is proficient in producing each new sound that you encounter in this course, a teacher who requires you to mimic, practice, recognize, and transcribe the sounds. Such practice allows you to internalize the sounds and the pitch patterns associated with them. In mimicry the goal is to be able to reproduce quickly and accurately sounds in words, phrases, and sentences in another language. In addition, you will also learn to transcribe, i.e., to write down, discrete sounds together with their pitch patterns.

Suppose you hear someone say something and then repeat it. You may judge that the two utterances were said exactly in the same way. However, at some level of detail, no two utterances are *ever* said in *exactly* the same way. It is best to have several different teachers so that you learn the speech patterns of more than one individual. Further, application of what you learn in this course to a language other than English is helpful and practical. You may be amazed at the new skills and abilities you develop as you read and follow this text.

Transcribing sounds

Over the centuries people have been very creative in the ways they have written down spoken language. In transcribing sounds and syllables, people developed early pictographs, cuneiform writing, syllabic writing systems (e.g., Korean, Amharic, and Japanese), the Mayan graphs, the *Ajami* script for writing Arabic, Devanagari script for writing Sanskrit, Cyrillic script used for writing Russian and related Slavic languages, the Greek alphabet, the Roman alphabet, and other lesser known scripts.

Phoneticians have long recognized the need for a common writing system that can be applied to languages throughout the world. Consequently, they developed the INTERNATIONAL PHONETIC ALPHABET (IPA) which combines individual letter symbols with superscripts, subscripts, and diacritics to represent speech sounds. The AMERICANIST PHONETIC ALPHABET (APA) is another useful writing system, designed to use symbols that are readily available on a typewriter. (See Appendices A and B for IPA and APA charts.)

This text uses IPA because it is the most widely used phonetic writing system. Also, the IPA continues to be refined as linguists encounter new sounds in various little-known, often endangered, languages. The goal of using the IPA is that the data collected are readily pronounceable and readable by any linguist who knows this system. It provides a consistent system that can be used when writing sounds in a wide variety of languages. It also introduces the SOUND-SYMBOL CONCEPT, with one sound represented by one symbol or a symbol plus one or more diacritics, with or without pitch marked. While it is not always possible to achieve this goal in a practical alphabet (an orthography used for writing a language by the general population), in phonetic writing this is the goal. In a practical ORTHOGRAPHY it may be necessary to use two or more symbols to write a particular sound, e.g., 'wh', 'th', 'sh', and 'ng'.

There are many symbols in IPA that look rather similar to others. Thus it is important to write phonetic symbols carefully, adhering closely to the standard shapes shown on the IPA chart. There are significant differences between how some phonetic symbols will look depending on whether they are handwritten, typed on a typewriter, or printed from a computer. One example is [ɡ], which on a standard typewriter is 'g'. In addition, the glottal stop symbol, 'ʔ', can be handwritten without the serif at the bottom; notice also that there should be no dot below this symbol as is present with a question mark '?'.

The symbol 't', when handwritten, needs to have a curved tail on it, not just a straight vertical line. This is to differentiate it from 'l' (which will sometimes have a horizontal line through it) and from other phonetic symbols with which it may be confused.

Key terms

    mother tongue
    Language of Wider Communication (LWC), trade language

1: Introduction

- phonics
- articulation
- phonetics
    - articulatory phonetics
    - instrumental phonetics
    - acoustic phonetics
- palatography
- language interference
- idiophone
- idiolect
- ideophone
- International Phonetic Alphabet
- Americanist Phonetic Alphabet
- sound-symbol concept
- orthography

2

Anatomy of the Vocal Tract and Phonetic Features of Sounds

Speech sounds group naturally into classes according to how speakers use different parts of their vocal tracts. Our understanding of the anatomy of the vocal tract and the functions of its parts in speaking provides us with a good foundation for learning field phonetics, including both articulatory and acoustic phonetics. This chapter introduces the anatomy of speech production. It also presents variables used by phoneticians to describe and identify specific sounds. In particular it introduces what occurs below the LARYNX, at the larynx, and above it. Chapter 23 goes into more detail about different types of voicing that are produced in the larynx.

Below the larynx

Take a very deep breath and hold it a moment. Now, start reciting something that you know so well you do not have to think about what you are saying and can concentrate on how you are saying it: for example, say your name, address, or telephone number. Keep talking without taking a breath until you are quite out of breath. Do this again and again until you have completed the observations described below.

In this exercise as you speak, think first about the origin of the energy that is the source of the power of the speech sound wave; where did the energy come from? When you took a very deep breath, you put appreciable energy into expanding your lung cavity. Surrounding your lung cavity are your ribs that are hinged to your STERNUM (breast bone) at the front, and to your spinal column at the back. When your respiratory muscles are at rest, your ribs droop downward like the leaves on a thirsty plant. When you took a deep breath in preparation for talking, you lifted your ribs and they spread outward, thus enlarging the volume of your rib cage. The EXTERNAL INTERCOSTAL MUSCLES, the outer layer of muscles running between adjacent ribs, contribute most to this movement. The INTERNAL INTERCOSTAL MUSCLES are more active in exhaling, as when you are speaking.

While you were tensing your external intercostal muscles to lift your ribs, you were also tensing your DIAPHRAGM, a dome-shaped muscle that separates your thoracic cavity from your abdominal cavity. Since your diaphragm is concave, contracting it added to the expansion of your thoracic cavity, but at the expense of some of your viscera having to move aside. Your abdominal muscles obligingly relaxed and bulged outward until the vocal tract again needed air pressure for exhalation. At that time your abdominal muscles began to tense, pushing inward on your viscera which pushed upward on your diaphragm which in turn pushed upward on your lungs which pushed upward on the air in your lungs, forcing the airstream out through your vocal tract. You needed that airstream so long as you were to keep on talking. See figure 2.1 for a diagram of the vocal tract.

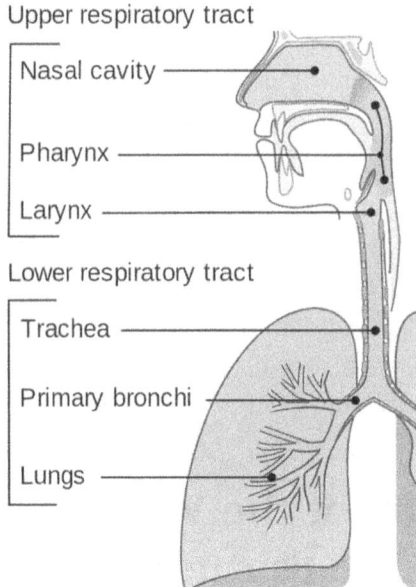

Figure 2.1. The vocal tract.
Wikipedia.org/wiki/Respiratory_tract#Lower_respiratory_tract.
Accessed 20 October 2009.

Thus the muscular effort you used to expand your lung cavity stored up energy. When you began to relax those muscles, the tensions that opposed expansion of your lung cavity during inhalation now provided the energy to force air to flow out of your lungs. As you continued to speak, the volume of air in your lungs depleted continually until the muscles of inhalation relaxed to the point of being barely able to supply the air pressure you needed in order to keep talking. At some point the muscles of exhalation began to contract, supplementing the waning effect of relaxing the muscles of inhalation in order to continue speaking.

Some of the energy in this airflow under pressure produces sound by causing the VOCAL FOLDS (also called the VOCAL CORDS) to vibrate, which in turn chops the airflow into pulses. Some of this energy becomes *noise* by forcing the air to pass through a narrow CONSTRICTION. Some of the energy becomes a burst that occurs when the air trapped under pressure behind a CLOSURE in its path is suddenly released, like the "Pop!" that occurs when a balloon is pricked with a pin.

In the exercise above, at some point you had to begin tensing muscles—a different set of muscles—to further reduce the volume of the lung cavity and maintain air pressure adequate to keep producing speech sounds.

The larynx

Many speech sounds are VOICED; air flowing from the lungs passes upward first through the TRACHEA, then through the LARYNX, and into the PHARYNX. As it passes between the *vocal folds,* the air causes them to vibrate if they are positioned and tensioned properly (*folds* is a more accurate descriptive term than *cords*). The vocal folds are located in the larynx. The open area between the vocal folds is called the GLOTTIS; and if there is no open area between them, the glottis is closed. Typically the vibrations alternately open and close the glottis, thus chopping the flow of air into pulses of air. See figure 2.2 for a diagram of the pharynx.

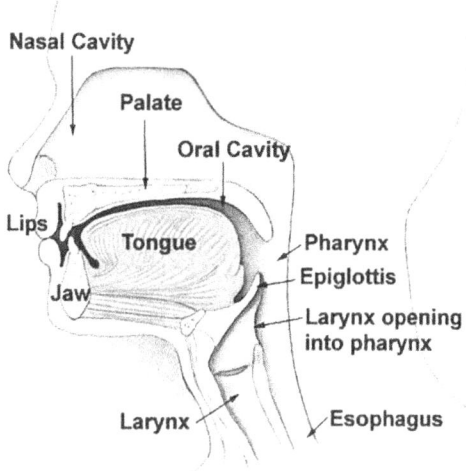

Figure 2.2. The head and neck.
Wikipedia.org/wiki/Pharynx
Accessed 20 October 2009.

Above the larynx

The TONGUE is so central to spoken language that we call languages "tongues." The tongue, aided by the jaw and collaborating with the lips and the soft palate, modifies the sound and airstream emanating from the larynx to produce a myriad of sounds. These sounds are the vehicles by which we instruct, console, entertain, reprimand, and command.

The SOFT PALATE or VELUM can be lowered to open the way into the nasal cavity, or raised to close it. The lips and the tongue can close or constrict the airstream and thus keep sounds from passing through the mouth, or they can so constrict the airstream that air turbulence generates significant noise. The quality of any speech sound depends on the shape of the tongue and the lips. Thus, in the remainder of this book, we will focus mainly on activities and configurations of the tongue, together with the lips and soft palate.

Phonetic features of sound

As described above, speech sounds are produced by an airstream in the vocal tract that is moved and modified by the tongue, the pharynx, and the glottis. Linguists identify and classify speech sounds according to several PHONETIC FEATURES. These features specify where the airstream is coming from (e.g., the lungs, the pharynx, or the mouth) and in which DIRECTION it is moving, whether inward or outward. Phonetic features also describe what happens to the airstream, resulting in audible vibrations (e.g., air passing through a constriction), what articulation modifies the vibrations (e.g., the narrowing of the opening through which the sound passes), and what parts of the vocal apparatus cause this. This book uses five main phonetic features to identify speech sounds: the airstream mechanism and direction of the airstream, state of the vocal folds and vocal cavities, velic opening or closure, manner of articulation, and place of articulation. Figure 2.3 presents parts of the vocal apparatus that should help you as the five main features of sound identification are discussed.

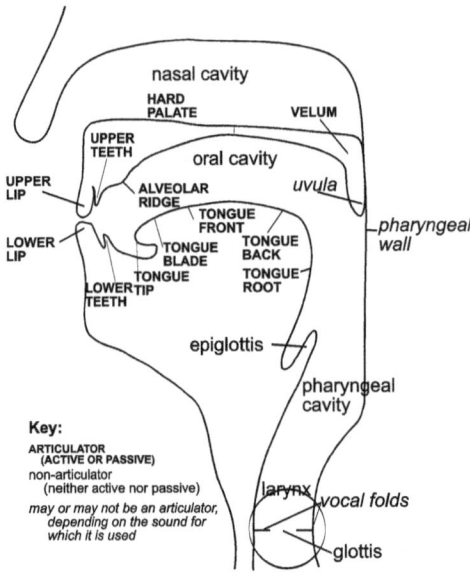

Figure 2.3. Parts of the vocal apparatus.

1. Airstream mechanism and direction of airstream

An AIRSTREAM MECHANISM initiates the motion of the air used in speaking. There are three ways in which air in the vocal tract can be set in motion and thus provide the energy for speech sounds. The airstream mechanism of a speech sound is PULMONIC if the air comes from the lungs in the PULMONIC CAVITY, GLOTTALIC if the air comes from the pharynx in the PHARYNGEAL CAVITY, and VELARIC if the motion is initiated by the back of the tongue against the velum in the ORAL CAVITY.

A CAVITY or chamber in the vocal tract changes size due to muscular contraction, thus initiating the motion of the air. Table 2.1 lists the three airstream mechanisms, the cavity, and the motion of the initiator. That which creates the airstream and sets it in motion is the INITIATOR. There may be more than one INITIATING ACTION occurring at the same time. Labels in figure 2.3 identify parts of the vocal apparatus. Note that the pulmonic airstream mechanism is the assumed default airstream mechanism used in the sound production unless it is specified that the sound uses the glottalic or the velaric airstream mechanism.

Table 2.1. Airstream mechanisms

Airstream mechanism	Cavity	Airstream direction	Closure	Initiators	Motion of Initiator
pulmonic	pulmonic	egressive	(n.a.)*	respiratory system (ribs, intercostal muscles)	down & in
				diaphragm	up
glottalic	pharyngeal	egressive	glottis	larynx	up
				pharynx walls	contract
glottalic	pharyngeal	ingressive	glottis	larynx	down
				pharynx walls	expand
velaric	oral	ingressive	tongue back against velum	back of tongue	back
				tongue body	down

* n.a. = not applicable

2: Anatomy of the Vocal Tract and Phonetic Features of Sounds

The airstream for a speech sound is EGRESSIVE if the air moves outward or INGRESSIVE if the air moves inward. In speech, pulmonic air is almost always egressive, and it is used for most speech sounds. A glottalic airstream may be either ingressive or egressive, and velaric air is always ingressive. For example, an air kiss uses an ingressive velaric airstream. A few speech sounds use a combination of airstream mechanisms.

Speech sounds use varying sizes and shapes of the vocal cavities, thus changing the RESONANCES (i.e., the tendency to reverberate at particular frequencies) of the vocal tract, in the same way that you can produce different pitches by blowing across the openings of different sized bottles or bottles with different levels of water.

2. State of the vocal folds and vocal cavities

As was mentioned in the anatomy of speech production, the *vocal folds* are located in the larynx. If they are close together and vibrating, the resulting sound is VOICED; otherwise it is VOICELESS. Examples of voiced sounds include 'b', 'd', and 'g'. Examples of voiceless sounds include 'p', 't', and 'k'. These six sounds form pairs that are the same except for voicing: 'b' and 'p', 'd', and 't', 'g' and 'k'.

PHONATION is the general term used to refer to the acoustic energy produced by the VIBRATIONS of the vocal folds. While initially this text focuses on voiced and voiceless sounds, there are other types of phonation as well, including whisper, creaky or laryngealized voice, falsetto, harsh voice, and combinations of these, such as whispery creaky falsetto voice. These phonation types will be discussed further in chapter 23.

The vocal tract consists of three cavities in which sounds resonate: the oral cavity (the mouth), the nasal cavity (the nose and sinus cavities), and the pharyngeal cavity (the throat) (or the supralaryngeal cavity) located just above the larynx. The walls of each cavity are mostly very flexible and muscular, and they change shape and size continually in speech. The size and shape of the cavities in which the airstream vibrates determine the quality of a speech sound, causing the hearer to perceive a certain sound as a particular consonant or vowel.

Experiment 2.1

To feel and hear the vibration of your vocal folds

Touch your fingertips lightly against your throat, just under your chin, and say these vowels: "aah," "ooh." Do you feel your vocal folds vibrating? Now pronounce these consonants: 'f, v, s, z, m, p, b, t, d, k, g'. Was there much difference between the different consonants? For which ones did you feel vibration?

To hear the vibrations instead of feeling them, put your hands firmly against your ears and say the same sounds as above.

---

3. Velic opening/nasal port

The soft palate is called the *velum*. There is VELIC CLOSURE when the velum is raised against the pharyngeal wall, closing the passageway to the nasal cavity. Sounds produced with velic closure, i.e., with sound waves resonating only in the oral cavity, are called ORAL. In contrast, when there is velic opening, SOUND WAVES resonate in the nasal cavity. Some phoneticians refer to the passageway between the oral and nasal cavities as the NASAL PORT; thus there is VELIC OPENING when the nasal port is open. Figure 2.4 represents a schematic side view of the vocal tract in a sagittal diagram, illustrating the velic opening and velic closure.

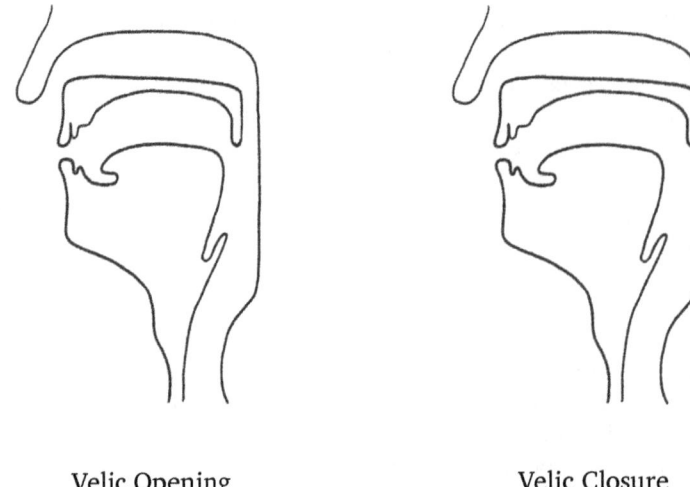

Velic Opening   Velic Closure

Figure 2.4. Sagittal diagrams illustrating the nasal port, open and closed.

There are two kinds of sounds produced with a velic opening, NASAL and NASALIZED sounds. *Nasal sounds* are produced with an open passageway through the nose only, with the passageway through the mouth blocked by some part of the vocal apparatus. For nasal sounds, the sound waves resonate in the nasal cavity and part of the oral cavity (up to the place in the mouth blocked by the lips or some part of the tongue). Nasals include [m], [n], and [ŋ] ('ng', e.g., the final sound in 'sing') in English. Note the contrast between a nasal and its oral counterpart, as between [m] and [b], [n] and [d], [ŋ] and [g].

Nasalized sounds are produced with an open passageway through both the nose and mouth. Thus, the sound waves of nasalized speech resonate in both the nasal and oral cavities. Nasalized sounds include French vowels in the words *dans* 'in', *vin* 'wine', and *un* 'a, an'.

4. Manner of articulation

The airstream can be constricted in the production of speech sounds. The degree of constriction of the airstream and the type of closure are used to identify the MANNER OF ARTICULATION.[1]

The airstream for a given sound may be produced with *complete closure* (complete constriction) when the airflow is completely obstructed. Sounds with the airstream completely blocked are called STOPS or PLOSIVES. These include 'p, t, k, b, d, g', and others that will be introduced later. For NASALS the airstream is completely blocked in the oral cavity, though not in the nasal cavity. Nasal sounds include 'm' and 'n'. *Intermittent closure* of the airstream is caused by vibration of part of the vocal tract, such as the tongue tip, thereby producing a FLAP or TRILL.

If the airstream is *partially obstructed*, such that turbulence of the air passing through the constriction produces audible noise, the airstream is said to have *incomplete closure*. FRICATIVES are a group of consonant sounds produced with partial closure. Examples of fricatives include 'v, f, z', and 's'. A LATERAL such as 'l', is also produced with partial closure.

If the airstream passes freely through the oral cavity with inaudible turbulence, there is only slight constriction. Examples include VOWELS such as 'a, e, i, o, u' and APPROXIMANTS such as 'y, w' and 'r'.

In the production of some sounds, such as 's, d, z, l', and 't', the position of the various parts of the vocal apparatus is essentially the same except for the distance of the tip and sides of the tongue to the upper ALVEOLAR RIDGE (gum ridge); the amount and type of constriction determines the manner

---

[1] K. Pike (1943:56–65) speaks of various degrees of stricture and structural function, and Ladefoged and Maddieson (1996) speak of contrasts in constriction. Bickford and Floyd (2006:3) speak of *impedance,* a term not used here, since in acoustics impedance refers to the energy absorbing property of an acoustical system. Impedance can be resistive and either capacitive or inductive in an acoustical system. An example of an impedance system is a car muffler where the resistive part of the system absorbs noise coming from the engine.

of articulation. For 't', a stop, the airstream is completely blocked by both the tip and the sides of the tongue pressing against the upper gum ridge. For 's', a fricative, the airstream is partially blocked because the sides of the tongue press against the gum ridge and air is forced to pass through a small space between the tongue tip and the gum ridge. For 'l', a lateral approximant, there is sufficient space between one or both sides of the tongue and the gum ridge to allow the airstream to pass over the sides of the tongue with only slight closure.

5. Place of articulation and articulators

PLACE OF ARTICULATION of a consonant refers to the combination of active and passive articulators that together form the constriction at a particular location.[2] There are two types of ARTICULATORS in the vocal apparatus—ACTIVE and PASSIVE. An *active articulator* is a moveable part of the vocal apparatus that obstructs or directs the airstream by coming close to or touching a relatively fixed part of the vocal apparatus, the *passive articulator*. The passive articulators are located on the upper surface of the oral cavity; these are the UPPER ARTICULATORS. Most of the active articulators are found beneath the upper articulators and are moveable; they are termed LOWER ARTICULATORS. In most instances, the word *articulator* alone refers to the active or lower articulator.

Table 2.2 contains a partial list of the places of articulation and the corresponding active and passive articulators. Figure 2.5 illustrates the places of articulation in which the active articulators move toward the passive articulators, as referred to by the numbers in table 2.2. As you review this table and figures 2.3 and 2.5, experiment with different speech sounds, paying close attention to what part of your mouth is moving to make the sound, and where that part is moving to. For example, the difference between the pronunciations of the words 'loop', 'loot' and 'Luke' is the place of articulation of the final sound: 'p' is bilabial, 't' is alveolar, and 'k' is velar.

Table 2.2. Articulators and places of articulation

	Place of articulation	Active articulator	Passive articulator
1.	bilabial	lower lip	upper lip
2.	labiodental	lower lip	upper teeth
3.	interdental	tongue tip	teeth
4.	dental	tongue tip	behind upper teeth
5.	alveolar	tongue tip	alveolar ridge
6.	postalveolar	tongue blade	behind alveolar ridge
7.	palatal	tongue front	hard palate
8.	velar	tongue back	front of velum
9.	uvular	tongue back	back of velum, uvula
10.	pharyngeal	tongue root	back wall of pharynx
11.	epiglottal	epiglottis	back wall of pharynx
12.	glottal	vocal folds	—

---

[2] Some phoneticians have used *point of articulation* rather than *place of articulation* as used here (Floyd 1986). Bickford and Floyd (2006) use place of articulation. We prefer place of articulation as the term *point* in geometry refers to an element having position but not dimensions, as the intersection of two lines. Place of articulation indicates that there is an area involved on one or more articulators.

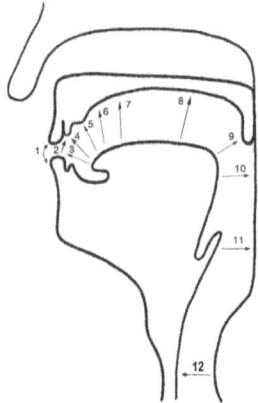

Figure 2.5. Places of articulation.

Some articulators, such as the tongue tip, may be involved in the production of sounds with more than one place of articulation. For example, a constriction between the tongue tip and the teeth produces a sound with an INTERDENTAL place of articulation; a constriction between the tongue tip and the back of the upper front teeth produces a sound with a DENTAL place of articulation; and a constriction between the tongue tip and the alveolar ridge produces a sound with an ALVEOLAR place of articulation.

In addition to the places of articulation shown in table 2.2, another place, with active and passive articulators, is LINGUOLABIAL. For consonants produced at this place of articulation the tongue tip is the active articulator and the upper lip is the passive articulator.

Phases of articulation

There are three distinct phases of articulation of a speech sound: the ONSET PHASE when an articulator is approaching the place in the vocal tract in which the maximum degree of closure will occur; the *medial* or STEADY STATE PHASE in which there is the maximum degree of constriction or closure; and the OFFSET or release PHASE in which the articulators are moving in transition to the following sound. The OFFSET or release phase is also called the CODA PHASE. The medial phase is the *nucleus*. When two sounds are adjacent to each other, the offset phase for the first sound is the same as the onset phase of the following sound. This results in an OVERLAPPING PHASE of the two segments. The onset and offset phases comprise the TRANSITION between the two sounds. These phases are important when eliciting primary phonetic data because the onset, offset, and transition phases are often primary clues to the places of articulation of particular sounds. They are also important when doing acoustic and perception studies of speech sounds.[3]

Key terms

external intercostal muscles	soft palate/velum
internal intercostal muscles	oral cavity
diaphragm	nasal cavity
vocal cords/vocal folds	pharyngeal cavity, supralaryngeal cavity
constriction	pulmonic cavity
closure	sternum
trachea	larynx
larynx	glottis
pharynx	epiglottis

---

[3] See chapter 33 on acoustic phonetics. Speech perception studies are not covered in this book.

phonetic features
    airstream mechanism and direction of the airstream
        egressive—pulmonic and glottalic—airstreams
        ingressive—glottalic and velaric—airstreams
        pulmonic air—pulmonary—diaphragm and/or muscles of rib cage, etc.
        glottalic air—pharyngeal—larynx with closed glottis, etc.
        velaric air—oral—back of tongue against velum, etc.
        initiating action
        initiator
    state of the vocal folds and vocal cavities
        phonation
            voiced
            voiceless
        resonance
    velic closure/velic opening
        velum/nasal port
        oral and nasal sounds; nasalized vowels
    manner of articulation
        complete closure (plosives, or stops)
        intermittent closure (flaps and trills)
        partial closure (fricatives and laterals)
        slight closure (vowels, approximants)
    place of articulation—see table 2.2 and figure 2.3
        articulator
            active (lower)
            passive (upper)
phases of sounds in context
    onset phase   release phase
    medial phase   coda phase
    steady state phase   transition between sounds
    nucleus   overlapping phases
    offset phase

Exercises

1. What are the three major airstream mechanisms and their initiators?

Airstream mechanism	Initiator
_____	_____
_____	_____
_____	_____

2. Learn the terms in table 2.2 and figure 2.3.

3. From what you have learned of these terms, without consulting the book, draw a blank sagittal diagram. Fill in the active and passive articulators and places of articulation. Check your answers with those in table 2.2 and figure 2.3.

4. Airstream identification:

   Describe the first sound in the word 'bottle' using the phonetic features in this chapter. (Remember, airstream mechanism and direction of airstream are two parts of a single feature!)
   _____

   Describe the first sound in the word 'thin.'
   _____

5. Name a possible passive articulator for each of the active articulators listed below.

tongue tip	_____
tongue root	_____
lower lip	_____
tongue blade	_____

6. Identify the <u>degree of constriction</u> for the following classes of sounds. The first is a completed example.

stops	<u>completely constricted</u>
fricatives	_____
vowels	_____
nasals	_____
laterals	_____

3

Sagittal Diagrams

A SAGITTAL DIAGRAM is a static schematic side view picture of the head used to show the action and position of the vocal apparatus in the production of a speech sound. Midsagittal diagrams, (hereafter called *sagittals*) are also referred to as *face diagrams* and *profile diagrams*. They illustrate what is happening in sound production with the articulators, the velum, the airstream mechanism, the direction of the airstream, the manner of articulation, and the vocal folds.

Phonetic features representation

A sagittal diagram graphically represents each of five phonetic features that identify a speech sound.

1. *Airstream and the direction of the airstream.* Traditionally, the source of the air used in producing an individual sound is represented schematically by an arrow near the source of the air. It also indicates the direction of the airflow. An arrow below the glottis indicates that the sound is produced with pulmonic air. Further, the arrow specifies the direction of the airflow, as seen in figure 3.1, indicating that the air is egressive.

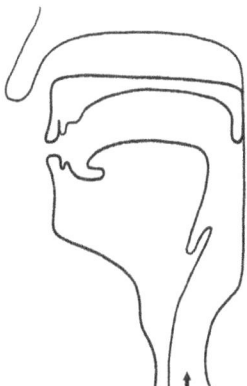

Figure 3.1. Airstream mechanism and velic closure.

2. *State of the vocal folds.* The action or inaction of the vocal folds is represented on a sagittal diagram either by a wavy line indicating that the vocal folds are vibrating, or by horizontal lines — — indicating that the vocal folds are open, at rest and not vibrating, as seen in figure 3.2.

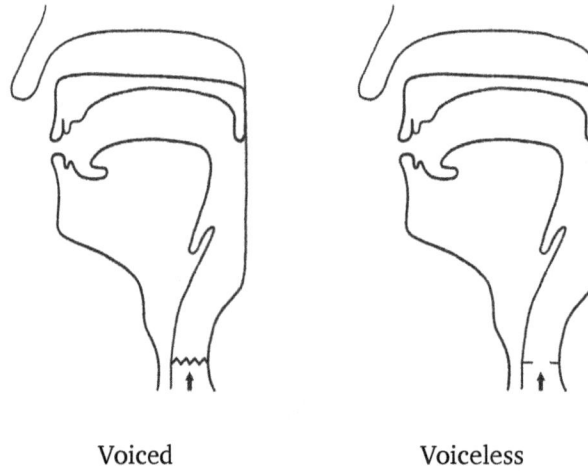

Voiced   Voiceless

Figure 3.2. States of the vocal folds.

3. *Nasal port.* The VELUM or NASAL PORT is either hanging down relaxed (open passageway) for a nasal or a nasalized sound, or pressed up against the pharyngeal wall (closed passageway) for an oral sound, as seen in figure 3.3.

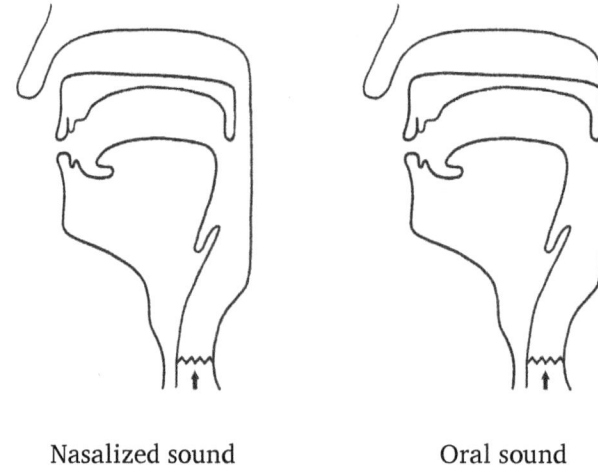

Nasalized sound   Oral sound

Figure 3.3. Placement of velum.

4. *Place of articulation.* The active articulator interacts with the passive articulator at a particular spot in the vocal tract. If the articulators are correctly portrayed, the sagittal diagram can be read to determine the PLACE OF ARTICULATION. In figure 3.4 the lips are the articulators in the diagram on the left for [ɸ], and the alveolar ridge and the tongue tip for [t] in the right-hand figure.

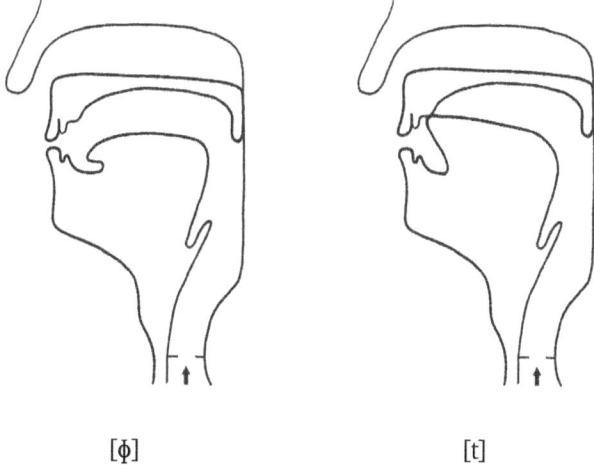

[ɸ]   [t]

Figure 3.4. Place and manner of articulation.

Since the narrowest space between an active articulator and a passive articulator in the diagram on the left in figure 3.4 is between the lower lip and the upper lip, they are the active and passive articulators, respectively; the diagram depicts the bilabial sound [ɸ]. In the right-hand diagram in figure 3.4, the tongue tip, drawn to touch the alveolar ridge, indicates that the sound, [t], is alveolar.

5. *Manner of articulation.* The MANNER OF ARTICULATION is reflected in the diagrams by how close the active articulator is to the passive articulator. For a stop, they should touch in the diagram, whereas there should be a small space between them for a fricative. Thus in figure 3.4 the left-hand diagram depicts a bilabial fricative and the right-hand one depicts an alveolar stop.

In sagittal diagrams all the articulators are represented, not just those that are directly involved in producing the sound depicted. For example, in figure 3.4, the tongue and teeth are drawn in the left-hand diagram, even though the lips are the active articulators for [ɸ] and the tongue and teeth are inactive in the production of that sound.

Limitations

Sagittal diagrams have a few significant limitations. A stream of speech is a continuum of sounds that very often slur together without clear-cut boundaries, whereas a sagittal diagram is a static cross-sectional representation of the vocal apparatus showing the articulation of only one speech sound.

A further limitation is that it is hard to represent vowels with sagittal diagrams because it is more difficult to describe articulatory positions of the tongue for vowels than for consonants. It is also difficult to represent certain positions of the lips and the sides of the tongue because sagittal diagrams are limited to a side view. Further, several modifications to the consonants in which vowels or other sounds are anticipated are not represented in these diagrams. Even given these limitations, such schematics have proved extremely helpful for the study of speech sounds.

Key terms and symbols

   sagittal diagrams, face diagrams
   arrow: placement of the arrow indicates which airstream mechanism is used; the direction of the arrow indicates the direction of the airstream
   representation of vocal folds with a wavy line is used to indicate a voiced sound, and – – is used to represent a voiceless sound

velum, nasal port
place of articulation
manner of articulation

Exercises

1. On the sagittal diagrams below, identify the following:

Articulatory features	Sagittal diagram A	Sagittal diagram B
State of the vocal folds		
State of the nasal port		
Place of articulation		
Active articulator		
Passive articulator		
Manner of articulation		

 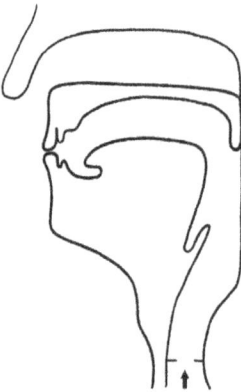

Sagittal diagram A   Sagittal diagram B

4

Fricatives

A FRICATIVE is a speech sound made by forming a constriction in the vocal tract and forcing the airstream through it, thereby producing audible air turbulence.[1] The sound of the turbulence is heard acoustically as noise. The auditory quality of the noise, which we hear as a certain pitch or 'color' of the sound, is determined by the size and shape of the vocal tract in front of and behind the constriction.

The difference in quality of the fricative noise produced at different places of articulation is one of the primary cues by which we perceive and identify the place of articulation of a fricative. For example, a voiceless fricative might have a hissing sound as in 'see,' a hushing sound as in 'she,' or a blowing sound as in 'fee,' and so on. Fricatives may be produced at almost any place of articulation.

For nearly every voiceless fricative, a voiced fricative may be produced at the same place of articulation, although not necessarily in the same language. For example, in English there are several sets of words that illustrate this contrast.

Voiceless	Voiced
sue	zoo
thigh	thy
feel	veal

Experiment 4.1

Purpose: This experiment is intended to acquaint you with the variety of fricative sounds that you can make.

Procedure:

1. Take a deep breath, so that you can make a continuous sound for an extended time. Then as you exhale, first make a voiceless alveolar fricative—an 's' sound. Without interrupting your continuous production of the fricative sound, glide quickly to 'sh.' Continue from there on back through the mouth until you reach the furthest back (and perhaps downward) that you can produce a fricative sound.
2. Repeat the first part, but start with a voiceless bilabial fricative by putting your lips close together as you blow, much as you would do in blowing out a candle flame.

Results: Did you notice any places where it was difficult to maintain a continuous fricative sound?

Table 4.1 introduces the International Phonetic Alphabet (IPA) symbols for eight fricatives. The columns indicate places of articulation and the rows indicate contrast in voicing. The bottom two rows indicate the articulators.

---

[1] An older term for a fricative consonant is SPIRANT (from Latin *spirans* 'blowing'). This term comes from the way fricatives are produced, namely, two articulators come so close together that turbulence is produced.

Table 4.1. Fricatives

	Bilabial	Labiodental	Interdental	Velar	
Voiceless	ɸ	f	θ	x	fricative with egressive pulmonic air (wepa)
Voiced	β	v	ð	ɣ	
Passive articulator	upper lip	upper teeth	teeth	front of velum	
Active articulator	lower lip	lower lip	tongue tip	tongue back	

Names of sounds

Each speech sound has a NAME, which summarizes the values of its phonetic features in a standard order.[2] In this book, you can find the name of a sound in a table, such as table 4.1, by reading the row and column headings clockwise around the table of sounds, beginning on the left. Thus, the name of the sound transcribed as [ð] is a 'voiced interdental fricative with egressive pulmonic air.' The phrase, 'with egressive pulmonic air,' may be abbreviated to *wepa*. However, egressive pulmonic air represents the most frequently used airstream mechanism and direction of the airstream for speech sounds; therefore, *"wepa"* may be omitted if no other airstream mechanism is used for a particular sound. If another airstream mechanism and direction of the airstream is used, then it must be specified.

Brackets

Placing brackets [ ] around a string of phonetic symbols indicates that the string constitutes a PHONETIC TRANSCRIPTION. Linguists differentiate between phonetic and other kinds of representations, e.g., a phonological transcription and a PRACTICAL ORTHOGRAPHY (a practical writing system for use by the general public). Symbols used in PHONOLOGICAL TRANSCRIPTIONS are set off by the use of diagonal lines / /. This distinction between phonetic and phonological representations is particularly significant as phonological transcriptions are also written with phonetic symbols. The distinction is that in a phonological representation the phonetic sounds have been analyzed into distinctive sound units or phonemes, whereas in phonetics they have not been analyzed; they simply represent the unanalyzed phonetic data.

Sagittal diagrams of fricatives

The sagittal diagrams in figure 4.1 depict phonetic features for [β] and [ɣ]. In these figures there is a small space between the passive articulators and the active articulators, indicating partial, but not complete, obstruction of the airstream at that place of articulation.

---

[2] The characteristics of speech sounds that distinguish one sound from another are called features of the sound, and the various possibilities for a feature are values of the feature. Thus 'place of articulation' is a feature; 'bilabial' is a value of that feature. This use of the terms *features* and *values of features* follows standard statistical terminology.

4: Fricatives

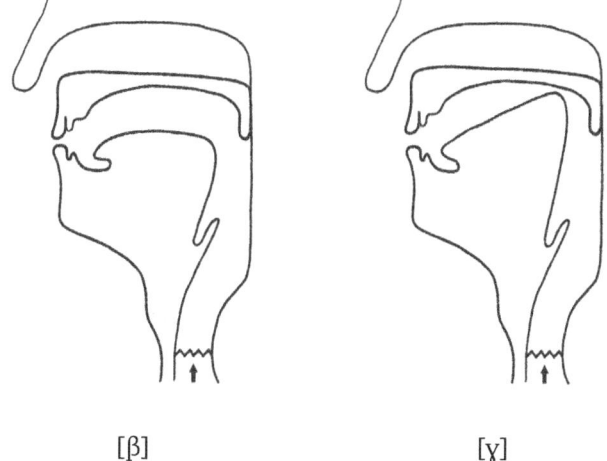

[β]   [ɣ]

Figure 4.1. Sagittal diagrams of voiced fricatives [β] and [ɣ].

Pronunciation guide

The following descriptions may help you with producing the fricatives introduced in this chapter.

1. [f] the lower lip is placed against the upper teeth for a voiceless labiodental fricative. For example, the initial sound in 'face', 'far', 'from'.
2. [v] the lower lip is placed against the upper teeth for a voiced labiodental fricative. For example, the initial sound in 'vase', 'vague', 'vogue'.
3. [θ] the tongue tip is inserted between the upper and lower teeth for a voiceless interdental fricative. Some speakers make this sound by placing the tongue directly behind the upper teeth. For example, the initial sound in 'thing', 'thistle', 'throne'.
4. [ð] the tongue tip is inserted between the upper and lower teeth for a voiced interdental fricative. For example, the initial sound in 'these', 'those', 'this'.
5. [ɸ] the lips are placed close together without touching; they are not rounded while you blow slightly. For example, blow out a candle gently without voicing.
6. [β] the lips are placed close together without touching and they are not rounded while you blow slightly with voicing added for a voiced bilabial fricative. For example, blow out a candle gently with voicing. The voiced and voiceless bilabial fricatives are not used in English as consonants, though they are present in Spanish, as well as in many other languages.
7. [x] the tongue is placed in the position for a voiceless velar stop as in the first sound in English 'cat,' but without it actually touching the roof of your mouth. There is a small constriction of the airstream sufficient to produce friction. This voiceless sound occurs as a consonant in many other languages, but not in English.
8. [ɣ] the tongue is placed in the same position as for a voiced velar stop as in the first sound in English 'gate' but without actually touching the roof of your mouth. There is a small constriction of the airstream sufficient to produce friction. This voiced sound occurs as a consonant in other languages, but not in English.

Differentiation drills

DIFFERENTIATION DRILLS are useful in learning to produce unfamiliar sounds. These are also referred to as FRAME DRILLS or CARRIER DRILLS. To compose a differentiation drill, first identify a series of sounds that include the new sound(s) in focus, such as the set of voiced fricatives [β, v, ð, ɣ]. These are called the SUBSTITUTION ITEMS. Next choose the substitution word, a constant context for the new sounds. The CARRIER word may precede the substitution item, e.g., [a__]; follow it, e.g., [__o]; or both, e.g., [a__o]. Then pronounce each of the substitution items in the context of the differentiation drill. When a differentiation drill is written out, it may look something like this, with the voiceless and voiced fricatives set between vowels:

    aˈɸo³   aˈβo
    aˈfo   aˈvo
    aˈθo   aˈðo
    aˈxo   aˈɣo

When constructing a differentiation drill, vary the way in which the substitution items are grouped. For example, in the differentiation drill above, the fricatives in the first column are voiceless and those in the second column are voiced. In constructing and using the items in a differentiation drill, sounds may be grouped by place of articulation. Two sounds such as [x] and [ɣ] are placed opposite each other, then read across the differentiation drill above, pronouncing them as a pair: [aˈxo], [aˈɣo], with the contrast between them being in voicing on the fricative. Continue working through the differentiation drill, reading the words as pairs contrasting with each other in whether the consonant is voiced or voiceless. Then read down each list in order to practice the difference in place of articulation for the focused sounds set in the same environment.

When using a differentiation drill, you learn best by repeating the examples. Therefore, put sounds that are hard for you to pronounce into the carrier word or phrase, since this is the part you will repeat over and over. This is especially important for new unfamiliar sounds, such as [ɣ] and [x] or [ɸ] and [β] which may not be found in your language. In order to practice these unfamiliar sounds, place them initially in the words as in the following differentiation drill. In this way you practice [ɣ] nine times instead of only once.

    ɣaˈɸo   ɣaˈβo
    ɣaˈfo   ɣaˈvo
    ɣaˈθo   ɣaˈðo
    ɣaˈxo   ɣaˈɣo

The carrier word for consonant substitution items needs to include at least one vowel in order to make the combination readily pronounceable. A vowel that is easy for you allows you to focus your attention on the consonant sounds. Any sound, whether consonant or vowel, which is difficult for you to pronounce, can profitably be put into a differentiation drill to give you practice by repeating it over and over.

Key terms

    fricative
    name, technical name
    phonetic representation, phonetic transcription
    phonological transcription
    practical orthography
    symbols of fricative sounds
    differentiation drill: carrier and substitution item, frame drill

---

[3] The small vertical stress diacritic [ˈ] before each fricative in the differentiation drill indicates stress on the following syllable. Stress will be discussed in more detail in chapter 8. For now, accent the stressed syllable. (In some writings, stress is indicated with an acute accent mark over the nucleus of the stressed syllable (usually a vowel), rather than the [ˈ] used in IPA, e.g., [aβó] rather than [aˈβo].

Exercises

1. Practice reading and pronouncing the following words from Pashto, Pakistan (Backstrom, personal communication). In pronouncing words with more than one syllable, be careful to stress the syllable that follows the stress mark.

xa	'good'	aˈya	'that, those'
xe	'right'	ɣax	'tooth'

2. Practice the following Castilian Spanish words (E. V. Pike 1963:7):

aˈxi	'chili pepper'	ˈuβo	'there were'
ˈoxa	'leaf'	ˈiβa	'he used to go'
ˈaxo	'garlic'	aˈɣaβe	'century plant'
ˈaɣo	'I make'	ˈθexa	'eyebrow'
ˈiðo	'went'	aˈɣuðo	'sharp'
ˈiθo	'he made'	oˈβexa	'sheep'
ˈixo	'son'	ˈfixa	'pay attention!'
ˈiɣo	'fig'	aˈɣuxa	'needle'
ˈoxo	'eye'	eˈðað	'age'
ˈaβe	'bird'		

3. Practice the following Foi words (Papua New Guinea; data from M. and J. Rule as cited in E. V. Pike 1963:7):

ˈfaɣa	'stomach'	ˈoɣo	'chest'

4. Practice the following Mende words (Sierra Leone; data from E. V. Pike 1963:7):

aɸ	'father'	ˈiβu	'he'

5. Practice the following Kamasau words (Papua New Guinea; data from Joy Sanders, personal communication):

ɸu	'pig'	ˈɸuɣɛ[4]	'what'
ˈɸuwo	'beetle nut'	ˈtuɣɛ	'who'
ˈoɸu	'area'	ˈɸaɣɛ ɸo	'we go down'
ɸas	'we sit'	ɸɛs ˈɸewo	'we go up'

---

[4] The vowel symbol [e] contrasts with [ɛ] in English. For example, [e] occurs in 'bake' (though in American English it glides to [eⁱ]) and [ɛ] occurs in 'Ed'.

6. Identify the following sound and give its name:

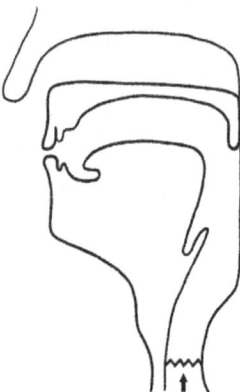

[ ] _____

7. Give names for the following:

[f] _____
[v] _____
[θ] _____
[x] _____
[ɣ] _____
[ð] _____

5

Stops

A STOP is a speech sound produced with complete obstruction of the vocal airstream. The term *stop* refers to any sound made with an oral closure, together with a simultaneous velic closure. Stops are the only type of consonants found in all of the world's languages (Ladefoged and Maddieson 1996:47).

A stop may be either voiced or voiceless, and aspirated or unaspirated. Table 5.1 organizes stops into four columns according to their place of articulation, whether bilabial, alveolar, velar, or glottal. In fact, stops may be produced along a continuum in the oral and pharyngeal cavities, so there are many more stops in languages than those included in table 5.1. Many of these will be introduced in later chapters.

Table 5.1. Stops

	Bilabial	Alveolar	Velar	Glottal		
Voiceless	p^h	t^h	k^h	$ʔ^h$	aspirated	
Voiceless	p	t	k	ʔ		stop (wepa)
Voiced	b	d	ɡ			
Passive articulator	upper lip	alveolar ridge	front of velum	(not applicable)		
Active articulator	lower lip	tongue tip	tongue back	vocal folds		

Aspirated and unaspirated stops

ASPIRATION on voiceless stops refers to an audible rush of air that occurs immediately following release of the stop. In order to help you be aware of aspiration, place your fingertips close to your mouth as you say the English words *pea, tea,* and *key*. You can feel the strength of the release of the puff of air that occurs immediately after releasing the stop. Another means of testing for the presence or absence of aspiration is to use a small piece of paper. Hold it directly in front of your lips and say the words [pop] and [p^hop^h]. For the second word you should notice movement of the paper. As indicated in the second word [p^hop^h], aspiration of stop consonants is indicated by use of a superscript diacritic [^{h}].

While initial voiceless stop consonants are normally aspirated in English, in many other languages this is not the case. Spanish and French are languages with initial unaspirated voiceless stop consonants, for example, Spanish [paf] 'bang!' UNASPIRATED stops also occur in English, though not initially in a word. Rather, they occur when the stop consonant is in the second position in a word, following [s], as in the words *spell, stop,* and *skill.* In some languages there is no such environmental conditioning. For example, note the contrasts in Kiowa in table 5.2.

Table 5.2. Kiowa stops[a]

	Bilabial	Gloss	Alveolar	Gloss	Velar	Gloss
Aspirated	pʰo	louse	tʰo	water	kʰi	day
Unaspirated	po	beaver	to	house	ki	meat

[a]from E. V. Pike 1963:11

Names of stops

The names of stops are derived from the labels in table 5.1, starting at the left and going clockwise around the chart. For example, [d] is a 'voiced alveolar stop,' and [kʰ] is a 'voiceless velar aspirated stop.' When the word 'aspirated' is not included in the identifying name for a stop, the default is an unaspirated consonant. The assumed airstream mechanism is egressive pulmonic air unless otherwise specified.

Sagittal diagrams of stops

Figure 5.1 presents sagittal diagrams of two consonants, a stop and a fricative. Notice that the following features are identical: the place of articulation is velar; the state of the vocal folds is voiced; the airstream mechanism and direction of the airstream is egressive pulmonic; and the nasal port is closed. These diagrams differ only in the degree of closure, with complete closure for the stop [g] and great constriction which produces air turbulence for the fricative [ɣ]. In a sagittal diagram of a stop, we draw the active articulator touching the passive articulator; this indicates complete closure of the airstream. The nasal port is closed. Aspiration is not shown on a sagittal diagram.

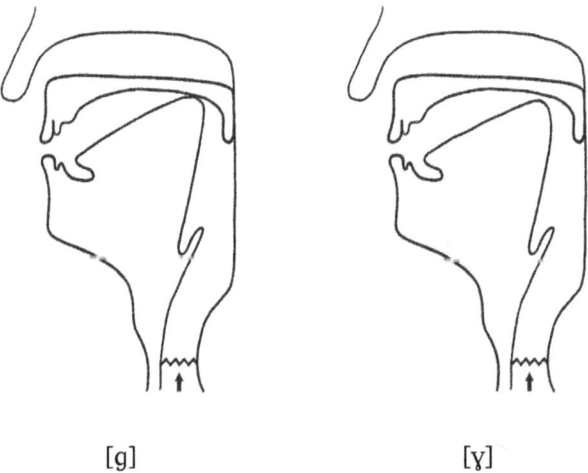

[g]   [ɣ]

Figure 5.1. Sagittal diagrams illustrating the contrast between a stop [g] and a fricative [ɣ] produced at the same place of articulation.

Glottal stops

A GLOTTAL STOP is produced by complete closure of the vocal folds with the airstream completely blocked. While glottal stops serve as consonants in many languages, they do not have this function in English, even though they occur frequently. Further, they are not usually included in the spelling of English. In order to become aware of your pronunciation of [ʔ] say 'oh-oh' [oʔo], such as you would say if something broke. The voiceless consonant between the two [o]s is a glottal stop. Another place where glottal stops occur regularly in English is in words that begin with a vowel, e.g., 'egg' [ʔeⁱg].[1] Repeat this word several times with a brief pause between repetitions. You will notice a slight blockage of the airstream in your throat just before the vowel; this is a glottal stop.

In languages where glottal stops serve as contrastive consonants they produce different words. For example, notice the difference in meanings of words (Tzotzil, Mexico) ending in a glottal stop and a voiceless alveolar stop (Laughlin 1975:149, 151):

    heʔ   'hah!' (exclamation of disbelief)
    het   'fork, shuttle, slingshot'

Because the presence or absence of a glottal stop indicates contrastive meaning in many languages, as in Tzotzil above, it is important to control your production of glottal stops and to recognize their presence or absence.

It is impossible to produce a voiced glottal stop. Thus the term *glottal stop* is sufficient as the name of this sound. Aspirated glottal stops [ʔʰ] do occur, but only infrequently.

Figure 5.2 is a sagittal diagram of a glottal stop. Besides the arrow indicating egressive pulmonic air, the only relevant part of the diagram is the straight line drawn across the larynx, indicating complete closure of the vocal folds, which function as the articulators of this sound. In this diagram the sound has the mid back tongue position, as for the word [ʔoʔo]; the tongue position depends on the preceding or following sounds.

[ʔ]

Figure 5.2. Sagittal diagram of a glottal stop.

Onset, closure, and release of stops

As was discussed in chapter 2 on phases of articulation, the production of stops may be divided into onset, closure or steady state phase, and release of the closure. During the onset the articulators are moving towards the place of articulation of the stop. During the oral closure, there is complete closure of the airstream. The nasal port is shut and air is trapped

---
[1] [eⁱ] represents a vowel with a short offglide. This will be discussed further in chapter 6.

behind the place of articulation. During release the articulators move apart, and the trapped air that has built up behind the closure is released. This release is sometimes referred to as a *burst* or *stop release*. Hence British phoneticians often refer to stops as *plosives* (see IPA chart Appendix A).

Stops may have an aspirated or unaspirated release, be unreleased, released into a fricative, or released into a nasal. The latter two types of release are discussed later in chapters 11 and 17.

Unreleased stops

When in final position in a word, usually at the end of an utterance, a stop often lacks an audible release. This is called an *unreleased stop,* represented by a small corner diacritic following the consonant, for example, [p̚, t̚, k̚].

Voice Onset Time (VOT)

VOICE ONSET TIME (VOT) refers to 'the interval between the release of a stop closure and the start of voicing' (Ladefoged 2001:125). VOT helps us understand more precisely the differences between voicing, voicelessness and voicelessness with aspiration. The following three sequences of sounds are presented graphically in figure 5.3.

[ba] Voicing begins from the beginning of the utterance (sequence 1). In some languages the first part of [b] is actually [p] and voicing begins part way through the production of the initial consonant (sequence 2). The critical factor is that voicing begins before the lips open for production of the vowel.
[pa] Voicing on the vowel begins immediately with the release of the stop (sequence 3).
[pʰa] Voicing begins after the release of the stop, with a short interval of voicelessness during the period of aspiration (sequences 4 and 5).

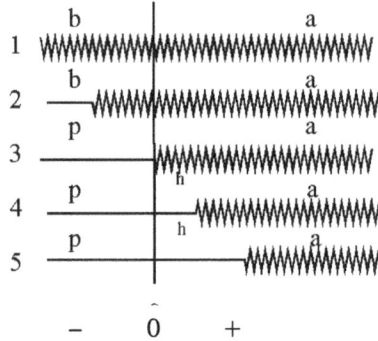

Figure 5.3 Voice Onset Time.

Hence, there are three types of VOT represented in the utterances above: voicing initiated on the vowel immediately following the release of the stop (sequence 3); voicing occurring before the stop is released into the vowel (sequences 1 and 2); and voicing delayed during the aspiration that occurs after the stop release (sequence 4). A fourth possibility is that voicing is delayed during a long aspiration period (sequence 5), perhaps as would occur in stressed pronunciation or emphatic speech in English. These represent possibilities along a continuum of VOTs.

VOT can be measured on a display of the sound wave. Measurement of VOT begins from the release of the stop to when voicing begins. For a voiced stop the VOT is a negative number, as shown in sequences 1 and 2.

Pronunciation helps

Because [ʔ] often occurs in English words preceding a vowel, practice pronouncing words that have a vowel initially with and without a glottal stop. Practice the following contrasts:

ʔaʔa   aʔa   tatʰa   tʰata
ʔatʰ   atʰa

Note the difference in production and perception of a word pronounced with and without a glottal stop word initially. The absence of the glottal stop has a smoother beginning to the word.

[pʰ], [tʰ], and [kʰ] occur initially in the English words 'peel,' 'teal' and 'keel.' When they occur initially, these stops are aspirated. However, when [p], [t], and [k] occur as the second sounds in the English words 'spill,' 'still,' and 'skill,' they are unaspirated. You can check this by holding a single piece of paper up in front of your lips and noting the difference in movement of the paper when you pronounce the following pairs of words:

pell	spell	pool	spool	Paul	sprawl
teal	steal	tool	stool	tall	stall
keel	skeet	cool	school	call	scald

In order to produce a voiceless unaspirated stop word initially, it may be helpful to begin by saying a word with an [s] initially, and then spread it out in these English words as follows:

spell . . . s...pell. . . .	s.......pell	(s)	pell	pell
steal . . . s...teal	s.......teal	(s)	teal	teal
skeet . . . s...keet. . . .	s.......keet	(s)	keet	keet

Next, think the [s] while saying the rest of the word. Check to see whether or not you are aspirating the initial consonant by holding a piece of paper in front of your mouth. Although you may feel a small burst of air when the articulators first part, allowing the pent up air pressure to be released, there should not be aspiration following the [p], [t], or [k].

One way to learn not to do something is first to do it vigorously. Thus, if you say a phrase such as "Peter, Peter, pumpkin eater" with a big puff of aspiration after each voiceless stop (think of the aspiration as a long 'h' sound between the consonant and the following vowel) you may become more aware when you are aspirating. Note that a minor danger in this exercise is hyperventilation. Now say the same phrase without aspiration.

While their environment conditions the occurrence of aspirated and unaspirated stops in English, in some languages, such as Spanish, there are only unaspirated stops. Another common result of conditioning by environment is a voiced stop becoming voiceless before voicelessness. These two examples of conditioning by environment are topics covered in phonology.

If you speak a language that has both voiceless unaspirated stops and voiceless aspirated stops, this distinction may be represented orthographically as a contrast between voiced and voiceless stops. It is important to check to see that you are really voicing sounds that are written as voiced. Say the following words while placing your fingers on top of your larynx: "bad," "dad," "gad." Now produce them again while exaggerating the voicing on the voiced consonants.

For some speakers of English the difference between an aspirated voiceless stop 'p' and a voiced stop 'b' word-initially is actually a contrast between an aspirated voiceless stop and an unaspirated voiceless stop; for example, voiceless 'p' in the word 'pea' [pʰi], and voiced 'b' in 'bee' [pi]. In other English dialects, the contrast is between an aspirated voiceless stop and a voiced stop.

It is crucial to learn to voice stops completely, because fully voiced stops occur in many languages. Say the following words: [abo], [ado], [ago]. Use the same technique described above by placing your fingers on your larynx to make sure that your vocal folds are vibrating throughout the production of these words. Now say these voiced stops word initially: [bo], [do], [go]. Check your vocal folds again to make sure they are vibrating throughout. If you are not sure whether you are really voicing these stops, say [apɑ], [atɑ], and [akɑ], again with your hand on your throat just below your jaw, and note what the cessation of vibrations feels like during these stops. Then go back to saying [abɑ], [adɑ], [ɑgɑ] and start the above practice cycle again.

Key terms

stop, plosive
names and symbols for all stops in table 5.1.
onset, closure, release
aspiration, aspirated stops, unaspirated stops

stop burst, stop release
unreleased stops
voice onset time (VOT)

Exercises

1. Practice the following differentiation drill three times, preferably with a partner:

atʰɑ	atɑ	apɑ	abɑ	adɑ
akɑ	akʰɑ	adɑ	aʔa	ɑgɑ
ta/tʰa	da	ba	pa	pʰa
ʔa/ʔaʔ	ka	ga	kʰa	aʔ

2. Practice the following words three times each:

apʰapʰa	'Apapa' (name of a city)
igɛdɛ	'Igede' (name of a language)
ibibio	'Ibibio' (name of a language)
pʰaʔa	'Pabir/Bura' (a Chadic language)
pʰitʰi	'Piti/Abisi' (a Niger-Congo language)

3. Practice reading and pronouncing the following Pashto (Pakistan) words (Backstrom, personal communication). In pronouncing words with more than one syllable, be careful to stress the syllable that follows the stress mark [ˈ].

paˈna	'leaf'	kəb	'fish'
goˈta	'ring'	aˈge	'egg'
uˈbə	'water'	pe	'milk'
uˈga	'garlic'		

4. What is the meaning of VOT? How does VOT help us to understand stops? _____
   _____
   _____

5. Give the phonetic symbols and the names for the sounds represented in the following sagittal diagrams:

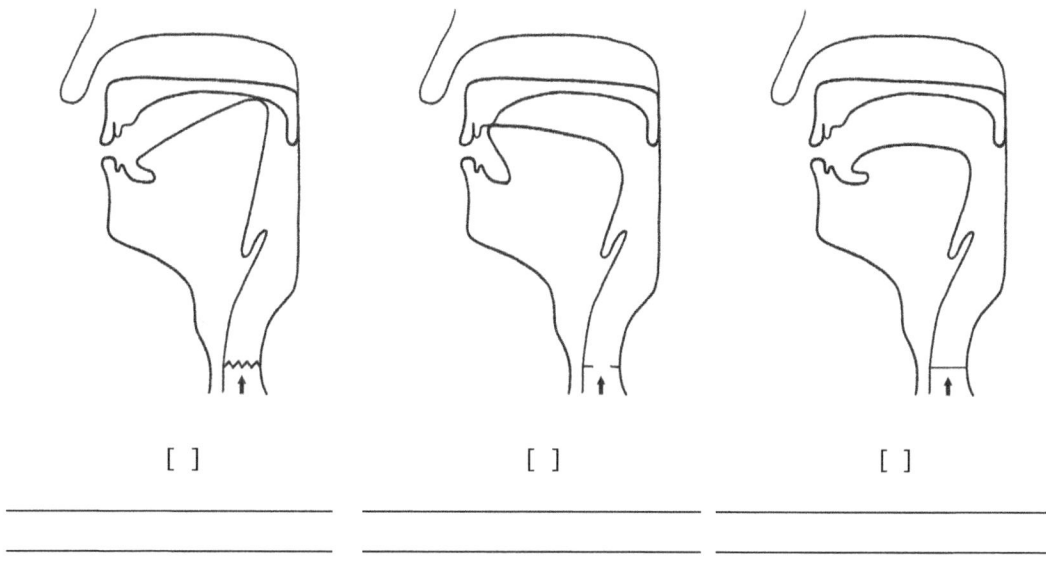

[ ]   [ ]   [ ]

_____ _____ _____
_____ _____ _____
_____ _____ _____

6. Give the technical name for the following stops:

[t] _____
[g] _____
[p] _____
[b] _____

6

Vowels

A VOWEL is a central oral resonant continuant (see table 6.1 for a summary of this definition). A vowel typically forms the nucleus of a syllable; hence phoneticians speak of vowels as being SYLLABIC. Phonetic vowels are also referred to as VOCOIDS (K. Pike 1943:78; Ladefoged 2001:215). In parallel with the term *vocoids,* consonants have been referred to as CONTOIDS (K. Pike 1943:78). The use of the term *vocoid* for phonetic data contrasts with 'vowel', used for phonological data. Here, the term *vowel* is used both for phonetic and phonological vowel sounds; IPA does not distinguish the two usages.

Vowels have articulatory features; that is, vowels can be described relative to the positions of the tongue in producing them. For example, figure 6.1 shows that the tongue may be humped up towards the alveolar and dental areas in the front of the mouth to produce a front vowel such as [i]; alternatively the tongue may be humped up towards the velum to produce a back vowel such as [u]. Phoneticians use these as relative places of articulation to describe the production of vowels.

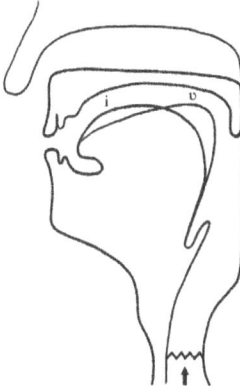

Figure 6.1. Relative tongue positions in production of [i] and [u].

Phoneticians use phonetic features roughly determined by the shape of the vocal tract to describe particular vowels, each of which has a particular VOWEL QUALITY. Vowel quality refers to all of the distinguishing phonetic features of a particular vowel resulting from the positions of the tongue and the lips. The term *vowel quality* does not include the pitch, loudness, or duration of the vowel. There is some discussion as to whether or not nasalization is a feature of vowel quality. IPA considers it an independent feature, while, acoustically, it is part of the vowel quality.

These places of articulation are similar to those presented in chapter 2, table 2.2. However, phoneticians describe a vowel as being made in the front of the mouth, in the central part of the mouth, or in the back of the mouth; hence a vowel may be FRONT, CENTRAL or BACK within a two-dimensional vowel diagram (see figure 6.2). Figure 6.2 also shows a difference in the height of the tongue, specifying the phonetic features of vowels, e.g., CLOSE, MID, and OPEN. Each of these tongue heights is further subdivided into *close* versus *open* at the vertical extremities of the diagram; these terms describe the relative degree of opening of the mouth and corresponding position of the jaw when producing a particular vowel. In addition, a vowel may be produced with ROUNDED or UNROUNDED (spread) lips. There is less precision of tongue position for vowel sounds, than for consonants. These articulatory descriptions are helpful, though inadequate for specifying the vocal tract shapes that produce different vowel qualities. More exact descriptions are best specified acoustically and auditorily.[1]

Figure 6.2 displays the IPA arrangement of English-like vowels. (The terms in parenthesis are not used in IPA.) Different dialects of English may have a different number of vowels. Notice that the diagram distinguishes seven degrees of openness of the vocal tract and three degrees of the tongue front and back dimension. The back vowels are rounded, with the exception of [ɑ] which is an 'open back unrounded vowel'.

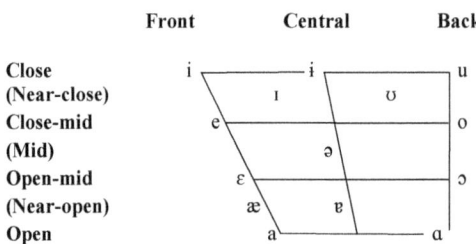

Figure 6.2. English vowel chart.

The IPA vowel diagram is a trapezoid with its top side considerably wider than its base. This trapezoidal shape corresponds to the acoustic characteristics of vowel sounds, as well as the way we perceive their quality.

If the perimeter of a vowel diagram represents the extreme limits of the vowel qualities that a particular person can produce, the area inside the diagram represents that person's VOWEL SPACE. This vowel space encompasses all the different vowel sounds that a person can produce. Another useful interpretation of a vowel diagram is to define the perimeter of the diagram, or at least three of its corners. Thus, three corners of the diagram for a speaker of midwestern American English might be determined by the person's vowels in words like 'hot' [ɑ], 'heat' [i], and 'hoot' [u] in the lower right, upper left, and upper right corners of the diagram, respectively.

The vowels on the IPA vowel chart are classified according to four main vertical positions along a scale of close, mid, and open, and three horizontal positions, front, central, and back.

For names of vowels read the labels clockwise around the vowel chart. For example, [e] is a 'close-mid front unrounded vowel,' and [u] is a 'close back rounded vowel.'[2] While in some languages, such as Athabaskan languages (North America), voiceless vowels are present, the default case is that vowels are voiced. Hence, we omit the word "voiced" in the name of a vowel unless it needs to be specified.

---

[1] Phonetic features of vowels are most accurately described acoustically in terms of their first three formants. This will be discussed in detail in chapter 33 on acoustic phonetics.

[2] [ɪ],[ʊ] and [æ] fall between the IPA levels and thus have no official names. Ladefoged (personal communications) has suggested that [ɪ] and [ʊ], which are somewhere between close and close-mid, be called *near-close*, and that [æ], which is between open-mid and open, be called *near-open*. We may infer from the official IPA chart of symbols that *mid* is the term for vowels between close-mid and open-mid.

Figure 6.3 is a sagittal diagram showing the tongue positions for the vowels [i] and [æ].

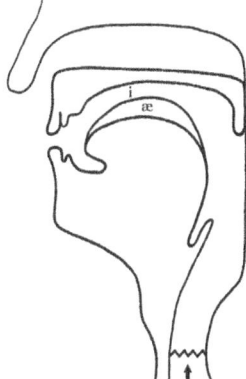

Figure 6.3. Tongue height positions for [i] and [æ].

The acoustical range of vowel sounds that a person can produce is determined by the dimensions of his or her vocal cavities. Thus, for example, just as the musical range of a small but articulate child's intonation is much higher than that of the mother, and the mother's range is usually higher than that of the father, so is the range of a child's vowel qualities quite different from those of his or her parents. Yet people can understand the child, the father and the mother equally well, because they listen to each person's vowels in terms of that person's vowel space, and they listen to each person's intonation patterns and vowel qualities relative to that person's pitch range. Similarly, different people's vocal cavities (including the nasal cavities and chest) are differently proportioned, making their vowel spaces significantly different acoustically and probably musically, but not linguistically.

Vowels as central oral resonant sounds

In reiterating and expanding the definition of a vowel, we note that a vowel's airstream flows over the central part of the tongue. That is, a vowel is a speech sound with three essential components: *central*, *oral*, and *resonant* (or SONORANT). It is CENTRAL because the airstream goes over the center of the tongue, not its sides.[3] It is ORAL because the airstream goes through the oral cavity. (This contrasts with a nasal consonant in which the airflow is blocked in the oral cavity but flows through the nasal cavity. A *nasalized* sound is one in which the airflow goes both through the oral cavity and the nasal cavity. Hence a nasalized vowel is considered oral even though it also has airflow through the nasal cavity.) It is a RESONANT in that it is a sound with relatively free airflow; any constrictions in the path of the airstream are insufficient to produce audible noise or friction, and thus the sound is not a fricative.

These distinctions of oral, central, resonant, and airflow over the tongue are represented in table 6.1. Note that a resonant contrasts with an obstruent, a sound produced with some constriction of the airstream, whether partial or complete.

---

[3] This indicates that the sound is not a lateral.

Table 6.1. Phonetic features of vowels

Phonetic feature	Description of phonetic feature	What the sound would be if this feature were not true
Central	airstream flows over the center of the tongue on a midsagittal plane	lateral
Resonant	no obstruction or constriction noise	fricative
Continuant	could be continued indefinitely	stop
Oral	airflow only through oral cavity	nasalized vowel

Figure 6.4, below, illustrates the place of vowels in the scheme of all speech sounds.

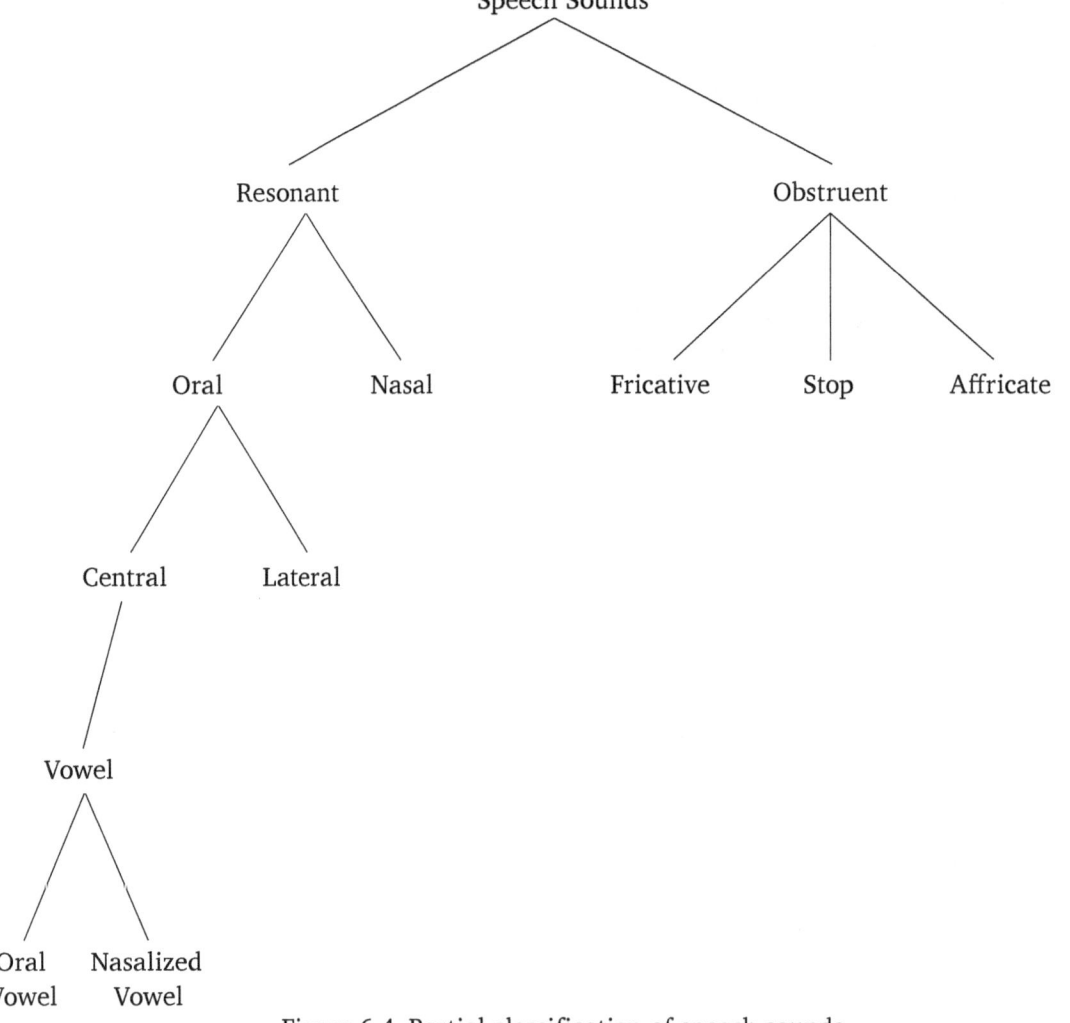

Figure 6.4. Partial classification of speech sounds.

Based on figure 6.4, consider whether the following sounds are vowels: [u, l, m, d, ɵ]. Considerations for each of these are as follows:

[u] is a vowel because it is a central oral resonant continuant.
[l] is an oral resonant but it is lateral rather than central, so it is not a vowel.

6: Vowels

[m] is a nasal resonant, so it is not a vowel.
[d] and [θ] are obstruents, so they are not vowels.

Discussion of nasals, nasalized vowels, affricates, semivowels, and laterals will be taken up in later chapters.

Cardinal vowels

Daniel Jones (1881–1967), a British phonetician, proposed the CARDINAL VOWEL system. Cardinal vowels serve as reference positions for use in analyzing vowels encountered in the world's languages. The cardinal vowels together with their numbers are shown in figure 6.5.

Jones hypothesized that vowels 2–4 are theoretically equidistant from each other between the extremes [i] and [ɑ]. [i] is defined as being produced as far forward in the mouth as possible with the tongue as high as possible without producing audible friction (Jones 1940:31-32). The vowel [ɑ] is produced with the tongue as low and as far back as possible. It occurs in a word like "father." Both [i] and [ɑ] are produced with unrounded or spread lips. The cardinal vowels [e], [ɛ], and [a] are equidistant from each other between [i] and [ɑ].

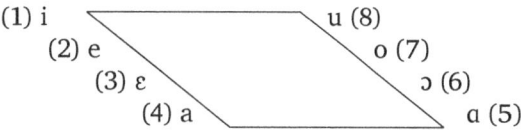

Figure 6.5. Cardinal vowels.

The cardinal vowels [u], [o], and [ɔ] are more rounded than cardinal vowels 1–5. The vowel [u] is defined as the highest back rounded vowel; it is produced as far back in the mouth as possible, with the tongue as high as possible without producing audible friction.

While these cardinal vowels have been very useful as a standard against which a field linguist can compare vowels in specific languages, they have the disadvantage in that they cannot be learned from reading about them. They must be learned from some auditory source, whether from a teacher or a recording.

Though the cardinal vowels are close to English vowels, because of dialectal differences in spoken varieties, these vowels should not be identified with any specific English dialect. For example, the [ɑ] in many English dialects is produced further forward in the mouth than in the cardinal vowel system. A further problem with this system is the question of how to define articulatory equidistance between vowels.

Within this vowel system there is also a series of secondary cardinal vowels. Cardinal vowels 9–12 are front rounded, cardinal vowel 13 is back rounded, and cardinal vowels 14–16 are back unrounded vowels.

(9)   y   the tongue position is the same as for [i] with lip rounding added
(10) ø   the tongue position is the same as for [e] with lip rounding added
(11) œ   the tongue position is the same as for [ɛ] with lip rounding added
(12) ɶ   the tongue position is the same as for [a] with lip rounding added
(13) ɒ   the tongue position is the same as for [ɑ] with lip rounding added
(14) ʌ   the tongue position is the same as for [ɔ] with the lips unrounded
(15) ɤ   the tongue position is the same as for [o] with the lips unrounded
(16) ɯ   the tongue position is the same as for [u] with the lips unrounded

Figure 6.6 shows the placement of all the vowels on the vowel chart. (Note: the terms in parentheses are not used in IPA.) Where vowel symbols appear in pairs, the one to the right represents a ROUNDED vowel and the one on the left an UNROUNDED one.

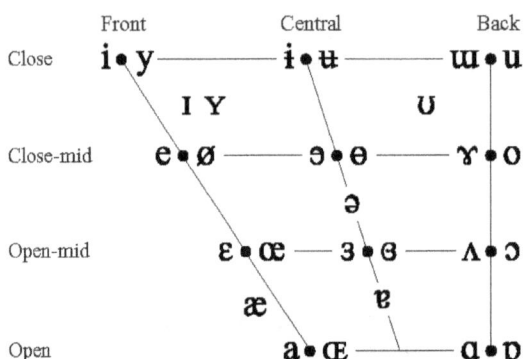

Figure 6.6. IPA vowel diagram.

Functions of vowels in syllables

While vowel placement in syllables is usually analyzed in phonology, it is helpful to consider the function of vowels briefly in phonetics. A vowel is usually the most prominent sound in a syllable, and it comprises the syllable nucleus. By contrast, consonants occupy the syllable onset and coda. Note, however, that a vowel may comprise a syllable without consonants surrounding it, e.g., 'a' in 'a plum' and in 'aplomb' [ə.pʰləm]. In phonetic notation a period [.] is used to separate syllables.

Although vowels are the typical syllabic sounds, some consonants may be syllabic (for further discussion see chapter 22).

The most common vowel

The most common vowel found in the world's languages is [ɑ]. While various sounds in language are written orthographically and in most computer fonts as [a], in transcribing phonetic data, it is important to be careful to distinguish [ɑ], [æ], and [a].

Because [ɑ] is the most common vowel in Jju, we introduced this vowel first in the primers, as it enabled us to include a large number of words. Consider the following Jju words both as citation forms and in context.[4]

á	'you'	á bá	'you came'
bá	'come, came' (verb)	bà bá	'they came'
bà	'they' (pronoun)	bàbà bá	'father came'
bàbá	'father'	bà bá bàʔ	'they didn't come'
bàʔ	'negative'	bàbà bá bàʔ	'father didn't come'

Glided vowels

The vowels on the chart in figure 6.2 represent *unglided vowels*. This means that the tongue is held in one position—it does not move. Vowel GLIDES refer to movement from one vowel to another, e.g., [ɑⁱ]. When producing a glided vowel, the tongue position changes, thus changing the vowel quality, e.g., [ɑⁱ, eⁱ]. Glided vowels are also called DIPHTHONGS.

Words in English such as 'bee,' 'too,' and 'tall' have unglided vowels in most dialects. However, in many words the vowels are glided; the tongue moves from one vowel position to another during the production of the vowel, as in 'boat,' 'take,' 'bite.' For an American English speaker learning a new language, the challenge may be to learn to pronounce these vowels as unglided, specifically pronouncing [oᵘ, eⁱ, ɐⁱ] as [o, e, ɐ]. While these glides are common in English, you may find other vowel glides in other languages.

IPA uses either a superscript or diacritic notation to represent a vowel glide. Thus the vowel glide 'o' in English, such as in 'oh,' can be transcribed as either oᵘ or [ou̯]. Similarly, vowel glide 'e' in 'eight' is transcribed either as [eⁱ] or [ei̯].

---

[4]In these data [´] indicates high tone and [`] low tone.

6: Vowels

Pronunciation helps

Figure 6.2 introduced symbols representing vowels that are quite similar to English vowels. However, they also differ from several English vowels in that all of the symbols given represent unglided vowels.

Listed below are some English words with various vowel sounds and some hints on how to produce unglided vowels.

- [i] 'skeet'
- [ɪ] 'nit'
- [e] 'late' For contrast, work to pronounce this vowel without gliding towards [eⁱ].
- [ɛ] 'let'
- [æ] 'that' Try to pronounce this word without the vowel gliding toward [æə], a vowel glide which is common in southern American English.
- [a] 'park' This occurs in a New England dialect, in which the 'r' sound is deleted.
- [ɨ] 'the' This vowel occurs only in unstressed syllables in English, though it is a contrastive vowel in many other languages. In some English dialects this vowel is closer to [ə] than to [ɨ]. It probably occurs most often as [ɨ] in southern American English, e.g., 'roses' [ɹoziz].
- [ə] 'lush, cup'
- [u] 'loot, too, hoot'
- [ʊ] 'look, took'
- [o] 'low, toe' This is often glided to [oᵘ]. Work to produce an unglided [o].
- [ɔ] 'caught, sought' In some English dialects this vowel is a glide, i.e., [ɔə].

In the Western dialect of American English, [ɔ] and [ɑ] have merged or are merging into one sound unit. For example, 'cot' and 'caught', or 'tot' and 'taught', are pronounced almost identically; the listener must use context to distinguish them. In midwestern and eastern American English these have retained separate vowel qualities.

Here are a few hints that a mother tongue speaker of American English may use to learn to say vowels without the common diphthongs.

1. Be aware that certain vowels in English are produced as diphthongs or with an offglide on the vowel. This information helps a great deal in being able to produce unglided vowels. First, learn to pronounce unglided [e, ɑ, o] in isolation. In order to do so with each vowel, be careful not to move your tongue or jaw. Perhaps you will find it helpful to look into a mirror as you pronounce them so that you know that your tongue and/or jaw do not move. Next, put these sounds into English words such as 'late,' 'ate,' and 'hoe,' and pronounce them without the offglide. You will sound like a non-native speaker.

2. Say each vowel in isolation, for example, pronounce a long [o:] and [e:]. When doing so, be careful not to glide each vowel. Practice also pronouncing [ɑ:] without an offglide.

3. Pronounce [o:h] and [e:h]. Adding [h] following the vowel may help you say the vowel without gliding it.

4. In order to be aware of the vowel continuum, alternate saying 'ee' [i] and 'oo' [u] as shown in figure 6.1. For which sound is your tongue further forward? What do your lips do, and on which sound? Lip rounding or lack of it is an important articulatory characteristic of vowels. In English front vowels are made with unrounded lips, while most back vowels are produced with rounded lips. The vowel [ɔ] is also produced with rounded lips, as in the word 'caught.' In figure 6.3 note the different height of the tongue in the production of [i] in 'beet' and [æ] in 'bat.'

Additional rounded and unrounded vowels

While the vowels introduced so far are those found in English, other vowels are contrastive in other languages in the world. These are the front rounded, central unrounded, and back unrounded vowels. Figure 6.6 displays a more complete set of IPA vowel symbols than are presented in figure 6.2. The pair [ɪ], [ʏ] are near-close front vowels, while [ʊ] is back. Since there is no symbol on the chart for a near-close back unrounded vowel to pair with [ʊ], which is rounded, we use a diacritic [ˌ] for lowering, placed below the close back unrounded vowel [ɯ] to represent the near-close back unrounded vowel.

Apical vowels, also called fricative vowels, are covered in chapter 22.

Slight modifications of vowels

When studying a language, you may find that the vowels you hear fall between those on the IPA vowel chart. In order to symbolize these vowel qualities, the IPA has a set of diacritics that are used to indicate a vowel that is slightly lower, slightly further back, slightly more fronted, or slightly higher than the IPA vowel. These are added to the closest vowel symbol. These diacritics are presented in table 6.2. Note that these diacritics are placed directly below the base character.

It is very unlikely that the only phonetic difference between two words with different meanings will be as slight as the difference between, for example, [e] and [e̝]. It is much more likely that, in a particular language, some vowels will consistently be pronounced a bit further forward than the ones in the phonetic vowel diagram, or a bit higher. That is, minor variations in tongue position on vowels are not likely to be PHONOLOGICALLY CONTRASTIVE. For example, after you have discovered that /e/ is always pronounced a bit higher in the mouth in the language you are studying than the norm, you may decide to stop writing [e̝] and simply write 'e,' while remembering that this vowel is pronounced higher than the auditory norm for this vowel. By pronouncing it like the native speakers do, you will not have a foreign accent (for that vowel); you will note that difference in papers you write about the language. However, it is inadvisable to ignore such phonetic detail too early in your language study because your initial hypotheses about what is phonologically contrastive may change with further analysis.

Table 6.2. Diacritics representing slight differences in vowel quality

Diacritics indicating shifted tongue position on vowels, using [e] and [o] as examples	
Advanced (fronted)	o̟
Retracted (backed)	e̠
Raised	e̝
Lowered	o̞

Pronunciation helps for additional vowels

In order to pronounce the front rounded vowels, first produce the unrounded one, i.e., [i], then add lip rounding to produce [y]. Do the same with each of the front rounded vowels, e.g., [e]→[ø], [ɛ]→[œ], [a]→[ɶ].

[y] Say 'She sees these seeds' which has several instances of [i]. Then say it again, with your tongue in the same position for [i] but your lips rounded for [u]. Now say [y] a few times in isolation.

6: Vowels

[ø] Say 'Kate sails by eight lakes' slowly without gliding the vowels. Then pronounce it again with your tongue in position for [e], but with your lips rounded for [o]. Now say [ø] in isolation a few times.

[œ] Say 'Fred said, Ned's dead!' Then say it again with your tongue in position for [ɛ] as before, but with lips rounded as for [ɔ]. Now say the vowel in isolation.

[ɯ] Say 'Who chooses coot?' Position your tongue as for [u] but with your lips slightly spread throughout, as for [i]. Do not let your tongue shift forward toward the [i] position. Now say the back unrounded vowel [ɯ] in isolation.

[ɤ] Say 'Moe, go blow the snow with the snowblower!' slowly without gliding. Say it again with your tongue consciously held back in the [o] position, and your lips slightly spread, as for [e]. Now say the close-mid back unrounded vowel [ɤ] in isolation a few times.

[ʌ] or [ɑ] or [ɒ] In learning how to differentiate these three, your pronunciation will depend on which one or two of these that you use in English.

   a. Do you make a distinction between the English words 'cot' [kʰɑt] with unrounded lips and 'caught' [kʰɔt] with rounded lips? Say [kʰɔt] again with your tongue kept back in the position for [ɔ], but with your lips slightly spread. The resulting vowel should be the back unrounded vowel [ʌ]. Repeat the vowel [ʌ] several times in isolation.

   b. If you do not make a distinction between the English words 'cot' and 'caught,' but pronounce both as [kʰɑt], say the words with your tongue kept back in the position for [ɑ], but with your lips slightly rounded. The resulting vowels should be the open back rounded vowel [ɒ]. Repeat the vowel [ɒ] several times in isolation.

If you find that your tongue and lips seem to work together as an English set and insist on making only front unrounded and back rounded vowels, the techniques of slurring and bracketing might help. SLURRING involves sliding your tongue back and forth or up and down through a whole range of vowel qualities while maintaining a constant lip position. For example, keeping your lip position constant and voicing continuous in a monotone, slide your tongue slowly back and forth between [i] and [ɯ]:

   i------------------------------ɯ

To practice front rounded vowels, keep your lips rounded and voicing going, while sliding your tongue slowly back and forth between [y] and [u]:

   y------------------------------u

Slurring may help you become aware of what your tongue is doing rather than focusing both on what your tongue and lips are doing. As you slur between vowels that are widely apart, you move through the whole continuum of possible vowel sounds at a given tongue height:

   i-------------------------------ɯ   y-------------------------------u
   i--------------ɨ-----------------ɯ   y--------------u̶---------------u
   i-------ɨ-------ɨ-------ɯ̟-------ɯ   y------y̠--------u------u̟--------u

When BRACKETING, concentrate on the extremes of your tongue positions; move from [i] to [ɯ]. You may also place your tongue at a point in the middle between them, i.e., [ɨ]. This is a way to locate vowels that are intermediate between other vowels and that may be difficult to find.

The examples of slurring and bracketing given so far have shown tongue movement along the front-central-back dimension. It is also possible and useful to slur and bracket up and down, from low to high or high to low.

In this case, you are keeping your lip position and tongue frontness-or-backness constant while moving your tongue up and down through the full range of possible vowel heights.

Key terms

vowel
- vocoid/contoid
- vowel quality
- tongue positions: front, back, central
- vowel space
- central
- resonant, sonorant
- continuant
- four primary degrees and three intermediate degrees of close – open
- lip positions: rounded, unrounded
- cardinal vowel
- vowel glide
- glided vowel, unglided vowel
- diphthong
- phonologically contrastive sounds
- diacritics for slight differences of vowel quality
- slurring, bracketing
- IPA symbols and names for all vowels in the chapter

Exercises

1. Practice the following differentiation drill three times:

baba	babu	babɨ	babʊ	bibɨ
tʰita	tʰitɨ	tʰita	tʰitɛ	tʰitɪ
kekʰu	kekʰə	kekʰɔ	kekʰæ	kekʰɐ
dædɔ	dæda	dædɨ	dædʊ	dædo

2. Practice making the contrasts between these words in French (from Tranel 1987):

de	'thimble'	fe	'fairy'
dɛ	'canopy'	fɛ	'fact'
epe	'sword'	ge	'ford'
epɛ	'thick'	gɛ	'happy'
ete	'summer'	pike	'to sting'
etɛ	'was'	pikɛ	'stake'

3. Practice pronouncing the following words from German and French:

ˈtɔnə	'ton'	German
gɔt	'God'	German
pat	'paw'	French
fas	'face'	French

4. Practice pronouncing the following Lao words (data from Roffe as cited in E. V. Pike 1963:17):

kɑk	'skin disease'	kɑt	'gnaw'
kʰək	'clear'	bɑp	'sin'
kʰop	'bite'	pʰət	'to brush'
tɔt	'to strike'		

5. Practice slurring and bracketing with any vowels that you have difficulty producing.

6. Practice saying the following word drills aloud three times each:

fitʰy	fitʰʉ	fɯtʰu
ɸɪgɤ	ɸegø	ɸɯgʊ

| vɛdœ | vɜdʌ | vɛdɔ |
| kʰabœ | kʰɤbo | kʰibɒ |

7. Practice pronouncing the following Shipibo data from Peru (Loriot as cited in E. V. Pike 1963:18), Norwegian (E. V. Pike 1963:18), and French (E. V. Pike 1963:17):

Phonetic transcription	English gloss	Language
ˈβɤte	'to take'	Shipibo
tɨɬɨ	'hawk'	Shipibo
bʏː	'town'	Norwegian
bʉː	'shack'	Norwegian
buː	'to live'	Norwegian
ty	'you'	French
tu	'all'	French
pat	'paw'	French
vøːl	'spineless'	French
vœl	'want'	French

8. Draw a vowel chart with the eight primary cardinal vowels and the eight secondary cardinal vowels. Include labels for seven degrees of openness of the vocal tract, three degrees of tongue frontness and backness, and lip rounding and unrounding.

9. Write the names for the following vowels:

[ə] _____

[ɨ] _____

[ø] _____

[ɰ] _____

[ɤ] _____

[e] _____

[ʊ] _____

[æ] _____

[ʉ] _____

[ʏ] _____

[ɪ] _____

7

Flaps, Taps, and Trills

FLAPS, TAPS, and TRILLS are speech sounds produced with a motion of the articulator(s) that is more ballistic and less controlled in detail than are otherwise similar sounds. As a result, the active articulator touches the passive articulator more briefly for a flap, tap, or trill than for similar sounds, e.g., stops and nasals.

For a tap or a flap, the active and passive articulators are in contact with each other only once. For a tap, the active articulator returns to its neutral position after touching the passive articulator. For a flap, the active articulator touches the passive articulator as it moves to another articulatory target. For a trill, the articulators typically contact each other more than once in rapid succession.

During production of a stop, nasal, or lateral approximant, the movement of the active articulator is under direct muscular control throughout the articulation. The active articulator moves to the passive articulator, maintains contact with it momentarily, and then draws away, all in a controlled manner. In contrast, in the articulation of a flap, tap, or trill, the movement of the active articulator is under direct muscular control moving toward the articulatory target, but the motion of the active articulator also depends considerably on its inertia and elasticity in combination with aerodynamic forces on it.

In producing a *trill,* controlled muscular tension positions the active articulator so that it comes very close to or lightly touches the passive articulator. Air pressure building up behind this constriction or closure forces the articulators apart, allowing air to flow through the opening. The increased velocity of air passing through the constriction between the two articulators creates a partial vacuum between them (the BERNOULLI EFFECT) which pulls the articulators back into contact with each other. This vibratory cycle repeats (at a rate of about one repetition every thirtieth of a second) as long as the airflow and the general position of the active articulator are favorable for sustained vibration. Thus the vibration of the lips, tongue tip, or uvula in producing a trill is much like the vibration of the vocal folds in voicing. Just as voicing may be so brief that it consists of just one pulse of air resulting from a single momentary opening of the glottis (see chapter 23), a trill may be so brief that it consists of a single contact between the active and the passive articulators (Ladefoged 1993:168).

During the articulation of a *flap,* the active articulator touches the passive articulator in passing on its way to another articulation. In American English a common flap begins with the tongue tip curled back. From this position, the tongue tip flops forward, propelled by a combination of muscular tension, elasticity of the tongue, and air pressure (during the time that the airstream is completely blocked). These forces are augmented by pressure from the airstream behind the closure as the tongue tip strikes the alveolar ridge (or just behind it) on its way to rest behind the lower front teeth. This describes a retroflex flap, the initial consonant of the third syllable of "Satur_d_ay." Thus, elasticity, inertia, muscular tension, and air pressure combine to produce a flap.

In articulating a *tap,* a burst of muscular tension throws the active articulator against the passive articulator, but the muscular tension does not continue long, and the active articulator promptly falls back to its resting position, again propelled by some combination of elasticity of the tongue and the air pressure that builds during the time that the airstream is completely blocked. Taps are probably simply shortening certain stops, nasals, or laterals. Table 7.1 summarizes some of the more common flaps, taps, and trills. The IPA does not distinguish between flaps and taps, since no language is known to contrast the two. The same symbols are used to transcribe both types of articulation.

Table 7.1. Flaps, taps, and trills

	Bilabial	Labiodental	Dental	Alveolar	Retroflex	Uvular	
Voiceless	p̥̆	v̥̆	r̥̆	ɾ̥	ʈ̥̆		flap and/or tap
Voiced	b̆	v̆	ɾ̪	ɾ	ɽ		
Voiced				ɺ	ɭ̆		lateral flap or tap
Voiced	m̆			n̆	ɳ̆		nasal flap or tap
Voiceless	ʙ̥		r̪̥	r̥		ʀ̥	trill
Voiced	ʙ		r̪	r		ʀ	

Table 7.2 illustrates three distinct trajectories of the tongue tip as the active articulator in producing taps and flaps:

Table 7.2. Tongue movements in taps and flaps

Tongue action	Direction of movement	Example
A. The tongue tip taps the alveolar ridge and returns to its resting position.	↗↓	[ˈkʰɪɾi] 'kitty'
B. The tongue tip flaps against the alveolar ridge on its way from front to back.	⤴→	[ˈbəɾɚ] 'butter'
C. The under side of the tongue tip flaps against the back of the alveolar ridge on its way from back to front.	←⤵	[ˈpʰɑɽi] 'party'

Type A movement occurs as a tap medially in many English words, e.g., [ˈhɪɾi] 'hilly', [ˈhaɾoᵘ] 'hollow', [ˈpʰəp̆i] 'puppy', and [ˈməm̆i] 'mummy'. Note that pronunciations of these words vary according to different dialects.

Type B movement occurs as a flap immediately preceding a syllabic 'r' in many English words, e.g., [ˈfɛɾɚ] 'fetter', and [ˈbæn̆ɚ] 'banner' (at least in fast speech). Type C movement occurs as a flap immediately following either a consonantal 'r' or a syllabic 'r' in many English words, e.g., 'barley' [ˈbɑɹɭi]. The first flap in 'Saturday' [ˈsæɾəɽeⁱ] is of Type B and the second flap is of Type C.

Usually the flaps in both members of a minimal pair of words such as 'latter' [læɾɚ] and 'ladder' [læˑɾɚ] are voiced. (Note that use of the small wedge following the vowel [æˑ] indicates added length on the vowel.) The phonetic contrast between these two words is vowel length: the vowel preceding the flap is longer in 'ladder' than in 'latter'. Length is discussed further in chapter 16.

The Type A tap and the Type B flap illustrated above are written with the same phonetic symbols (the four flap symbols found in the alveolar column in table 7.1), even though their trajectories are somewhat different. That is, a voiced alveolar lateral tap or Type B flap is written as [ɺ], a voiced alveolar nasal tap or Type B flap as [n̆]. Probably this is because the first part of the trajectory and the place of articulation are similar for the two and because the two types have not been found to be contrastive in any language.

7: Flaps, Taps, and Trills

Type C flaps are retroflex flaps, and they are written with symbols different from those used for types A and B, because they involve a different active articulator (the bottom side of the tongue tip rather than the top side), and because they are used in contrast with the other two types. To produce a retroflex flap the tongue tip moves forward from the retroflex position.

Pronunciation helps

To produce a trill you must do three things: position the active articulator(s) correctly, relax it (or them), and blow between with the right rate of airflow. You cannot produce a trill by firing off a rapid series of short stops, taps, or flaps, because each one requires a separate controlled muscular contraction, and the neuromuscular system is unable to repeat individual contractions at that rate.

- [ɾ]—Say [kʰəˈdɑ] faster and faster to [kʰɾɑ]. Do the same for [guˈdu] to [gɾu] and for [dɑˈdɑ] to [dɾɑ].
- [ɾ̥]—Try [h] before and perhaps during the voiceless flap.
- [r]—For the expression, 'brrr', used to express how cold you feel, relax your tongue to produce this trill, because it needs to be set in vibration by the moving airstream. Keep your jaw fairly closed. Try saying 'butter up' or 'put it on', more and more rapidly, until they become [bəɾɚ əp] and [pɾɑn/pɾɔn].
- [ɺ]—Say 'Billy' [ˈbɪɺi] or 'Kelly' [ˈkʰɛɺi] rapidly.
- [ɭ̆]—Say 'Merlin' [ˈmɚɭ̆ɪn] or 'early' [ˈɚɭ̆i] rapidly.
- [ñ]—Say 'fainting' [feiñĩŋ] rapidly.
- [ʙ]—Imitate the sound a horse makes with its lips.
- [ʙ̥]—When it's cold, you may say [ʙ̥]. Your lips need to be looser than for [β]. Note that in Southeast Asia this sound has been found to function as a vowel [ʙ̩] (Edmondson 2000, lecture given at GIAL). Alexander reports that in Mixtec (Mexico) this sound is used to call turkeys (Ruth Mary Alexander as cited in Bickford and Floyd 2003:143).
- [ʀ]—When a person snores, the sound is produced with ingressive air rather than egressive, and it is produced with the same articulators as an egressive trill. Try alternating between a snore and a voiceless uvular trill. Gargling can produce an egressive uvular trill, voiced for some people, voiceless for others.

Key terms

flap
tap

the Bernouilli effect
trill

Exercises

1. Practice the following Spanish words:

pɛɾo	'but'	bɛɾɛða	'path'
pero	'dog'	bɛɾɑko	'boar'
pɑhɑɾo	'bird'	fɑɾɑ	'salmon trout'
buɾo	'donkey'	fɑɾolɑ	'lighthouse'
pɑɾlɑɾ	'to speak with facility'	bɛɾuɣɑ	'wart'
poro	'joint'	bɛɾuɣo	'miser'

2. Practice the following Jju words (Nigeria; McKinney data):

kʰɾɑkʰukʰɑ	'sound of train wheels going over railroad ties'
əʃiʃɾɪm	'cold'
dɾɑm	'red monkey'
ɾotʰ	'because'
dʒɾɪŋ	'one'
tʰɾɪm	'to tremble'

kʰəɾam	'when, time'
ətʰɾo	'cloth, clothe'
kʰəŋkʰɾaŋ	'town'
sɾaŋ	'to be without'
ɾan	'to be better than'

3. Tongue twister. Practice saying this English tongue twister rapidly:

   'Daddy dutifully dated a dotty Dane dame.'

4. Practice the following Amharic data (Ethiopia, data from Pete Unseth, personal communication):

abɜru	'they made it shine'
abarɜɾu	'they chased away'

5. Give symbols for the following (some have two possible symbols):

   1) Voiced bilabial trill   [   ]
   2) Voiceless bilabial trill   [   ]
   3) Voiced uvular trill   [   ]
   4) Voiceless uvular trill   [   ]
   5) Voiced alveolar lateral flap [   ]
   6) Voiced retroflex lateral flap [   ]

6. Give names for the following sounds:

   [b̌] _____

   [R] _____

   [r̥] _____

   [t̥] _____

   [ň̩] _____

   [ɽ] _____

8

Stress

In many languages one or more syllables in an utterance may be perceived as having more PROMINENCE than other syllables in that same utterance. This prominence is called STRESS. A speaker produces stress on a syllable by exerting greater effort than in producing an otherwise similar unstressed syllable. This extra effort results in increased pressures in the vocal tract, particularly the transglottal pressure in the case of sounds made with egressive pulmonic air. This greater effort requires greater tension in the muscles of the larynx, in the intercostal muscles which help to force the air out of the lungs, and perhaps also in the muscles of articulation.

A listener perceives a STRESSED SYLLABLE as having more *prominence* than an otherwise similar unstressed syllable because of one or more of the following physical differences:

- It is longer in duration.
- It has greater intensity.
- Its prominence may be from a combination of characteristics: loudness, longer duration and pitch variations.
- The vowel quality may be different from that of unstressed vowels in an otherwise similar phonetic environment. For example, in English, the vowel in an unstressed syllable is often a centralized vowel, e.g., [ə]. Usually the vowels in stressed syllables lie somewhere near the periphery of the two-dimensional vowel space.

Whereas in most languages the length of a syllable is the primary cue that a syllable is stressed, in some languages other parameters may contribute more to the perception of prominence. For example, the pitch contour may play a crucial role. On the other hand, many languages have contrastive length on consonants or vowels or both that is independent of stress.

A technique to help identify the stressed syllables in an utterance is to ask a mother tongue speaker of the language to tap with a finger or an object (e.g., a pencil or a percussion instrument such as a drum) while speaking the utterance. The bursts of physical energy exerted in tapping often correlate in timing with the bursts of physical energy that produce stressed syllables. If the speaker exhibits this correlation, the identification of the stressed syllables by tapping may lead to identification of the correlates of stress in that language.

A syllable may be stressed for various reasons. In a given language, stress placement may function to indicate a meaning (lexical) difference in words. A speaker may also stress a certain syllable to call the listener's attention to the particular syllable, word, or phrase in which it occurs. Stressing a syllable may also intensify the meaning of the word.

In IPA, a small raised vertical mark ['], the stress mark, placed just before a syllable, indicates that the syllable is stressed. Some stressed syllables may appear to have a greater degree of stress than others. These syllables have PRIMARY STRESS. Syllables with less prominence have SECONDARY STRESS; the lowered IPA stress symbol [ˌ] identifies these less-stressed syllables in the transcription. The IPA symbol chart gives the transcription [ˌfoʊnəˈtɪʃən] 'phonetician' as an example of primary and secondary stress. Some linguists also mark *tertiary stress*.

Correlates of stress in English are pitch, vowel length, and vowel quality. In the following pairs of words the pitch rises and vowels lengthen in stressed syllables, while vowels in unstressed syllables are often reduced to [ə] or [i]. Note that a change in stress placement in English correlates with a meaning difference in the following examples.[1]

ˈcontract	[ˈkʰɑːntɹækt̪ʰ]	'a legally binding agreement'
conˈtract	[kʰənˈtɹæːkt̪ʰ]	'to reduce in size'
ˈreject	[ˈɹiːdʒɛkt̪ʰ]	'that which is rejected'
reˈject	[ɹiˈdʒɛːkt̪ʰ]	'to refuse, shun'
ˈcommune	[ˈkʰɑːmjun]	'a collective farm'
comˈmune	[kʰəˈmjuːn]	'to communicate intimately'

Most languages have a metrical structure, a rhythm of stress placement that is vital to intelligibility as well as to sounding natural when speaking that language. The metrical structure leads to the phonetic correlates of the rhythm or stress placement in the language in focus.

Timing in languages: Syllable-timed, stress-timed, and mora-timed

In a SYLLABLE-TIMED language *consecutive* syllables tend to occur at regular timed intervals, whereas in a STRESS-TIMED language the *stressed* syllables tend to occur at regular timed intervals.

The timing of stressed syllables in a phrase gives that phrase a distinctive rhythm. Consequently, variations in the use of stress cause different languages to have different rhythms. English and other Germanic languages are stress timed languages, with stressed syllables occurring at roughly evenly timed intervals regardless of the number of intervening unstressed syllables. This occurs because the duration of the unstressed syllables between them varies; the more unstressed syllables there are between the two consecutive stressed syllables, the shorter the unstressed syllables are.

In contrast with Germanic languages, languages such as French and Spanish are syllable-timed, with all syllables tending to have approximately the same duration. For example, in the Spanish sentence, *'¿Como se llama usted?'*, 'What is your name?', each syllable is given about the same duration of time and the same amount of stress.

When hearing a syllable-timed language spoken, speakers of stress-timed languages may think that the language is spoken very rapidly, because there is no difference in the timing of the syllables. Conversely, speakers of syllable-timed languages think those who speak stress-timed languages speak rapidly, as some syllables are shorter than others.

A MORA is a phonological unit that is longer than a single segment but typically shorter than a syllable. Crystal states that "The analysis of SEGMENTS into moras is usually applied only to the syllabic NUCLEUS and CODA (the RHYME), and not to the onset ('onset/rhyme asymmetry')" (Crystal 2003:299, upper case in the original). The RHYME or RIME is the part of

> **Experiment 8.1: Rhythm**
>
> Select a short passage of English text and arrange for a good speaker of English to assist you. Have the speaker read the text in a normal manner while simultaneously tapping the stressed syllables audibly. The first reading of the text should be for practice. The second reading can be for data acquisition. Record this reading. Next, listen to the audio recording focusing on the taps. Do the taps come at relatively regular intervals or does the interval between taps depend on the number of syllables? Is English a syllable-timed or stress-timed language?
> When you have completed the experiment for English, carry out the same procedure for Spanish or French. How do the results for the two languages compare? You may wish to quantify the observations of timing. You can do so using any of several waveform editors.

---

[1] A colon following a segment indicates the segment is long. Length on vowels and consonants will be discussed further in chapter 16.

the syllable that consists of its nucleus and any following segments. In dealing with moras, there is a contrast between a LIGHT SYLLABLE which has one mora, and a HEAVY SYLLABLE which consists of two moras. A MORA-TIMED language is one in which moras recur at regular intervals. It is the syllable weight, whether a light or heavy syllable, that is significant in the rhythm. Moras are important as part of the rhythm in some languages, such as Japanese.

In our definition of a *mora,* note that it is a phonological definition, not a phonetic one, per se. However, in our discussion of different types of timing in languages, it is appropriate to mention mora timing here.

In order for you to develop a good accent when learning to speak another language, mimic carefully the rhythm of the language, including the relative pattern of stresses and duration of its syllables. By doing so, you will avoid sounding foreign to native speakers.

Key terms and symbols

stress
stressed syllable
stress mark
stress-timed
syllable-timed
mora-timed

mora
rhyme/rime
light syllable, heavy syllable
primary stress [']
prominence
secondary stress [ˌ]

Exercises

1. Practice the following English words, paying particular attention to stress differences:

'contract	[ˈkʰɑːntɹæktʰ]	'a legally binding agreement'
conˈtract	[kʰənˈtɹæːktʰ]	'to reduce in size'
'reject	[ˈɹiːdʒɛktʰ]	'that which is rejected'
reˈject	[ɹiˈdʒɛːktʰ]	'to refuse, shun'
'compact	[ˈkʰɑːmpʰækt]	'a formal agreement or contract'
comˈpact	[kʰəmˈpʰæːkt]	'to join or pact together'
'permit	[ˈpʰɚːmɪt] or [ˈpʰəːɹmɪt]	'a document granting permission'
perˈmit	[pʰɚˈmɪːt]	'to allow, to consent'

2. Practice reading a paragraph from any English book. First, read it normally. Second, read it placing the stress on the second word of each phrase or sentence only. Third, read it giving each syllable the same length of time. Notice how each of the second and third modifications results in your sounding less like normal English pronunciation.

3. Name four ways that a listener perceives stress on a syllable:

   a. _____
   b. _____
   c. _____
   d. _____

4. What vowels tend to be in unstressed syllables in English?

   [ ]
   [ ]

5. Name two syllable-timed languages: _____

   Name a language in which moras are important to the rhythm: _____

6. Name two stress-timed languages: _____

9

Pitch and Intonation

PITCH is our auditory perception of a sound in terms of where it is on a scale from low to high. It corresponds to the rate at which the vocal folds complete each vibration cycle, namely the acoustic fundamental frequency. In language, the RELATIVE pitch of the voice is significant, not the ABSOLUTE pitch.

Proper use of the pitch of your voice is extremely important for good pronunciation. When you are learning a language, it is important for you to mimic the relative pitches as carefully as you pronounce individual segments. Failure to use correct pitch will result in your sounding foreign. It may also communicate a message different from what you intend or communicate simply nonsense! For example, in Nigeria, when we asked a local person the way to a particular town, we inquired whether we were near [óyò] (a high-low pitch pattern). He looked at us with a complete lack of understanding. With our phonetics background in mind, we began to ask the name of the town by changing the tones on the two vowels. Were we near [óyò], [òyò] or [òyó]? We were, in fact, quite close to [òyó], (a low-high pitch pattern). That lesson reinforced for us the importance of having correct tone for communicating specific lexical items.

In addition to pitch signaling which syllables of a word are stressed, as discussed in chapter eight, pitch is used in languages in two additional ways, as INTONATION and as TONE. *Intonation* is the use of pitch over an entire sentence or utterance to convey emotions, attitudes, the relative urgency of the information, and, in almost all languages, it also has grammatical functions. For example, in American English it distinguishes statements and yes-no questions. The following examples illustrate two sentences, identical except for intonation.

> *Tone and a traffic checkpoint*
>
> Carol and a friend were stopped at a police check-point in Nigeria on their way home at about 10 p.m. When the driver greeted the officer with "[sánù]', Carol thought, "We'll never get through this check-point tonight," for she knew that the driver had used the wrong pitch pattern. In fact, the driver should have said "[sànú]," with a low-high pitch pattern followed by a glottal stop. They had to turn around and drive home the long way, because the policeman would not let them through. Using the correct tone might have made a difference! The word the driver used was not a word in the language.

Statement: She's going skiing today. (Intonation begins low, rises toward the end, before falling again.)
Question: She's going skiing today? (Intonation begins low and rises, reaching the highest point at the end.)

Intonation does not distinguish one word's meaning from another. By contrast, in languages with *contrastive tone,* pitch on individual syllables indicates a meaning difference between words. The examples [óyò] and [òyó] cited above illustrate how speech errors in tone can occur.

When we study tone and intonation in languages, we focus on whether the pitches used are higher than, lower than, or the same as those surrounding them, not the absolute musical pitch used in a particular word or phrase. For both intonation and tone, meaning is conveyed by relative pitch.

Different people speak in different VOICE REGISTERS, or voice qualities. Women usually have higher voice registers than men, and children's voices are usually higher yet. There is wide variation of registers within these groups as well, and sometimes even by one person moving from one situation to another. It sounds strange to hear someone speaking in a register other than that of his or her natural speaking voice, e.g., a man attempting to mimic a woman's speech.

Declination

Often during an utterance, as air is expelled from the lungs, the pitch of the utterance goes down gradually due to lessened air pressure. This gradual lowering of the pitch over an utterance is referred to as DECLINATION; declination affects all the pitches in the utterance. This is true for both tone and intonation in language. The unit over which the pitch gradually lowers is called a BREATH GROUP or TONE GROUP.

Intonation notation

Intonation may be represented by a continuous line just above a string of segmental characters, just below them, or even right through them.[1] The relative height of the line represents the relative pitches of the voice with the lower line drawn to indicate low pitch, the next level up is the next higher pitch, and so on. The highest line represents the highest pitch of the voice. For example, in the sentence shown below, the first two words are depicted with low pitch, the third with a high pitch falling to a lower pitch; the fourth and fifth words are low.

Susan does not want to go!

Say this sentence aloud, using the intonation pattern indicated. With the above pitch pattern it indicates emphasis. Say it again, using the pitch pattern below:

Susan does not want to go!

This time, the voice starts high, drops lower for the next four words, then rises and falls during the last word. With this intonation pattern it sounds more like a simple statement. Now say this sentence with the following intonation pattern:

Susan does not want to go!

Here, the voice starts low, rises on the second syllable of the first word and stays up for the next four words; then it climbs even higher on the last word. This intonation pattern communicates that the speaker thought Susan really did or would want to go; perhaps the person is startled to hear that she does not want to go, or perhaps the speaker does not want to believe it.

---

[1] Drawing pitch contour lines right through the characters in a segmental phonetic transcription, indicating phonetic tone or intonation or both, makes it easier to "read the contour lines," to identify the relative heights of the graphical contour for each syllable, and thus the relative height of the pitch contour. For each syllable the contour indicates whether the pitch is level or (as is almost always the case) changing as a contour spreads. The reference levels could be as follows: tone 1) below the descenders; tone 2) the bottom of the descender; tone 3) the base line, on which all the characters 'sit'; tone 4) half way between the base line and the top of the body of characters; tone 5) the top of the body of characters; tone 6) the top of ascenders; and tone 7) above the tops of the ascenders. Thus, this system gives reference lines for several levels, sufficient to represent contrastive pitch contours in most human languages.

9: Pitch and Intonation

The meaning of an utterance can change depending on the intonation pattern with the same sequence of vowels and consonants. In the three intonation examples above, punctuation reflects the different intonation contours. Often in written texts punctuation is the only clue to INTONATION CONTOURS for reading the material aloud, although the context may also indicate attitudes or emotions. When you transcribe an unfamiliar language, include the pitch contour as well as the segments so that you and other field linguists will be able to reproduce the pitch pattern of the language accurately as well as the vowels and consonants present.

The following examples illustrate information conveyed by different intonation contours in the Rumanian phrase 'What is your name?' (K. L. Pike 1948:16):

kum te kyama — normal unemotional style with interrogative first word

kum te kyama — polite, reserved

kum te kyama — polite, familiar

kum te kyama — protective, confiding or tender

kum te kyama — carefully spoken, as to a foreigner who does not know the language well

kum te kyama — indicating surprise

kum te kyama — Implying, "Is that what you asked me?"

kum te kyama — implying, "I am surprised that you asked me; I know your name"

kum te kyama — threatening, as if spoken by a policeman

kum te kyama — implying perturbation.

A TONIC SYLLABLE is one that stands out in an intonation pattern over an utterance, usually due to a major pitch change. This is illustrated by the following Spanish examples. If a Spanish speaker asks you where you are from and your response has a normal English narrative intonation contour,

Soy de América   ('I am from America.')

instead of the normal Spanish narrative intonation contour,

Soy de América

you might be inadvertently indicating annoyance with having been asked. Contrastively, if an English speaker asks a Spanish speaker what is for dinner and gets the reply with the normal Spanish narrative intonation contour

macaroni, tomatoes, and cheese

instead of the usual English intonation,

macaroni, tomatoes, and cheese

the information conveyed is that you should not have asked or that the speaker is not looking forward to dinner.

The lines over the sentences above indicate both level and contour tones. The use of the highly schematic lines does not imply that the tone does not change even over segments and words where a level tone is indicated. Rather, these are more or less accurate. Some scholars have focused on level tones as the units of intonation, while others have dealt more with tone contours. In intonation both types of pitch patterns are used.

Key terms

pitch
   relative
   absolute
intonation
tone

voice register
breath group or tone group
intonation contour
tonic syllable

Exercises

1. Practice the following stressed English sentences and transcribe the intonation contour that you use:

   'I'm not going!
   I'm 'not going!
   I'm 'going!

   Do 'you want to go with 'me?
   Do you 'want to go without me?
   Do you want to go with 'him?

2. Transcribe the intonation patterns on the above six sentences as spoken by another person.

3. Match the letters for the phrases on the right with the terms on the left. Note: a letter may be used more than once.

   1) _____ pitch
   2) _____ tone
   3) _____ intonation

   a. distinguishes one word from another
   b. represented by a continuous line
   c. extends over an entire utterance
   d. indicates emotions or attitudes
   e. includes both tone and intonation
   f. indicates grammatical functions
   g. important for lexical meanings
   h. uses relative pitch
   i. auditory perception of a sound in terms of where it is on a scale from low to high.

10

Tone

Tone is the use of pitch on a word or syllable to indicate lexical or grammatical meaning distinctions between words. Thus tone acts similarly to individual segments with the pitches intrinsic to the meanings of words. When pitch functions to distinguish words, it is termed LEXICAL TONE; and when it functions to indicate differences in grammar, it is termed GRAMMATICAL TONE. Lehiste distinguishes lexical tone, grammatical tone, and morphemic tone, though she notes that the latter two may be collapsed into one category (1970:83).

Thai is a tone language in which the single syllable [kʰɑː] can have five different meanings, depending on the pitch of the voice (Ed Robinson, cited in Floyd 1986:55).

    kʰɑː   'to engage in trade'

    kʰɑː   'medicinal herb, a cooking herb'

    kʰɑː   'a grass'

    kʰɑː   'to kill'

    kʰɑː   'leg'

The segments are identical in these words such that the pitch of the voice makes the difference in the meanings of the words. By contrast, in an intonational language this would not be the case. For example, you can say the word 'cow' with a high pitch, low pitch, high falling pitch, low rising pitch, or any other pitch combination, and you would still be referring to a 'mooing female bovine animal'!

Intonation contours are distributed over entire phrases, clauses, and sentences, e.g.,

Come here!

She's coming here!

He told me that she's coming here.

By contrast, tones occur on a single syllable or word rather than an entire phrase, clause, or sentence. For example, in the following Jju examples, the tone distinguishes between singular and multiple action verbs and nouns.

zùk^h	'misery' (noun, sg.)	zòk^h	'to quarrel'
zúk^h	'miseries' (noun, pl.)	zók^h	'to quarrel multiple times/quarreling'

Relative pitch studied in context

The pitch used in tone languages is relative to the tones on surrounding syllables. For example, when you practice or analyze tone, use a citation phrase, a frame, with a pitch pattern that you are sure of and that remains constant. Then place words whose tones you are unsure of into that citation phrase or sentence, as substitution items, so that you can compare the tone of the substitution item with the tone(s) of the citation phrase.

In some languages the tones on adjacent syllables or words influence each other phonetically. For example, if one syllable has low tone and the next has a high tone, the high tone may cause the low tone to be somewhat higher. When this type of influence of one tone upon another occurs, it is termed TONE SANDHI.

Most tone languages also have intonation superimposed over individual tone contours. It is through use of a constant citation phrase or sentence that you can figure out the basic lexical tones. Further, transcription and pitch analysis will aid you in discovering the intonation patterns present, and their meaning.

Etic and emic tone patterns

An etic approach to tone focuses on the minute pitch detail. An emic approach to tone focuses on tones that provide meaning contrasts between utterances. When first writing down the phonetic transcription of an utterance, a fieldworker needs to do so etically. After analyzing these data to decide the role of tone and finding the number of contrastive (meaningful) tones present, the analyst will write the emic tone patterns present and omit the minute detail that is not contrastive.

Types of tone languages

Some tone languages have only level tones; that is, pitches are perceived to be unchanging on individual syllables. These languages are traditionally called REGISTER TONE languages. Other languages have TONE GLIDES instead of, or in addition to, level tones; that is, the pitch is perceived to rise or fall or both, within a single syllable.[1] When a language utilizes tone glides or a combination of level and contour tones, it is traditionally called a CONTOUR TONE language. Some languages use both level tones and one or more tone glides.

Languages differ as to the number of contrastive tones they have. For example, Igbo and Jju (Nigeria) have two levels, high and low; Trique (Mexico) has five levels; Thai has three levels and two glides; and Mandarin Chinese has four tones: level, rising, falling, and falling-rising tone.

Field linguists analyze the data, looking for the number and type of pitches, whether level or contour. For example, they may place words into citation phrases to ascertain the number of contrastive tones, whether it is a contour or register tone language, and what the various tone patterns are.

---

[1] Note the two different uses of the word *glide*. In this chapter, a glide refers to a rising or falling pitch contour of the voice, with no reference to vowel quality. Chapter 6 on vowels refers to a continuous change or glides of vowel quality caused by a shift in the tongue and/or lip position, with no reference to pitch.

Downstep and upstep

In some tone languages, particularly in Africa, there is DOWNSTEP, in which a high (H) tone or mid (M) tone is lowered after a similar high or mid tone syllable. Sometimes this is due to a loss of an intervening tone, and sometimes a high following another high is lowered. Downstep is marked with the diacritic [ꜜ]. Thus in a two-tone language with downstep, the combinations HH without downstep, HL, and HꜜH with downstep may occur.

Just as downstep has been found to occur in language, so too has UPSTEP, though more rarely. It has been found primarily when two high tones occur together. The first is often realized as a mid tone, with the second high produced slightly higher in pitch or as a high upglide (Schuh 1978:247).

Tone notation

When transcribing a language phonetically, begin writing pitch patterns early. In the beginning it may be easiest to use the continuous pitch contour lines suggested in the previous chapter, placing tone lines above, through, or below the string of segments. This is one way of TONE NOTATION.

There are many ways to write tone. Table 10.1 summarizes some of the main phonetic notations in use.

Table 10.1. Tone notation

Level pitches	IPA numbers	Diacritics	Tone symbols	Tone letters	APA[a] numbers
Extra high	a^5	a̋	a˥	a^{HH}	a^1
High	a^4	á	a˦	a^H	a^2
Mid	a^3	ā	a˧	a^M	a^3
Low	a^2	à	a˨	a^L	a^4
Extra low	a^1	ȁ	a˩	a^{LL}	a^5
Glide sequences					
Extra high-low	a^{52}	â	a˥˩	a^{HHL}	a^{14}
High-low-mid	a^{423}	ā̂	a˦˩˧	a^{HLM}	a^{243}
Mid-high	a^{34}	ā́	a˧˦	a^{MH}	a^{32}
Low-high	a^{24}	ǎ	a˨˦	a^{LH}	a^{42}
Low-mid	a^{23}	à̄	a˨˧	a^{LM}	a^{43}

[a]APA = the Americanist Phonetic Alphabet.

When using a number system for tones, we begin with "1" for the lowest pitch level and use higher numbers for higher pitch levels. However, some linguists use the Americanist Phonetic Alphabet, with the highest tone level numbered "1" and lower tones with higher numbers. In both systems, the numbers are written as superscripts following the syllables they relate to. Numbers used for tone glides are written as a series of levels, e.g., 423 for a high-low-mid glide.

Another means to mark tone is to use diacritics, written directly above the syllables. Diacritics slant toward the tone level they indicate. For example, the high tone diacritic [´] slants upward to the right, the low tone diacritic [`] slants downward to the right, and the mid tone diacritic [¯] is a horizontal line above the vowel. Diacritics may be combined to indicate contour tones. For example, [ˇ] represents low followed by high tone, indicating a glide from a low pitch to a high pitch, and [ˆ] represents a high-low pitch glide.

Tone letters and tone contour markings are used in several different ways. Usually tone letters follow the syllable they are part of.

According to the number of tones you find in a particular language, any of the above tone notation systems can be adapted for use in your transcription. Further, if you have been writing four or more phonetic pitch levels in a language, and then discover that there are only three contrastive tone levels, you can readily adapt your tone notation system.

Consonants may affect etic tone. For example, the etic tone on a vowel following a voiced stop tends to be lower than that following a voiceless stop. Other consonants also have a tone-lowering effect. This lowering affect does not seem to apply to consonants that follow vowels (Hombert 1978:92).

Is a language tonal?

When beginning to work with an unwritten language or one that has been only superficially analyzed, you must decide how pitch functions in the language. For example, does it function as tone or intonation or some combination of tone and intonation? Looking at how tone and intonation function in a language is part of the phonological analysis of a language, but writing pitch is a phonetic task, whether the pitch is used as tone or intonation or both.

The following are suggestions for making a decision concerning whether or not a language is tonal. Begin by looking for sets of words with identical segments, having different meanings, reflected only by pitch differences, as shown in the Thai and Mandarin Chinese examples. If you can find these kinds of words, they are excellent evidence that the language is tonal. Contrast this with the Rumanian data in the previous chapter in which pitch change reflects change in meaning, but not *lexical* meaning. When this is the case, it is an intonational language. Be aware that both tone and intonation are often present in the same language.

Eunice V. Pike (1974:169ff) provides some further guidance to aid in making this decision:

- Most intonational languages have some correlation between stress and high pitch. This is not necessarily the case with tone languages. Hearing stress on a low pitch is a good indication that the language is tonal.
- In a language where high pitch tends to co-occur with stress, a stressed syllable is also frequently lengthened, as in English. Such languages are usually not tonal. However, in a tone language, syllables with high pitch are often shorter in duration than syllables with non-high pitches, as is the case in Cantonese, Thai, Fasu, Chatino, and Popoluca.

These suggestions represent tendencies only. It is important to analyze the data you collect and then make carefully thought-out decisions based on the data.

Hearing pitch

In order to hear contrastive pitch, compare one syllable's tone with another syllable's tone. Are they the same or do they differ? If they are different, is the second syllable's tone higher or lower than the first or does it glide? If there is a pitch glide, how does the contour of the glide differ from that of another glide? Is it a high-low glide, a mid-low, a high-low-mid glide or does it have another pitch pattern?

If you are unsure of the tone(s) on a word, make a list of several words that you guess probably have the same tone as the word that you are unsure of. Then ask a speaker of the language to say the words on the list, one right after the other. If you guessed right, the tone on the word in question will be the same as those in the list. If your guess is wrong, the tone of the word will stand out clearly as being different. If that occurs, then set up another list of words with some other tone pattern until the tone patterns match. This list-making technique can be very effective in identifying tones.

To study tone, place a word, the CITATION FORM, into a CARRIER PHRASE. Insert other words into the same carrier phrase, then compare their tones. Make lists of words with the same tone pattern in the carrier phrase. This will enable you to discover how many contrastive tones are present in the language, and whether or not tone glides are contrastive.

If you have difficulty hearing pitch differences and writing them down accurately, but find that you are able to mimic the pitch, seeing the pitch displayed on a computer screen may help. (See chapter 33 on acoustic phonetics.)

Pitch accent

A PITCH ACCENT language is one in which the pitches contrast on certain accented syllables. The pitches on other syllables are predictable (by phonological rule). The syllables or moras have one of a particular permitted sequence of pitches. This contrasts with a tone language in which the pitches in words are significant and must be marked. For example, in Japanese, a pitch accent language, only the position where the pitch falls must be marked, with all the other pitches being predictable.

Key terms

tone
    lexical
    grammatical
    tone sandhi
    tone glide
    tone notation
tone languages
    register tone languages
    contour tone languages
citation form, carrier phrase
downstep
upstep
pitch accent

Exercises

1. Practice the following words from Highland Mazatec of Mexico (E. V. Pike 1963:12). Pitch 1 is high; pitch 4 is low.

$^|ki^2$	'he went'	$^|to^2$	'fruit'
$^|k^hi^2$	'it appears'	t^ho^1	'gun'
$^|ti^{21}$	'boy'	$ti^{4|}ka^2$	'he is falling'
$^|t^hi^2$	'round'	$\beta i^{2|}t^ho^2$	'he goes out'

2. Practice the following Ibibio words (Nigeria; Urua 1995:335):

èkà	'mother'
èkǎ	'go' (2nd person pl.)
ídém	'body'
ídêm	'masquerade'
ítèm	'he has placed us'
ítêm	'advice'
è kǎ ùdùà	'you (pl.) are going to (the) market'

3. Practice the following Ejagham words (Nigeria; K. Watters, lecture 2003):

èbhì	'mongoose'	èbhî	'palm nut cluster'
èbhí	'cooking pot'	ébhí	'red'

4. Practice the following Trique words (Mexico; data from R. Longacre as cited in E. V. Pike 1963:27):

ˈʒã¹	'eleven'	ʒi³ˈŋgɑ⁴	'fence'
ʒɑ³ˈto³	'rabbit'	ˈʃi³	'big'
me⁴ˈsɑ³	'table'	gi³ˈzi³	'she's finished'
si³ˈki⁵⁴	'incense'		

5. Define the following:

   a. Register tone languages

   _____
   _____

   Write three sets of symbols that could be used with register tone languages.

   _____
   _____

   b. Contour tone languages

   _____
   _____

11

Nasals

NASALS are sounds made by opening the nasal port (i.e., lowering the velum) while blocking the airstream at some place of articulation in the oral cavity. This configuration forces air coming up through the larynx and the pharynx to flow through the nasal cavity and out through the nose. Sound waves going through these passages resonate in each cavity, including the oral cavity behind the place of articulation. However, much of the intensity of the sound at the glottis is lost as the sound waves impinge on the soft tissues of the nasal cavity.

Nasals are consonants and although they are sonorants, they are not oral sonorants. Some linguists classify nasals as stops, termed nasal stops, because the airstream is completely blocked in the mouth; others classify them as continuants, because the air flows freely through the nose without being obstructed.

Table 11.1 lists the twelve nasals presented in this chapter. The names for the nasals may be found by reading clockwise around the edges of the table. For example, [m] is a *voiced bilabial nasal* and [ŋ̊] is a *voiceless velar nasal*.

There is no base character in the IPA for the postalveolar nasal. This is laminal, since the tongue blade is the active articulator. So it can be represented by using the base character [n] and adding the under-box diacritic [◌] below the base character to symbolize laminal, i.e., [n̠]. Alternatively, some have chosen to transcribe it with the tilde diacritic [˜] above the base character [n], i.e., [ñ]. This is often used in Latin American linguistics.

The base symbol for the velar nasal has a descender, a part of the character that extends below the base line. Placing a diacritic below a base character may result in the diacritic overprinting the descender. Whenever such a conflict occurs, IPA allows the diacritic to be placed above the base character, thereby making both the base character and the diacritic easier to read, i.e., [ŋ̊].

Table 11.1. Nasal consonants

	Bilabial	Labiodental	Alveolar	Postalveolar	Palatal	Velar	
Voiceless	m̥	ɱ̊	n̥	n̠̥	ɲ̊	ŋ̊/ŋ̥	nasal
Voiced	m	ɱ	n	ñ	ɲ	ŋ	
Passive articulator	upper lip	upper teeth	alveolar ridge	behind alveolar ridge	hard palate	front of soft palate	
Active articulator	lower lip	lower lip	tongue tip	tongue blade	tongue front	tongue back	

Figure 11.1 displays sagittal diagrams for the sounds [b] and [m]. The only difference between the two diagrams, and between production of the two sounds, is the position of the velum. For the stop, the velum is raised, preventing the sound from resonating in the nasal cavity; for the nasal, it is lowered, allowing the sound to resonate in the nasal cavity.

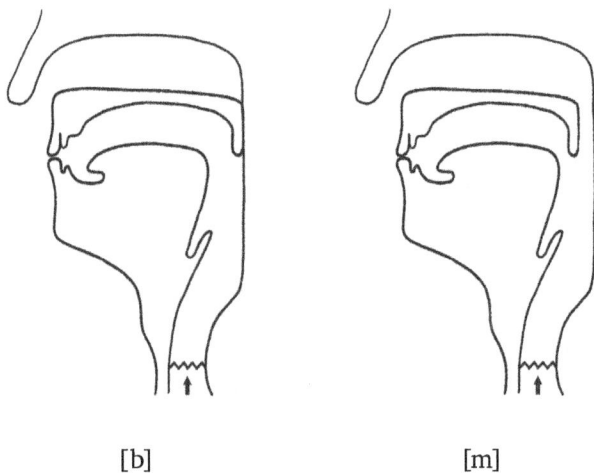

[b]　　　　　　　　　[m]

Figure 11.1. Sagittal diagrams illustrating the
difference between a stop and a nasal.

Since sounds tend to be modified by the environments in which they occur, a nasal often conforms to the same place of articulation as a stop which follows it. Sequences of [mp, nd, ŋg] are common. Phonologists speak of the nasal assimilating to the place of articulation of the following stop. Hence, we are less likely to find combinations such as [mt] or [nk] occurring in language. (For further discussion of sounds assimilating to the same place of articulation, see Burquest 1998:3.) Suffice it to say that in phonetics, you can expect to find that a nasal and a stop occurring together will be at the same place of articulation.

Nasal plosion

When a stop is released into a nasal, it is termed a NASAL PLOSION or NASAL RELEASE. Examples of nasal plosion in English include 'button' [bətn̩], written with [̩] underneath the [n], indicating that [n̩] is SYLLABIC. Other examples of words with nasal plosion include 'hidden' [hɪdn̩], 'kitten' [kʰɪtn̩], and 'Cap'n' [kʰæpm̩]. For further discussion of syllabic nasals see chapter 22.

Voiceless nasals with other consonants

Voiceless nasals tend to either precede or follow a voiced nasal at the same place of articulation, e.g., [m̥ma], [n̥na], [amm̥], [ann̥]. However, voiceless nasals do sometimes occur without their voiced counterparts, e.g., [m̥a], [n̥a], [am̥], [an̥]. Voiced nasals can also occur in combination with an [h], e.g., [hma], [hna]. Control of nasals includes being able to hear, produce, and transcribe all of these combinations as phonetically distinct.

Pronunciation helps

For [ɱ] place your lower lip against your upper teeth in a position to say [f], but then say 'mimaw' (a southern American English form of address for 'grandmother'). For some English speakers, this sound occurs in emphatic speech.

　　For postalveolar [ñ] and [ñ̥] place your tongue tip behind your lower teeth while raising your tongue blade to form the closure on the roof of your mouth and open the nasal port. One tendency is to have

11: Nasals

a [ʲ] offglide when producing this sound. If the offglide is present in the language you are studying, it is appropriate for the [ʲ] to follow the [ñ]; however, if it is not present, be careful to omit it from your pronunciation. Practice [ñ] with and without a [ʲ] offglide.

Velar [ŋ] occurs in English in the middle or at the ends of words, but never word initially. To learn to make this sound at the beginning of a word, say 'a song', repeating the phrase several times, gradually shifting the [ŋ] from the end of 'song' onto the beginning of the next word 'a' (i.e., [ə sɔŋ ə sɔŋ ə sɔ ŋə sɔ ŋə sɔ ŋə sɔ ŋə]).

When producing voiceless nasals, take care not to add voicing to them. You may also pronounce a nasal while thinking [h] simultaneously.

Key terms

nasal, nasal stop
tilde
laminal
descender

all the symbols in table 11.1
nasal plosion
syllabic nasals

Exercises

1. Practice the following words from Majang (Ethiopia; data from Peter Unseth, personal communication):

móːmónón	'weed,' n.	ŋántàn	'split vines,' n.
mòːɲókán	'booger'	ŋòɾŋ	'let go'
nòmɛ́ŋ	'follow'	ŋònòkɛ́ŋ	'hug,' n.
ɲèːpɛ́ŋ	'teach'	ŋònì	'vegetation'
ɲìgìm	'chin'	káŋtàn	'snare,' n.
ɲúgùɾ	'darkness'	múktàn	'wedding song'
ɲúːɲánák	'boiled maize'	mìkíŋ	'pierce'
ŋàːkà	'aroma'	ɛ̀ŋɛ́n	'nose'
ŋáːŋá	'your mother'	ŋáːŋáːɾáːŋ	'I'm going now'
ŋón	'women'		

2. Practice the following words from African languages (Westerman and Ward 1933:63, 65):

Kikiyu (Kenya)
    ŋanɔŋanɔ   'stories'
Mende (Sierra Leone)
    ŋɔna   'bitter'
    ŋɔni   'bird'
Ewe (Ghana)
    ŋe   'to break'
    ŋu   'outside'
    ŋɔti   'nose'
    ŋɔ   'to perforate'

Kwanyama (Angola and Namibia)
    na   'with'
    n̥a   'quite'
    n̥ano   'five'
    omunue   'finger'
    omuɲu   'man'
    om̥ito   'escape'
    om̥epo   'wind'

3. Practice the following words from Australian languages:
Gunwinggu (data from W. and L. Oates as cited in E. V. Pike 1963:21):

ˈgiɲa	'crocodile'	ŋaˈŋunɛŋ	'I sat'
ˈmanmɛ	'food'	ŋaˈgiñɛ	'I cook'
ˈmiñ	'negative'	ŋaˈbuñma	'I kiss'
ˈŋabɔm	'I hit'	mənˈbaːnba	'throwing stick'
ˈguñ	'kangaroo'	ŋaboːnaŋ	'my son'

Pitjantjatjara (data from Douglas as cited in E. V. Pike 1963:21):

| ˈpaña | 'that' | ˈñɪnŋa | 'frost' |
| ˈpina | 'ear' | ˈmiñma | 'a woman' |

4. Practice the following labial consonants from Xiŋkuna, a dialect of Tsonga (from Baumback 1974, 1987, as quoted in Ladefoged and Maddieson 1996:18):

| kuvumba | 'to guess' | ɱfutsu | 'tortoise' |
| ɱɸfʰuka | 'distance' | tiɱɸfuβu | 'hippos' |

Note: [ɸ] is a non-IPA symbol for "voiceless labiodental stop".

5. Write the names for the following sounds:

[m̥] _____

[ŋ̊] _____

[n] _____

6. Complete the sagittal diagrams for the following sounds and write their names:

[ŋ]   [ɱ]   [ñ̥]

_____
_____
_____

12

Nasalized Vowels

A NASALIZED VOWEL is produced when the velum is lowered in the oral cavity. This opens the nasal port, the passageway into the nasal cavity. Any vowel may be nasalized. A vowel symbol with a tilde [˜] over it represents a nasalized vowel. It is produced with the same articulation as that represented by the basic vowel symbol, except for the velic opening. The phonetic name of [ĩ], a nasalized vowel, is a *close front unrounded nasalized vowel*.

A nasalized vowel has two passageways: the open passageway through the oral cavity in which there is no significant constriction to the air passing through it, and through the velic opening, which allows the sound to resonate in the nasal cavity in addition to the oral cavity.[1] The velic opening distinguishes *nasalized vowels* from NON-NASALIZED VOWELS, which have no velic opening, and the open oral passageway distinguishes *nasalized vowels* from NASALS, which have a complete closure somewhere in the mouth.

When producing vowels, nasalized or otherwise, a speaker can produce a wide range of vowel qualities. The speaker does this by positioning the jaw and moving and shaping the lips and tongue to form an extensive variety of shapes (and to some extent, lengths) of the oral tract. This varies the resonances of the oral tract, and thus the vowel quality, over a wide range.

In contrast with the vowel quality, a speaker may control only the presence and degree of NASALIZATION, but not its quality. By opening or closing the nasal port, the speaker may control whether or not the resonances of the nasal tract affect the formation of a vowel. The speaker may also control the perceived degree of nasalization by varying the size or timing of the nasal port opening. However, the size and shape of the nasal tract are essentially fixed. Thus the speaker is unable to vary significantly the frequencies of the nasal tract resonances, which determine the quality of nasalization.

Nasal resonances and anti-resonances[2] often nullify or mask the effects of some oral tract resonances. Thus, the vowel quality of a nasalized vowel is often more difficult to identify than the vowel quality of a non-nasalized vowel. Nasal resonances may also change the perceived quality of a vowel, usually in the direction of making it sound more open.

Nasalized vowels, non-nasalized vowels, non-nasal consonants (other than stops), stops, and nasals contrast with one another in manner of articulation according to whether the nasal port is open or closed and whether the oral passageway is open or blocked. Table 12.1 illustrates this relationship.

---

[1] Even if the nasal cavity is congested, preventing air from passing through it, the sound will still resonate in the remaining (back) part of the nasal cavity when there is a velic opening, producing a distinctly nasalized sound. You can demonstrate this by an experiment suggested in the pronunciation helps section of this chapter.

[2] Anti-resonances are valleys in the spectrum's energy profile produced by the mouth absorbing energy at those particular frequencies.

Table 12.1. Passageways and manners of articulation

	Nasal port open	Nasal port closed
Oral passageway open	nasalized vowel	non-nasalized vowel, non-nasal consonant (other than stops)
Oral passageway blocked	nasal	stop

Contrastive nasalization

In some languages the presence or absence of nasalization on a vowel is the only difference between words with different meanings. The following example shows three minimal pairs from Ewe spoken in Ghana (Westerman and Ward 1933:43). Notice that in each pair, the words have different meanings, and the only phonetic difference between the two words is whether or not the vowel is nasalized; this indicates that nasalization on vowels is contrastive in Ewe:

dɔ	'belly'	du:	'in heaps'	ma	'not'
dɔ̃	'be weak'	dũ:	'staring'	mã	'divide'

A binary distinction between nasalized vowels and non-nasalized vowels, symbolized by presence or absence of a tilde over the vowel symbol, is often sufficient for purposes of phonological analysis. Sometimes, however, a phonetic description of nasalization in a language needs to distinguish two degrees of nasalization. A vowel may be fully nasalized, represented by a tilde over the vowel [ã], or have light late nasalization (represented here by the Americanist symbol with the Polish hook under the vowel [ą]. Palantla Chinantec, a language spoken in the District of Tuxtepec, Oaxaca, Mexico, is a case in point. With light late nasalization, nasal resonances begin late in the syllable and gradually increase to their greatest level at the end of the syllable, then decline rapidly. With full nasalization, nasal resonances remain constant throughout the syllable. Examples from Palantla Chinantec (Merrifield 1963:14 as cited in Merrifield and Edmondson 1999:306) illustrate this contrast:

[hɑ[LM]]   'so much'
[hą[LM]]   'he opens it wide'
[hã[LM]]   'foam'

> **Experiment 12.1: Control—watch your velum in action**
>
> For this experiment you will need a handheld mirror to see into your own mouth, and a flashlight, preferably bright, to illuminate the inside of your mouth.
>
> Open your mouth fairly wide and say a long vowel [ɑ:::], as a doctor asks you to say in order to see the back of your throat. Using the flashlight and mirror, look in your mouth for the structures in the oral cavity, in the pharyngeal cavity, and the oro-pharyngeal cavity:
>
> back molars
> two pairs of faucal pillars[3]
> uvula
> velum
> back of your oropharynx[4]
>
> Just possibly, if you make your tongue lie very far down at the midline, you will also be able to see the top edge of your epiglottis. Now say [aãaãaãaãaã...] and watch your velum move up and down—up for the non-nasalized vowel [a], and down for the nasalized vowel [ã]. If you have difficulty making alternately nasal and non-nasal vowels, try the suggestions in the previous Pronunciation helps.

---

[3] The part of the pharynx just behind the oral cavity. The faucal pillars consist of two pairs of muscles that run vertically at the back of the oral cavity on each side of the pharynx. One pair is in front of the uvula and one pair is behind it. The tonsils lie between each pair of the faucal pillars.

[4] This part of the vocal tract is more specifically the oropharynx. The pharynx is the passageway just in front of the spinal column. It extends from the top of the larynx up into the nasal cavity. Although there are no sharply

12: Nasalized Vowels

In other cases, perceptually heavier nasalization, symbolized as [ã], results from full velic opening from beginning to end of the vowel sound, whereas gradual velic opening during the vowel enunciation results in perceptually lighter nasalization, as in English:

[bɑb]   'Bob'   [mãm]   'mom'
[bɑ̃m]   'bomb'

The name of a nasalized vowel is the same as that of the corresponding non-nasalized vowel, but with the word 'nasalized' preceding 'vowel'. Thus [ẽ] is a *close-mid front unrounded nasalized vowel*. Inserting 'lightly' or 'heavily' before 'nasalized' in the name distinguishes degrees of nasalization.

Pronunciation helps

Pronounce the word 'sudden', with a vowel in the second syllable. The difference between the presence or absence of a vowel between [d] and [n] is the presence or absence of a velic opening. Next, say the second syllable of 'sudden' repetitively, [dndndndndn], without intervening vowels. Can you feel your velum move down and up, thereby opening and closing the passageway to the nasal cavity? Next, pronounce [bmbmbmbmbm]. Another exercise for this purpose is to say [tn̩tn̩tn̩tn̩tn̩], similar to the way some people blow their noses.

To practice saying and hearing nasalized vowels, say [mĩ mĩ mĩ mĩ ĩ ĩ ĩ ĩ ĩĩ]. Pronounce other nasalized vowels, e.g., [ã ẽ ĩ õ ũ]. Next pronounce nasalized vowels adjacent to [n], then adjacent to [ŋ]. Most people can pronounce nasalized vowels adjacent to nasal consonants, and non-nasalized vowels adjacent to oral consonants. However, pronouncing non-nasalized vowels adjacent to a nasalized consonant, or pronouncing nasalized vowels adjacent to a non-nasalized consonant, is harder. For example, try saying [mɑmɑmɑ] without any nasalization on the vowels, or [bẽbẽbẽbẽ] with nasalization on the vowels but not on the consonants. It helps to say this combination slowly during which you lengthen the entire utterance. Place your thumb and finger on each side of your nose below the hard cartilage. During nasalization you should feel some vibration of your nose, and an absence of vibration when you pronounce an oral sound. Finally, to test the idea that nasalization does not depend upon an unobstructed air passageway through the nasal cavity, gently pinch your nose closed and hold it closed while you pronounce a series of alternating nasalized and non-nasalized vowels such as [ææ̃ææ̃ææ̃ææ̃].

Key terms

nasalized vowel   non-nasalized vowel
nasal   nasalization

Exercises

1. Practice saying the following words from Mixteco (Mexico; Priscilla Small, personal communication, 2000):

   ɑtɑ   ɑ̃tɑ   ɑ̃tɑ̃   ɑtɑ̃
   mã̃tʰã   matʰa   mifi   mĩf̃ĩ
   tʰõdɑ   tʰõmõ   ŋĩgæ̃   ŋĩbo

   Note that in [mĩf̃ĩ] the [f] is also nasalized. While fricatives have not been found to have contrastive nasalization, phonetic nasalization can occur as is the case in Mixteco.

---

defined divisions in the pharynx, it is helpful to divide it into three parts: the oropharynx is the part behind the mouth, or oral cavity; the laryngopharynx extends from the oropharynx down to but not including, the larynx; the naso-pharynx is the part at the back of the nasal cavity, above the velum, which divides it from the oropharynx.

2. Practice the phrases from Mixteco (Mexico; data from Floyd 1981:36):

   ku u kɨ tɨ kʷa a   'The blind animals will die.'
   kũ ũ kɨ tɨ kʷa a   'four blind animals'
   ku u kɨ tɨ kʷã ã   'The yellow animals will die.'
   kũ ũ kɨ tɨ kʷã ã   'four yellow animals'

3. Write the names for the following sounds:

   [ẽ] _____

   [ĩ] _____

   [ɔ̃] _____

4. Assume these two sounds occur in contrast in a language. Write the names of each.

   [ɑ̃] _____

   [ɑ] _____

5. Give one contrast and one similarity between nasals and nasalized vowels:

   Contrast _____

   Similarity _____

6. Practice the following words from Kashinawa[5] (Brazil and Peru; Richard Montag, personal communication):

isi	'unending'	isĩ	'to cut the edge of'
isĩ	'pain, to hurt'	kapɑ	'squirrel'
isɑ	'type of bird'	kapã	'to mix'
isã	'type of palm'	piʃi	'rib'
isu	'spider monkey'	piʃĩ	'palm mat'
isũ	'urine'	ui isikiki	'rain continues unending'
isĩ	'head-painting'	isĩkiki	'it is hurting'

---

[5] Kashinawa is a more recent spelling for the name Cashinahua, a term found in the literature (Richard Montag, personal communication).

13

Sibilants

SIBILANTS are fricatives made in the front part of the mouth with a narrower passageway for the airstream than is used for other fricative sounds. Sibilants are also called GROOVED FRICATIVES because the tongue tip and tongue blade are typically grooved to form a narrow passageway. By contrast, other fricatives are sometimes called FLAT FRICATIVES, because, in their production, the surface of the tongue is either grooved less or not grooved at all. Figure 13.1 illustrates this contrast in tongue shapes.

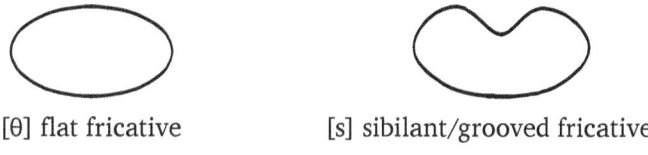

[θ] flat fricative   [s] sibilant/grooved fricative

Figure 13.1. Typical tongue shapes for flat fricatives and sibilants.

Table 13.1 presents symbols for four frequently occurring sibilants. The names of these sibilants may be found by reading the row and column labels clockwise around the table. For example, [s] is a *voiceless alveolar sibilant* and [ʒ] is a *voiced postalveolar sibilant*.

Table 13.1. Sibilants

	Alveolar	Postalveolar[a]	
Voiceless	s	ʃ	sibilant
Voiced	z	ʒ	
Passive articulator	alveolar ridge	behind alveolar ridge	
Active articulator	tongue tip	tongue blade	

[a]You will also encounter the terms *alveopalatal* and *palato-alveolar* for sounds produced with this place of articulation. They are roughly equivalent, indicating shades of differences not treated in this text.

Alveolar sounds typically are articulated with the tongue tip and postalveolar sounds with the tongue blade. Some speakers produce sibilants with the tongue tip behind the lower teeth. Sibilants produced with the tongue tip up are the norm. A sibilant produced with the tongue tip behind the lower teeth tends to be pronounced with the upper articulator further forward in the mouth than one produced with the tongue tip up at the alveolar ridge. However, they sound similar to each other.

73

Practice producing these sounds both ways; this will prepare you to observe this difference in others' articulation of sibilants.

Sibilants are distinguished from other fricatives by having louder noise at a higher pitch. Their distinctive sound has led some phoneticians to call the voiceless sibilants hissing and hushing sounds, as in the English words 'hiss' and 'hush'. The voiced counterpart of hissing sounds could likewise be called 'buzzing' sounds, as in 'buzz'. Alveolar sibilants have a higher pitched noise than postalveolar ones because the cavity or passageway in front of the noise source for an alveolar sibilant is shorter and has a smaller volume, causing the sound to resonate at a higher frequency.

In sagittal diagrams of sibilants a dotted line represents the sides of the tongue which are making closure at the alveolar ridge around the sides of the mouth. This is in addition to the solid line that represents the center line of the tongue with an opening which forms the narrow passageway to produce the sibilant.[1]

Pronunciation helps

[s], [z], and [ʃ] are common sibilant sounds in most dialects of English. The words 'sue' [s], 'zoo' [z], and 'shoe' [ʃ] illustrate these sounds.

[ʒ] occurs word medially in English, as in 'pleasure', and word finally in some words borrowed from French, such as 'rouge' and 'garage', but it does not occur word initially. English speakers, when trying to pronounce a word with initial [ʒ], insert [d] before the [ʒ], as in 'gym' [dʒɪm]. Practice initial [ʒ] by saying [ʒɑʒɑ] or the name Dr. Zhivago. Or say a word such as 'measure' slowly, pausing between the syllables, until you can say the second syllable alone: [ˈmɛʒɚ ... ˈmɛ ʒɚ ... ˈmɚ ... ʒɚ ... ˈʒɚ].[2]

Many English speakers pronounce initial [ʃ] and [ʒ] with rounded lips. Such is not the case in every language. Watch in a mirror as you say words beginning with initial [ʃ] followed by an unrounded vowel, e.g., 'shake' and 'sheet', to see whether you round your lips. If you do, practice controlling this feature of sibilants by not allowing your lips to round.

Key terms

sibilant (grooved fricative)   postalveolar, alveopalatal
non-sibilant (flat fricative)

Exercises

1. Practice this drill three times:

ˈʃɑso	ˈʒɑsɑ	ˈsuzu
ˈʒɑzɑ	ʒɛˈʒu	ˈsutʰ
siˈʃo	ˈʒɑʃɑ	ˈzãnã
ˈzu	ˈʒɑʒɑ	tʰoˈzɑ

2. Practice the following Jju words (Nigeria; McKinney data):

sɑ	'ring'	ʃe	'until, except'
sɑkʰ	'to put, keep'	ʃekʰ	'to move a small distance'
zɑ	'rain' (n.)	zokʰ	'famine, hunger'
zɑpʰ	'to buy' (v.)	zukʰ	'millet'
ʃɑpʰ	'to sharpen, carve, peel'		

---

[1] In this book, the less detailed but more common diagram is used, with a line indicating only the center line of the tongue.
[2] [ɚ] represents a mid central unrounded rhotacized vowel, the '-er' of American English.

13: Sibilants

3. Practice the following Biangai words (Papua New Guinea; data from R. and M. Dubert 1973:8–22):[3]

sɑbi	'long cucumber'	kisi	'to split firewood'
kozɑ	'bone'	sisik	'mad'
poβu	'here'	pəβɑ	'father'
təɣi	'therefore'	puɣusi	'to remove'
iβik	'weeds'	kozoβək	'ash box'

4. Fill in the following table for four grooved fricatives:

Symbol for a grooved fricative	Name for the symbol	Active articulator
[ ]		
[ ]		
[ ]		
[ ]		

5. Fill in the following table for six flat fricatives:

Symbol for a flat fricative	Name for the symbol	Active articulator
[ ]		
[ ]		
[ ]		
[ ]		
[ ]		
[ ]		

---

[3] Note that some data used in some of the exercises in this book do not have stress marked because the source for those data did not mark it.

14

Palatal, Velar, and Uvular Consonants

Sounds articulated by the tongue front coming close to or contacting the hard palate, forward of the velum, have a PALATAL place of articulation. Sounds articulated by the tongue back coming close to or contacting the back part of the velum, including the uvula, have a UVULAR place of articulation. Between the palatal and uvular places of articulation is the VELAR place of articulation, in which the tongue back moves towards or touches the front of the velum in the production of a sound. These consonants are stops, fricatives, affricates, and nasals produced at the palatal, velar, and uvular places of articulation. Table 14.1 presents the symbols that represent these sounds.

Table 14.1. Palatal, velar, and uvular consonants

	Palatal	Velar	Uvular		
Voiceless	c^h	k^h	q^h	aspirated	stop
Voiceless	c	k	q		
Voiced	ɟ	g	ɢ		
Voiceless	ç	x	χ		fricative
Voiced	ʝ	ɣ	ʁ		
Voiced	ɲ	ŋ	ɴ		nasal
Passive articulator	hard palate	front of velum	back of velum		
Active articulator	tongue front	tongue back	tongue back		

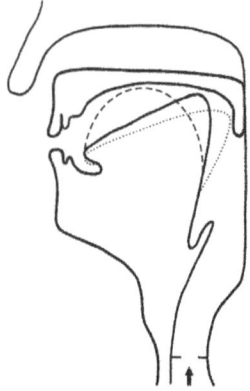

Figure 14.1. Three voiceless fricatives: palatal [ç] (dash line), velar [x] (solid line), and uvular [χ] (dotted line) consonants.

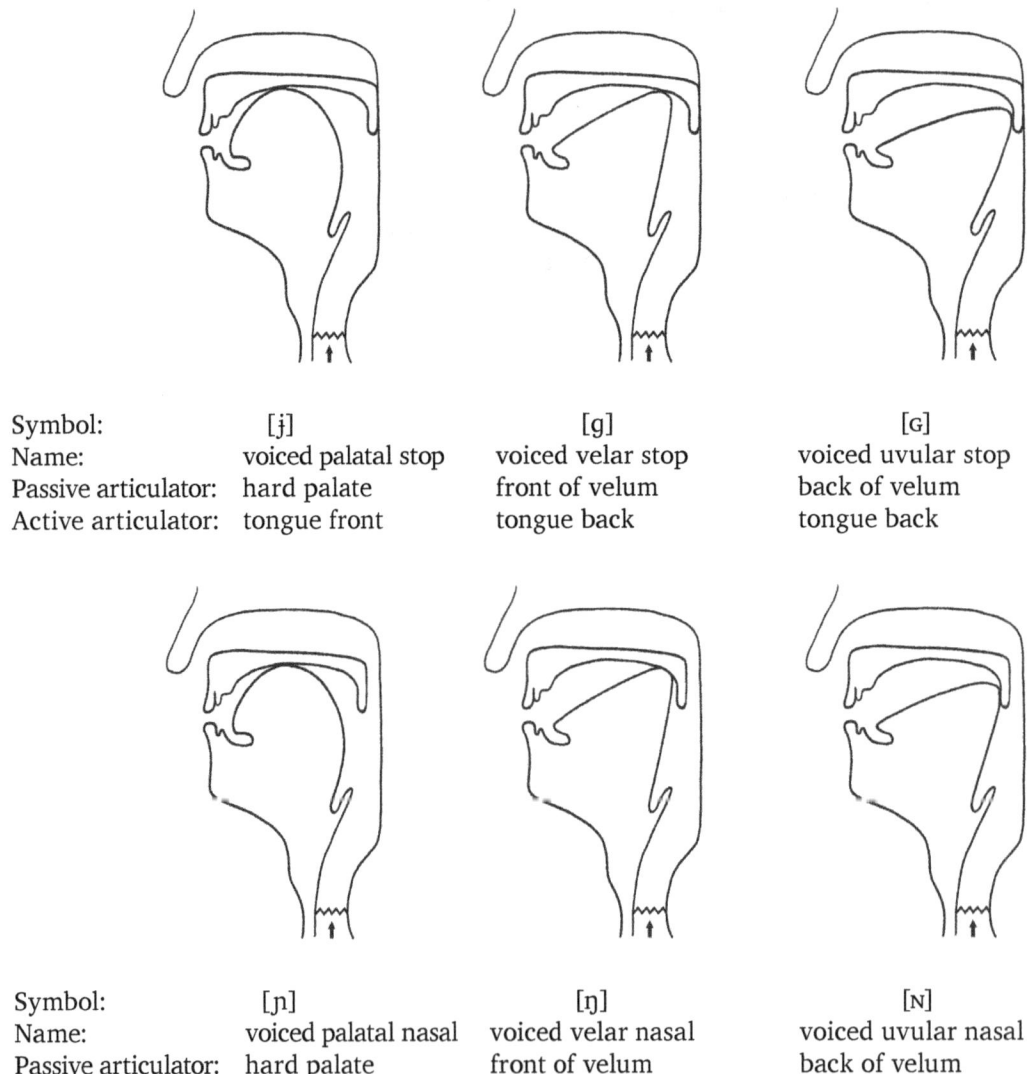

Symbol:	[ɟ]	[g]	[ɢ]
Name:	voiced palatal stop	voiced velar stop	voiced uvular stop
Passive articulator:	hard palate	front of velum	back of velum
Active articulator:	tongue front	tongue back	tongue back

Symbol:	[ɲ]	[ŋ]	[ɴ]
Name:	voiced palatal nasal	voiced velar nasal	voiced uvular nasal
Passive articulator:	hard palate	front of velum	back of velum
Active articulator:	tongue front	tongue back	tongue back

Figure 14.2. Sounds with palatal, velar, and uvular places of articulation.

Speakers of English often pronounce a palatal stop when it precedes a front vowel, such as in 'keep' [cʰip]. During the formation of [c] the articulators are already moving in transition to the following vowel, in this example, to the place of articulation of [i]. This is an example of ANTICIPATORY COARTICULATION of the consonant with the following front vowel. Typically, English speakers use a velar stop in pronouncing a word such as 'coop' [kʰup], where there is coarticulation of the consonant with the following back vowel [u]. Likewise, some English speakers pronounce words such as 'caw' [qʰɔ] (the sound produced by a crow, rook, or raven) or 'coffee' [qʰɔfi] with an initial uvular stop. These three voiceless aspirated stops are all variants of the same /k/ sound unit in English, though in other languages they may be contrastive.

Pronunciation helps

Start by producing the voiceless velar fricative [x]. Continue pronouncing a fricative as you move your tongue forward to the palatal place of articulation and back to the uvular place of articulation. The pitch of the fricative sound rises and falls as you produce this series of voiceless fricatives: [xçxχxçxχxçxχ...].

The pitch that you hear going up and down in this experiment is the result of reverberation in the vocal tract. It changes because the different positions of your tongue vary the size of the chamber in front of the turbulent noise source within the oral cavity. Since different sizes of cavities have different resonances, a listener may distinguish between different places of articulation based on the sound quality, as shown in table 14.2. This is different from the musical pitch of voiced sounds that are determined by the rate of vibration of the vocal folds that convey tone, intonation, and stress.

Table 14.2. Effect of place of articulation on chamber size and sound quality

Place of articulation	Chamber size	Sound quality
palatal	small	high pitch
velar	medium	medium pitch
uvular	large	low, hollow-sounding pitch

Sounds produced at the palatal, velar, and uvular places of articulation are more closely related to each other than to sounds produced further forward or further back in the mouth. In the experiment above you experienced a gliding continuity in the transition between the sounds at these three places of articulation. By attempting to produce the same gliding transition from a palatal fricative to one further forward, or from a uvular fricative to one further back, you may experience the discontinuities that set these three places of articulation apart from their closest neighbors.

Key terms

palatal place of articulation
uvular place of articulation
velar place of articulation
anticipatory coarticulation

Exercises

1. Practice aloud the following Dutch words (Rotterdam dialect) (Floyd 1986:61):

dʁi	'three'	ʁœym	'space'
fyχ	'fire'	ʁøˈzɪn	'giantess'
mɑχ	'but'	xχɑx	'gladly'
fχintʰ	'friend'	ˈɑndəʁə	'other'

2. Practice aloud the following Quiche words (Guatemala; data from David G. Fox, in Bickford and Floyd 2003:112):

kʰukʰ	'squirrel'	cʰinuˈmicʰ	'I'm hungry'
kʰuqʰ	'their skirt'	wiˈcʰan	'my uncle'
qʰuqʰ	'our skirt'	tsʰɪç	'word, truth'
kʰaˈtʃʰotʃʰ	'their house'	icʰ	'moon, month'
qʰaˈtʃʰotʃʰ	'our house'		

3. Practice aloud the following Wakhi words (data from Peter Backstrom, personal communication):

çik	'Wakhi person'
çʉj	'sister'
ɟaːɾ	'stone'
ɟiɾ	'rotate'
niçit	'extracted'
ɾuçʉp	'sleep'
ˈveɟĭnə	'finished'
ɾiˈɟɛð	'fingernail'
teç	'soul, last breath'
zăç	'thorn'
ðiːɟ	'buttermilk'
qɨlaˈgiɟ	'difficult, characterized by obstacles'

14: Palatal, Velar, and Uvular Consonants

4. Complete sagittal diagrams and give the names for the following sounds:

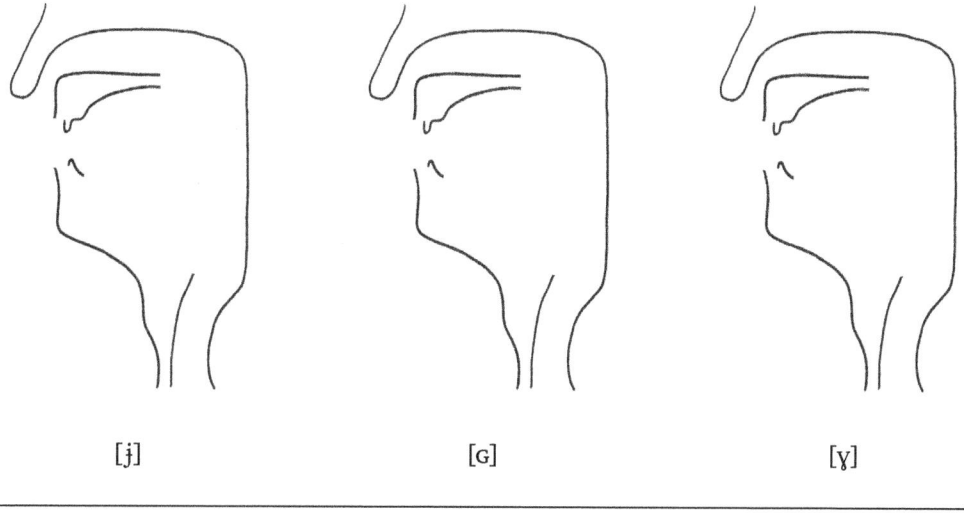

[j]   [ɢ]   [ɣ]

_____

_____

5. Complete the following table:

Symbol for a voiceless sound	Symbol for its voiced counterpart	Technical name	Active articulator
[c]	[ ]		
[x]	[ ]		
[ɲ̊]	[ ]		
[q]	[ ]		
[χ]	[ ]		
[ç]	[ ]		
[ɴ̥]	[ ]		

15

Laterals

A LATERAL is a speech sound made with the airstream flowing over one or both sides of the tongue, with complete closure some place along the midline of the tongue. Thus the airstream is prevented from passing over the tongue's midline. Ladefoged and Maddieson (1996:182) state "[laterals] are sounds in which the tongue is contracted in such a way as to narrow its profile from side to side so that a greater volume of air flows around one or both sides than over the center of the tongue." They go on to say that in most laterals there is no central air that escapes over the tongue, though that is not essential for a definition of a lateral.

For laterals the tongue is up against the roof of the mouth at some place along the medial plane, preventing the airstream from flowing over the centerline of the tongue. For other consonants the rim of the tongue is up against the alveolar ridge along both sides of the mouth, keeping the airstream from flowing over the side of the tongue. But for laterals an occlusion on the centerline forces the airstream to divert from the central path through the mouth, and it flows between the alveolar ridge and the rim of the tongue somewhere along one or both sides of the mouth.

If there is audible noisy turbulence of the airstream, the sound is a LATERAL FRICATIVE; otherwise it is a LATERAL APPROXIMANT. The most common lateral is the voiced alveolar lateral approximant [l], as in English 'leak', 'lock', 'Luke' [lik^h, lɑk^h, luk^h]. An approximant is a speech sound produced by one articulator coming close to (i.e., approximating) another, but not so close as to cause audible turbulence. See chapter 19 for further discussion of approximants.

The shape of the tongue for an alveolar LATERAL FRICATIVE [ɬ] may be compared with that of an alveolar sibilant [s] and an interdental (flat) fricative [θ]. See figure 15.1. For the sibilant, the surface is down at the midline of the tip, and up making a closure along both sides, forcing the airstream to flow close to the midline. For the interdental fricative, the surface of the tongue tip is neither down at the midline forming a grooved channel for the airstream, nor up against the alveolar ridge blocking the airstream and diverting it to the side. Rather it forms a wide aperture across the alveolar ridge.

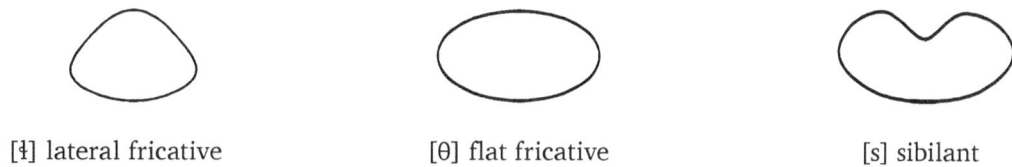

[ɬ] lateral fricative   [θ] flat fricative   [s] sibilant

Figure 15.1. Tongue shapes for fricatives and laterals.

Except in the chapter on sibilants, sagittal diagrams have represented the alveolar ridge only at the front of the mouth. They have not represented the alveolar ridge along the sides of the mouth, where there is closure in articulating most oral consonants, but an opening for the airstream to flow through in producing a lateral speech sound. Just as for sibilants, the position of the sides of the tongue can be represented by a dashed or dotted line.

Names and symbols

Table 15.1 presents printed symbols for seven of the most common laterals. The names of these sounds may be found by reading the row and column labels clockwise around the table. For example, [ɮ] is a *voiced alveolar lateral fricative,* and [l̥] is a *voiceless alveolar lateral approximant.*

Table 15.1. Laterals (printed style)

	Alveolar	Velar	
Voiceless	l̥	ʟ̥	lateral approximant
Voiced	l	ʟ	
Voiceless	ɬ		lateral fricative
Voiced	ɮ		
Voiced	ɺ		lateral flap
Passive articulator	alveolar ridge	front of velum	
Active articulator	tongue tip	tongue back	

When transcribing laterals by hand, use a cursive [l]. This will aid in differentiating it from a cursive [t]. Table 15.2 displays handwritten symbols for these sounds.

Table 15.2. Laterals (handwritten style)

	Alveolar	Velar	
Voiceless	*l̥*	*L̥*	lateral approximant
Voiced	*l*	*L*	
Voiceless	*ɬ*		lateral fricative
Voiced	*ɮ*		
Passive articulator	alveolar ridge	front of velum	
Active articulator	tongue tip	tongue back	

To our knowledge, no contrast has been reported in a language between the two voiceless alveolar lateral sounds, [l̥] and [ɬ]. Voiceless laterals are usually fricatives; consequently, it is common to represent both sounds by one symbol [ɬ].

Pronunciation helps

The sound [l] occurs in English in words such as 'leap', 'lop', and 'loop', in which a lateral is prevocalic, that is, it occurs before a vowel. English commonly uses a velar lateral or a velarized lateral (a lateral in which the tongue back humps up towards the velum) in postvocalic positions, where the lateral follows a vowel in the same syllable, or when the lateral is used as the syllable nucleus, e.g., the final [lˠ] in 'little'. When the lateral forms the syllable nucleus, it is a SYLLABIC LATERAL. For example, compare your pronunciation of the initial lateral with the second lateral in the words 'Lil' (a woman's name) and 'lullaby'. Phoneticians call the initial voiced alveolar lateral [l] a 'CLEAR L', and the velar or velarized lateral, a 'DARK L'. English laterals will be discussed further in chapter 21 on secondary articulations.

In Spanish there is a voiced dental lateral, or less commonly, an alveolar lateral, as in the word [sol] 'sun'. Since this difference contrasts with the lateral in the postvocalic position in English, an English speaker learning Spanish should be careful to pronounce this sound as native Spanish speakers do.

The contrast between [l̥] and [l] is voicing; otherwise they are produced identically. Practice [lel:el:e] and [l̥el̥:el̥:e].

[ɬ] and [l̥] are produced with similar articulation, but [ɬ] has sufficient constriction of the airflow to cause audible noise due to air turbulence. Start with the voiceless lateral, and then move the sides of your tongue toward the roof of your mouth to narrow the constriction thus producing fricative noise. Keep the tip of your tongue on your alveolar ridge. [ɮ] is produced with voicing added to the voiceless alveolar lateral fricative [ɬ].

Some English speakers use only velar laterals [ʟ] in their normal speech. To practice pronouncing velar laterals, begin by pronouncing words that start with 'gl,' as in 'glide' and 'glue', being careful to keep your tongue tip down on the bottom of your mouth. Say these words again, while lengthening the laterals. Isolate the velar lateral and say it by itself. Next insert it between [ɑ] vowels: [ʟɑʟɑ], as the refrain [falalalala-lala-la-la] in the Christmas song "Deck the Halls with Boughs of Holly."[1] To make the voiceless velar lateral sound, pronounce the same sequence by whispering 'cl' words, such as 'club' and 'clasp', then whisper the [ʟ̥ɑʟ̥ɑ] sequence. Pronounce the voiceless velar lateral in isolation, and then place it between two voiced vowels [ɑʟ̥ɑʟ̥ɑ].

Another technique for learning to pronounce [ʟ] is to say "lalala" fairly slowly. Then gradually shift the place of articulation further and further back in your mouth until you can feel that in producing the lateral your tongue is touching the same place on the palate as when you make a [k], except that there is an airstream pathway between the tongue and one or both sides of the tongue.

Key terms

lateral
lateral approximant
approximant
lateral fricative

syllabic lateral
clear l
dark l

Exercises

1. Practice these English words with [l̥], [ʟ], and [ʟ̥]:

pl̥i	'plea'	ˈvəlˠgɚ	'vulgar'
pl̥eⁱ	'ply'	mɪʟkʰ	'milk'
pl̥eᵘ	'plow'	bɔʟ	'ball'
pl̥iz	'please'	sɪʟkʰ	'silk'
gloᵘ	'glow'		

---

[1] It was while singing this song as a primary school student that Norris McKinney discovered that he made only velar laterals. His teacher objected to his singing this refrain, but to no avail.

2. Practice the following Balti words aloud three times (Pakistan; data from Backstrom and Radloff 1992:220–233):

loˈŋa	'leaf'	Balti
ɬok	'lightning'	Balti
loxso	'different'	Balti
ɬtoks	'he was hungry'	Balti
ɬuŋ	'wind'	Rondu Balti
bləŋ	'breast'	Western Balti
pl̥əkˈpə	'arm'	Western Balti
pl̥u	'child'	Balti
ləxˈtʰɪl	'palm'	Khapalu Balti

3. Practice the following Zulu words (South Africa; data from Westermann and Ward 1933 as cited in E. V. Pike 1963:36):

ʛula	'pass'		isiɬaɬa	'bush, tree'
iʛelo	'pasture ground'		ɬupʰa	'trouble'
amaʛozi	'spirits'			

4. Practice these additional Zulu words (South Africa; data from Dent and Nyembezi 1969:184, 334–335, 344, 368, 376–377):

ɬaba	'stab'		ʛulela	'pass on towards'
ɬaɬa	'cut down trees'		inʛuzele	'hartebeest'
ɬaɬela	'cut up carcass'		ʛonʛobalal	'become enraged'
inɬakanɬaka	'things in disorder'		ɬepʰula	'tear off'
ʛuʛuʒa	'boil' v.		ɬupʰeka	'experience hardship'
isiʛuka	'feather head dress'		isiɬutʰanʛebe	'bat' n.
kʰuɬane	'common cold'			

5. Practice the following Tyap words (Nigeria; data from Bulus Tauna, personal communication):

lìpʰ	'to sell', singular action verb		ɔ́lílì	'eyes'
lírə́m	'to sell', multiple action verb		ə̀làm	'mud bench'
ə̀lí	'eye'		lóŋ	'fire'

6. Give the symbol and name for two lateral fricatives:

   [ ] _____
   [ ] _____

7. Give the symbol, name, and articulators for the four lateral approximants:

Symbol	Name	Articulators
[ ]		
[ ]		
[ ]		
[ ]		

16

Length

A vowel or consonant has PHONETIC LENGTH if it lasts perceptibly longer than the same speech sound (or a similar one) in a different expression. Phonetic length is physical duration, the length of time of a phonetic segment. Duration is measured in milliseconds, a topic discussed further in chapter 33 on acoustic phonetics.

In some languages there are pairs of words in which the words are the same except for the phonetic length of one of the sounds. That is, one of the vowels or consonants lasts noticeably longer in one of the words than it does in the other. This difference in length results in a difference in meaning between the two words. For example, in Jju, the phonetic difference between the verb forms [natʰ] 'went' and [naːtʰ] 'going' is the length on the vowel in [naːtʰ]. The pair of triangles [ː] following the vowel character is a LENGTH MARK; it indicates that the vowel is LONG in contrast with the vowel in [natʰ], which is SHORT. An analysis of the sound system of a language may find certain phonetically long sounds to be phonologically long, or it may find them to be sequences of short sounds.

Phonetically long versus short sounds are long or short in relation to each other. It is *relative* length that is important in language, rather than *absolute* length.

In many languages a stressed vowel is long. In the English noun 'reject' [ˈɹiːdʒɛktʰ], the vowel in the first syllable is longer than in the first syllable of the verb 'reject' [ɹiˈdʒɛːktʰ]. This difference in phonetic length combines in English with a difference in pitch pattern and vowel quality to make us hear the first syllable as stressed on the noun and unstressed on the verb.

IPA provides three symbols for marking degrees of length. Leaving one degree of length unmarked allows transcription of four degrees of length. Table 16.1 presents this system of representing length.

Table 16.1. Symbols and names for length

Degree of length	IPA symbol		Alternative symbol	
Long	aː	length mark	aː	colon
Half-long	aˑ	half-length mark	aˑ	dot
Short	a	unmarked	a	unmarked
Extra-short	ă	breve	ă	wedge

Typically the majority of sounds in a language have short length, and a description refers to them as *short* and leaves them unmarked. Likewise, a description calls the other sounds *long,* and the transcription employs the colon or the IPA length mark to represent their length.

IPA provides two other symbols for distinguishing different degrees of phonetic length. A single triangle [ˑ] following the symbol signifies that the length of the sound is half-long, i.e., intermediate in length between long and short. The breve diacritic [˘] placed above the symbol marks it as extra-short, compared with other similar sounds unmarked for length at the same overall rate of speaking.

Since a colon [:] is easier to write than the IPA pair of triangles [ː], and since the colon is available on word processors, we use the colon rather than the IPA length mark, except in professionally printed materials. Similarly, people have often preferred to use a dot or raised period for transcribing *half-long*.

Contrastive vs. non-contrastive length

For English, phoneticians identify at least three degrees of phonetic duration of a vowel. This non-contrastive difference is contingent upon whether a syllable ends with a voiced consonant, a voiceless consonant, or a vowel. Consider the words 'he,' 'heed,' 'heat.' The [i:] vowel in 'he' is the longest, the [iˑ] in 'heed' is next longest, and the [i] in 'heat' is shortest.[1]

This difference in length may not be applicable to another language. A field worker would need to check out how length functions in the language.

In some languages, such as Jju mentioned above, the difference in vowel or consonant length is not predictable based on the phonetic environment. The following Jju examples contain both long vowels and long consonants (Nigeria; McKinney data):

nàtʰ	'went'	nà:tʰ	'going'
sótʰ	'clan'	só:kʰ	'to glean, pick'
súpʰ	'large water pot'	s:úkʰ	'to paint, color, purify'
ʃétʰ	'to slip, to slide'	ʃ:ékʰ	'to wake up'
zóŋ	'famine, hunger'	z:óm	'elephant'
zápʰ	'to cut into pieces little by little'	z:ápʰ	'to sell'

Length differences are found in Koasati words (Louisiana; Gene Burnham, personal communication, 2002):

ɪlalːahõ	'I'll arrive'	paˈlaːna	'plate'
ɪlalahõ	'he'll arrive'	palaˈna	'beans'
ɪlːalahõ	'we'll arrive'		

Consonants with contrastive degrees of length are also found in Zuñi (New Mexico) words (Bickford and Floyd 2003:84):

ˈlatanːɛ	'feather'	ˈtatːanːɛ	'a tree'

Estonian has three degrees of phonetic length on both vowels and consonants (Laver 1994:444).[2] The following sets of words exemplify these contrasts:

linɑ	'flax'	jɑmɑ	'nonsense'
linːɑ	'of the town'	jɑːmɑ	'of the station'
linːːɑ	'to the town'	jɑːːmɑ	'to the station'

---

[1] It has been found through acoustic study that the length of a vowel depends on the structure of the syllable in which the vowel occurs: a vowel in an *open syllable* (a syllable that ends in a vowel) is the longest; the same vowel in a syllable ending in a phonemically voiced consonant will be next longest; and the same vowel will be shortest if the consonant following it is voiceless.

[2] Languages with three phonologically contrastive degrees of length are rare, and authorities have not been unanimous in attributing three degrees of length to Estonian.

16: Length

An *affricate* is a stop followed by a fricative.[3] If an affricate is marked for length, only part of the affricate complex may actually be lengthened, as shown in the following Koasati words:

[ɪltoˈt͡ʃinan]   /iltot͡ʃinan/[4]   'work'
[toˈt͡ʃːinan]   /tot͡ʃːinan/   'three'

and in the Jju word:

[d͡ʒːu]   'Jju'

Length in phonics vs. phonetic length

In phonics, *long* vs. *short* refers to a contrast in vowel quality, not a difference in length as we are using the terms here. In English phonics, a short vowel occurs in the middle of a word spelled with a consonant-vowel-consonant sequence such as in 'mat', and a long vowel occurs in the middle of a word spelled with a consonant-vowel-consonant-silent [e] sequence, such as 'mate'. Although the vowels classified as 'long' by this criterion may have greater duration than those classified as 'short', the difference between these long and short vowels is primarily a difference in vowel quality, and only secondarily one of phonetic length. For example, the vowel in 'mat' is [æ], and the vowel in 'mate' is a glided vowel [ei̯] or [eˈ]. In our discussion of significant differences in phonetic duration of vowels as the physical correlate of a phonological contrast in vowel length in some languages, we are not referring to the terms *long vowels* and *short vowels*, as used in phonics.

Names of sounds

The terms to use for degrees of length are LONG, HALF-LONG, and EXTRA SHORT. To specify a length other than SHORT, one of these terms is placed immediately before the last word in the name of the sound:

[iː] close front unrounded long vowel
[tˑ] voiceless alveolar half-long stop

Just as short vowels are usually left unmarked in a phonetic transcription, they also are assumed by default when the name of a sound does not specify the relative length of the sound.

The terms *lengthened* and *shortened* refer to processes that change sounds from one length to another. Such phenomena belong to the study of phonology and are not treated in this phonetics book.

Pronunciation helps

In English, increased duration together with a higher pitch are significant phonetic features that identify stress. In another language these two phonetic features may not co-occur, but rather, pitch and length may be independent variables. It is important for you to separate these two features by practicing words from a language where these do not co-occur. The following words are from Comanche (Oklahoma, data from Elliot Canonge, as cited in E. V. Pike 1963:55).

ˈmasiˑto   'fingernail'   ˈhaniˑβi   'corn'

Key terms

duration, phonetic length   half-length mark [ˑ], raised period [ˑ]
long, half-long, short, extra-short   breve [˘], wedge [˘]
length mark [ː], colon [ː]   length in phonics vs. phonetic length

---

[3] Affricates are discussed in more detail in chapter 17.
[4] The curved symbol over the [t͡ʃ] indicates that these two sounds function as one consonant, an affricate.

Exercises

1. Practice the following words from Belgian French (Tranel 1987:50):

tus	'all'	ɑmi	'friend' (masculine)
tuːs	'cough'	syʁ	'sure' (masculine)
ɑmiː	'friend' (feminine)	syːʁ	'sure' (feminine)

2. Practice the following Norwegian words (E. V. Pike, 1963:56):

sè·ntʰ	'late' (neuter)	sè·n	'late'
sèn·tʰ	'sent'	sèn·	'send!'

3. Practice the following Navajo words (United States; data from Edgerton as cited in E. V. Pike 1963:55):

nà·ʃá	'I travel around'	ʔákő:	'over there'
dàsìzí	'he is standing up'		

4. Practice the following Amharic words (Ethiopia; data from Peter Unseth, personal communication):

ɑlːɜ	'it is there'	asɜmːɑ	'call a witness'
ɑlɜ	'he said'	asːɜmːɑ	'cause to hear'
gɜnɑ	'not yet'	sɜbːɜkɜ	'preach'
gɜnːɑ	'Christmas'	sɜbɜkɑ	'parish, diocese'
sɜfːi	'wide'	tamːɜmɜ	'he was pained'
sɜfi	'tailor'	kɜsːɜsɜ	'he accused'
bimɜtɑl	'if he will hit'	bɜsɜbːɜsɜ	'it rotted'
bimːɜtːɑl	'if he will be hit'	sɜbɜsːɜbɜ	'he gathered'
bibɜsɑl	'if he will bore a hole'		
bibːɜsːɑl	'if it will be bored'		

5. Practice the following Tyap words (Nigeria, data from Bulus Tauna, personal communication):

kʰáːtʰ	'to fry in oil'	vːóŋ	'to restrain'
bàn	'grinding stone'	fːúŋ	'to rest'
vːòn	'to be different'	ʃòːtʰ	'moving'
zːò	'crocodile'	ɣːúɣːúkʰ	'tree bark'
fáːtʰ	'to cut'	nàːtʰ	'going'

17

Affricates

Central affricates

An AFFRICATE is a sequence of a stop followed by a fricative; that is, the stop has a FRICATIVE RELEASE. All stops, whether voiced or voiceless, may be affricated.[1] Voiceless affricates may be aspirated or unaspirated. Affricates often function as single units in language with no syllable boundary between the stop and fricative. If a stop and a fricative are produced either at the same place of articulation, as in [ts], or at adjacent places of articulation, as in [tʃ], the affricate is HOMORGANIC. If the stop and fricative places of articulation differ, it is a HETERORGANIC affricate, e.g., [ps, bz]. Some linguists (e.g., Ladefoged 1993:291) consider only homorganic stop-fricative sequences to be affricates because of how they pattern in languages, whether as one or two phonological units.[2]

If an affricate functions as a phonological unit in a language, both the stop and the fricative will be fully voiced as in English [dʒoᵘk] 'joke' or fully voiceless as in [tʃʰoᵘk] 'choke.' However, it is quite common for phonetically-voiced units such as fricatives, stops, and affricates to be at least partially DEVOICED; that is, there is an absence of voicing during part or the whole of a phonologically voiced sound. This is especially true when the sound is contiguous to a voiceless environment, such as at the beginning or the end of an utterance. For example, a speaker might pronounce 'joke' as [tʃoᵘk]. If you are a native speaker of a language such as English, in which there is a strong tendency to devoice sounds, pay careful attention to maintain voicing when it is important to do so in another language.

An explanatory note on the IPA chart of symbols (2015; see Appendix A) allows that "affricates… [that function as sound units in a language] can be represented by two symbols joined by a tie bar [͡] if necessary." In a BROAD TRANSCRIPTION, one that leaves out much of the fine phonetic detail, a tie bar might be useful for distinguishing 'Why choose?' [weɪ.t͡ʃuz] from 'white shoes' [weɪtʃuz]. A NARROW TRANSCRIPTION is one that includes considerable phonetic detail.

Symbols and names

If a stop is released into a fricative over the midline of the tongue, the sequence is a central affricate. If the stop is released into a fricative over one or both sides of the tongue, the sequence is a lateral affricate. Table 17.1 lists some of the more widely found homorganic central affricates. Although it is

---

[1] The exception to this statement is double stops such as [k͡p] and [g͡b], discussed in chapter 20, which have not been found to be affricated.
[2] In Jju, [ps] and [bz], while heterorganic affricates, function as phonological units.

possible to aspirate any voiceless affricate, only the alveolar and postalveolar affricates are commonly found with an aspirated release.

The names for affricates may be read from the tables in the usual manner. For example, [tʃʰ] is a *voiceless postalveolar aspirated affricate.* Notice that the name for the place of articulation of an affricate is that of the *fricative,* which is not necessarily the same as that of the stop. A heterorganic stop-fricative sequence has no widely recognized name.

Table 17.1. Homorganic central affricates

	Bilabial	Labiodental	Interdental	Alveolar	Postalveolar	Velar		
Voiceless				tsʰ	tʃʰ		aspirated	affricate
Voiceless	pɸ	pf	tθ	ts	tʃ	kx		
Voiced	bβ	bv	dð	dz	dʒ	gɣ		
Passive articulator	upper lip	upper teeth	back of teeth	alveolar ridge	behind alveolar ridge	front of velum		
Active articulator	lower lip	lower lip	tongue tip	tongue tip	tongue blade	tongue back		

Because we have used sagittal diagrams to represent only one moment in a single articulation, and it would take two diagrams to represent an affricate, one for the stop and another one for the fricative, we have not included them in this chapter.

Lateral affricates

Some stops are released into a lateral fricative, thus producing a LATERAL AFFRICATE. Table 17.2 lists the most common lateral affricates. The term *lateral* is needed in the names for lateral affricates, to distinguish them from central affricates.

Table 17.2. Lateral affricates

	Alveolar	Velar		
Voiceless	tɬʰ		aspirated	lateral affricate
Voiceless	tɬ	kʟ̥		
Voiced	dl	gʟ		
Passive articulator	alveolar ridge	front of velum		
Active articulator	tongue tip	tongue back		

The sequence [dl] occurs in many languages. According to the definition that an affricate is a stop followed by a fricative, [dl] is not an affricate since [l] is not a fricative. The definition of an affricate would lead us to expect that a voiced alveolar lateral affricate would be [dɮ]. However, [dɮ] has not been found to occur in languages, whereas [dl] does occur quite frequently and in contexts similar to those of other affricates. Therefore [dl] has been included here as an affricate rather than [dɮ], though technically speaking, [dl] and [gʟ] are not affricates.

Pronunciation helps

When you pronounce an affricate, be careful when releasing the stop, to do so directly into the fricative without an intervening vowel or aspiration. For example, when pronouncing [tsʰat], be careful that you do not say [tʰsat]. Also, depending on the language, you may need to make the fricative fairly short, if the stop and fricative together form a single phonological unit.

The following English phrases contain alveolar and postalveolar affricates for practice:

[tsʰ]	'the cat's here'	[tʃʰ]	'change'
[ts]	'the cat's ear'	[tʃ]	'exchange'
[dz]	'the lad's ear'	[dʒ]	'see James'

When pronouncing alveolar lateral affricates, try substituting [d] for initial [g] in English words like 'glade' (i.e., [dleⁱd]), and [t] for initial [k] in words like 'close' (i.e., [tɬoᵘs]). When you practice this exercise, be careful that the initial stop is indeed alveolar rather than velar.

Note that the [dl] *affricate* is different from the [dl̩] *sequence* that occurs in English words like 'waddle' [wadl̩].

A difference between [dl] and [gl], or [tɬ] and [kɬ] have not been reported to make a difference in meaning of words in language. In transcription, if you seem to hear [gl] or [kɬ] as we have in English, check carefully to see whether the sequence is actually [dl] or [tɬ], which do not occur in English.

Key terms

affricate
fricative release
homorganic affricate, heterorganic affricate
devoicing
broad phonetic transcription, narrow phonetic transcription
lateral affricate

Exercises

1. Practice the following affricates from American English:

    | ˈkʰætʃəp | 'ketchup, catsup' | dʒeˈmz | 'James' |
    | ˈtʃʰɪmni | 'chimney' | sɛts | 'sets' |
    | ˈtʰitʃɪŋ | 'teaching' | ˈpʰeˈdʒɪz | 'pages' |

2. Practice the following Kiowa words (United States; E. V. Pike 1963:37):

    | pʰod͡l | 'lie' | tʰõ·gud͡l | 'soda water' |
    | to·gud͡l | 'young man' | tad͡l | 'skunk' |

3. Practice the following Northern Totonac words (Mexico; data from Reid as cited in E. V. Pike 1963:38):

    | laɬ | 'it became' | taˈtɬax | 'wages' |
    | ˈɬuku | 'cave' | ɬtuˈlulu | 'thick' |
    | ˈʃa·lu | 'pitcher' | tɬunˈtɬulu | 'furry, hairy' |
    | ˈtɬo· | 'he does it' | ɬtaˈta | 'he sleeps' |
    | tɬaˈxa | 'he earns it'| ˈmiʃli | 'he put it out' |

4. Practice the following Jju words (Nigeria; McKinney data):

    | əbvún | 'unripe, raw, uncooked' | pfò | 'ear' |
    | tʃòtʰ | 'goods carried on one's head' | tsáŋ | 'crocodile'|
    | tʃóŋ | 'python, walk' (n.) | kʰədzà | 'God' |

dʒípʰ   'bush fowl, partridge'   kʰə́pfùn   'today'
dʒìpʰ   'bush fowls, partridges'

5. Practice the following Tyap words (Nigeria; data from Bulus Tauna, personal communication):

tʃĩntʃòn   'smoke'   tsà̰ŋ   'crocodile'
tʃètʃó   'mermaid'   tsùpʰ   'spitting cobra'
tʃĩntʃín   'fly'   tsúpʰ   'spitting cobras'
tʃĩntʃìn   'flies'

6. List the symbol and the name for eight homorganic affricates at six different places of articulation represented:

[ ] _____
[ ] _____
[ ] _____
[ ] _____
[ ] _____
[ ] _____
[ ] _____
[ ] _____

7. For each of the following pairs of phonetic segments, identify homorganic, heterorganic, and non-affricates, stating the reason for your decision.

[pʰ] _____
[gɣ] _____
[ðd] _____
[dt] _____
[sʃ] _____
[pɬ] _____
[pɸ] _____

18

Voiceless Vowels and Glottal Consonants

Voiceless vowels

A VOICELESS VOWEL results when two conditions are met: first, the rate of airflow through the glottis and the degree of constriction at the glottis are sufficient to produce audible air turbulence there but without voicing, and second, a vowel is articulated. It may sound somewhat like a voiceless fricative, because both start out as random noise resulting from air turbulence at the constriction. It usually has the same vowel quality as a voiced vowel made with the same articulation.

Some phoneticians distinguish three kinds of voiceless vowels. (1) A voiceless vowel may be *inaudible* because there is little or no airflow to produce a sound; this is termed NIL PHONATION. (2) In addition to its vowel quality, the noise of a voiceless vowel may have the low-pitched quality of a gentle flow of air called BREATH PHONATION. (3) Alternatively, the voiceless vowel noise may have the high-pitched quality of air rushing through the narrow glottis under high pressure, in which case it is a WHISPERED VOWEL. Whispered vowels seldom occur in casual speech. They are used primarily in whispered speech, a speech style in which all the sounds are voiceless. In the transcriptions in this book, the diacritic for voicelessness means 'made with breath phonation' unless specified otherwise.

When voiceless vowels are present, transcribe them by placing a small circle diacritic below the symbol for the voiced vowel with the same quality, e.g., [ɪ̥] and [e̥]. The name of a voiceless vowel is the same as for its voiced counterpart, with the term *voiceless* added at the beginning. Thus, [i̥] is a *voiceless close front unrounded vowel*.

When a voiceless vowel occurs next to a voiced vowel, the two vowels are produced with the same articulation, and thus have the same vowel quality. In this case, the quality of a voiceless vowel is PREDICTABLE from its environment. The voiceless vowel may be transcribed with [h] instead of an explicit voiceless vowel symbol, in this case. Many words in English have a predictable voiceless vowel, spelled with 'h' or [V̥] for a voiceless vowel in phonetic script. 'h' is also used in the orthography for the following examples:

> *Cheyenne*
>
> When Carol worked with Mr. Ed Riggs, a Cheyenne language associate, in a linguistic field methods class, she missed hearing a voiceless vowel. Mr. Riggs leaned over the desk, pointed to the place of the missed segment in her transcription, and said, "If I were you, I'd write a voiceless 'a' there."

    [æ̥æt]   [hæt]   'hat'
    [i̥it]   [hit]   'heat'
    [ɑ̥ɑt]   [hɑt]   'hot'

Many languages have voiceless vowels in positions where their vowel quality is not predictable. In such languages the vowel should be written with a vowel letter rather than with [h]. The following example from Comanche (Oklahoma) (from Elliott Canonge 1957 as cited in E. V. Pike 1963:41) illustrates a contrast in final voiceless vowels:

['tɯpi̥] 'stone'   ['tɯpe̥] 'lips'

This difference cannot be accounted for by any environmental phonetic conditioning. Because this contrast in voiceless vowels correlates with a meaning difference, the quality of the voiceless vowels must be written. The use of [h] to represent this difference is not possible in this language. Usually a consonant immediately preceding a syllable-final voiceless vowel is also voiceless.

Pronunciation helps

Often speakers of languages such as Comanche and Cheyenne (Oklahoma) pronounce voiceless vowels softly such that a field linguist may fail to notice them (see Cheyenne side-box). The main clue to their presence may be slight lip movement. In order to pronounce voiceless vowels like a native speaker of the language, make them more softly than you are inclined to do, and make syllables with voiceless vowels as long as syllables with voiced vowels. In some languages, voiceless vowels may be shorter than syllables with voiced vowels. Pronounce the words below (from E. V. Pike 1963:41–42; Canonge 1957:67):

Cheyenne	βi̥pots̥i̥	'leaf'	matɑ̥	'cactus'
	i̥stɑɢpi̥	'brain'	mato̥	'again'
Comanche	'kaɢpe	'bed'	'pukuki̥ni	'stable'
	mɑ'muɸisiika	'when he blew his nose'	'puhakɯ̥ni	'church'

Glottal consonants

This section focuses on three sounds involving the glottis: the GLOTTAL STOP [ʔ], the VOICELESS GLOTTAL FRICATIVE [h], and the BREATHY GLOTTAL FRICATIVE [ɦ]. Although the glottal stop is quite different from the two glottal fricatives, it is closely related to them, both in the way it is produced and in the way it functions in the sound systems of languages. To produce a glottal stop, press the vocal folds tightly together; to produce a glottal fricative, keep the vocal folds slightly apart.

The adjustment of the larynx to produce *ordinary voicing*, as the term has been used up to this point, is intermediate between that for [ɦ] and that for [ʔ]. The adjustment that produces the breathy voice of the glottal fricative is intermediate between that for [h] and that for other voiced sounds.

The [ɦ] sound is produced in the same way as [h], but with BREATHY VOICE (also called MURMUR). This kind of voicing will be discussed in more detail in a later chapter on phonation.

When [h] functions as a consonant, it is a glottal fricative made at the same place of articulation as the breathy glottal fricative [ɦ] and the glottal stop [ʔ].[1] In some languages through coarticulation [h] assimilates to the place of articulation of the following vowel. This is true in English, as seen in the 'hat', 'heat', 'hot' examples.

Table 18.1. Glottal stop, glottal fricative, and breathy glottal fricative

	Glottal stop	Glottal fricative	Breathy glottal fricative
	ʔ	h	ɦ
Voicing	voiceless	voiceless	breathy voice

---

[1] Traditionally the symbol [h] has been used for a voiceless vowel in some languages and in other languages it functions phonologically as a consonant.

[ʔ] may be released with aspiration, i.e., [ʔʰ]. Pronounce [ʔɑʔ] and [ʔɑʔʰ], with and without aspiration. So far linguists have not found aspirated glottal stops prior to vowels, e.g., *[ʔʰɑ].[2] An aspirated glottal stop does occur before another consonant in some languages, e.g., in the Pame words [ˈbɑhoʔʰkʰ] 'they see me' and [ˈbɑhoʔʰtʰ] 'they see them' (Mexico, data from Lorna Gibson as cited in E. V. Pike 1963:72).

Pronunciation helps

We produce glottal stops by closing the glottis completely. Glottal consonants occur in the English expression [ʔoʔo] 'oh oh'. The challenge is to recognize a glottal stop when you or others produce one, and to control whether you make one or not.

In English words beginning with a vowel, we pronounce a glottal stop prior to that vowel. In order to practice inserting or deleting a vowel-initial glottal stop, use one or more of these techniques:

say [hɑ]; then gradually shorten the [h] until you have [ɑ] in isolation;
think the [h] but do not say it; say [ɑ];
practice yawning and saying [ɑ].

Helps for detecting the presence of [ʔ] include listening for the following three things:

abrupt onset of voicing
abrupt cutoff of voicing
interruption of either voicing or the 'continuity' of a segment.

Pronounce the following words with and without an initial glottal stop:

| ʔæm | oᵘkʰ | æm | ʔoᵘkʰ |

It is important to be able to control the presence or absence of a glottal stop in order to be able to mimic words in a language you are studying in which a glottal stop functions differently than it does in English.

Key terms

voiceless vowel
nil phonation
breath phonation
whispered vowel
predictable quality [h]

non-predictable quality (explicit vowel symbol)
glottal stop [ʔ]
voiceless glottal fricative [h]
breathy glottal fricative [ɦ]
breathy voice, murmur

Exercises

1. Practice the following words:

ɑʔakʰ	aʔkʰ	ɑhkʰ	aʔʰkʰ
ɛhɛpʰ	ɛʔpʰ	ɛhpʰ	ɛʔʰpʰ
oʔɪtʰ	oʔtʰ	ohtʰ	oʔʰtʰ

2. Practice the following Cuicatec words from Oaxaca (Mexico; data from May Morrison and Voila Waterhouse as cited in E. V. Pike 1963:51):

   ˧ ˧
   ˈiβiʔ   'boss'

   ˧ ˩
   ˈiβi   'large rat'

---
[2] An asterisk prior to a linguistic form indicates that it is unattested in language in general or in a specific language.

˧ ˥		
toˈʔo	'my hand'	
˥ ˧		
ˈtoʔoʔ	'our hand'	
˩		
ˈtuˑʔ	'thick'	
˧ ˧		
ˈtuʔu	'chicken'	

3. Practice the following Shoshone words (Utah; data from Floyd 1981:38):

ˈtɪmpe̥	'mouth'	ˈsapɯ	'belly'
ˈtɪmpi̥	'stone'	ˈtaɸe̥	'sun'
ˈnəmpe̥	'foot'	ˈtuku̥	'flesh'
ˈnəmpɑ̥	'shoe'		

4. Practice the following Paez words (Colombia, data from Marianna Slocum, personal communication):

uʔʰ	'to go away'	ˈtʃihmɛ	'white'
ũʔ	'to eat'	ˈtʃihmɛʔ	'it is white'

5. Practice the following Comanche words (United States, data from Canonge 1957:65, 67):

ˈkupi̥taʔ	'light'	ˈpapinɯː	'heads'
ˈɑɑʔniː	'beaver'	ˈnakinɯː	'ears'
ˈɯɯki̥	'brush arbor'	ˈtoʔinɯː	'pipes'

6. Name the following:

[ɦ] _____
[h] _____
[i̥] _____
[u̥] _____
[ɔ] _____
[i̥] _____

List and define three kinds of voiceless vowels:

_____
_____
_____

19

Central Approximants and Labial Flaps

An APPROXIMANT is a speech sound produced by one articulator coming close to (approximating) another, but not so close that closure of the airstream causes audible turbulence. A CENTRAL APPROXIMANT is one for which the passageway for the airstream is centered along the midline of the tongue. See chapter 15 for lateral approximants.

Central approximants are similar to vowels, but there are important differences. Like vowels, they are central oral sonorants, and sometimes they are called SEMIVOWELS or *non-syllabic vowels*. Phonologically, however, a vowel functions as the nucleus of a syllable, but an approximant does not. The active articulator generally moves more rapidly and comes closer to the passive articulator for an approximant than it does for a vowel.

Table 19.1. Central approximants

	Single articulation				Double articulation		Sound quality
	labio-dental	inter-dental	palatal	velar	labial-palatal	labial-velar	alveolar (rhotacized)
Voiceless	ʋ̥		j̊	ɰ̊	ɥ̊	ʍ	ɻ̊	approximant/ semivowel/ non-syllabic vowel
Voiced	ʋ	ð̞	j	ɰ	ɥ	w	ɻ
Passive articulator	upper teeth	upper teeth	hard palate	front of velum	upper lip	upper lip	
Active articulator	lower lip	tongue blade	tongue front	tongue back	lower lip	lower lip	
Passive articulator #2					hard palate	front of velum	
Active articulator #2					tongue front	tongue back	

Table 19.1 presents four categories of common central approximants: LABIODENTAL, INTERDENTAL, PALATAL, and VELAR APPROXIMANTS. They are produced by a single pair of articulators. LABIAL-PALATAL and LABIAL-VELAR APPROXIMANTS each involve two constrictions, at the lips (*labial*) and with the tongue (*palatal* or *velar*).

Examples of names of the central approximant [w] are *voiced labial-velar approximant, voiced labial-velar non-syllabic vowel,* and *voiced labial-velar semivowel.* The term *central* need not be included in the names of semivowels; an approximant is central unless specified as lateral.

Rhotacized speech sounds are ones that have RHOTICITY, i.e., an 'r' quality; thus *rhotacized approximants* are ones with an 'r' quality. Rhotacized vowels and semivowels may be produced in at least two rather different ways: by RETROFLEXION, curling the tongue tip upward and backward toward the back of the alveolar ridge, or by humping the center of the tongue up.[1] We do not know of any language in which the difference between these two articulations is contrastive. However, recognizing which articulation someone is using can help explain some rule of how the language works. Also, typically American English speakers round their lips in producing the 'r' sound when it comes before a vowel in the same syllable, but not when the 'r' sound comes after a vowel in the same syllable.

Table 19.2 gives examples of approximants in a midwestern American dialect of English known as General American. When American English speakers say 'ye' and 'woo' the approximant is made with greater constriction than the similar vowel in the same syllable. This helps to distinguish the approximant or semivowel from the syllabic vowel that follows it.

Table 19.2. Examples of approximants in English

[j] syllable initial		[w] syllable initial		[ɹ] syllable initial		[ɹ] syllable final	
'you'	[ju]	'woo'	[wu]	'rue'	[ɹu]	'tour'	[tʰuɹ]
'yacht'	[jɑt]	'watt'	[wɑt]	'rot'	[ɹɑt]	'tar'	[tʰɑɹ]
'ye'	[ji]	'we'	[wi]	're-'	[ɹi]	'hear'	[hɪɹ]

The voiced-voiceless contrast between [w] and [w̥] distinguishes words in some languages. For example, in Jju, [wan] 'to cook' contrasts with [w̥an] 'to perish'. Some dialects of American English have this voiced/voiceless contrast, too. For example, check how you say the following pairs of words: 'which' – 'witch', 'where' – 'wear.' Do you make a voiced/voiceless distinction? Many English speakers pronounce both as [w]. If this is true for you, then you may need to pay special attention to whether the language you are studying makes this distinction and produce it appropriately.

When we produce a voiceless approximant, our articulators cannot form as great a constriction at the place of articulation as they often do for a voiced approximant. This is because the air can flow more rapidly when the glottis is wide open for a voiceless approximant than it does when the glottis opens only a little, and for only part of the time for a voiced approximant. The more rapid airflow through the wide-open glottis produces noisy turbulence as it forces its way through the maximum constriction for the voiceless approximant. Experiment 19.1 is a way for you to experience this.

> **Experiment 19.1**
>
> Say "ye" (the archaic plural form of 'you') a few times. Then say just the first part of the word a few times, making sure not to move the articulators (i.e., don't glide the vowel). This should be approximately the cardinal vowel [i]. After you have gotten the feel of the voiced vowel that corresponds to the beginning of the approximant, take a deep breath and say the vowel again. Then, while continuing to hold the vowel articulation, stop voicing and allow the air from the lungs to rush freely through your open glottis. You should find yourself making a strong palatal fricative [ç] rather than a voiceless [j̥].

---

[1] The symbol for the retroflex version is [ɻ]. Retroflex sounds are covered in chapter 26.

Voiced interdental approximant

The *voiced interdental approximant* [ð̞] occurs in at least ten languages in the Philippines. In producing it, the tongue body moves forward and protrudes between the teeth or to the lips. The highest degree of narrowing occurs between the tongue blade and the upper teeth. There is no lip spreading in its production. While the symbol [ð̞] has not yet been accepted as an IPA symbol, Olson (2007, lecture at GIAL, Dallas) has suggested this symbol as a way to represent this sound. Previously it was variously described. For example, Gieser (1958:17) classified it as a *central resonant oral vowel;* Olson and Mbomate, as a *near-open front unrounded approximant* (2006); Harmon, as an *L-colored glide* (1979:17); Wiens (1976:41) called it a *palatal lateral;* Gallman (1974:8) transcribed it as [lᶸ]; and Everett (1982:94) described it as a *sublaminal labial* or a *voiced lateralized apical*. It functions as a consonant in the languages where it occurs.

Correspondence between vowels and approximants/semivowels

Table 19.3 shows the most common semivowel symbols and their corresponding syllabic vowel symbols. Just as for voiceless nasals, the circle diacritic denoting voicelessness may be placed over the base character if that character has a descender.

Table 19.3. Correspondence between vowels and approximants/semivowels

Semivowel quality or place of articulation	Voiced vowel	Voiced semivowel	Voiceless semivowel
Palatal	i	j	j̊
Labial-palatal	y	ɥ	ɥ̊
Labial-velar	u	w	w̥
Rhotacized/Alveolar	ɚ	ɹ	ɹ̊
Velar	ɯ	ɰ	ɰ̊

Labial flaps

LABIAL FLAPS involve the lower lip as the active articulator flapping against the upper lip or the upper teeth. Two versions of labial flaps occur: [ⱱ] is a *voiced labiodental flap* and [w̬] is a *voiced bilabial flap*. In producing the labiodental flap, the lower lip is retracted behind the upper teeth, and then it is brought forward rapidly and strikes the upper teeth in passing. While the basic flap is labiodental, a bilabial variant has also been found in some languages. A bilabial flap has not been found to contrast with a labiodental flap; hence both are referred to as labial flaps.

Olson and Hajek (1999:106) reported only one instance where a labial flap has been reported as voiceless. It is in an ideophone in the Zezuru dialect of Shona, a Bantu language spoken in Zimbabwe, e.g., in [ⱱ̥a] 'a report of a gun'. It has been found in contrast with the voiced bilabial and labiodental fricatives [β] and [v], and with the labial-velar approximant [w] in some languages. A further feature of a labial flap in some languages is that there is backing of the tongue that co-occurs with the articulation of the flap.

Linguists have found labial flaps primarily in north central Africa in Niger-Congo, Afro-Asiatic (Chadic), and Nilo-Saharan (Eastern Sudanic) languages. Though it may be voiceless word-initially, in over 90% of its occurrence it is voiced. It has spread to the various languages in this area. It has also been found in at least one Austronesian (Malayo-Polynesian) language, Sika, in Indonesia.

Pronunciation helps

In order to pronounce a voiceless labial-velar approximant [w̥], think of producing [h] and [w] simultaneously, or [hw]. The same technique will facilitate saying the other voiceless central approximants. For example, to pronounce [j̊]; think of saying [h] and [j] simultaneously, or [hj].

To practice rhotacized sounds, try pronouncing 'raw' [ɹɔ], first with the tongue tip retroflexed and then with the tongue tip low and the center of the tongue humped up. (See experiment 19.2.) One way to retroflex your tongue is to touch the tip of your tongue to the alveolar ridge, then slide it back until it is touching the hard palate. Keep the tip curled back but let the tip come away from the palate so that the sound is central rather than lateral. If you make a sound with the tongue in this position, it will be rhotacized, i.e., it will have an 'r' quality. To make the rhotacized sound with the back of the tongue humped up instead of the tip curled up and back, start with the mid central vowel [ə]. Then, continuing to voice and keeping your tongue tip, blade, and front all very low in your mouth, pull the body or back of your tongue up and back toward the position for a close back vowel. This should produce an 'r' quality, and by experimenting with variations in the tongue position you can learn to make a very acceptable [ɹ] without retroflexing your tongue.

Experiment 19.2

In this experiment you will (1) discover different ways in which you make an 'r' sound, (2) practice making the same 'r' sound quality in two very different ways, and (3) challenge a friend to tell you which way you are making the sound as you make it differently in random order. You will use *introspection* and *proprioception* to discover what you are doing with your tongue and your lips as you pronounce English words with the 'r' sound in various contexts. Then you will use visual observation with a mirror to check your results. In this context, *introspection* is consciously thinking about how you shape your lips and your tongue in producing the 'r' sound without physically articulating the word. *Proprioception* is your ability to feel what you are doing as you physically articulate the 'r' sound.

Prepare a list of words that have the 'r' sound in them. Some of the words should have the 'r' sound before the vowel as in 'read,' 'rod,' 'rude.' Some should have it after the vowel as in 'peer,' 'par,' 'poor.' And in some the 'r' should be syllabic, as in 'her,' 'sir,' 'cur.'

Begin by watching your lips in a mirror as you say: 'ray' vs. 'hair'; 'rid' or 'reed' vs. 'deer;' 'rear,' 'rare.' Draw out the length of each word so that you can observe what you are doing with your mouth. When do you round your lips in making the 'r' sounds, and when do you not?

When you round your lips, where is the tip of your tongue, and where is the middle or back of your tongue—what are they doing? When you make the 'r' sound without rounding your lips, what are the tip and back doing? Is the shape of your tongue about the same or quite different?

(1)   Practice making the 'r' sound first with your tongue tip curled upward, and then with it lying down behind the lower teeth. Try to make the 'r' sound with the same vowel quality with the two very different articulations. Practice until they sound the same to you both ways.

(2)   Then enlist a friend to watch you as you make the 'r' sound with the two very different articulations. If possible, help your friend to visually detect a difference between the two.

(3)   Finally, the acid test of your phonetic prowess—challenge your friend to look away as you make the same sound in the two different ways in random order and to tell you just by listening which way you made the sound each time.

Key terms

approximant, central approximant, interdental approximant
semivowel, non-syllabic vowel
retroflex, retroflexion
rhotacized, rhoticity
labial-velar, labial-palatal, labiodental
labial flap

Exercises

1. Practice the following English words:

ɹu	'you'	wu	'woo'	ɹu	'rue'
jatʰ	'yacht'	watʰ	'watt'	ɹatʰ	'rot'
ji	'ye'	wi	'we'	ɹi	're-'
wɛɹ	'wear'	w̥ɛɹ	'where'	wɪtʃ	'witch'
w̥ɪtʃ	'which'	ju	'you'	j̥u	'hue,' 'Hugh'
tʰʊɹ or tʰuɹ	'tour'	tʰɑɹ	'tar'	tʰɪɹ or tʰiɹ	'tear'

2. Practice the following French words (Atkins, et. al 1987):

Phonetic spelling	French spelling	English gloss
ɥil	huile	'oil'
ɥi	huis	'door'
juˈpi	youpi	'yippee'
juˈju	youyou	'dinghy'
ɥit	huit	'eight'
wagaˈdugu	Ouagadougou	'Ouagadougou' (a city in Burkina Faso)
wananiʃ	ouananiche	'lake trout,' 'salmon'

3. Practice the following Jju words (McKinney data):

ɥap	'to err'	ɥ̊ap	'to sell'
ɥ̊an	'moon, month'	jɑːn	'another'
ɥ̊otʰ	'arrow'	ɥ̊ːotʰ	'to be close to'
ɥ̊apʰ	'to blow'	ɥ̊okʰ	'to approach'
wapʰ	'an ethnic group'	wːaŋ	'granite rock'
wan	'to cook'	wan	'to perish'
jakʰ	'grain'	jːakʰ	'to press'
wi	'to fail'	wi	'to burn'
w̥ːoŋ	'an underwater cave'	w̥ːom	'to crush'
ji	'you' (pl. subj. pron.)	jːi	'to steal'
w̥a	'to think'	w̥ːa	'to eat rapidly, to scramble for'
jːa	'to do'	ja	'to eat'

4. Practice the following Mono words (Democratic Republic of the Congo; data from Olson and Schrag 1997, as quoted in Olson and Hajek 1999:108):

àw̌éɲè	'rainbow'	w̌átò	'queen ant'
áw̌árá	'wisdom'	kə́w̌ì	'to throw'
áw̌ūrūŋgù	'vehicle'	kə́kàw̌a	'to snap'
àw̌ɨ́	'hyena'	w̌ɨ́tɨ́	'calf of leg'
w̌à	'to send'	wà	'to cut'

5. Practice the following Tzotzil words (data from Laughlin 1975:381, 444, 473, 500, 533, 536):

jijil	'Never mind, forget it! What's the use?'	jo	'shoo' (as shooing chickens by waving)
jaʃuʃ	'garlic'	wɛj	'ox'
joʔtʰo	'until, whenever'	jɑj	'male term of address to women of Chenalhó, Mitonic, and Tzeltal towns'

6. Practice the following Foi words (Papua New Guinea; data from M. and J. Rule as cited in E. V. Pike 1963:63):

waʔohaʔoˈjoʔo	'don't laugh'	faʔabɪdaˈʔæ	'I am hungry'
waʔoʔoˈjoʔo	'don't dig'	oʔodaˈʔæ	'I want to go'
waʔobubaˈʔæ	'he is digging'	nobaʔæˈjoʔo	'in order to eat'

7. Practice the following Lubuagan Kalinga words (Philippines; data from Gieser 1958:13, 15, 17, 19):

laðaki	'man'	koðtoj	'epilepsy'
pɸuðan	'moon, month'	takðai	'arm'
ʔapuð	'lime for betel nut chewing'		

8. Practice the following Kagayanen words (Philippines; data from Olson lecture 2007):

pɑðɑd	'palm of the hand'	wɑðəŋ	'face'
ðɑðɑ	'weave'	uðu	'head'
ɑððu	'pestle'	sɑðɑg	'nest'
dɑðɑ	'send'	sɑlɑ	'living room'

9. List three acceptable names for [ɹ]:

_____

_____

10. Fill in the following table with the central approximants produced with a single articulation:

Symbol	Name	Articulators
[ ]		
[ ]		
[ ]		

11. Fill in the following table with two voiceless central approximants with double articulations:

Symbol	Name	Articulators (four for each)
[ ]		
[ ]		

20

Double Stop and Double Nasal Articulations

DOUBLE STOP and DOUBLE NASAL articulations occur in the production of speech sounds by forming two constrictions with the same degree of closure at two different places of articulation at the same time. When a double stop or double nasal articulation is produced, at some point in the articulation both closures are simultaneous. However, one articulation may close before the other or be released before the other. For example, in the Jju word [ə͡gbə́dàŋ] 'big' the velar closure for the [g͡b] occurs first followed by the bilabial, and both closures are released at the same time. This differential timing in closure or release for the two places of articulation is often the primary clue for an outside researcher that a double stop articulation is present. In other languages both closures occur together, with the velar closure released first, resulting in air coming into the oral cavity from the lungs and the cheeks tending to puff out. This is the pattern in Vietnamese.

While speakers of a language with double stop and double nasal articulations can readily identify if one is present initially in a word, it tends to be more difficult for non-native speakers, especially when first hearing the language. If the double stop or double nasal occurs initially in a word, it helps to place that word into a frame with a vowel immediately preceding the word being studied in order to be able to hear that there is a double stop or double nasal articulation present. For example, when the Jju word [k͡pà] 'to fall' is placed in the frame [à k͡pá] 'you fall' it can be more readily heard that the double stop [k͡p] is present.[1]

A double nasal is produced with the nasal port open (i.e., without velic closure) and two complete closures in the oral cavity. A double nasal can be continued as long as there is breath to continue it. A *double stop* is produced with the nasal port closed. Thus a voiced double stop can be continued only as long as there is space left behind the rear place of the articulation to store up the air coming through the glottis. Note that in a double articulation, both components have the same voicing. Some sounds produced with double stop and double nasal articulations are presented in table 20.1.

---

[1] Note that the tone on [k͡pa] changes due to the grammatical context.

Table 20.1. Double stops and double nasals[a]

	Labial-alveolar	Labial-velar		
Voiceless	t͡pʰ	k͡pʰ	aspirated	
Voiceless	t͡p	k͡p		stop
Voiced	d͡b	g͡b		
Voiced	n͡m	ŋ͡m		nasal
Passive articulators	upper lip, alveolar ridge	upper lip, front of velum		
Active articulators	lower lip, tongue tip	lower lip, tongue back		

[c]Bickford and Floyd (2006:174) report that the voiceless implosive [kɓ̥] and the voiced implosive [gɓ] may also occur in language. There are no documented cases of alveolar-velar double stops. The Zezuru dialect of Shona has sequences [tk, dg] which may possibly be interpreted phonologically as a single unit, but as Ladefoged and Maddieson (1996:345) note, phonetically they are clearly sequences.

Doubly-articulated fricatives do not appear to exist, though Laver (1994:316–318) notes several reports of such, and even the International Phonetic Alphabet includes the symbol [ɧ] which is supposedly simultaneous [ʃ] and [x]. Ladefoged and Maddieson (1996) note that physiologically, it is quite difficult to produce simultaneous frication at two places of articulation, and also to hear such. They have investigated several of the supposed cases and found them to have either a sequence of fricatives, or frication at only one place, often with labialization as a secondary articulation (see chapter 21).

The stops and nasals presented in earlier chapters are singly articulated. If two of them occur in sequence without open transition between them, the closure for one of them necessarily overlaps the closure for the other at least for a moment, resulting in COARTICULATION of the two consonants, e.g., [æptʰ] 'apt'. Thus, in coarticulation there is often complete constriction at two places at the same time, just as there is in a double articulation. The difference is that in double stops and double nasals the release of the two articulations is usually nearly simultaneous, whereas in coarticulation the first articulation is released well before the second, and the degree of overlap is less.

In table 20.1, for each double stop or double nasal, the place of articulation further forward in the mouth comes first in the name of the consonant but second in the symbol for the consonant.[2] For example, the bilabial articulation of a labial-velar stop is named first but symbolized second: [k͡p] is a *voiceless labial-velar stop*. A tie bar or ligature drawn over the two symbols indicates that the two articulations function as a unit in a language. This distinguishes a double articulation, e.g., [k͡p], from a consonant cluster that consists of two articulations in a sequence, e.g., [kp].

Labial-velar double articulations are the most common type of double stop. If there is a difference in release timing, the velar articulation is often released before the bilabial one, as is evidenced in Vietnamese.

Sagittal diagrams in figure 20.1 illustrate single articulations for [p] and [k] and double articulations for [k͡p].

---

[2] The reason that the articulation further to the back is first in the digraph transcription may be that there is a tendency for that articulatory closure to be completed first.

20: Double Stop and Double Nasal Articulations

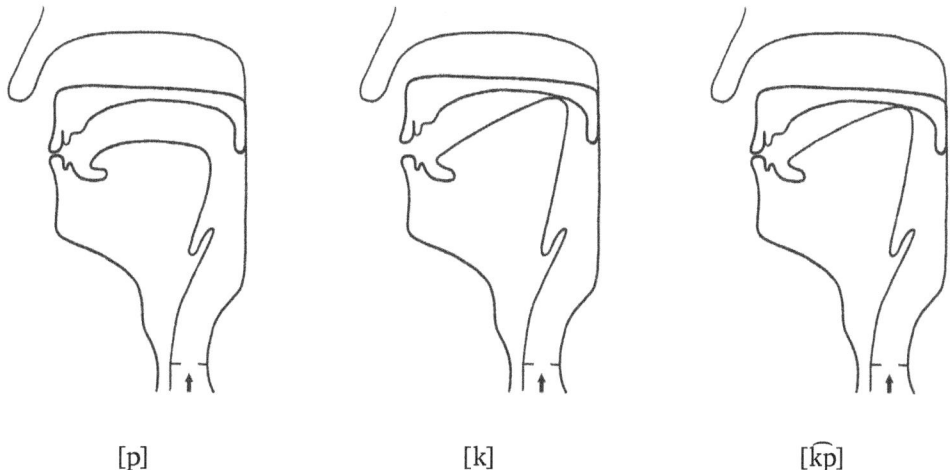

Figure 20.1. Stops [p], [k], and labio-velar double stop [k͡p].

Pronunciation helps

One way to achieve simultaneity of release is to let the jaw move the two active articulators without any additional motion. For the simultaneous release, let the breath stream blow the articulators apart.

Imitate a hen clucking: [k͡pək͡pək͡pək͡p]. Say 'big, big, big', gradually lengthening the vowel until the two stops are articulated simultaneously.

When you have learned to produce the voiced labial-velar double stop, by analogy, try to say the voiceless double stop [k͡p] and the double nasal [ŋ͡m]. Then, substitute other double articulations.

Practice with other sequences such as 'bed, bed, bed,' 'men, men, men,' 'pick, pick, pick.'

Key terms

double articulation   labial-alveolar
double stop   labial-velar
double nasal   coarticulation

Exercises

1. Practice the following sequences:

pʰa	pa	k͡pa	ak͡pa	akʰpʰa
	ba	g͡ba	ag͡ba	agba
pʰa	pa	t͡pa	at͡pa	atʰpʰa
	ba	d͡ba	ad͡ba	adba
	ma	ŋ͡ma	aŋ͡m	aŋma
	ma	n͡ma	an͡ma	anma
	na	ŋ͡na	aŋ͡na	aŋna

2. Practice the following Jju words (Nigeria; McKinney data):

g͡bə̀g͡bán	'far'	kʰá	'to divide'
əg͡bádàŋ	'large'	k͡pà	'skin, book; to fall'
g͡bàŋ	'to pound, distant'	à k͡pá	'you fell'
tʰàkʰ	'leg, foot'	k͡pàtʰàkʰ	'shoe' (lit. 'skin of the foot/leg')

3. For each of the following symbols, give the name of the sound it represents.

   [d͡b] _____

   [n͡m] _____

   [k͡pʰ] _____

   [ŋ͡m] _____

4. Complete the sagittal diagrams and write the names and articulators for the following double articulatons:

Symbol:	[k͡p]	[tp]	[ŋ͡m]
Name:	_____	_____	_____
	_____	_____	_____
Passive art(s).	_____	_____	_____
Active art(s).	_____	_____	_____

21

Secondary Articulations

Most of the consonants introduced so far are articulated at a single place of articulation, with the exception of the double articulations and the central approximants. Most of these sounds have one active articulator that comes close to or touches the passive articulator, significantly shaping the vocal tract, thus affecting the resonances, and, except for sonorants, constricting the airstream.[1]

By contrast, some consonants are produced with two simultaneous articulations, one which constricts or blocks the airstream's flow through the pharynx or the mouth and the other which shapes the vocal tract significantly without constricting the airstream. The articulation that blocks or severely constricts the airstream is the PRIMARY ARTICULATION, and the one that shapes the vocal tract without blocking or constricting the airstream is the SECONDARY ARTICULATION. In addition, some consonants are articulated with a primary articulation and two secondary articulations.

A secondary articulation produces something very similar to a semivowel at the same time that the primary articulation occurs, and alters the sound of the primary articulation. For example, the [p] at the beginning of 'piano' is palatalized, i.e., the tongue blade or center humps up toward the hard palate at the same time that the bilabial articulation is occurring. There is a significant difference between the sounds of the bilabial stops in [p^{jh}æno] and [p^{h}æno]. (The superscript [^{j}] symbolizes palatalization.) Try saying 'piano' with and without palatalization on the [p^{h}]. An initial [b] can be labialized, with lip rounding added, e.g., [b^{w}it^{h}i] 'Bwiti, a syncretistic religious cult in Gabon'. (The superscript [^{w}] indicates labialization.)

Typically, the primary articulation is released first, then the secondary articulation is released, producing an off-glide sound, as in [p^{jh}æno]. In other instances, both releases occur at the same time in which case the secondary articulation is symbolized with a subscript, e.g., [$_{\text{w}}$]. For example, many English speakers labialize the postalveolar sibilant [ʃ] in words such as 'she', 'sheep', and 'shoe'. When speakers labialize [ʃ], the lip rounding is released at about the same time as the fricative articulation. While watching yourself in a mirror, slowly say 'she' and 'sheep' to see if you round your lips. If you do not, find someone to observe who does labialize when pronouncing words with [ʃ]. Next, observe yourself or the other person's difference in timing of the release of the lip rounding relative to the release of the sibilant in the pronunciation of these words. In 'she' and 'sheep' the labialization is released simultaneously with the sibilant, while in the word 'schwa' the labialization continues for a short time after the release of the sibilant. Try pronouncing the words 'coo' and 'cue' and note the different timing of the releases.

Seven types of secondary articulation are LABIALIZATION, PALATALIZATION, VELARIZATION, PHARYNGEALIZATION, LABIODENTALIZATION, LABIAL-PALATALIZATION, and LABIAL-VELARIZATION. Each of these involves a primary articulation and a secondary articulation with less closure. Below we

[1] By the active articulator coming close to or touching the passive articulator it significantly shapes the vocal tract and affects the resonances, i.e., the formants, which will be discussed in chapter 33.

describe the seven secondary articulations together with ways to transcribe them, including both a simultaneous release of the secondary articulation and an off-glide release.

Labialization

Labialization is the addition of lip rounding and sometimes lip protrusion during articulation of a primary consonant. Any consonant may be labialized, including bilabial ones. Labialization is symbolized as follows:

- Simultaneous release   [t_w]
- Off-glide release   [t^w]

Both [s_w] and [s^w] are *voiceless alveolar labialized sibilants*. Their active articulators are the tongue tip for the primary alveolar articulation and the lips for the secondary labialized articulation. Examples show the difference between simultaneous and secondary articulation including (for those who round their lips when saying these words) words such as [ʃ_wip] 'sheep,' [s^wip] 'sweep,' and [ɹ_wid] 'read.'

Palatalization

In palatalization the body of the tongue moves close to the hard palate during the primary articulation often resulting in an off-glide [j] following the release of the primary articulator. Most consonants can be palatalized, except for those consonants produced at the epiglottal or pharyngeal places of articulation (see chapter 27). Their primary articulation requires the whole body of the tongue to be so low in the mouth that the central portion of the tongue cannot be simultaneously humped up toward the hard palate. Palatalization is symbolized as follows:

- Simultaneous release   [t_j]
- Off-glide release   [t^j]

Both [p_j] and [p^j] are *voiceless bilabial palatalized stops* and their articulators are the lips (for the primary bilabial articulation) and the tongue blade or center for the secondary palatalization articulation. The sagittal diagrams in figure 21.1 show the contrast between [p] and [p_j] or [p^j].

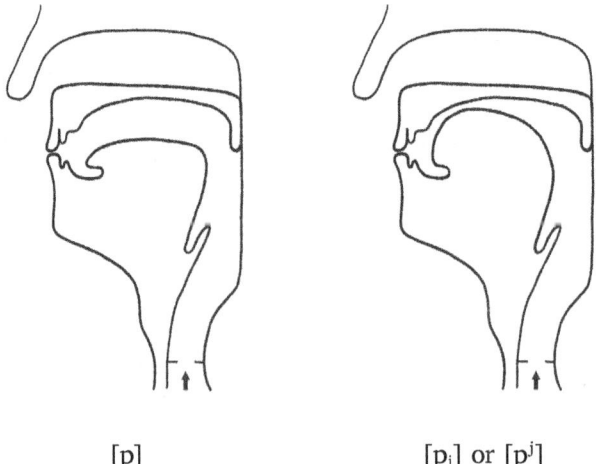

[p]   [p_j] or [p^j]

Figure 21.1. Sagittal diagrams of [p] and [p_j] or [p^j].

Velarization

Velarization is a secondary articulation in which the tongue back rises toward the velum simultaneous with a primary articulation; there is a greater degree of constriction or blocking of the airstream towards the front of the mouth. During velarization the tongue back moves towards the position for producing the high back unrounded vowel [ɯ]. Consonant sounds that do not have this secondary articulation include velar and uvular sounds in which the tongue back is the primary active articulator. The articulation of epiglottal and pharyngeal consonants requires the whole body of the tongue to be too low in the mouth to permit the tongue back to approach the velum.

Velarization is symbolized as follows:[2]

- Simultaneous release   [t̰]
- Off-glide release   [tˠ]

Both [d̰] and [dˠ] are *voiced alveolar velarized stops;* their articulators are the tongue tip for the primary alveolar articulation and the tongue back for the secondary velarization articulation. The sagittal diagrams in figure 21.2 contrast [d] and [d̰] or [dˠ].

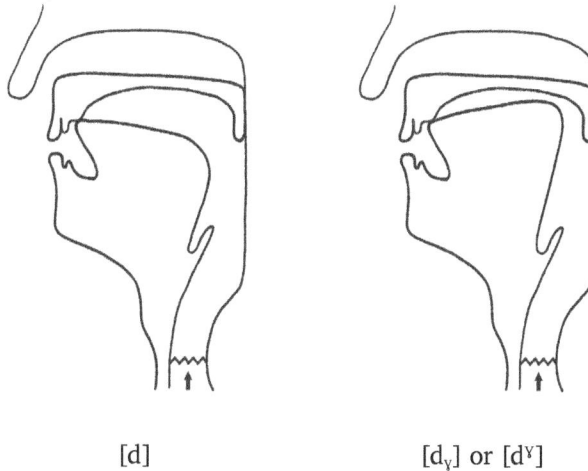

[d]   [d̰] or [dˠ]

Figure 21.2. Sagittal diagrams of [d] and [d̰] or [dˠ].

In learning to velarize consonants without simultaneously labializing them, say the English words 'schwa', 'swim', and 'Swiss' without lip rounding.

Pharyngealization

Pharyngealization is produced by the TONGUE ROOT being retracted toward the back wall of the pharynx as for a pharyngeal fricative. Pharyngealization typically involves off-glide timing, though both a simultaneous release and an off-glide release are presented below. Only consonants articulated fairly far forward in the mouth may be pharyngealized.

Pharyngealization is indicated as follows:

- Simultaneous release   [tˤ]
- Off-glide release   [tˤ]

---

[2] Although traditionally a subscript [ʃ̰] or superscript [ʃˠ] is used to symbolize velarization, the secondary articulation is an approximant [ɰ].

The names and articulators of pharyngealized sounds are the same regardless of the relative timing of the releases. Both [$t^{ʕ}$] and [$t_{ʕ}$] are *voiceless alveolar pharyngealized stops* and their articulators are the tongue tip for the primary alveolar articulation and the tongue root for the secondary pharyngealization articulation. The sagittal diagrams in figure 21.3 illustrate the contrast between [d] and [$d^{ʕ}$] or [$d_{ʕ}$].

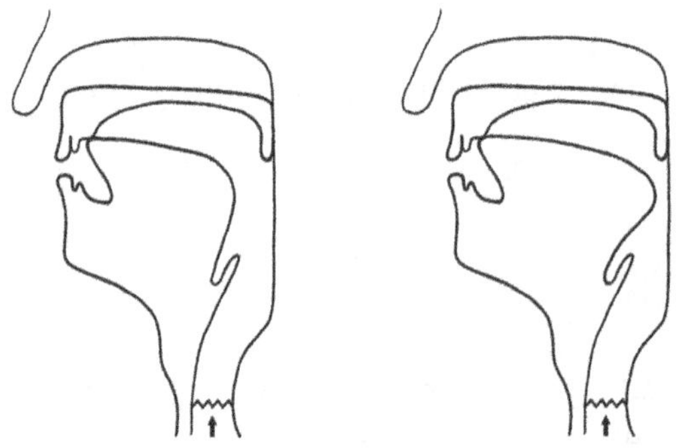

[d] [$d_{ʕ}$] or [$d^{ʕ}$]

Figure 21.3. Sagittal diagrams of [d] and [$d_{ʕ}$] or [$d^{ʕ}$].

Labiodentalization

Laver (1994:322) describes an uncommon type of secondary articulation termed *labiodentalization,* in which "the lower lip is brought into open approximation with the upper front teeth simultaneously with some other more primary stricture." It is found in Abkhaz in the Northwest Caucasus and in some neighboring languages. It is symbolized as follows:

- Simultaneous release [$t_{ʋ}$]
- Off-glide release [$t^{ʋ}$]

Labial-palatalization

Labial-palatalization combines palatalization and labialization on a consonant with a primary articulation. For labial-palatalization the lips are rounded and the blade or center portion of the tongue is humped up toward the hard palate. It is as though a high close front rounded vowel, [y], and rounded palatal semivowel, [ɥ], occur at the same time as the primary articulation.

Labial-palatalization is symbolized as follows:

- Simultaneous release [$t_{ɥ}$]
- Off-glide release [$t^{ɥ}$]

The name and articulators of labial-palatalized sounds are as follows: [$t^{ɥ}$] is a *voiceless alveolar labial-palatalized stop,* and its active articulators are the tongue tip for the alveolar articulation, and the lips and tongue blade for the secondary labial and palatal articulations.

Labial-velarization

Labial-velarization has the secondary articulations of labialization and velarization on the same primary consonant. That is, a labial-velarized consonant is produced with lip rounding, and the tongue back is humped toward the velum. Any velarized consonant may have labial-velarization. There is a non-simultaneous release of the articulators typically resulting in a 'w' off-glide.

Labial-velarization is written with the same symbol as labialization. It is questionable whether labial-velarization is used contrastively with labialization in a particular language. IPA does not distinguish between labialization and labial-velarization (because both are symbolized with 'w' as in [tʷ] or [t_w]).

Sound combinations

Secondary articulations can occur with other qualities of consonants, such as aspiration, and the glottalic airstream mechanism, making it necessary in phonetic transcription to combine symbols. When combining symbols, place the secondary articulation symbol closest to the primary consonant articulation, followed by any other relevant symbol, e.g., [pʲ, pʷʰ].

Table 21.1. Summary of symbols for secondary articulations

Secondary articulation	Articulatory positions of the tongue and lips	Symbols	
		simultaneous	off-glide
Labialization	lips rounded	t_w	tʷ
Palatalization	tongue front humped up toward [i] or [j]	t_j	tʲ
Velarization	tongue back humped up toward [ɯ]	t_ɣ	tˠ
Pharyngealization	tongue root back toward pharynx wall as for [ʕ]	t_ʕ	tˤ
Labiodentalization	lower lip approximates the upper front teeth	t_ʋ	tᶹ
Labial-palatalization	lips rounded; tongue front humped up toward [y]	t_ɥ	tᶣ
Labial-velarization	lips rounded, tongue back humped up toward [w] or [u]	t_w	tʷ

Velarized laterals

The velarized lateral approximant without an off-glide [l_ɣ] is often called a *dark l* to distinguish it from a *clear l* [l], i.e., an alveolar lateral approximant with no secondary articulation.³ Both sounds occur in English; the clear [l] occurs in a syllable before a vowel which is the nucleus of the syllable, and the dark [l_ɣ] occurs elsewhere. Most English speakers do not have trouble pronouncing these sounds. By contrast, palatalized and velarized laterals occur in other positions in other languages. Because of this it is important to be able to produce them in any position in a word.

In order to learn to pronounce both nonvelarized and velarized alveolar laterals, practice the following words:

    tʰɔl_ɣ   'tall'
    tʰɔl
    leɪtʰ   'late'
    l_ɣeɪtʰ

As already mentioned, some languages place velarized and non-velarized consonants in positions other than those found in English. In Russian, laterals are velarized, including word-initially. In

---
³ The traditional IPA transcription for the voiced alveolar velarized lateral approximant is [ɫ].

Spanish there are no velarized laterals. So, in order not to sound foreign when speaking Spanish, use clear non-velarized laterals.

Key terms

primary articulation, primary articulator
secondary articulation, secondary articulator
labialization
palatalization
velarization

pharyngealization
labiodentalization
labial-palatalization
labial-velarization
tongue root

Exercises

1. Practice the following English words aloud (remember that a subscript indicates simultaneous articulation and a superscript represents sequential articulation):

ʃwoᵘ	'show'	tʷʰɪstʰ	'twist'
ɹweⁱs	'race'	sʷæm	'swam'
kʷʰɑm	'qualm'	kʷʰin	'queen'

2. Practice the following Amharic words (Ethiopia; data from Peter Unseth, personal communication):

bʷambʷa	'pipe'	gʷɜd:ɜlɜ	'was lacking'
fʷafʷate	'waterfall'	gɜd:ɜlɜ	'killed'
kɜn:ɜnɜ	'be parched'	anʷ:anʷaɾ	'way of living'
kʷɜnɜnɜ	'condemn'		

3. Practice the following velarized Russian words (Floyd 1981:103):

ˈlˠoɘʃkə	'spoon'	ˈlˠapa	'paw'
lˠukʰ	'garlic'		

4. Practice the following palatalized Russian words (Sivertsen as cited in E. V. Pike 1963:129):

ˈbʲitʲʰ	'to beat'	ˈpʲil̥ or ˈpʲiʎ	'take it'
ˈbʲitʰ	'beaten'	ˈpʲil	'he drank'

5. Practice the following Jju words (Nigeria; McKinney data):

kʲʰaŋ	'thing'	mʷi	'to smell'
tʲʰoŋ	'run'	tʲʰej	'to put; to give birth' (pl.)
mʲ:i	'to lie'	tᵗʰeⁱ	'to sew'
ʃʲ:a	'to find'	k͡pukp͡ʷej	'broad bean soup'
nᵗon	'hen'	k͡pʲokʰ	'to pluck'
nʲat	'to hide'	gbʲaŋ	'naked'
nᵗat	'guinea corn'	ɾan	'to be better than'
kʷʰaŋ	'to grind'	ɾwan	'to be tired'
tʷʰaŋ	'to count'		

6. Practice the following Nii words (Papua New Guinea; data from A. and D. Stucky 1973:42):

mʷíni̋	'lizard'	kʷì	'rat'
ŋʷìmbí	'grasshopper'	nùmbʷí	'I will eat'
tʷì	'ax, knife'		

7. Practice the following Southern Gumuz word (Ethiopia; data from Peter Unseth, personal communication):

bᵗa	'rat'

21: Secondary Articulations 115

8. Practice the following Kamasau words (Papua New Guinea; data from Joy Sanders, personal communication):

ʔʷat	'thorn'	ʔat	'crayfish'
ˈʔʷaji	'man'		
ʔʷet	'wild cane'	wet	'stone'
ʔʷem	'white'		
wand tʷan	'vernacular'	tan	'sword grass'
bʷañʲ	'sugar cane'		
ñʲes	'yellow'	nes	'he stands up'
ŋʷan	'ripe, mature'	ʔʷan	'many, much'

9. Complete the following table for six different secondary articulations:

Symbol	Name of secondary articulation	Tongue and lip position
[ ]		
[ ]		
[ ]		
[ ]		
[ ]		
[ ]		

10. Name the following:

   [tʸ] _____

   [gʷ] _____

   [dˤ] _____

11. Explain the timing difference between the following representations:

   [ʃʷ] _____

   [ʃw] _____

22

Syllabic Consonants, Prenasalization, Preplosion of Nasals, and Apical Vowels

Before discussing syllabic consonants, it is important to define a SYLLABLE. Trask defines a syllable as a "fundamental but elusive phonological unit typically consisting of a short sequence of segments, most typically a single vowel or diphthong possibly preceded and/or followed by one or more consonants" (1996:345). Linguists have found syllables difficult to define, yet clearly people recognize individual syllables. This is evident in that the scripts of some languages are syllabic in nature, e.g., Amharic in Ethiopia and Hiragana in Japan. Most syllables contain one or more consonants and one vowel, though some contain only one sound, a vowel or a syllabic consonant. The study of syllable patterns is an important topic within phonology. A syllable is divided into optional onset, obligatory nucleus, and optional coda. Syllables are described with C representing any consonant and V representing any vowel, with syllable patterns such as V, CV, CCV, CVC, CCVC, VC, found in specific languages. Some words are monosyllabic, for example, [ɪtʰ] 'it' and [tʰu] 'too', 'to', 'two' in English; some are disyllabic, for example, [bɪ.tʷʰin] 'between' and [ə.loᵘd] 'aloud'; and some are trisyllabic or polysyllabic, [lɪŋ.gʷɪs.tʰɪks] 'linguistics'.

While it is not common, some consonants serve as syllable nuclei; when this occurs they fulfill the same function as a vowel does in the syllable nucleus. Consonants that fill a syllable nucleus are SYLLABIC CONSONANTS. To indicate that a consonant is syllabic, place a small vertical line, a syllabicity mark, under the consonant, e.g., [m̩], [l̩].

Even though we defined a syllable, it continues to remain an elusive concept. On occasion people disagree on the number of syllables in a particular word or phrase. Ladefoged suggested that one way to define a syllable is in terms of the inherent SONORITY of each sound. "The sonority of a sound is its loudness relative to that of other sounds with the same length, stress, and pitch" (Ladefoged 2001:227). As stated in chapter 8 on stress, loudness relates to the acoustic intensity or energy present. Further, acoustic intensity in speech varies with different speakers. As an example of sonority, note that the vowel [ɑ] has greater sonority than the vowels [i] and [u]. This relates to the mouth being wider open in producing [ɑ] than it is for [i] and [u]. Peaks of sonority coincide with peaks of syllables. There are some words that do not follow this, however. Perhaps we should speak of peaks of PROMINENCE, namely the degree to which a particular sound or syllable stands out from surrounding sounds or syllables, based on pitch, whether higher or lower, greater loudness, longer duration, and stress. While we do not want to belabor the difficulties with the definition of a syllable, the above discussion illustrates that there is not agreement on any one definition.

Indications that a consonant is syllabic include the fact that it may have its own tone, intonation, or both of these. Furthermore, a syllabic consonant is of similar duration as a syllabic vowel. The consonants that are syllabic are usually the voiced sonorants, but other kinds of consonants, e.g., [s] in Japanese, may also function as the nucleus of a syllable. American English words below contain syllabic voiced sonorants.

The word [θɹ̩d] 'third' in table 22.1 has the consonant [ɹ̩] in it. Alternately, this syllabic consonant could be written as the (syllabic) rhotacized vowel [ɚ]. With this vowel symbol there is no need for the syllabic stroke under it because [ɚ] is already syllabic. The schwa symbol alone represents a (mid central) syllabic vowel, and the right hook diacritic added to it indicates that the vowel is rhotacized, i.e., it has an 'r' quality. There are a number of English words in which [ɹ̩] / [ɚ] is syllabic; for example, [fɹ̩] 'fir', and [tʰɚn] 'turn'. Examples of syllabic nasals include [mɑᵘntʰn̩] 'mountain', and [bətn̩] 'button'. Fricatives and laterals may also be syllabic.

Table 22.1. English syllabic consonants

hədl̩	'huddle'
pʰɪdl̩	'piddle'
ˈlɪdl̩/ lɪtl̩	'little'
ˈməʔn̩	'mutton'
ˈθɹ̩d/ˈθɚd	'third'
ˈspænɹ̩/ˈspænɚ	'spanner'
sədn̩	'sudden'

Apical vowels and syllabic fricatives

Apical vowels, also termed *fricative vowels,* are sometimes termed *syllabic fricatives.* An apical vowel is produced with the airstream sufficiently constricted by the tongue blade so close to the roof of the mouth that audible friction results. Though there are no officially recognized IPA symbols in use for these vowels, some linguists write them as [iz] and [yz] or one of the symbols below. They occur in Sino-Tibetan languages (Ladefoged and Maddieson 1996), Salish languages on the Pacific Northwest coast of North America (Hoard 1978), Sudanic languages (Kutsch Lojenga 1989, 1994), Afro-Asiatic languages (Coleman 1996), and some Bantu languages (Blench 1993). In some languages these may occur, or there may be syllabic fricatives that lengthen and occupy a vowel position following the loss of a vowel. Those found in languages include the following:

[ɿ] apical dental (or alveolar) unrounded vowel = [z̩] voiced alveolar syllabic sibilant, also referred to as [ɹ̩] be apico-laminal or laminal denti-alveolar syllabic approximant when following [s, ts, tsʰ] or [z̩] voiced dental syllabic fricative;

[ʮ] apical dental (or alveolar) rounded vowel = [z̩ʷ] voiced alveolar labialized syllabic sibilant;

[ʅ] apical retroflex (or postalveolar) unrounded vowel = [ʐ̩] voiced retroflex syllabic sibilant, also referred to as [ɻ̩] voiced retroflex syllabic approximant when following [ʃ, tʃ, or tʃʰt] or [ɻ̩] voiced retroflex syllabic approximant.

[ʯ] apical retroflex (or postalveolar) rounded vowel =[ʐ̩ʷ] voiced retroflex labialized syllabic fricative.

summary chart

	unrounded	rounded
alveolar	ɿ = z̩	ʮ = z̩ʷ
retroflex	ʅ = ʐ̩	ʯ = ʐ̩ʷ

The following examples are from Lendu (Kutsch Lojenga 1989:120–121).

ìsẓ̄	'woman'	rř̩	'folly'
rītsẓ̀	'something'	lirr̩	'dove'
dzẓ̄	'black'	dzẓ̀dzẓ́	'type of banana'
rr̩̀	'earthquake'	tsẓ́	'cow'

Similarly in Ngiti (Democratic Republic of the Congo; data from Kutsch Lojenga 1989:12; 1994:90, 436, 495), a language related to Lendu, examples of syllabic consonants are given in the following list. These represent the surface forms, the way they are pronounced. Kutsch Lojenga posits that in their underlying forms there was a vowel, but when the vowel deleted, tone on the syllabic consonant remained.

| ˈndrr̩̀ | 'goat' | sẓ̀tà | 'sweet potato' |
| adzẓ | 'earth' | | |

Prenasalized stops

In some languages there is a series of PRENASALIZED STOPS, contrasting with other stops by having a short nasal onset. This nasal onset is articulated the same as a nasal consonant, but it is shorter than either a syllabic nasal (described above) or a nasal consonant, and it does not carry contrastive tone. The place of articulation of the nasal in a prenasalized stop is the same as that of the following stop. The nasal is almost always voiced, but the stop may be either voiced or voiceless.

The symbol for a prenasalized stop is a superscripted nasal preceding the stop symbol, e.g., [ᵐb, ⁿd, ᵑg]. This method of representing prenasalization is widely used; however, IPA does not specify how to symbolize prenasalization.

A prenasalized stop in a transcription, e.g., [ɑːᵐbe], implies a syllable boundary just before the prenasalized stop, in this case immediately after the [ɑː]. This reflects a phonological decision. However, the person writing a phonetic transcription may not wish to imply that a certain nasal-stop sequence is necessarily a prenasalized stop. If the same sequence of sounds were transcribed as a nasal followed by a stop, [ɑːmbe], the transcription would be ambiguous as to location of the syllable boundary. The location of a syllable break as above can be made explicit by adding a period to indicate the perceived syllable break, as in [ɑː.ᵐbe]. Many languages in Africa have prenasalized stops, and they also occur elsewhere in the world.

It is important to distinguish phonetically between prenasalization of stops and a nasal-plus-stop combination. With the nasal plus a stop, the nasal may carry its own tone and may have the same length as most other consonants in the language. The following Jju examples are illustrative:

| m̩bâː | 'welcome' (female greeting) | n̩tʲʰèŋ | 'waterfall' |
| n̩tʷʰákʰ | 'salt' | ŋ̩kʲʰàŋ | 'things' |

Other prenasalized consonants

While the previous section focused on prenasalization of stops, prenasalization can also occur on other consonants, such as fricatives. (See the Ngiti data from Kutsch Lojenga in exercise 3 below.) Prenasalization may also occur on affricates. Ladefoged and Maddieson (1996:130) report prenasalization with [ⁿdr] and [ᵐbβ] consonant clusters in Kele, spoken in Papua New Guinea.

Preplosion of nasals

During the PREPLOSION OF A NASAL the place of articulation of the stop is the same as that of the following nasal. Ladefoged and Maddieson (1996:128) speak of prestopped nasals. The stop is almost always voiced, but the nasal may be either voiced or voiced-fading-to-voicelessness.

In the representation for preplosion of a stop, the stop symbol is written as a superscript preceding the nasal symbol. Although this symbolization for preplosion may be used, IPA does not specify how to symbolize preplosion of nasals. In exercise 4, the raised superscript represents preplosion before the nasal. In Bonggi, an Austronesian language spoken in Malaysia, [nõɪᵈn] means 'to swallow' (data from M. Boutin, Academic Forum, January 24, 2005, Dallas). Preplosion of nasals has been found in other Austronesian languages as well as elsewhere.

Key terms

syllable
syllabic consonant
apical vowels, syllabic fricatives

prenasalized stop
preplosion of nasals

Exercises

1. Practice the following Jju words (Nigeria; McKinney data):

n̩dà	'to sleep'	ɲ̩yàkʰ	'cow'
m̩bà	'them'	ɲ̩yákʰ	'cows'
ŋ̩gá	'take it'	ɲ̩tʲʰén	'examples'
ŋ̩wán	'you'	m̩wí	'open area at top of house'

2. Practice the following Ibibio words (Nigeria; Urua 1995:330, 333–334):

m̩bɔk	'please'	ŋkó	'personal name' (fem.)
m̩bɔ́k	'wrestling' n.	òkôn	'personal name' (masc.)
n̩sámà	'a type of beans'	ŋkêt	'lead' (a metal)
ŋkánìká	'clock'		

3. Practice the following Ngiti prenasalized fricative consonants (Democratic Republic of the Congo; data from Kutsch Lojenga 1994:50–51, 61, 98):

àᵐvǔvà	'chimpanzee'	pfɔ̀ᵐvɔ́	'water spirit'

4. Practice the following Bongii preplosion of nasals (Malaysia; data from M. Boutin, Academic Forum presentation, Dallas, January 24, 2005):

ˈdaɪᵈn	'path, way, trail'	ˈlatəᵈn	'will you wait?'

5. Give three indicators that suggest that a consonant is syllabic:

   _____

   _____

   _____

6. Name the following sounds:

   [ᵐb] _____

   [ⁿg] _____

   [n̩] _____

   [ɹ̩] _____

   [ɚ] _____

23

Phonation and Supralaryngeal Activity

PHONATION is any vocal activity in the larynx. Languages use different types of phonation to differentiate words that are otherwise articulated in the same or a similar way but have entirely different meanings or different pitch patterns. Previous chapters introduced only the binary distinction between VOICED (or MODAL) PHONATION and VOICELESS PHONATION. This chapter distinguishes other phonation types, focusing on four types of voiced phonation and three types of voiceless phonation. It also presents aspects of the laryngeal anatomy and physiology that are particularly relevant to speech. We briefly describe each type of phonation, voiced and voiceless, along with the settings of the larynx that produce these types. Finally, we describe and give examples of some ways in which different kinds of non-modal phonation combine with vowel and consonant articulations to produce speech data rich in complexity, considerably beyond what has already been presented. This is an area of current research—using fiber-optic laryngoscope instruments—to examine what is happening at the vocal folds and in the supralaryngeal vocal tract. What is presented here will likely need updating based on on-going research in this area.

The larynx: Heart of phonation

The *larynx* hangs in the neck like the basket of a tethered hot air balloon. Suspended between the *pharynx* above and the *trachea* below, it stands guard with two lines of defense against any intrusion, lest anything but air enters the trachea and finds its way into the lungs. Should anything slip past the epiglottis and touch the true vocal folds or their backup just above, the FALSE VOCAL FOLDS or VENTRICULAR FOLDS, both pairs of folds immediately slam together to secure the lungs and the passageways leading to them. Meanwhile, much of the body responds to the alarm, and the intruder is forthwith ejected unceremoniously from the premises by violent coughing.

The larynx consists primarily of cartilages, soft tissue, and muscles with just one bone, the HYOID BONE at the top of the larynx. Its shape resembles a stirrup, and it is fastened to the THYROID CARTILAGE at the back. The thyroid cartilage is located between the hyoid bone and the cricoid cartilage and is shaped somewhat like a shield or pair of wings to protect the vocal folds and the delicate mechanism that controls them with precision. The upper front corner of the thyroid cartilage that protrudes outward is the "Adam's apple." See figure 23.1.

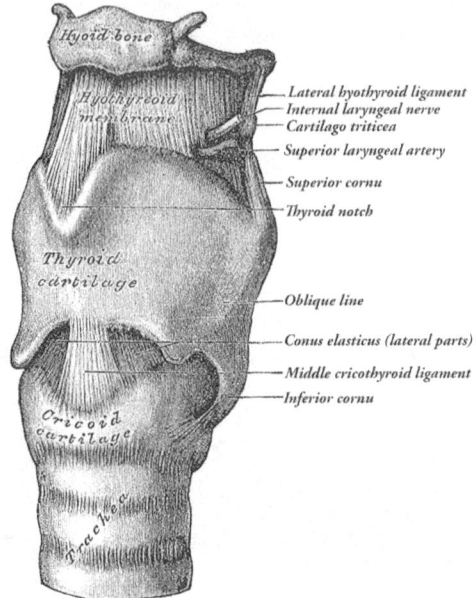

Figure 23.1. Antero-lateral view of the larynx.
http://fr.wikipedia.org/wiki/Fichier:Gray951.png
Accessed 20 October 2009.

The TRACHEA is a stack of ring-shaped cartilages, open toward the back and joined by soft tissue. The top of the trachea attaches to the larynx, the bottom of which is the CRICOID CARTILAGE, shaped like a signet ring, with the narrow part toward the front and the large part to the back. It is located at the top of the trachea, commonly called the *windpipe*. See figures 23.2 and 23.3.

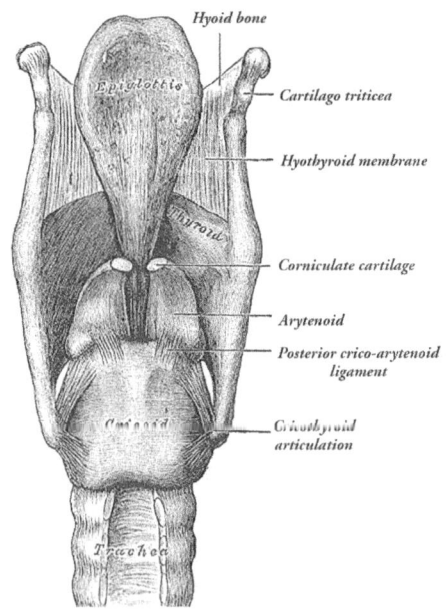

Figure 23.2. Posterior view of the larynx.
http://fr.wikipedia.org/wiki/Fichier:Gray952.png
Accessed 20 October 2009.

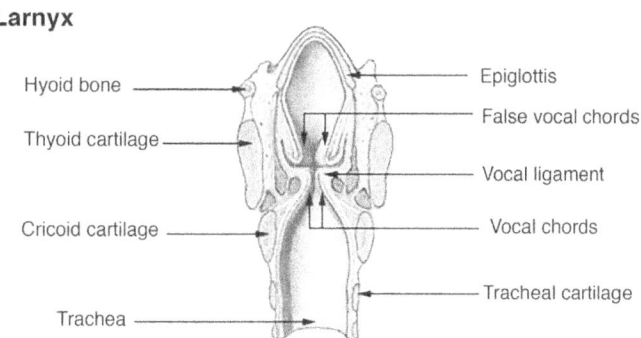

Figure 23.3. The larynx.
http://en.wikipedia.org/wiki/File:Illu_larynx.jpg
Accessed 20 October 2009.

The *vocal folds,* often called *vocal cords,* are located in the larynx; the GLOTTIS is the space between them. The sounds that come out of the mouth depend very much on what goes on in the larynx.

The front ends of the vocal folds are attached together to the front inside of the thyroid cartilage. See figure 23.4. The back or anterior ends of the vocal folds are attached to a pair of arytenoid cartilages that move in two important ways, under the control of various muscles. They rotate in opposite directions, and they slide inwardly toward the centerline and outwardly away from the centerline. As they move, they slide sideways and also swivel around a vertical axis. Thus, when the arytenoid cartilages slide outward away from the centerline, this opens the glottis; and when they slide inwardly toward the centerline, this closes the glottis. Rotation of the arytenoid cartilages adds to the effect of their sliding. Their adjustment for voicing is somewhere between that for an open glottis and for glottal stop.

> **Where is your larynx**
>
> To locate your larynx, place your thumb on your neck just under your chin, and place your forefinger in the same place on the opposite side of your neck. Press your thumb and finger gently inward and try to feel the hyoid bone and thyroid cartilage and the space between the two. Then, with your forefinger still pressing gently against your neck, use it to trace forward along the top of the thyroid cartilage and toward the center until you find the notch at the midline of the neck. Now sing a high note and feel (or see in a mirror) the larynx go up.
>
> If you have already learned to make ejective and implosive speech sounds (to be discussed in chapter 24), try making some of them while your fingers are placed as described above.

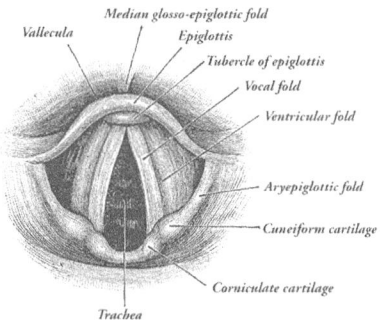

Figure 23.4. The vocal folds.
http://en.wikipedia.org/wiki/Vocal_folds
Accessed 20 October 2009.

The CRICOTHYROID MUSCLE runs along the outer front surfaces of the thyroid cartilage and the cricoid cartilage. It is fastened to the cricoid cartilage at one end and to the thyroid cartilage at the other (hence its name).

Tension on the vocal folds is a primary control on their rate of vibration. (Another control is TRANSGLOTTAL PRESSURE, i.e., the difference in pressure between just below the glottis and just above it.) Flexing the cricothyroid muscle pulls the front of the thyroid cartilage closer to the front of the cricoid cartilage. This lengthens the distance between the two ends of the vocal folds, putting them under more tension. Meanwhile, if voicing is continuous, the increased tension increases the rate of vibration, and thus it raises the *pitch* of the sound.

Just above the vocal folds are the VENTRICULAR FOLDS; these are also referred to as the FALSE VOCAL FOLDS. Above and surrounding the ventricular folds are the ARYEPIGLOTTIC FOLDS, and the spoon-shaped cartilage, termed the EPIGLOTTIS, that sticks up behind the tongue root. It stands ready to move down and block passage of anything except air that might intrude into the lungs and cause choking or pneumonia. Recent research has found that the ventricular folds, the aryepiglottic folds, and the epiglottis are far more active in speech production than has traditionally been thought. For example, there are EPIGLOTTAL stops in some dialects of Arabic in which the epiglottis moves down and closes off the larynx. In some Sudanese languages and in Somali there is an aryepiglottic folds trill. And in the production of an English glottal stop, the vocal folds, the ventricular folds, and the aryepiglottic folds are all involved. This does not happen in the production of glottal stops in all languages; for example, it does not occur in Pame, in Mexico. Most often the supralaryngeal area is involved in contrastive voice qualities, a topic covered here under phonation and supralaryngeal phonetic features.

Phonation types

Voiced phonations include modal voice, CREAKY voice, BREATHY voice, FALSETTO voice, and HARSH voice (also called TENSE voice). Voiceless phonations include NIL PHONATION, BREATH PHONATION, and WHISPER. Some combinations of two, three, or even four types of phonation can be produced simultaneously. However, combinations of three or more types apparently have not been reported to function linguistically. In the Yi languages of China harsh voice and breathy voice contrast with each other as well as with modal voice.

Modal phonation

A speech sound is *voiced* if vibration at the glottis breaks up the flow of air coming up from the lungs into repetitive pulses or puffs superimposed on a steady airflow. Otherwise the sound is voiceless, that is the vocal folds are apart and not vibrating. The repetitive nature of the glottal pulses in voiced speech gives sounds a readily perceptible musical pitch. Voiced sounds are also termed MODAL PHONATION (or MODAL VOICE) in which the air flowing through the glottis causes the vocal folds to vibrate without audible turbulence. In normal speech, modal phonation produces the vowels and semivowels and a majority of the consonants. For example, in the English word [ˈhɑbi] 'hobby' the vowels and the medial consonant are normally produced with modal phonation.

In modal voice the vocal folds vibrate along most or all of their length. The laryngeal muscles separately control the initial separation of the vocal folds, their length, and the tension on the vocal folds. Figure 23.5 shows the difference between the vocal folds in breathing and speaking.

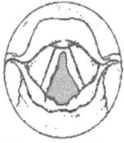 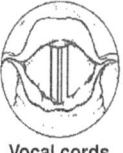

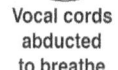

Vocal cords abducted to breathe   Vocal cords adducted to speak

Figure 23.5. The vocal folds in breathing and speaking.
http://en.wikipedia.org/wiki/vocal_folds
Accessed 20 October 2009.

When the vocal folds are in position to produce modal voice, but before air pressure has built up from below, they are in contact with each other. Then, they separate briefly and a pulse of air comes through the glottis. As the air flows briefly through the glottis, the air pressure between the vocal folds drops, producing the Bernoulli effect, and they again make contact with each other. This process repeats over and over, producing a series of GLOTTAL PULSES. In modal phonation the vocal folds are close together and vibrating. Modal voice sounds normal to most people.

A wedge [ˬ] placed under the symbol for an otherwise voiceless sound indicates that the sound is voiced, presumably with modal phonation unless specified otherwise. For example, [s̬] can be used to represent [z] in a language having no phonological contrast between [s] and [z] and where the sound unit /s/ is phonetically voiced in some environment, e.g., intervocalically.

Creaky phonation

In *creaky voice* the vocal folds are held tightly together at the back but vibrate at the front with the supralaryngeal area constricted. In addition, the sound may also have vibration of the false vocal folds (also termed the *ventricular folds*), action of the epiglottis, or the aryepiglottic folds rather than the true vocal folds. Creaky voice is also called LARYNGEALIZATION, VOCAL FRY, and TENSE VOICE. The arytenoid cartilages are held tightly together with a small opening on the front side of the vocal folds. Ladefoged and Maddieson (1996:55) state that the term STIFF VOICE can be used to describe a slight degree of laryngealization.

The glottal pulses in creaky voice frequently are somewhat random in volume and timing, so that they are also called GLOTTAL FRY. In another type of creaky voice, a glottal pulse of one size and shape and with one time interval alternates with glottal pulses of a different size and shape and time interval. When this is the case there is an alternation of long and short intervals between glottal pulses. Thus the pulses can be considered to come in pairs, with a strong one followed by a weak one.

Creaky voice can function to contrast individual segments (primarily vowels and other sonorants), as well as to characterize an overall speech style. In IPA a segmental symbol with a tilde diacritic underneath it represents a sound made with creaky voice, e.g., [ḁ], [m̰]. Hausa, a language widely spoken in West Africa, has a contrastive series of voiced versus creaky voiced stops [b d ʄ] versus [ɓ ɗ ʄ̰].

When people first wake up in the morning or are tired and in need of more sleep, their voice quality is often creaky or laryngealized. The voicing of some individuals is predominantly creaky, especially if their voices are low pitched.

Breathy phonation

Breathy voice sounds somewhat like the speech of someone who has just been running and is talking while still out of breath. The rush of air flowing through the glottis causes noisy air turbulence, giving speech sounds that are ordinarily modal a breathy quality. Also, because the glottal pulses in breathy voice are less sharp than in modal voice, breathy sounds are not as loud as modal sounds, and they are less distinct. They have a muffled quality due to an increased *spectral tilt*. Breathy voice is also called

MURMUR. In breathy phonation the glottis is apart but the vocal folds are vibrating producing a [h] type quality. The vocal folds vibrate in front, and are closed or nearly closed in back.

Many languages of the Indian subcontinent have a series of breathy stops and breathy affricates that contrast with voiced stops and voiced affricates at the same places of articulation. Because the rate of airflow is greater for sounds produced with breathy voice than for those produced with modal voice, the pulses of air coming through the glottis in breathy phonation are not as sharp, giving breathy sounds a softer quality. Breathy sounds sometimes have audible noise due to air turbulence.

The breathy phonation of a stop or affricate necessarily extends part of the way into the following vowel; a stop or affricate alone would ordinarily not be loud enough for a listener to hear the difference between a voiced one and a breathy one. Breathy stops and affricates have sometimes been called *voiced aspirated* because the breathy vowel release is similar to the voiceless vowel following a voiceless aspirated stop or affricate.

An umlaut [̤] diacritic placed under the basic symbol for a voiced sound indicates that the sound is breathy rather than modal, e.g., [g̤] and [d̤]. It is unlikely that a contrast will be found between a breathy affricate with a breathy stop and a breathy affricate with a voiced stop. Therefore the convention followed here in transcribing breathy affricates is that only the stop symbol has the umlaut diacritic under it. The symbol [ɦ] may be used for a breathy vowel if its quality is predictable from that of an adjacent voiced vowel, e.g., as in English words 'ahead' [əˈɦɛd] and 'hand' [ɦænd]. Here the breathy vowel serves as a non-syllabic breathy glottal fricative.[1]

Table 23.1 contrasts some of the most commonly found breathy stops and affricates with voiceless aspirated, voiceless and voiced stops and affricates at the same places of articulation. The names of the sounds can be found by reading the labels clockwise around the table. For example, [b̤] is a *breathy bilabial stop* and [d̤ʒ] is a *breathy retroflex affricate*.

Table 23.1. Breathy stops and affricates

	Bilabial	Dental	Alveolar	Retroflex	Post-alveolar	Velar		
Voiceless	pʰ	t̪ʰ	tʰ	ʈʰ		kʰ	aspirated	
Voiceless	p	t̪	t	ʈ		k		stop
Voiced	b	d̪	d	ɖ		g		
Breathy	b̤	d̪̤	d̤	ɖ̤		g̤		
Voiceless				t͡ʂʰ	t͡ʃʰ		aspirated	
Voiceless				t͡ʂ	t͡ʃ			affricate
Voiced				d͡ʐ	d͡ʒ			
Breathy				d͡ʐ̤	d͡ʒ̤			
Passive articulator	upper lip	upper teeth	alveolar ridge	behind part of alveolar ridge	behind alveolar ridge	front of velum		
Active articulator	lower lip	tongue tip	tongue tip	underside of tongue tip	tongue blade	tongue back		

---

[1] A literal interpretation of the IPA consonant chart would imply that [ɦ] is voiced rather than breathy.

The first position in the name for any speech sound specifies the type of phonation. For example, a vowel articulated with the tongue, lip, and jaw position for [ɑ] can have the following names, depending on the type of phonation:

[ɑ̥] — *voiceless* open back unrounded vowel (wepa)
[ɑ̤] — *breathy* open back unrounded vowel (wepa)
[ɑ] — (voiced) open back unrounded vowel (wepa)
[ɑ̰] — *creaky* open back unrounded vowel (wepa)

Falsetto phonation

Falsetto voice is a type of phonation probably not used in everyday speech, but it certainly is used on special social situations. Falsetto is very high pitched due to high tension and stretching of the vocal folds, which are often very slightly open giving it a breathy quality. In languages where it occurs, it is used as a speech style, thereby functioning similar to intonation. As such it does not make a lexical difference between words. For example, Fulani women often use falsetto voice, and we have heard falsetto voice used in singing in Hyam (also known as Jaba, a Nigerian Middle Belt language).

Harsh voice

Harsh voice is a type of phonation in which there is hypertension in the larynx resulting in approximation and irregular vibrations of the vocal folds and sometimes vibration of the ventricular folds and aryepiglottal folds. The type of sound produced is deep and hoarse sounding. Harsh voice sounds somewhat like the speech of someone with a bad case of laryngitis trying to shout. There is considerable muscular tension and audible turbulence. Harsh voice occurs in many of the languages in Southeast Asia.

Discussion on types of voiced phonation

Harsh voice may be combined with creaky voice or falsetto. According to some phoneticians, some muscles of the larynx may be especially tense when producing harsh voice, creaky voice, or falsetto. It seems to us, however, that none of these types of phonation necessarily requires strenuous effort.

Another difference between modal, creaky, and breathy voice is in the average rate of airflow. In producing breathy voice the vocal folds are close enough to each other that the air passing between them causes them to vibrate, as for modal voice. However, the glottis is open wider and during more of the vibratory cycle for breathy voice than for modal voice. Sometimes the vibrating vocal folds do not even touch. Because the average glottal opening is larger for breathy voice than for the other voiced phonation types, more air passes through the glottis. This gives breathy voice a gushy sound. Similarly, because the average glottal opening is smaller for creaky voice than for modal voice, the airflow rate is less for creaky voice.

One difference between these three types of phonation is that in contrast with modal voice, the glottal pulses in breathy voice do not have as narrow pulses as in modal voice, whereas the glottal pulses in creaky voice are sharper than in modal voice. This difference can be seen on a sound spectrogram (see chapter 33 on acoustic phonetics). A second difference is the average rate of airflow. The resultant three-way contrast in the shape of the acoustic speech wave has the outcome in a three-way difference in voice quality due to differences in the spectra of the speech wave, and the degree of spectral tilt. The glottal pulses of modal voice are fairly uniform in shape, volume, and timing.

Both consonants and vowels can be pronounced with modal, breathy, creaky, or harsh voice. Breathy vowels are contrastive in Dinka, Maasai, Nuer, and other Nilotic languages spoken in east Africa. A series of breathy consonants (stops and affricates) contrasts with voiced consonants in many languages of India.

Voiceless phonation types

In this section we discuss three types of voiceless phonation: *nil phonation, breath phonation,* and *whisper phonation.*

Nil phonation

A speech sound is produced with *nil phonation* if there is no audible sound coming from the larynx. This can occur in any of three ways. (1) The glottis may be tightly closed, producing a glottal stop [ʔ]. (2) The glottis may be open wide enough that air flowing through it produces neither vibration of the vocal folds nor audible turbulence in the larynx. This second condition may occur with voiceless vowels and voiceless fricatives. In these cases, there may be some sound, but it is not due to any constriction at the glottis. (3) The airstream is completely blocked in both the oral and nasal tracts, resulting in voiceless stops (e.g., [p, t, c, k]).

Breath phonation

In *breath phonation* the vocal folds are close enough to each other to cause audible turbulence as air flows between them, but not so close that they vibrate. There is very minimal sound due to slight involvement of the vocal folds in the airflow. Laver (1994:189) describes it as "a very gentle rustling sound." This condition may occur with the voiceless glottal fricative [h] or other voiceless sounds (except stops). The sound [h] at the beginning of 'had' [hæd] (said in isolation) is usually produced with breath phonation. Many times the difference between nil phonation and breath phonation will be indeterminable, as the sound of turbulence elsewhere in the mouth masks the sound of any turbulence at the glottis.

Whisper phonation

In *whisper phonation* the vocal folds are pressed tightly against each other, closing the main part of the glottis, but the arytenoid cartilages are rotated beyond the position necessary for complete glottal closure, leaving a small glottal opening between them. The vocal folds remain open at their posterior end. By tensing certain muscles as in forceful exhalation, air is forced through this small glottal opening with considerable noisy turbulence. Laver (1994:191) suggests that a subscript dot diacritic under the whispered vowel or consonant may be used to mark whisper phonation.

Discussion of voiceless phonation

Voiceless vowels in a language such as Cheyenne may be produced with either nil phonation or breath phonation, but probably not whisper. In most languages people whisper only in special contexts, such as when trying to converse with just one person while a meeting is in progress and they do not want to disturb those around them.

Voicelessness of one or another of these three phonation types (nil phonation, breath phonation, or whisper) is implicit in the symbols of many consonants in the IPA, e.g., [f], [s], [x], [p], [t], [k]. The UNDERRING diacritic [̥] beneath a symbol that is otherwise voiced, denotes voicelessness, e.g., [m̥], [ɡ̥], [ɣ̥]. Some linguists distinguish between such pairs as [b̥] and [p], though phonetically these are the same sounds. In such cases, they are probably discussing a phonological contrast that they then specify through a phonological rule where context results in a regularly voiced segment becoming voiceless.

Throat singing, overtone singing, harmonic singing, harmonic chanting

Throat singing is produced with regular vibrations by the vocal folds in which the vocal folds stay open for shorter lengths of time and closed longer, thus giving greater amplitude to the harmonics.[2] They often add the vibrations of the ventricular folds, and/or the aryepiglottic folds. The root of the epiglottis and the arytenoid cartilages are also involved in phonation by throat singers. The use of these structures allows throat singers to produce one, two, three, or even four tones simultaneously, as well as additional overtones. High-pitched throat singing sounds like whistling, which occurs in the larynx with modifications by the tongue in the vocal cavity. In making the whistling sound singers focus on strengthening a single harmonic through placement of the tongue. When singing the lower harmonics, a throat singer places the base of his tongue near the rear of his throat. As throat singers age, they often end up with hoarse voices.

Throat singing has been found among the Tuvan people in Siberia, central Asia, who are nomadic herders. Today both men and women do throat singing, though traditionally it was only men who did it. Women use throat singing to lull their infants to sleep, whereas men often do throat singing while out herding their reindeer, camels, horses, or yak, depending on where in central Asia they live. They also use throat singing when young people gather and in other ceremonial occasions. The content of their songs centers around nature, horses or reindeer, and beautiful women.

In addition to Tuva, throat singing occurs widely. It occurs as far east as the Chukchi Penninsula and as far west as Hungary, the Balkans, Khazakhstan, and Uzbekistan. Tibetan Buddhist monks use a form of throat singing in their chants, and it used to be practiced by the Ainu in Hokkaido, Japan, though it has recently died out there. Xhosa women in South Africa also do throat singing.

Airflow gradient in phonation

Phonation types introduced above can be arranged in order of increasing airflow due to decreasing glottal constriction, as follows:

- falsetto
- harsh voice (stiff voice) with tension on the vocal folds with the ventricular and aryepiglottal folds also vibrating; this is often associated with high pitch
- creaky voice
- modal voice with the vocal folds vibrating along their entire width and with no friction at the glottis
- breathy voice
- whisper
- breath phonation
- nil phonation with the glottis wide open, either for voiceless stops or other voiceless sounds with no breathiness.

---

[2] For futher information on throat singing, see Levin and Edgerton, 1999, "The Throat Singers of Tuva," *Scientific American* 281(3):80–87.

Summary of types of phonation

Table 23.2. Types of phonation in terms of airflow

Glottal airflow	Phonation	Comments	Examples	Phonation types
Least	nil phonation (no airflow)	[ʔ] or voiceless stops	ʔ, p, t, c, k, q	voiceless
⇓	creaky		ḭ, ɑ̰, n̰	voiced
⇓	modal		i, ɑ, d, n	voiced
⇓	breathy		i̤, ɑ̤, d̤, g̈	voiced
⇓	breath phonation	[h] or other voiceless sounds	h, i̥, ɑ̥, n̥, s, ʃ, x, χ	voiceless
Greatest	nil phonation (no turbulence at vocal folds)	voiceless vowels or fricatives	i̥, ɑ̥, ɸ, f, θ, x	voiceless

In Bai, spoken in Hunan province, China, there are four contrastive voice qualities. The first is modal voice; in the second the ventricular folds are sphinctered together. The third involves the aryepiglottic folds that trill, and the fourth is an epiglottal fricative. In Dinka (Sudan and Somalia in east Africa) the difference between various vowels is best described as a difference in the shape of the SUPRALARYNGEAL CAVITY rather than articulation of the vowel. While the tongue root is involved in [+ATR] (advanced tongue root) and [–ATR] (retracted tongue root) vowels, its role is secondary to what is going on in the supralaryngeal cavity that affects the vowel quality. The tone is independent of the supralaryngeal phenomena. In Bor Dinka, the following words contrast (data from J. Edmondson, lecture, September 8, 2003):

Breathy voice
tɔf⁴² 'go ahead'

Modal voice
tɑf⁴² 'diarrhea'

Tense voice
tdɛt⁴² 'scorpion'

Hollow voice[3]
tʲef⁴² 'swallow'

Compound phonation types

According to Laver (1994:198), several phonation types may co-occur. He specifically mentions whispery falsetto and whispery creaky voice as examples of two co-occurring types. A triple co-occurring phonation type is whispery creaky falsetto voice.

Pronunciation helps

Creaky voice: Imitate the voice of someone waking from sleep. Try to imitate the sound of a slowly opening door with creaky hinges. In order to learn to control creaky voice, use a word with two nearly identical syllables. On the first syllable use creaky voice while on the second use modal voice, e.g., [ˈd̰ɑ̰dɑ]. Now use several other two-syllable words. Pronounce each word with creakiness on one syllable and modal voice on the other.

Creaky speech sounds are easiest to produce at low pitch. However, they also occur at high pitches in many languages, e.g., Mazatec and Zapotec. Repeat exercises above at a higher pitch.

Breathy voice: Inhale deeply, and then exhale with a sigh, making sure that you hear your vocal folds vibrating as well as the rush of air. Then try the technique outlined in the paragraph for creaky voice; say a word with two syllables that differ only in that the first syllable is breathy and the second is voiced.

---
[3] See chapter 28 for discussion of vowels described as having hollow voice.

23: Phonation and Supralaryngeal Activity

Say 'ahead' [əˈfiɛd] and 'behind' [bəˈfiɛi̯nd], drawing out the 'h' sound and making sure that you hear or feel the vocal folds continue to vibrate throughout.

Harsh voice: In order to produce sounds with harsh voice, tense your vocal folds and the musculature in your larynx, including the ventricular folds and aryepiglottal folds. Then say [haɚʃ vois].

Key terms

phonation, phonation type
voiced, voiceless phonation
ventricular folds, false vocal folds
hyoid bone
thyroid cartilage
cricoid cartilage
trachea
glottis
arytenoid cartilages
cricothyroid muscle
transglottal pressure

aryepiglottic folds
epiglottis
nil phonation, breath phonation, whisper phonation
supralaryngeal cavity
breathy voice, murmur
creaky voice, laryngealization, vocal fry, glottal fry
harsh voice, tense voice, stiff voice
modal phonation, modal voice
glottal pulse
diacritics: underring, tilde, umlaut, wedge

Exercises

1. Try each of the techniques described in Pronunciation Helps for learning to pronounce breathy and creaky speech sounds.

2. Practice the following Shilluk words (Sudan; Tucker and Bryan 1966:403):

    | kʷɔ̄mī̠ | 'chairs' | tsā:kɔ̠ | 'to begin' |
    | kʷɔ̄mī | 'your chair' | kótsàkū̠- | 'don't begin!' |
    | tsɑ̀:gē̠ | 'his milk' | nē:nɔ̠ | 'to see' |
    | tsɑ̀:gē: | 'our milk' | nè:ná | 'my sight' |

3. Practice the following Lango and Shilluk words (Sudan; Tucker and Bryan 1966:404–409):

    | kɔ́m | 'chair' | pé̠:ɑ̀pòá | 'it is not a feeble-minded man' |
    | kó̠mê̠ | 'chairs' | jálíɲá̠ gùòk | 'I hear the dog' |
    | kó̠m:í | 'your chair' | | |

4. Write a phonetic symbol for each sound:

    [ ] breathy open back rounded vowel (wepa)

    [ ] creaky velar approximant (wepa)

    [ ] voiceless open front rounded vowel (wepa)

    [ ] voiced alveolar approximant (wepa)

5. Listen to your own speech and that of others, to observe occurrences of breathy and creaky states of the glottis being used in everyday conversation. Describe one such observation, including a transcription of the word or phrase in which you noticed the breathy or creaky sound.

6. Name four states of the glottis in order, from least glottal airflow to greatest airflow. Write the symbol of a sound made with each state.

    [ ] _____

    [ ] _____

    [ ] _____

    [ ] _____

7. List five types of voiced phonation:
   a. _____
   b. _____
   c. _____
   d. _____
   e. _____

8. List three types of voiceless phonation:
   a. _____
   b. _____
   c. _____

24

Ejectives and Implosives

All of the sounds introduced so far are produced with an egressive pulmonic airstream. Here we introduce a new airstream. EJECTIVES are sounds made with an EGRESSIVE GLOTTALIC AIRSTREAM; that is, they are produced by raising the larynx with the glottis closed. Because ejectives are produced with a glottalic airstream, some phoneticians refer to them as glottalized sounds. IMPLOSIVES are sounds made with an INGRESSIVE GLOTTALIC AIRSTREAM; that is, they are produced by lowering the larynx with the glottis closed except for voicing.

Ejectives

An *ejective* is a sound produced with an egressive glottalic airstream resulting from raising the larynx with a *closed glottis*. To produce an ejective, air is trapped between the closed glottis and the articulatory constriction or closure which occurs at some place of articulation in the mouth. The nasal port must also be closed. Then the larynx, with a closed glottis, is raised, increasing the pressure of the air trapped between the closed glottis and the articulatory constriction. Contracting the muscles of the pharynx and retracting the tongue root also contribute to raising the air pressure in the mouth. If the tongue or lips completely block the passage of air through the mouth, when the articulation is released, the sound of the air bursting forth is that of an EJECTIVE STOP. If the articulatory closure is partial, the audible turbulence of the air rushing out of the constriction produces an EJECTIVE FRICATIVE. If an ejective stop is released into a fricative, the pair of sounds is an EJECTIVE AFFRICATE.

Table 24.1 lists common ejectives. The name of each may be read from its row and column labels, going clockwise around the table. For example, [t'] is an *alveolar ejective stop,* [s'] is an *alveolar ejective fricative,* and [tʃ'] is a *postalveolar ejective affricate.* The apostrophe diacritic ['] symbolizes the egressive glottalic airstream mechanism.

Voiced ejectives are not known to occur in any language, presumably because they are impossible to produce. Table 24.1 presents the ejectives. (There are no voiced ejectives in this table; it is redundant to specify 'voiceless' in the name of an ejective.)

Table 24.1. Ejectives

Bilabial	Labiodental	Dental	Alveolar	Postalveolar	Retroflex	Palatal	Velar	Uvular	Ejective
p'			t'		ʈ'	c'	k'	q'	stop
	f'	θ'	s'	ʃ'		ç'	x'	χ'	fricative
	pf'	tθ'	ts'	tʃ'	tʂ'	cç'	kx'	qχ'	affricate
			ɬ'						lateral fricative
			tɬ'		tl̥'				lateral affricate

In sagittal diagrams of ejectives the closed glottis is indicated by a straight line across the larynx. An upward arrow *through* the glottis line indicates that the initiator of the glottalic airstream is the vocal folds. A sagittal diagram of [ʔ] also has a straight line across the larynx, but the arrow is *below* the glottis line, indicating that the airstream mechanism is pulmonic. Figure 24.1 illustrates differences in [k], [k'], and [ʔ] as examples of these diagramming conventions.

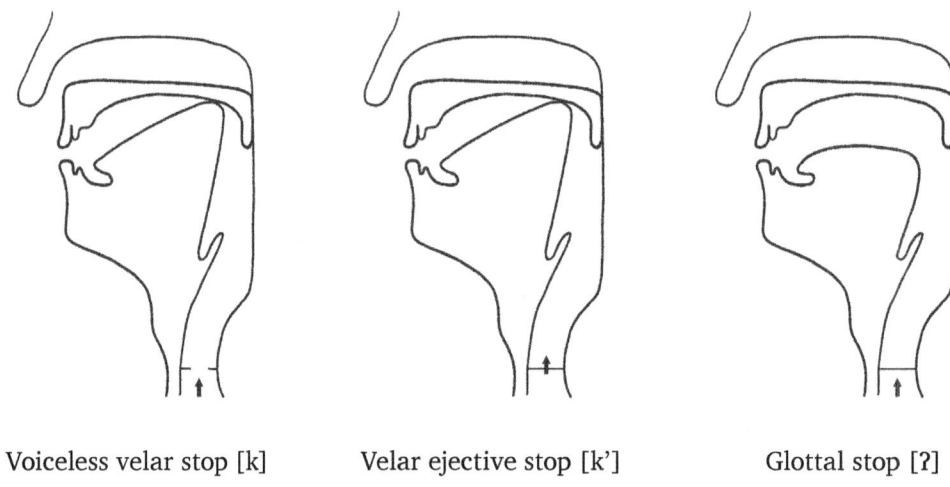

Voiceless velar stop [k]   Velar ejective stop [k']   Glottal stop [ʔ]

Figure 24.1. Sagittal diagrams of [k], [k'], and [ʔ].

Pronouncing and recognizing ejectives

Since producing an ejective involves raising the larynx, it is important to learn conscious control of this maneuver. One way to observe upward and downward movement of your larynx is to watch or feel your Adam's apple move up and down. You can see fairly well with one mirror, but better yet, use two mirrors for a profile view. If you cannot see the movement of your larynx clearly in this way, place the tips of the four fingers of one hand lightly along the midline of the front of your neck, so that you can feel the up or down movement of the larynx. Keep your fingers there, or keep watching in the mirror, as you do the exercises described below.

One way to learn to raise your larynx begins with your singing a low note. Continue to sing as you glide quickly from the low note up to a high note. Watch in the mirror to *see* your larynx move upward, and rest the fingertips of one hand gently on your Adam's apple to *feel* it move upward. Again sing a low note, but this time end the low note with a glottal stop. Just think and silently make the laryngeal adjustment for a rapid change from low to high. As you do so, you should still observe the larynx move upward. Repeat the rapid glide from low to high, but this time add a velar stop [k] closure to the glottal stop before beginning the glide. When you release the [k] at the end of the glide, the result should be either the ejective stop [k'] or the ejective affricate [kx'].

Another way to learn to produce an ejective affricate [kx'] is to first say [kx], then try to say [kx'] while holding your breath, i.e., keeping your glottis tightly closed. The same technique can be of help in learning to pronounce any of the ejectives. For example, hold your breath while trying to say [k], [p], or [t]. This should result in [k'], [p'], or [t'].

A related technique develops the ability to say an ejective in context. Begin by saying [aʔ:a]. Lengthen the glottal stop so that you can articulate another sound while maintaining the glottal closure. For example, if you superimpose [k] on a glottal stop, you get [aʔk'ʔa]. When you can produce this sequence at a normal rate of speaking, then eliminate the glottal stop preceding the ejective by ending the initial vowel with a velar closure. Finally, shorten the glottal stop that follows the release of the stop or fricative until it is only a necessary part of producing the ejective. In transcribing an ejective, this brief but necessary glottal stop is not symbolized.

You can produce many ejectives during a long glottal stop without depleting the air in the lungs, because pulmonic air is not being used. For practice, see how many of the sounds in table 24.1 you can pronounce while you hold just one breath. (If you learn to exercise exceptional control in producing these sounds, you might even be able to produce all the ejectives in the table twice with just one breath!)

There are certain differences between the way an ejective sounds and the way its pulmonic counterpart sounds. These perceptions can help you to recognize which you are hearing, as follows.

- The explosive burst of air when an ejective stop is released has a quality different from that of the burst or aspiration of a pulmonic stop.
- An ejective usually ends with the release of a glottal stop, whereas the corresponding pulmonic stop seldom does.
- Ejective fricatives are short compared with fricatives made with pulmonic air, because raising the larynx displaces only a relatively small volume of air.

Implosives

An *implosive* is a stop sound produced with an *ingressive* glottalic airstream resulting from lowering the larynx with a closed glottis. To produce an implosive, air is trapped between the closed glottis and the articulatory constriction occurring at some place of articulation in the mouth. The nasal port must also be closed. Then the larynx, with a closed glottis, is lowered, decreasing the pressure of the air trapped between the closed glottis and the articulatory constriction, creating a partial vacuum in the vocal tract. As the articulatory constriction is released, the sound produced is that of air bursting inward, resulting in a *voiceless implosive*.

VOICELESS IMPLOSIVES contrast with voiceless *stops* in two ways. The airstream mechanism for voiceless implosives is GLOTTALIC and the airstream direction is *ingressive,* while the mechanism for voiceless stops is *pulmonic,* and the direction is *egressive.* VOICED IMPLOSIVES, however, are similar to *voiced stops* in that both involve voicing produced by an egressive pulmonic airstream. With a *voiced implosive* the vocal folds are not held as tightly together as for a voiceless implosive. Some air leaks upward through the glottis, causing the vocal folds to vibrate. Hence voiced implosives are made with both ingressive glottalic airstream as well as egressive pulmonic airstream.

Table 24.2 presents implosives found in natural languages. To represent the ingressive glottalic airstream mechanism, we add a hook bending to the right to the top of the pulmonic stop symbol with the same place of articulation.[1]

---

[1] A voiceless implosive can also be symbolized using the voiced symbol with a small circle underneath it indicating voicelessness, e.g., [ɓ̥], since the IPA does not specify symbols for these sounds. The symbols presented here for the voiceless implosives, while very common, are not IPA symbols. Rather, the voiced equivalent symbol with a voiceless circle beneath each, is used in IPA.

Table 24.2. Implosives

	Bilabial	Labial-alveolar	Alveolar	Post-alveolar	Palatal	Labial-velar	Velar	Uvular	
Voiceless	ɓ̥		ƭ		ƈ		ƙ	ʠ	implosive
Voiced	ɓ		ɗ		ʄ		ɠ	ʛ	
Voiceless						k͡ɓ̥			
Voiced		d͡ɓ				ɠ͡ɓ			
Voiced				d͡ʒ					

Implosives are common in languages of Africa, Vietnam, Central America, and the Caucasus. Voiced implosives are much more common than voiceless ones. Roglai, spoken in Vietnam (Ken Gregerson, personal communication), is a language which has a voiced implosive affricate [d͡ʒ]; it also occurs in Komo, spoken in the Democratic Republic of the Congo (Bickford and Floyd 2003:151). Because implosive affricates and other sounds, other than stops, are rare, the manner of articulation is not specified in the names: for example, [d͡ʒ] is a *voiced postalveolar implosive.*

The sagittal diagrams in figure 24.2 show voiceless velar implosive [ƙ] and voiced velar implosive [ɠ]. An arrow pointing down through the glottis represents the ingressive glottalic airstream mechanism. For voiceless implosives, the straight line goes straight across the larynx, representing complete closure of the glottis. For voiced implosives, the simultaneous action of two airstream mechanisms is diagrammed by drawing a straight line halfway across the larynx with a downward arrow drawn *through* it representing the ingressive glottalic airstream mechanism. A wavy line with an upward arrow below it is also present, indicating that there is also egressive pulmonic air involved in the production of this sound, as it is voiced.

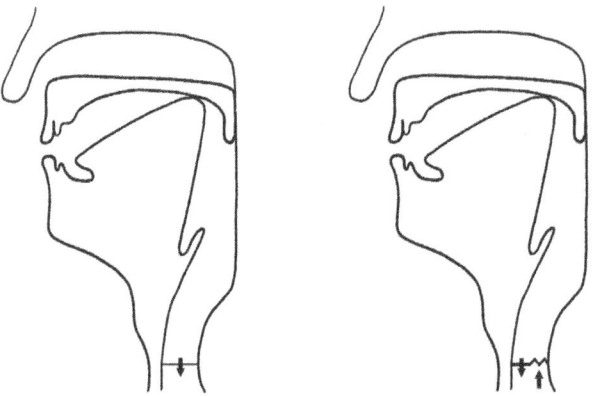

Voiceless velar implosive [ƙ]   Voiced velar implosive [ɠ]

Figure 24.2. Sagittal diagrams of [ƙ] and [ɠ].

Pronouncing and recognizing implosives

Just as watching and feeling movement of the larynx is useful for recognizing ejectives, it can also help you to know whether you are pulling your larynx down as is necessary for pronouncing implosives. Try imitating a frog or a bottle emptying using voiced implosives, [ɠə ɠə ɠə ɠə]. If you can produce a voiced velar implosive in this way, you can probably produce voiced implosives at other places of articulation.

You may find it easier to pull your larynx down to produce a voiceless implosive if you have just pulled it up to produce an ejective. Alternatively produce voiceless velar implosives and ejectives by alternately raising and lowering the larynx in a 'tick-tocking' exercise, [k' ƙ k' ƙ k' ƙ k' ƙ].

In order to put voiceless implosives in context, whisper a sequence such as [ɓAɓA]. The result will be [ɓqɓq]. The next step is to produce a voiced vowel following the voiceless implosive. Try to do it by analogy, saying [ɓaɓa], then immediately [βaβa].

Another useful technique to help you produce implosives is to hold your breath while you are producing a long glottal stop [ʔ]. At the same time use your laryngeal muscles to push and pull the airstream by muscle action, being sure to keep the glottis closed. Try producing several sounds while pushing and pulling the airstream, such as [s, f, ʃ].

With a simple experiment you can verify whether the air pressure behind the place of articulation is higher than atmospheric pressure, as for a pulmonic obstruent or an ejective, or whether the pressure is lower than atmospheric pressure, as for an implosive. Partially fill a cup with a colored drink such as orange soda. Put one end of a clear, flexible drinking straw into the drink and the other end into your mouth behind the place of articulation. This is easiest to do for bilabials, a bit harder for alveolars, and a challenge for velars. If the liquid rises in the straw when the sound is produced, the pressure in the mouth is lower than atmospheric pressure. If the liquid goes downward in the straw, the pressure in the mouth is higher than atmospheric pressure. If you are the one pronouncing the sounds, watching in a mirror may help you see the movement of the liquid more clearly.

Since the larynx is lowered and the tongue root pushed forward for implosives, the pharyngeal cavity is enlarged resulting in a lower pitch and hollow sound for implosives than for ejectives. This pitch difference between implosives and ejectives is a clue for deciding which consonant sound is being produced.

Ken Pike teaches his teacher implosives

"With the Linguistic Society of America meeting in Ann Arbor again that summer, lots of other people were providing stimulus[,] of course. There was the day Ken was walking across the campus with Professors Fries and Trager. George Trager (a leading young theoretician of that time) was teaching the course in phonetics, and he told Fries that he had never learned how to make the "implosive" sounds. Those were the sounds that had taken Ken a year to learn and which he had taught numerous students at the Summer Institute of linguistics school in Arkansas with no trouble at all.

"Ken was sure that Trager would like to learn, and he was completely confident that he could teach him, so, feeling rather brash, he offered. Trager thanked him for the offer and invited him up to his office.

"Part of the reason that Ken was confident that he could teach Trager quickly was because he knew that there were glottalized stops in Taos, the language Trager had been studying. A glottalized stop also used the closed larynx, but it pushed the air outward instead of drawing it in. Ken figured that it would be very easy to show Trager the difference.

"So, the first thing he did as he sat facing the professor was to tell him to make a glottalized stop. Trager responded, but to Ken's horror, he didn't make the kind of sound that Ken called a glottalized stop. It was a sound sort of halfway between a glottalized stop and an implosive—the larynx was closed but it was not moving either up or down. There was no way for Ken to turn back. The only thing he could do was to go ahead and tell this teacher of phonetics that he wasn't making a glottalized stop either.

"Trager listened, willing to receive help, and followed Ken's instructions. In a very short time he was making both glottalized stops and implosives. He thanked Ken and asked him to present ideas to the phonetics class.

"In getting ready for the class presentation, Ken lined up the material more carefully. He talked about the number of places the airstream was closed off as each sound was made—the number of 'mechanisms,' and whether or not the airstream was moving inward or outward—'ingressive' versus 'egressive.' Then he saw that he had a system in which all sounds of the human voice could be classified (except for whistles and trills)." (E. V. Pike, *Ken Pike: Scholar and Christian*, 1981, pp. 108–109)

Key terms

egressive glottalic airstream ejective stop
ingressive glottalic airstream ejective fricative
ejective ejective affricate
implosive voiceless implosive, voiced implosive

Exercises

1. Practice the following sound drills, going first across the rows and then down:

ata	atʰa	at'a	atsa	as'a
apa	apʰa	ap'a	atʃa	atʃ'a
aθa	aθ'a	afa	af'a	apf'a
aka	ak'a	axa	ax'a	aχ'a
aba	aʕa	ada	aɗa	aga
aɠa	aɢa	aɠ'a	aqa	aʛa

2. Practice the following Aguacatec words (Guatemala; data from McArthur as cited in E. V. Pike 1963:99):

kʰaʔ	'grinding stone'	ʔaq'	'vine'
k'aʔ	'bitter'	sak'	'grasshopper'
qʰaˑʔ	'our water'	sakʰ	'gunny sack'
q'aʔ	'bridge'	saqʰ	'white'
ʔak'	'wet'		

3. Practice the following Tabasco Chontal words (Mexico; data from Keller as cited in E. V. Pike 1963:100):

   | tʃʰɛŋ | 'do it!' | p'os | 'sweepings' |
   | tʃ'ɛŋ | 'hole, well' | pʰos | 'it is pale' |

4. Practice the following Tlingit words (Alaska; data from Naish and Story as cited in E. V. Pike 1963:102):

s'ix	'dirt'	tʰax'	'bite'
t'ix'	'ice'	tʰaχ'	'snail'
x'at'	'island'	χ'aɬ'	'skunk cabbage'
tʰiɬ	'dog-salmon'	tɬ'atɬ	'yellow'
kx'utɬ	'boiling tide'	kʰuˈtʃ'et'a	'ball'

5. Practice the following Tojolobal words (Mexico; data from Mendenhall and Jackson as cited in E. V. Pike 1963:99):

   | k'ak' | 'fire' | kʰakʰ | 'my grass' |
   | kʰak' | 'my tongue' | k'akʰ | 'flea' |

6. Practice the following Kiowa words (United States; data from Gibson and Sivertsen as cited in E. V. Pike 1963:99):

t'ɔdl	'liver'	k'op	'mountain'
tʰɔdl	'thin'	kom	'friend'
tɔ̃ː	'sibling'	ˈgomba	'behind'
ˈdɔːtʰɔ	'he is singing'		

24: Ejectives and Implosives

7. Practice the following Nangere words (Chad; data from Brotherton as cited in E. V. Pike 1963:106):

ɗɛgɛ	'covered them'	ɓeⁱ	'pour out'
dɛgɛ	'with them'	ɓɛl	'lead'
di	'with him'	ɓaŋ	'he'
ɗi	'negative'		

8. Practice the following Hausa words (Nigeria; Bargery 1934:xxii):

da	'formerly'	ɗa	'a son'
dauda	'David'	dauɗa	'dirt'
babe	'a locust'	ɓaɓe	'become estranged'
baɾi	'leave off'	ɓaɾi	'trembling'

9. Practice the following Amharic words (Ethiopia; data from Peter Unseth, personal communication):

kokʰ	'peach'	atːɨtʼɨtʼutʰ	'you (pl.) don't drink it!'
kʼokʼ	'partridge'	tʼɜmɜtʼːɜmɜ	'he wrapped'
tʼitʼ	'cotton'	tɜmɜtːɜmɜ	'he tamped the earth level'
tʼutʰ	'breast'	tʃʼɜbɜtʃʼːɜbɜ	'it sprouted'
tʼatʰ	'finger'	tʃɜbɜtʃʼːɜbɜ	'he threshed grain'
mɜtʼːa	'he came'	tʃʼat	'semi-narcotic plant'
mɜtːa	'he hit'	tʃat	'patient, capable'

10. Practice the following Majang words (Ethiopia; data from Peter Unseth, personal communication):

ɗàndàmàŋ	'pray'	ámɗ	'stomach'
ɗàmà	'food'	émɗ	'boat'
dáːmé	'yellow'	ɓáːɓá	'your father'
dúk	'dew'	bàːbéj	'my father'
ɗúk	'forest'	ɓàdàjìɗíŋ	'break' v. trans.
ɗùŋéɗ	'hyena'	ɓóɓókán	'ant' (a specific type)
ɓùɓùɗíŋ	'fall' v.	ɓújbùs	'fish' (a specific type)

11. Practice the following Igbo words (Nigeria; Floyd 1981:113):

āk͡pōk͡pō	'bone'	ìk͡pô:	'fish hook'
āk͡pók͡pó	'to mold'	ák͡pók͡pá	'animal skin'
k͡pák͡pándò	'star'	ōk͡pāɾàː	'grasshopper'
ák͡pòɾòk͡pò	'long'	mk͡pōɾōmk͡pō	'short'
ák͡pók͡pá	'rashes'	ūk͡pútánk͡pō	'crooked'
ɔ̄k͡pâːlà	'peanuts'	ēk͡péɾē	'prayer'
āk͡pàː	'bag'	ɔ̄k͡pākɔ́	'smoking pipe'
ìk͡pùɾù	'maggots'	àk͡pòk͡pā	'weaving'

12. List two types of sounds made with the glottalic airstream and tell how they are produced:

   a. _____
      _____

   b. _____
      _____

13. Complete sagittal diagrams and give the names for the following:

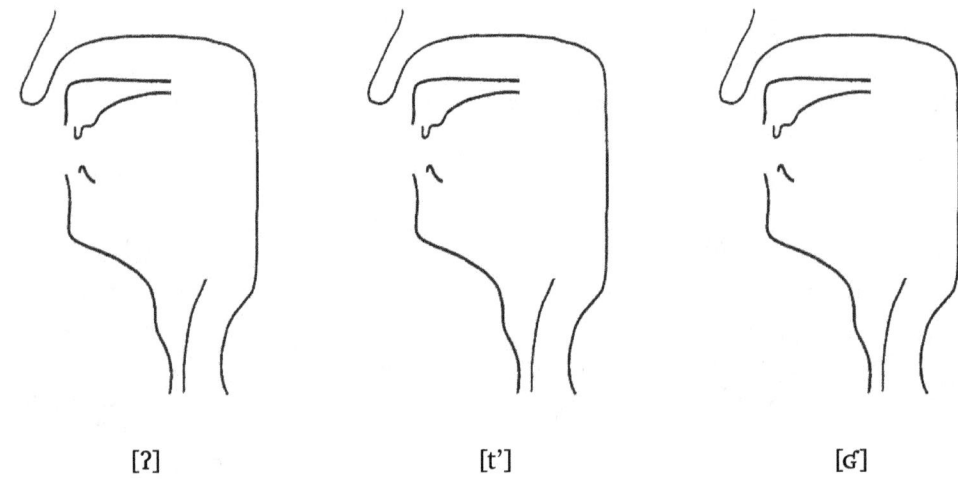

[ʔ] [t'] [ɢ]

_____ _____ _____

25

Releases, Transitions, Clusters, Glides, Gemination, and Juncture

In phonetics a continuous stream of speech is presented as a sequence of phonetic segments, which we represent by a string of discrete phonetic symbols, each representing a single segment. The concept extends naturally to suprasegmental features such as tone and subsegmental events, e.g., a feature that ends in the middle of a segment, such as the nasalized portion of a prenasalized stop. Laver expresses this well:

> The concept of the **segment** is that of a linear unit typically anchored in a short stretch of speech by a set of phonetic feature-values which are relatively unchanging. The segment is a construct of phonetic theory which relies here on a related concept of three different phases of articulation of any segment....segments are articulatorily classified partly in terms of the maximum degree of constriction of the vocal tract reached during the production of the segment. The period during which the maximum constriction is achieved defines the **medial phase** of the performance of the segment. Preceding this medial phase, an **onset phase** embodies the approach of the vocal organs to the medial phase, and an **offset phase** shows the movement of the organs towards the medial phase of the next segment (and hence constitutes an **overlapping phase** with the onset phase of that next segment). A given feature may therefore run right through several segments (as a **suprasegmental** feature), or may be limited to the medial phase of a single segment (as a **segmental** feature). More seldom, it may begin or terminate within a particular phase (as a **subsegmental** feature). (Laver 1994:112, bolding in original)

Laver's model gives us a useful basis for understanding and describing transitions from one phonetic segment to the next, including suprasegmental features and the transition from a segment to a pause. An important concept to understand about transitions is release of a segment.

Release

When the articulation of a consonant is released, the airstream may produce an audible sound that is judged not to be a full-length vowel or another consonant following soon after the first one, but rather a particular way of ending the consonant, possibly with an AUDIBLE RELEASE. In this case, the consonant is said to be RELEASED. If no such sound immediately follows the consonant, it is described as having no audible release. Sometimes a consonant with no audible release is called UNRELEASED, though this is inaccurate because every consonant articulation must be released eventually.

The audible release of voiceless consonants typically is voiceless and is written as aspiration, e.g., in [sækʰ] 'sack'. Voiced consonants often release into a brief voiced sound, typically an epenthetic vowel in the mid central region of the vowel space. The brevity of the release by comparison with the length of a syllabic vowel can be indicated by placing the diacritic for non-syllabic under the vowel symbol, as in [hiˈdɪdə̯] 'He did!' Or it may be indicated by superscripting a vowel symbol after the consonant symbol, as in [hiˈdɪdᵊ].

The diacritic called a *corner* [˺] indicates that a consonant has no audible release, e.g., [mɑp˺] 'mop' and [mɑb˺] 'mob'. It is used sometimes at the end of an utterance, just before a pause. Elsewhere in a transcription the absence of an explicitly transcribed audible release implies that there is none. Often a phonetic transcription of an utterance that ends with a consonant will not symbolize either that the final consonant was released or that it was not unless it is contrastive phonologically. That is, the final consonant symbol will stand alone without a diacritic, and the transcription is ambiguous. For example:

Table 25.1. Release of consonants

Audibly released	Not audibly released	Ambiguous
itʰ	it˺	it
idᵊ	id˺	id
ɑvᵊ	ɑv˺	ɑv
ɑzᵊ	ɑz˺	ɑz

Pronounce each of the above syllables, concentrating on the release of the consonant. Note that voicing on unreleased consonants, especially fricatives, has a tendency to fade into voicelessness.

Close and open transitions

In a sequence of two consonants, there is an OPEN TRANSITION between the two consonants if there is an audible release of the first consonant before the second consonant is fully established. There is CLOSE TRANSITION if there is no audible release of the first consonant.

When reading words with a syllable break between consonants, be careful not to insert open transitional elements such as aspiration or an extra vowel, such as a short schwa, between adjacent consonants unless the phonetic pronunciation so indicates. Practice reading aloud the following English examples, paying attention to the transition:

      sik.hɪm   sikʰ.hɪm   'seek him'

      hæd.gɔn   hædᵊ.gɔn   'had gone'

Segmental clusters

A CLUSTER is a sequence of two or more segments, either of vowels or consonants. Thus a CONSONANT CLUSTER is a sequence of two or more consonants and a VOWEL CLUSTER is a sequence of two or more vowels. A cluster may include transitions with open or close release, as is found in Chinook (see exercise 8 below).

Consonant clusters

In English, only a few words have clusters of more than three consonants, and word-initial clusters of more than two consonants occur only if the first consonant is [s], as in 'splash, scratch, splay, spleen, spray.' The second consonant in an initial consonant cluster is drawn from a limited set of consonants such as [p, l, k, w]. The third consonant is [ɹ] or [l] in an initial consonant cluster. On the other hand, in final consonant clusters, [l] or a fricative plus a stop occur. Other consonant clusters in English occur in words such as 'draw, glade, trade, milk, world.' See table 25.1 for other examples in English.

Table 25.2. Consonant clusters in English words

kɹæʃtʰ	'crashed'	bændz͡s	'bands'
æsktʰ	'asked'	bɪldz͡s	'builds'
mɪɫktʰ	'milked'	kʰɑɹvdᵊ	'carved'
pɹ̥eⁱ	'pray'	spɹeⁱ	'spray'
kl̥eⁱ	'clay'	skɚtʰ	'skirt'

Note that for words such as 'bands' and 'builds', [z] usually becomes voiceless [s] midway through the pronunciation of the final segment.

In other languages different combinations of consonant clusters occur. For example, consonant clusters in Jju are shown in the following examples:

dɾam   'brown monkey'   kʰɾ̥um   'money'
tʰɾ̥ɪm   'to shake'

Vowel clusters

In Roglai, spoken in Vietnam, two vowels occurring together in some words have a syllable break between them (Lee 1966:47–48). This syllable break is marked by increased force in pronunciation on the second vowel, as in the words:

si.iuam   'to whip'   ka.iua   'because'

Syllable breaks are marked between two adjacent consonants or vowels by placing a period on the line between the two sounds, as in the Roglai examples, and in Jju [ə.kʰɪŋ.kʲʰɪm] 'clay pot drum'.

When reading words with a syllable break between consonants, be careful not to insert open transitional elements such as aspiration or an extra vowel, such as a short schwa, between adjacent consonants unless the phonetic pronunciation so indicates. Likewise, be careful not to glide vowels in a vowel cluster such that you break up the cluster with semivowels such as 'w' and 'y'. Another error to avoid is inserting glottal stops between clustered vowels.

Glides: Vowel, central approximants, pitch, transitional sounds, and secondary articulations

The term *glide* refers to several different phonetic phenomena. A vowel glide refers to movement from one vowel to another, e.g., [ɑⁱ]. In producing a glided vowel the tongue position changes, thus changing the vowel quality, e.g., [aⁱ, eⁱ]. Glided vowels are also called DIPHTHONGS. An unglided vowel is one in which the tongue is held in the same position throughout the articulation of that vowel. See chapter 6 for discussion of vowel glides.

The sounds [j, j̊, w, w̥, ʋ, ʋ̥], which are also called *glides,* have been addressed under the topic of central approximants in chapter 19. These sounds function as consonants in language, though without many of the features usually associated with consonants in which the partially constricted airstream has audible friction. In the case of these glides, also called *semivowels*, there is no such audible friction, rather the air flows unconstricted through the oral cavity as it does for a vowel. However, a glide is produced with a narrower constriction than the constriction for a vowel. Phoneticians also use the term *glide* to refer to movements of the formants within a sound (see chapters 19 and 33).

Glide is also used to describe pitch changes in contour tone languages, e.g., a low-high glide, a high-low glide, a high-low-mid glide, and so on, depending on the particular tone system.

Finally, *glide* refers to a transitional sound in which the speech apparatus moves from one sound to another, i.e., an on-glide or an off-glide. Secondary articulations (see chapter 21), such as palatalization or labialization, are also referred to as glides.

Gemination

When there is a sequence of identical segments, whether consonants or vowels, within one morpheme, GEMINATION occurs. Two identical sounds coalesce into one long sound. The word geminate comes from the Latin word *geminare* 'to double.' A geminate consonant sequence cannot have an open transition, in particular an epenthetic vowel, between the two segments. An example of a geminate consonant sequence is in Italian /notte/ [notːe] 'night'. Italian [atːo] 'act' also has a geminate consonant. In practice, knowing when you are dealing with a geminate consonant or a sequence of two identical sounds depends upon the phonological analysis of the data. When writing phonetically, use the symbol for length [ː] for a geminate consonant; after the data have been analyzed phonologically as a geminate consonant, write it as two consonants. Examples include the following Hausa words:

sábó (adj., sg.)	'new'	gàrí	'town'
sàbàbːí (adj., pl.)	'new'	gàːɾí	'flour'

Note also the following Italian words:

notːe	'night'	faṭo	'fate'
belːo	'beautiful'	faṭːo	'made'

Juncture

JUNCTURE is any phonetic feature that marks the existence of a grammatical boundary. For example, in American English, a declarative sentence boundary is marked by low pitch at the end of the sentence, and an interrogative sentence boundary is marked by a high or rising pitch at the end of the sentence if there is no question word present ('who, what, when, where, why, how'). Different types of juncture may be distinguished. For example, CLOSE JUNCTURE refers to the normal transitions between words. INTERNAL OPEN JUNCTURE occurs within word boundaries, and EXTERNAL OPEN JUNCTURE occurs at utterance boundaries. Examples of juncture are illustrated by the following contrastive examples:

nitrate	night rate	The first has close juncture, while the second represents internal open juncture.
white shoes	why choose	Both are examples of internal open juncture which occurs at different places.

Further examples of juncture are given in exercises 9 and 10 below.

Key terms

released consonant (audible release)
unreleased consonant
open transition
close transition
consonant cluster

vowel cluster
glides
diphthong
gemination

juncture
    close juncture
    internal open juncture
    external open juncture

Exercises

1. Read aloud the following vowel glides (E. V. Pike 1963:59):

ɛu̯	(ɛw)	æi̯	(æj)
ou̯	(ow)	ɑi̯	(ɑj)
ɑu̯	(ɑw)	ɔi̯	(ɔj)
æu̯	(æw)	ei̯	(ej)
əu̯	(əw)	æi̯	(æj)
ɔu̯	(ɔw)	oi̯	(oj)
iu̯	(iw)	ɑi̯	(ɑj)
ɛu̯	(ɛw)	ei̯	(ej)
iu̯	(iw)	ui̯	(uj)
eu̯	(ew)	ɔi̯	(ɔj)

2. Practice the following Gogodala words (Papua New Guinea; data from Neuendorf as cited in E. V. Pike 1963:64):

ˈgaǫbə	'tree'	ˈgæǫ	'angry'
ˈgaųbə	'small kangaroo'	ˈgaǫ	'kind of coconut'
ˈbai̯ə	'sago, food'	ˈbaų	'kind of coconut'
ˈsæ.jə	'boy's name'	ˈwaǫ	'smoke'
ˈsæi̯jə	'fish trap'		

3. Practice the following Zambali words (Philippines; data from Minot as cited in E. V. Pike 1963:66):

ˈta.ib	'a kind of wall'	hikaˈina	'we (excl.) already'
taˈiʔataˈi	'a grass'	baˈba.i	'woman'
hiˈhi.ɑn	'to blame for something'	luˈbaj	'loincloth'
binaˈi.ɑn	'to ripen'	ˈta.inep	'dream'
kataˈo.ɑn	'person'	ˈlajnet	'a bird'
kataˈwan	'God'	kaˈta.o	'person'
paʔamuˈkawan	'place of wild banana'	kaˈtaw	'rafter'
hiˈkajnɑ	'you already'		

4. Practice the following Oaxaca Chontal words (Mexico; data from Morrison and Waterhouse as cited in E. V. Pike 1963:64):

ˈpojpa	'he went out'	lajˈwax	'my hair'
ˈpoj̊pa	'he cried out'	akaj̊ˈmaʔ	'gourd bowl'
ˈpaxpa	'she washed it'	ɛlˈwi̥j̊	'the fiesta'
ˈpoʃpa	'he went on out'	ˈjɛɣuj	'she is beating'
ˈxojpa	'now'	ˈw̥ɛðuj	'she wants it'
ˈxoxpa	'he wept'	hoˈlajʔuj	'he lives there'
ˈxoj̊pa	'it got used up'		

5. Practice the following Kickapoo words (Texas, Oklahoma and Mexico; data from James Klumpp as cited in Bickford and Floyd 2003:169):

waiˈjewi	'it is round'	juːhiˈɑijɑ	'he is here'
owiinɑki	'horns'	maːmɑjɑ	'early'
suːˈniɑhi	'money'	eːhˈpiɑɑːni	'unknown'

6. Put a check next to each of the following pairs of symbols that are written correctly and pronounced the same:

a̯i	aʲ	ɥu	y̯u
o̯u	ow	io	yo
əu	əw		

7. Practice reading the following Lao words with unreleased stops (data from Roffe as cited in E. V. Pike 1963:66):

ˈkat̚	'gnaw'	ˈkɑk̚	'skin disease'
ˈkʰək̚	'clear'	ˈbap̚	'sword'
ˈbaʔ̚	'sin'	ˈpʰət̚	'to brush'
ˈkʰop̚	'bite'	ˈtɔt̚	'to strike'
ˈpak̚	'month'		

8. Practice the following Chinook (Canada) words (Floyd 1986:76):

iɬˈtʃkʷa	'water'	ˈokʃt	'louse'
ˈitʰkʷʰti	'house'	ˈekʰtʰkʰ	'head'
ˈitʰkʰpʃ	'feet'	ektʃamxtʃ	'my heart'
iˈgel̪c̪ʃutkʰ	'flint'	ˈnukstx	'smallness'
oˈʔɨolɛptʃkiç	'fire'	olˈxakxalpʰtʃʰkiç	'our fire'
ˈtʰgakʰtʰkakʃ	'their heads'	aˈtʃokʰtʃʰkʰtamit̚	'he roasts her'
ʃˈtxɑxɑmuks	'our dogs'	aˈklokʃtʰtʰpʰtʃʰkʰ	'she carries it up from the beach'

9. Practice the following English words (Lehiste 1959:vi):

si me̯i bl̩	'see Mabel'	ho̯u me̯i kɚ	'hoe maker'
sim e̯i bl̩	'seem able'	ho̯um e̯i kɚ	'home acre'
ho̯umˈe̯i kɚ	'homemaker'		

10. Try saying the English phrases below in two different ways, in separate phases of this experiment: (Some of the data below are from Ilse Lehiste, *An Acoustic Phonetic Study of Internal Open Juncture*, U. of Mich. 1959.)

   (1a) First, read down through the list in Column 1 aloud at a normally rapid rate. Don't try to resolve any ambiguity that you might notice; that comes in the second phase.

   (1b) Then read down Column 2. By this time you will surely recognize ambiguities in what a listener might hear as you read the list aloud.

   (1c) Do the same for Column 3.

   (2) Read each triplet again. This time pronounce the phrases in a way that resolves, if possible, any ambiguity between them. Be careful not to let differences in spelling mislead you into pronouncing in an abnormal way. What phonetic differences do you use to distinguish which phrase you are saying? Are some pairs of phrases harder to disambiguate than others? If so, why? Conversely, are there some that do not seem at all ambiguous? Can you generalize on any of the ways you and others disambiguate the pronunciations? You may also want to enlist others to do the same procedure, to see whether they use the same phonetic contrasts that you use.

Column 1	Column 2	Column 3
beef-eater	bee-feeder	beef-feeder
by-law	by law	bile law
Dick's pots	Dick spots	Dick's spots
Free Danny	freed Annie	freed Danny
Grade A	gray day	grade day

25: Releases, Transitions, Clusters, Glides, Gemination, and Juncture

home-acre	hoe-maker	home-maker
it sprays	its praise	its sprays
it swings	its wings	its swings
keeps ticking	keep sticking	keeps sticking
night-rate	nitrate	night trait
Plato	play toe	plate toe
plump eye	plum pie	plumb pie
its school	it's cool	its school / it's school
see the meat	see them eat	see them meet
see zoos	seize ooze	seize zoos
see lying	seal eyeing	seal lying
white shoes	why choose	white chews
Sarah falls	seraph awls	seraph falls

26

Fronted and Retroflex Consonants; Comprehensive Framework for Places of Articulation

The places of articulation of some consonants may be fronted or retroflexed with respect to a specific reference point in the oral cavity. Part 1 of this chapter describes fronted and retroflex sounds and their articulations in a large number of languages. Part 2 presents a more comprehensive framework for describing places of articulation of all the sounds that Ladefoged and Maddieson have observed as described in their book *Sounds of the World's Languages* (1996).

Part 1: Fronted and retroflex consonants

FRONTED sounds are those sounds produced with a place of articulation further forward than a certain reference, usually either alveolar or postalveolar. Because of this difference in place of articulation, the active articulator is moved forward, making a new pairing of articulators with the passive articulator (when compared to the non-fronted sound). *Dental* sounds are classified as 'fronted' because they are articulated by the tongue tip forward of the alveolar ridge. A fronted alveolar sound is a dental sound. *Fronted postalveolar sounds* are also classified as 'fronted' because they are articulated by the tongue blade at the alveolar ridge, which is forward of the passive articulator for unmarked (non-fronted) postalveolar sounds.

Retroflex sounds are sounds produced with the tip of the tongue turned upward, and sometimes backward. Some part of the tongue tip is the active articulator. The passive articulator for retroflex sounds is behind the alveolar ridge. These sounds usually have *rhoticity*, an *r* sound quality.

Dental sounds

For DENTAL sounds the tongue tip goes either between the upper and lower front teeth (in which case it is more specifically an INTERDENTAL sound), against the back side of the upper front teeth, or against the gum just behind the upper front teeth. Spanish and French are examples of languages with dental consonants. The symbol for dental point of articulation is [̪] centered under the main consonant, e.g., [n̪], the *voiced dental nasal*.

Retroflex sounds

For RETROFLEX consonants, the tongue tip turns up and sometimes backward, usually toward an area behind the alveolar ridge, creating a slightly larger cavity both behind and in front of the tongue tip, thereby producing the characteristic rhoticity of the retroflex sound. Retroflex consonants occur in many languages of India, Pakistan, Nepal, Bangladesh, and in some African languages such as Gimira (now generally referred to as "Bench") in Ethiopia. Varying degrees of retroflexion are possible when producing retroflex consonants. For example, some Dravidian languages of south India have retroflex stops in which the underside of the tongue tip contacts the area behind the alveolar ridge (Ladefoged and Maddieson 1996:27). The IPA has one recognized set of symbols for retroflex sounds, each of which has a right-hook tail at the bottom of the symbol. One Dravidian language (Toda) has four contrastive sibilants demonstrating how close the contrasts within one language can be. Ladefoged and Maddieson (1996:154-160) give palatographic and linguographic records to support these four places of articulation: laminal alveolar [s̻] (also called fronted postalveolar) with tongue blade to the alveolar ridge, apical postalveolar [s̺] with tongue tip behind the alveolar ridge, laminal postalveolar [ʃ] with the blade contacting behind the alveolar ridge, and what they call a sub-apical palatal fricative [ʂ] with contact of the underside of the tongue tip behind the alveolar ridge. This they consider "a genuinely retroflex gesture" which we call the retroflex place of articulation.

Some sibilants and affricates that are commonly referred to as retroflex, for example in Mandarin, are not actually made with the tongue tip turned up, but rather with a relatively flat alveolar or postalveolar articulation while the body of the tongue is pulled back slightly with the sides raised.[1] This allows for the formation of a small resonating cavity under the front portion of the tongue which contributes to the characteristic rhoticity of the sound.

Sagittal diagrams in figure 26.1 contrast the tongue positions for dental, alveolar, and retroflex-voiceless stops.

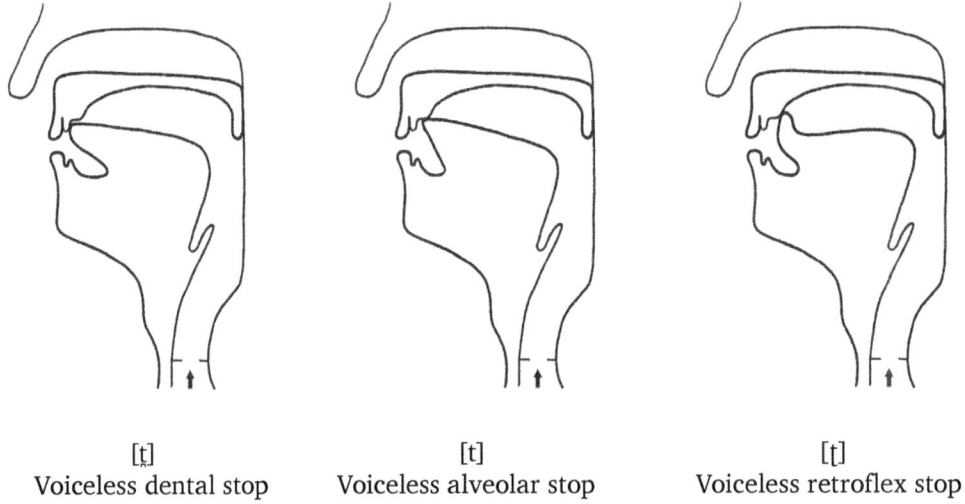

[t̪]
Voiceless dental stop

[t]
Voiceless alveolar stop

[ʈ]
Voiceless retroflex stop

Figure 26.1. Sagittal diagrams of dental, alveolar, and retroflex stops.

Fronted postalveolar consonants

For FRONTED POSTALVEOLAR consonants, the tongue blade moves forward from its normal postalveolar position to the alveolar ridge.

The tongue positions for fronted postalveolar and "normal" postalveolar consonants are illustrated in the sagittal diagrams in figure 26.2. The rectangular diacritic used for fronted postalveolar stops, e.g., [d̪], indicates that the sounds are LAMINAL, i.e., that the tongue blade is the active articulator.

---

[1] For this reason, some phoneticians say that these sounds are not true retroflexed sounds (cf. Ladefoged and Maddieson, 1996:153).

26: Fronted and Retroflex Consonants; Comprehensive Framework for Places of Articulation

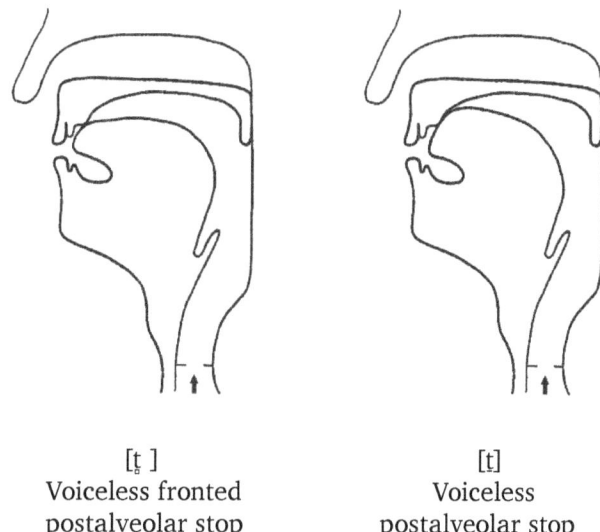

[t̻]
Voiceless fronted postalveolar stop

[t̠]
Voiceless postalveolar stop

Figure 26.2. Sagittal diagrams of fronted postalveolar and postalveolar stops.

Table 26.1 presents symbols for fronted and retroflex sounds in the six places of articulation discussed so far. Our reference to the dental fricatives articulated with a grooved tongue, e.g., [s̪], as *sibilants* rather than *fricatives,* distinguishes them from the dental fricatives that are not sibilants, e.g., [θ], [ð]. Thus [z̪] is a *voiced dental sibilant*.

Table 26.1. Dental, alveolar, and postalveolar consonants; fronted and retroflex consonants

	Dental	Alveolar	Retroflex	Fronted postalveolar = Laminal alveolar	Post-alveolar		
Voiceless	t̪ʰ	tʰ	ʈʰ	t̠ʰ	tʰ	aspirated	stop
Voiceless	t̪	t	ʈ	t̠	t		stop
Voiced	d̪	d	ɖ	d̠	d		
Voiced	r̪	r					trill
Voiced	ɾ̪	ɾ	ɽ				flap
Voiced		ɺ	ɺ̠				lateral flap
Voiceless	s̪	s	ʂ	s̠ (ʃ)	ʃ		sibilant
Voiced	z̪	z	ʐ	z̠ (ʒ)	ʒ		
Voiced	l̪	l	ɭ	l̠	l		lateral approximant
Voiceless	t̪s̪ʰ	tsʰ	ʈʂʰ	t̠s̠ʰ (tʃʰ)	tʃʰ	aspirated	affricate
Voiceless	t̪s̪	ts	ʈʂ	t̠s̠ (tʃ)	tʃ		
Voiced	d̪z̪	dz	ɖʐ	d̠z̠ (dʒ)	dʒ		
Voiceless	n̪̊	n̥	ɳ̊	n̠̊	ŋ̊ (n̥)		nasal
Voiced	n̪	n	ɳ	n̠	ñ (n)		
Voiced		ɹ	ɻ				approximant
Passive articulator	upper teeth	alveolar ridge	behind alveolar ridge	alveolar ridge	behind alveolar ridge		
Active articulator	tongue tip	tongue tip	underside or end of tongue tip	tongue blade	tongue blade		

Note that in constructing the symbol for an affricate, only the fricative needs detailed diacritics because the name of an affricate is based on the place of articulation of the fricative release.

Pronunciation helps

One way to learn to produce fronted or retroflex consonants is to practice a speech style in which the tongue is fronted or the tongue tip is retroflexed. Fronted and retroflex sounds often result automatically by adopting the corresponding speech style. For example, try saying the tongue twisters, "She sells seashells by the seashore" three times, first with a normal English alveolar tongue position, second with a fronted tongue position, and third with a retroflexed tongue tip. On your second time through, use no alveolar or postalveolar consonants; instead, substitute dentals and fronted postalveolars. Say the phrase, "Tilly tells the tailor to tailor the tux for Tex," for the same purpose.

Next, read down each column in table 26.2, pronouncing each consonant between two vowels.

Table 26.2. Articulator modifications

Dental	Alveolar	Retroflex	Fronted postalveolar	Postalveolar
ɑs̪ɑ	ɑsɑ	ɑʂɑ	ɑʃ̟ɑ	ɑʃɑ
ɑt̪ʰɑ	ɑtʰɑ	ɑʈʰɑ	ɑt̠ʰɑ	ɑt̠ʰɑ
ɑd̪ɑ	ɑdɑ	ɑɖɑ	ɑd̠ɑ	ɑd̠ɑ
ɑn̪ɑ	ɑnɑ	ɑɳɑ	ɑn̠ɑ	ɑn̠ɑ

Next read across the rows so that you learn to produce the contrast between these sounds. In addition to those included in the table above, practice other sounds in table 26.1.

Interdental consonants

Chapter 4 introduced interdental fricatives [θ] and [ð] as variants of dental fricatives. Nasal and lateral approximants at the interdental place of articulation have been reported in several languages of Australia (Dixon 1980:135ff). They can be transcribed using the same diacritic as for dental stops, i.e., [n̪], and [l̪]. They are produced by extending the tongue tip so that it protrudes between the front teeth, as for interdental fricatives, rather than touching the roof of the mouth at the alveolar ridge or behind the upper front teeth.

Retroflex consonants and their effects on vowels

There is *coarticulation* in every language. That is, the position of the articulator of one sound carries over to some extent into the following sound(s), or begins during the preceding sound(s), or both.

Retroflexion of consonant articulations is anticipated on preceding vowels or carried over onto following vowels. When retroflexion is carried from a consonant to a preceding vowel, the tongue tip begins to curl up and sometimes back for the retroflex consonant during that preceding vowel. In some cases it remains curled after the release of the main articulator of the consonant, resulting in retroflexion of the following sound(s). When we retroflex vowels, we produce RHOTICITY, symbolized by a right hook diacritic [˞] on the vowel symbol, e.g., [ɚ] or [ɝ], or by using the symbol [ɚ] for a rhotacized vowel with unspecified position in the vowel space. The right hook is occasionally used by IPA, but only on [ɚ] and [ɝ]. To indicate retroflexion of other vowels, IPA recommends superscripting the vowel symbol with an inverted 'r', e.g., [ɑʵ].

Part 2: Comprehensive framework for describing places of articulation

Ladefoged and Maddieson (1996:12) begin their description of places of articulation by identifying "five groups of moveable structures forming the active articulators in the vocal tract." These are juxtaposed with a diagram of "the nine regions of the vocal tract that can be considered as target areas for the moveable articulators. The numbered lines show some of the seventeen articulatory gestures, including those in the glottal region." They also zoom in with the two "more detailed diagrams of the anterior part of the vocal tract...showing articulation involving the tongue tip and blade." The articulatory gestures then are presented in tabular form under "terminology summarizing the place of articulatory gestures" (1996:15). See table 26.3. It summarizes the relationship between the major places and the individual places of articulation. These groupings of places of articulation correspond both to anatomical relationships of the various articulators and to the relationships between places of articulation in the languages where they have been observed.

Table 26.3. Terminology summarizing the place of articulatory gestures

Place of articulation	Articulatory target region	Moving articulator	Symbol examples
1. Bilabial	Labial	Lower lip	p b m
2. Labiodental	Dental	Lower lip	ɸ β ɱ
3. Linguolabial	Labial	Tongue blade	t̼ d̼ n̼
4. Interdental	Dental	Tongue blade	t̪ d̪ n̪
5. Apical dental	Dental	Tongue tip	t̺ d̺ n̺
6. (Laminal) denti-alveolar	Dental and alveolar	Tongue blade	t̪ d̪ n̪
7. Apical alveolar	Alveolar	Tongue tip	t d n
8. Laminal alveolar	Alveolar	Tongue blade	t̻ d̻ n̻
9. Apical retroflex	Postalveolar	Tongue tip	t̺ d̺ n̺
10. Palato-alveolar	Postalveolar	Tongue blade	t̠ d̠ n̠
11. Sub-apical (retroflex)	Palatal	Tongue underblade	ʈ ɖ ɳ
12. Palatal	Palatal	Front of tongue	c ɟ ɲ
13. Velar	Velar	Back of tongue	k g ŋ
14. Uvular	Uvular	Back of tongue	q ɢ ɴ
15. Pharyngeal	Pharyngeal	Root of tongue	ħ ʕ
16. Epiglottal	Epiglottal	Epiglottis	ʔ ʜ ʢ
17. Glottal	Glottal	Vocal folds	ʔ

Ladefoged and Maddieson (1996:15) Reproduced with permission, by John Wiley & Sons Ltd.

Key terms

fronted
retroflex
dental and interdental consonants
fronted postalveolar
laminal
rhoticity

Exercises

1. Practice the following Darai words (Nepal; data from C. and S. Kotapish 1973). Read each word three times:

ṭoɾike	'to pick' (e.g., corn)	ɳɑpike	'to measure'
ṭʰel	'backwaters of a river'	tɑn	'loom'
gəɖuɾə	'heavy'	kosṭɑ	'corn's husk'

2. Practice the following Malayalam words (India; data from Ladefoged 1975:139):

muṯ:u	'pearl'	kən:i	'virgin'
mut:u	'density'	kəɳ:i	'link in chain'
muṭ:u	'knee'	kəɲ:i	'boiled rice and water'
kuṯ:i	'stabbed'	kəŋ:i	'crushed'
kut:i	'peg'	eɳ:ə	'named'
kuṭ:i	'child'	en:ə	'me'
kəm:i	'shortage'	eɲ:ə	'oil'

3. Practice the following words (data from Ladefoged and Maddieson 1996:24–26):

   Isoko (Nigeria)
úd̬ù	'farm'	údù	'chest'

   Dahalo (India)
taʔadi	'fruit of *shitenké*'	ṭaːmi	'grass, thatch'

   Ewe (Nigeria)
é d̪à	'he throws'	é ḍà	'he cooks'

4. Practice the following Gimira words (Ethiopia; data from Breeze 1988):

ʃoʔ²	'be beautifully adorned'	ʒeg⁴	'salt'
ʃoʔ³	'to give birth'	ʒeg¹	'to move to and fro'
gatʃ⁴	'teff (a grain)'	kobʃ¹	'small'
gatʃ³	'shoulder'		

5. Draw sagittal diagrams for the following sounds: [ñ], [t̪], [d̪].

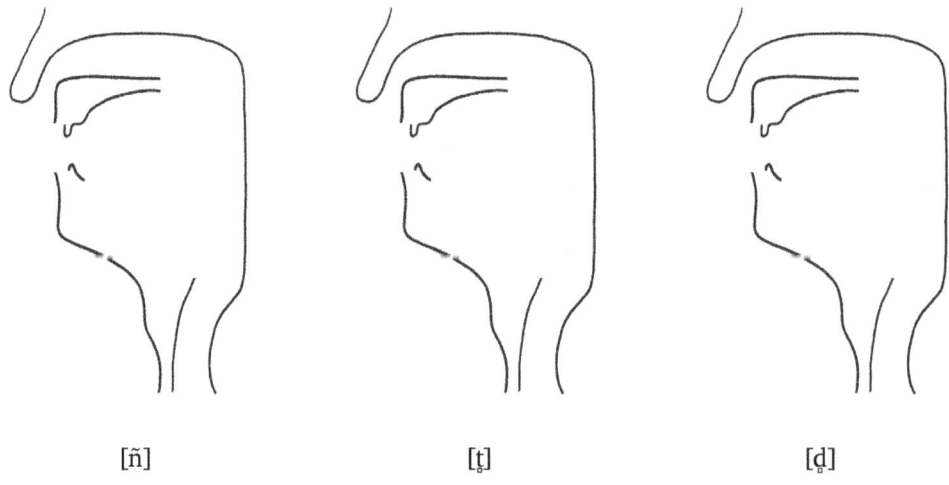

[ñ]　　　　　　　　[t̪]　　　　　　　　[d̪]

6. Give the phonetic names for the following:

[ɻ] _____

[l̥] _____

[ʒ] _____

[d̪] _____

[n̪] _____

[ɭ] _____

[t͡ʂʰ] _____

7. Write two symbols for the voiced postalveolar nasal: [ ] [ ].

27

Pharyngeal and Epiglottal Consonants

There are two places of articulation in the pharynx—PHARYNGEAL and EPIGLOTTAL. The back wall of the pharynx is the passive articulator for both pharyngeal and epiglottal sounds. If the constriction is between the *tongue root* and the back wall of the pharynx, the place of articulation is *pharyngeal*. If the constriction is between the *epiglottis* and the back wall of the pharynx, the place of articulation is *epiglottal*.

Pharyngeal and especially *epiglottal fricatives* occur frequently in Arabic and a few other languages of the Middle East and the Caucasus. They are also found in Nootka and Columbian of North America.

A speech sound is an OBSTRUENT if the articulation obstructs the airstream at least enough to form a fricative. Thus fricatives, affricates, and stops are obstruents. IPA does not include symbols for pharyngeal or epiglottal approximants, indicating that they have not been found to be contrastive in any language. (See pharyngealization in chapter 21 in which a pharyngeal approximant is an offglide from another consonant, indicated by a superscript pharyngeal fricative symbol.) The sagittal diagram in figure 27.1 illustrates a voiceless pharyngeal fricative.

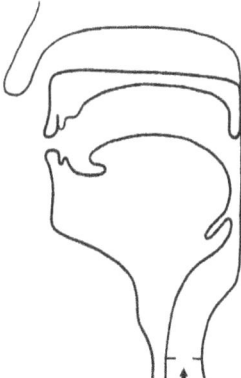

Figure 27.1. Sagittal diagram of a voiceless pharyngeal fricative [ħ].

The pharyngeal fricatives are:

- [ħ] voiceless pharyngeal fricative
- [ʕ] voiced pharyngeal fricative

The constriction between tongue root and pharyngeal back wall for producing a PHARYNGEAL FRICATIVE, such as [ħ], is lower and further back than the constriction between tongue back and soft palate for producing a uvular sound, such as [χ]. Because the part of the vocal tract in front of the noise source is longer for a pharyngeal fricative than for a uvular fricative, it resonates at a lower frequency; the noise of a pharyngeal fricative has a lower pitch than a uvular fricative.

Research has shown that the epiglottis is the active articulator for some fricatives that were previously thought to be pharyngeal. IPA provides symbols for three epiglottal consonants:

- [ʔ] EPIGLOTTAL STOP
- [ʕ] VOICED EPIGLOTTAL FRICATIVE
- [ʜ] VOICELESS EPIGLOTTAL FRICATIVE

In the production of any voiced stop, the volume of air enclosed between the glottis and the place of articulation must expand to accommodate the air coming through the glottis. There is so little capacity for the air volume between the glottis and the epiglottal or pharyngeal place of articulation to expand that an epiglottal stop or a PHARYNGEAL STOP must be essentially voiceless.

Ladefoged and Maddieson (1996:168), following Laufer and Condax (1979, 1981), report that in Semitic languages these sounds are often approximants rather than fricatives. Further, while traditionally called *pharyngeal,* they are more often epiglottal approximants. The constriction involves the epiglottis and the posterior pharyngeal wall rather than the tongue back. Caucasian languages have contrasts between pharyngeal and epiglottal fricatives. Catford (1983:347) reports that in the Burkekhan dialect of the Dagestanian language Agul there are seven contrastive pharyngeal and laryngeal sounds.

Pronunciation helps

Since pharyngeal fricatives are articulated by the tongue root coming close to the pharyngeal wall, one way to learn to pronounce them is to draw the whole tongue back. Another method is to depress the center of the tongue, which tends to squeeze the tongue root toward the rear. Pharyngeal fricatives are produced without turbulence or trilling at the velum or uvula. When you succeed in producing a pharyngeal fricative, it may sound as if someone is strangling you. This should not be too surprising, since the location of the articulatory constriction is roughly the same as the usual location of a stranglehold.

It may be helpful to use a mirror and a flashlight to check your throat during pronunciation of these sounds. If you hear a *voiceless fricative* sound deep in your throat, but at the same time you can still see your uvula, then you must be producing either a pharyngeal fricative, an epiglottal fricative, or a whisper.

Many people find it helpful to listen to the descending pitch of the fricative noise while gliding through a series of voiceless fricatives at places of articulation progressively farther back in the vocal tract—palatal, velar, uvular, and finally either pharyngeal or epiglottal, i.e., [ç: x: χ: ħ:] or [ç: x: χ: ʜ:]. The increasing volume and length of the resonating cavity for the sounds makes the pitch of the noise you hear go down as the place of articulation moves back and down.

Another approach for finding your pharyngeal place of articulation is to start with the voiced [ɑ] vowel and pull your tongue further and further back until the tongue root constricts the airstream at the back wall of the pharynx sufficiently to produce a fricative sound. This will produce [ɑ: ɑ̱: ʕ].

To produce epiglottal sounds some people have found it helpful to swallow. This action causes the epiglottis to move towards the pharyngeal wall while also voicing the sound. Practice pronouncing [ɑ: ɑ̱: ʕ]. With practice a person can learn to control the movement of the epiglottis.

Key terms

pharyngeal
epiglottal
obstruent
pharyngeal fricative

pharyngeal stop
epiglottal fricative (voiced/voiceless)
epiglottal stop

Exercises

1. Practice the following Columbian words (British Columbia; Kinkade 1967:228ff):

   ħamp   'fall off'   snħtstħˈtanaʔ   'earrings'
   tsiˈpaħː   'cloud of mosquitoes'

2. Practice the following Arabic words (Floyd 1981:93):

   ˈħaːɾab   'he fought'   ˈħəgəɾə   'stone'
   ħaˈmiːɾ   'donkeys'   ˈʕəgəɾə   'he left me'
   ħaˈɾiːɾ   'silk'   ħalˈla   'right away'
   ˈʔaħmaɾ   'red'   ʕala   'on'
   ħam: 'concern'   ʔatˤˈta   'God'
   ʕam: 'paternal uncle'

3. Write the names for the following symbols:

   [ʕ] _____
   [ʔ] _____
   [ʜ] _____
   [ʢ] _____
   [ħ] _____

4. Draw sagittal diagrams for the following sounds:

         [ʔ]   [ʕ]

28

Advanced and Retracted Tongue Root Vowels

Earlier chapters describe how the tongue root functions as an active articulator and the back wall of the pharynx as a passive articulator in producing pharyngeal consonants and in pharyngealization of consonants. This chapter discusses the effects of varying positions of the tongue root, the actions of the aryepiglottic folds, and the height of the larynx; these three effects sometimes combine in various ways in the production of vowels.

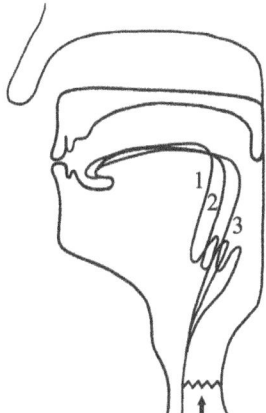

Figure 28.1. Tongue root positions.

Traditionally the features ADVANCED TONGUE ROOT [+ATR] and RETRACTED TONGUE ROOT [−ATR] have been used to describe the position of the tongue root. For [−ATR] vowels the tongue root is retracted toward the back wall of the pharynx, in the throat above the larynx; this reduces the volume of the pharynx, and the larynx is raised reducing the length of the pharynx, as well as its volume. For [+ATR] vowels the tongue root is advanced away from the back wall of the pharynx (thus increasing its volume) and the larynx is lowered, increasing the length of the pharynx and further increasing its volume. This has the opposite effect on the sound of vowels.

Traditionally, phoneticians have taught that it is convenient to distinguish three tongue root positions, *advanced, retracted,* and *neutral* (see figure 28.1). In table 28.1 the advanced and retracted positions are contrasts. The neutral position is intermediate between the other two. The NEUTRAL position is the default and needs no diacritic to indicate [+ATR] or [−ATR].

Recent research on what is happening in the pharyngeal cavity and at the glottis is adding to and modifying the above descriptions. In the production of [+ATR] and [–ATR] vowels, it increasingly looks as though the tongue root is the passive articulator in their production. For example, in Dinka [+ATR] vowels appear to be produced by lowering the larynx, thus producing a hollow sound. In West African vowel harmony languages, [+ATR] vowels have a breathy sound, resulting from the wide open pharynx that results from open aryepiglottic folds. In some languages (not all), [–ATR] vowels have a "choked" sound due to cinching of the aryepiglottic folds. To sum up, the supralaryngeal aryepiglottic folds narrow for the [–ATR] vowels and open for the [+ATR] vowels. This is in addition to the raising and lowering of the larynx. Since there are different though similar features taking place in various vowel harmony languages, one phonetic description does not apply to all cases.

Table 28.1. Possible phonetic features for advanced and retracted tongue root vowels

Advanced Tongue Root (+ATR)	Retracted Tongue Root (RTR, –ATR)
Tongue root is forward, away from the back wall of the pharynx, expanding the cross-sectional area of the pharynx.	Tongue root is back, close to the back wall of the pharynx, reducing the cross-sectional area of the pharynx.
Articulation also described as wide pharynx or non-faucalized.	Articulation also described as narrow pharynx or faucalized.
Often the larynx is lowered, lengthening the pharynx.	Often the larynx is raised, shortening the pharynx.
The supralaryngeal aryepiglottic folds open for the [+ATR] vowels.	The supralaryngeal aryepiglottic folds narrow for [–ATR] vowels.
Formant pitches are lower.[a]	Formant pitches are higher.

Vowel quality is sometimes called:
    hollow
    muffled
    loose
	Vowel quality is sometimes called:
	    choked
	    bright
	    tight, shrill

Musical pitch may be lower.	Musical pitch may be higher.
Phonation is often breathy (murmur).	Phonation is often creaky (laryngealized).
Sounds like the cartoon character Yogi Bear.	Sounds like the cartoon characters Fozzie Bear and Kermit the Frog.
Represented in a transcription by placing the diacritic [̫] under the vowel base character.	Represented in a transcription by placing the diacritic [̬] under the vowel base character.

[a]See chapter 33 on acoustic phonetics for a definition of *formant*.

Although the tongue root position is significantly different for what linguists sometimes call TENSE vowels, e.g., [i, e, o, u], than it is for what are called LAX vowels, e.g., [ɪ, ɛ, ɑ, ɔ, ʊ], the difference is less extreme than that associated with contrastive advanced and retracted tongue root positions.

The names of vowels with advanced and retracted tongue root are the same as for the corresponding neutral vowels, with the addition of *advanced tongue root* or *retracted tongue root* inserted before *vowel*, e.g., [i̫] is a 'close front unrounded vowel with advanced tongue root,' and [i̬] is a 'close front unrounded vowel with retracted tongue root.' If neither term is included in the name, the vowel is articulated with a neutral tongue root position. In phonetics three positions of the tongue root are distinguished;

28: Advanced and Retracted Tongue Root Vowels

however, most languages with a contrast in the tongue root position have a two-way contrast, e.g., [+ATR] vs. [−ATR].

Tongue root position produces contrastive effects on the quality of vowels in many African and Southeast Asian languages. Tongue root contrasts have been found in the Akyem dialect of Akan and Twi in Ghana, Igbo in Nigeria, and Dinka in Sudan, as well as other African languages. Phonologically, much vowel harmony is based upon the feature of an expanded or retracted tongue root [±ATR]. Some Niger-Congo languages exemplify the fullest form of this feature with five advanced tongue root vowels and five retracted tongue root vowels (Williamson 1989:23). In Ijaw, spoken in Nigeria, a set of [±ATR] vowels is further expanded to include both oral and nasal varieties (Jenewari 1989:110).

In Akan, as well as in other Kwa languages, there is VOWEL HARMONY. In table 28.2, set 1 differs from set 2 by having the tongue root advanced and the larynx lowered, while the second set has the tongue root retracted with a raised larynx. We know that the aryepiglottic folds are involved in the [±ATR] feature in both Dinka and Akan.

Table 28.2. Akan vowel harmony sets (Lindau 1979:163)

Set 1 [+ATR]		Set 2 [−ATR]	
i̭	ṷ	ɪ	ʊ
ḙ	o̭	ɛ	ɔ
	a		

The distinctions of the Akan vowel harmony sets are important for exercise 2 below. Note that the underlying mechanism for producing similar English vowels and Akan vowels differs. Akan vowels have [+ATR] and [−ATR] features which English vowels do not have. Lindau states that the production of [+ATR] vowels in Akan is similar to that of "the production of pharyngalized [*sic*] or 'emphatic' consonants in Arabic" (1979:175).

Key terms

advanced tongue root [+ATR]
retracted tongue root [−ATR]
tense and lax vowels

neutral tongue root position
vowel harmony

Exercise

1. Practice saying the following Yala words (Nigeria; Armstrong 1989:330). Note that the unmarked vowels below are [−ATR].

ó múm̀	'he saw me'	ó múʔlò	'he saw us'
o múò̭	'he saw you'	ó múʔnò	'he saw you' (pl.)
ó mó̭ò̭	'he saw him'	ó muúwa	'he saw them'

2. Practice the following Akan words (Ghana; Lindau 1979:165). See table 28.1 for assistance with this exercise.

fi̭	'to leave'	ʃṷḙ	'to pour'
fɪ	'to vomit'	pɛ̀	'to like'
bṷ	'to break'	mó	'well done'
bʊ	'to be drunk'	bɔ́	'to strike'

3. Practice saying the following Kru words (Liberia; Floyd 1981:108):

Advanced Tongue root		Retracted Tongue Root	
˥ fi̘	'to leave'	˥ fɪ	'to vomit'
˥ bu̘	'to break'	˥ bʊ	'to be drunk'
˥ mo̘	'well done'	˥ bɔ	'to strike'
˩˥ je̘fi̘	'we leave'	˩˥ jɛfɪ	'we vomit'
˥˩ wu̘fi̘	'you leave'	˥˩ wʊfɪ	'you vomit'
˩˥ o̘fi̘	'he leaves'	˩˥ ɔfɪ	'he vomits'
˩˩˥ o̘ko̘tu̘	'he goes and pulls it out'	˩˩˥ ɔkɔtʊ	'it goes and lays'

4. List four features of [+ATR]:

   a. _____
   b. _____
   c. _____
   d. _____

5. List four features of [−ATR]:

   a. _____
   b. _____
   c. _____
   d. _____

6. Give the technical names for the vowels:

   [i̘] _____
   [ɛ̘] _____
   [ʊ̘] _____
   [ɤ] _____

29

Clicks

A CLICK is a speech sound made with an *ingressive lingual airstream* (sometimes referred to as a velaric or oral airstream mechanism) and with two closures in the mouth that trap a small volume of air in the space between them. The back of the tongue forms one of the closures by pressing against the back of the velum, and it serves as the initiator of the ingressive velaric airstream. Meanwhile, the lips press together or the tongue presses against the roof of the mouth, forming the other closure at some place of articulation. Then the tongue pulls downward and sometimes toward the rear, forming a partial vacuum in the oral cavity. When the other closure is released, air bursts through the opening into the oral cavity between the two closures, producing a sharp sound called a *click*. Table 29.1 presents some of the more common clicks found in human language.

This book describes only the basic articulations of clicks and a few variations that occur in human language. For further discussion of clicks see Ladefoged and Maddieson (1996:246–280).

Table 29.1. Clicks

	Bilabial	Dental	Alveolar	Post-alveolar	Retroflex		
Voiceless	ʘ	ǀ	ǃ	ǂ	ǃ̢		
Voiced	g͡ʘ	g͡ǀ	g͡ǃ	g͡ǂ	g͡ǃ̢		
Voiced	ŋ͡ʘ	ŋ͡ǀ	ŋ͡ǃ	ŋ͡ǂ	ŋ͡ǃ̢	nasal	click
Voiceless			ǁ			lateral	
Voiced			g͡ǁ				
Voiced			ŋ͡ǁ			nasal lateral	
Passive articulator	upper lip	back of upper teeth	alveolar ridge	behind alveolar ridge	behind alveolar ridge		
Active articulator	lower lip	tongue tip	tongue tip	tongue blade	under side of tongue tip		

To find the name of a click, read the row and column labels clockwise around table 29.1. For example, [ǀ] is a *voiceless dental click,* and [ŋ͡ǁ] is a *voiced alveolar nasal lateral click.* The term *click* implies that the sound is made with the ingressive velaric airstream which, in turn, implies velar closure. Since an egressive pulmonic airstream is inherent in the term *voiced,* it need not be specified separately in the names of voiced clicks.

It is relatively easy to produce sounds with an egressive velaric airstream, but they have not been reported to function as contrastive units of sound in ordinary speech. (Not so long ago there was a teaching assistant on N. McKinney's phonetics staff who frequently expressed her ambivalence about some decision by making a bilabial click. Just for fun, try making one yourself. It can be very expressive!)

The velaric airstream mechanism acting alone produces a voiceless click, e.g., [!]. If, in addition, an egressive pulmonic airstream is causing the vocal folds to vibrate, and if the nasal port is open, the sound is a VOICED NASAL CLICK, e.g., [ŋǁ]. If, on the other hand, the nasal port is closed, the sound is a *voiced click,* e.g., [g͡!].

A nasal click can be repeated for as long as there is breath to sustain voicing, because the two airstreams do not share the same paths. A non-nasal voiced click is like a voiced stop in that the voicing can continue for only a relatively short time, because there is little space in which to hold the air that has passed through the glottis to produce voicing.

In the preliminary phase of producing a click, the back of the tongue contacts the velum, blocking the air passage at the back of the mouth. At the same time, a contact further forward in the mouth blocks air passage there. Thus either the lips are fully closed, or the tongue is in contact with the roof of the mouth, entrapping any air between the places where the air passage is blocked. Sometimes most or even the entire upper surface of the tongue is in contact with the roof of the mouth, leaving little or no air space between the tongue and the roof of the mouth.

The second phase of producing a click is the initiation phase, in which the two closures are maintained and a partial vacuum is formed between them. The tongue does this by muscular tension pulling downward on the tongue body and often toward the rear on the back of the tongue.

In the third phase one of the two closures is opened, and air rushes in, producing the click sound. A click is usually released orally by releasing the forward closure first. Releasing the velar closure first produces a NASALLY RELEASED CLICK. In Nigeria, Bajju men, when they are listening to someone talking, affirm the speaker or express pity by producing nasally released clicks.

The final phase in producing a click is the release of the second of the two closures. Except for nasally released clicks, this is the velar closure.

During the production of the click, air from the lungs may be passing up through the glottis, producing voicing. If the nasal port is open, there will be a voiced velar nasal sound simultaneous with the click. If the nasal port is closed, the sound simultaneous with the click will be a voiced velar stop. In transcribing such a combination, a tie bar over the pulmonic and the velaric symbols shows that they were produced simultaneously, e.g., [ŋ͡ʘ].

Ladefoged and Maddieson report that although the contact between the tongue and the roof of the mouth may cover a broad area in producing a click, the place of contact between articulators that most heavily influences the sound quality is the front edge of the forward area of contact just as the contact is broken, allowing air to burst into the cavity where the partial vacuum had been formed. They also report, "In all the languages that we have heard, the dental and lateral clicks are affricated, whereas the alveolar and palatal clicks are sharply released" (Ladefoged and Maddieson 1996:256).

English speakers do not use clicks in normal speech. However, a few clicks have widely recognized meanings to English speakers, though they are not part of the regular consonant inventory of English. A voiceless bilabial click [ʘ] is the sound of a kiss. A voiceless dental click [|], popularly written as "tsk, tsk, tsk!," expresses disapproval in some dialects of English, pity in others. Someone riding or driving a horse may use voiceless alveolar lateral clicks [ǁ] (also known as "clucking") to urge the horse(s) to start moving or to move faster. (When N. McKinney was a child, he and his friends imitated the sound of a horse trotting on a hard surface with alternately labialized and plain voiceless retroflex clicks.)

Clicks function as contrastive consonants in normal speech in only a few languages. Khoisan languages of southern Africa have the most clicks, but also some Bantu languages in central, eastern, and particularly in southern Africa have them. Bantu languages, Zulu and Xhosa, have borrowed clicks from their Khoisan neighbors.

29: Clicks

The sagittal diagrams in figure 29.1 illustrate bilabial clicks. The diagram of the voiced *bilabial click*, [g͡ʘ], is like that for the voiced *labial-velar stop*, [g͡b] (not shown here), except for the inward arrow drawn on the tongue back, indicating that the tongue back is the initiator of an INGRESSIVE VELARIC AIRSTREAM. The upward arrow drawn below the larynx for the voiced click indicates that an egressive pulmonic airstream is also active. There is no arrow drawn below the larynx for the voiceless click, [ʘ].

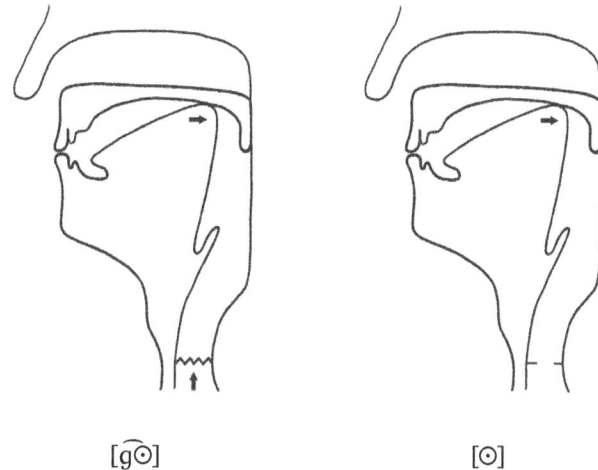

Figure 29.1. Sagittal diagrams of voiced and voiceless bilabial clicks.

Pronunciation helps

When practicing clicks, begin those mentioned earlier in the chapter for urging a horse to move on (a voiceless alveolar lateral click), for expressing pity or disapproval (a voiceless dental click), and for a kiss (a voiceless bilabial click).

Voiceless clicks may be released in several ways: directly into a vowel, or into [h], [l], [x] or [k] before the next vowel. Using each of these release possibilities, pronounce each voiceless click. All except the lateral click can also be released nasally by releasing the velar closure first. A superscript nasal symbol represents a nasal release, e.g., [!ⁿa].

To produce a nasal click, try humming [ŋ] while simultaneously producing a click. There is a natural tendency to leave a velic opening throughout the vowel following a nasal click; work at keeping the nasalization from spreading onto the vowel.

Finally, try to pronounce voiced non-nasal clicks. Think of saying [g] simultaneously with a voiceless click. Try saying a series of plain voiced velar stops alternating with a vowel, e.g., [gagaga], then superimpose a click articulation on top of the [g], resulting in [gagag͡!a]. It may be helpful to say a voiced click first, and then a voiced nasal click by consciously adding opening of the nasal port. Voiced (oral and nasal) clicks usually release directly into a vowel.

Key terms and symbols

click, voiced click, voiced nasal click   inward arrow on the tongue back
nasal release   upward arrow below the larynx
ingressive velaric airstream

Exercises

1. Practice each of the following click sequences:

	dental	alveolar	lateral
voiceless stop	u|o	u!o	u‖oo
voiceless aspirated stop	u|ʰo	u!ʰo	u‖ʰo
voiced	ug͡|o	ug͡!o	ug͡‖o
voiced nasal	uŋ͡|o	uŋ͡!o	uŋ͡‖o

2. Practice the following Zulu words (South Africa; Ladefoged 2001:264–265):[1]

dental		alveolar		alveolar lateral	
|á:gà	'to whitewash'	!à:!á	'to undo'	‖á:gà	'put into a fix'
|ʰà:gá	'to identify'	!ʰà:!ʰà	'to rip open'	‖ʰá:gà	'link horses'
g͡|ò:ɓá	'to grease'	g͡!ò:ɓá	'to milk'	g͡‖ò:ɓá	'to beat'
ìsì:ŋ͡|é	'kind of spear'	ìsì:ŋ͡!é	'rump'	ìsì:ŋ͡‖é:lè	'left hand'

3. Practice the following Xhosa words (South Africa; Ladefoged 2001:121):

Dental	Postalveolar	Alveolar lateral	Phonation	Click type
ukú|ola 'to grind fine'	ukú!oɓa 'to break stones'	úko‖o 'peace'	voiceless	unaspirated
uku|ʰóa 'to pick up'	ukú!ʰola 'perfume'	ukú‖ʰóa 'to arm oneself'	voiceless	aspirated
ukug͡|ôɓa 'to be joyful'	ukúg͡!oba 'to scoop'	ukug͡‖oba 'to stir up mud'	murmured	murmured
ukúŋ͡|oma 'to admire'	ukúŋ͡!ola 'to climb up'	ukúŋ͡‖iɓa 'to put on clothes'	voiced	nasal
ukúŋ͡|olla 'to be dirty'	ukúŋ͡!ala 'to go straight'	ukúŋ͡‖iɓa 'to lie on back, knees up'	murmured	nasal

---

[1] Ladefoged inserts the symbol [k] before a voiceless click; this is not standard IPA symbol usage, though we can see the logic of his notation. It is parallel to that of a voiced click symbol preceded by [g]. We have taken the liberty to change Ladefoged's transcription to be more in line with standard IPA usage of click symbols. Further, we have changed the column label of 'Alveolo Palatal' to 'Postalveolar'. We have also added a tie bar with the voiced and nasal clicks.

29: Clicks

4. Practice the following Zulu children's song, substituting a different click of your choice for each # (Smalley 1989:438):

5. Complete the following sagittal diagrams and write the names of the sounds and the articulators:

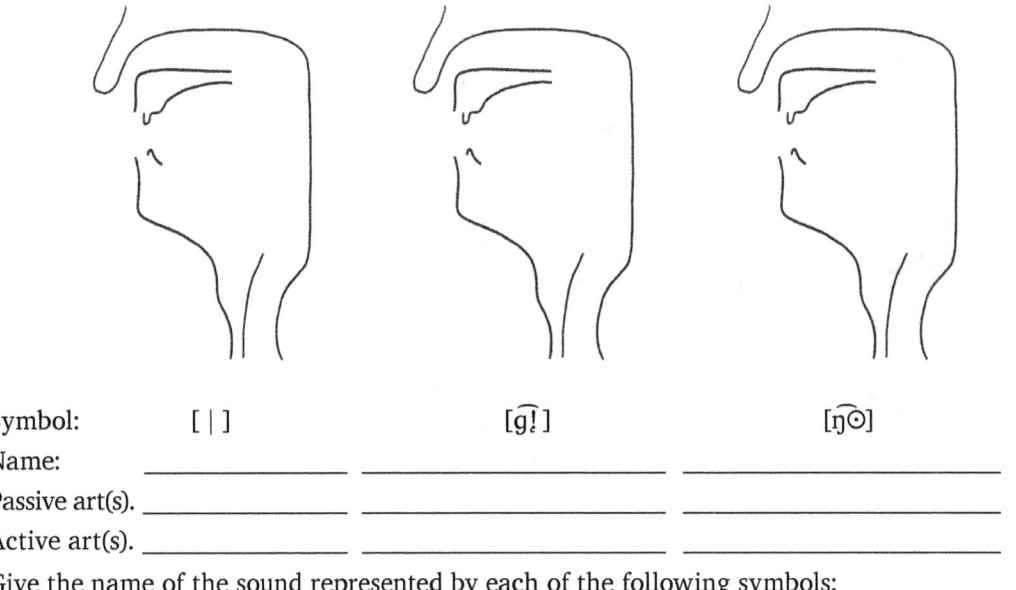

Symbol:	[	]	[g͡ǃ]	[ŋ͡ʘ]
Name:	_____	_____	_____
Passive art(s).	_____	_____	_____
Active art(s).	_____	_____	_____

6. Give the name of the sound represented by each of the following symbols:

[ʘ] _____

[ŋ͡ʘ] _____

[|] _____

[g͡|] _____

[ŋ͡ǃ] _____

[ɲ͡ǃ] _____

[ŋ͡‖] _____

[‖] _____

[ǃ] _____

30

Fortis and Lenis Consonants; Controlled and Ballistic Syllables

Fortis and lenis consonants

FORTIS consonants and their counterparts, LENIS consonants, are both phonetic and phonological features of some languages. A fortis consonant is produced with greater energy that is potentially realized as longer duration, greater frication or affrication, labialized or palatalized release, and a longer release of the fricative part of an affricate. There is usually a difference in the relative amount of effort (i.e., muscular tension) a speaker exerts in producing a fortis consonant. In descriptions of some languages where there is a contrast between fortis and lenis consonants, fortis refers to greater effort in phonation. For other languages fortis refers to greater effort in articulation, or both articulation and phonation.

Linguists have used the terms *fortis,* meaning strong, and *lenis,* meaning weak, to name and describe collective phonetic differences. For example, some phonological descriptions of English have called the consonants /p, t, k/ fortis and /b, d, g/ lenis. This follows the general pattern of identifying the voiceless consonants in a voiced/voiceless contrast as fortis. These linguists claim that something other than voicing must be the phonetic feature that distinguishes the two words in such pairs as 'see' and 'zee' (the name of the letter z in American English), since the initial consonants in both words, when pronounced in isolation, will very often be phonetically voiceless. They submit as evidence for their claim the fact that an English speaker has little difficulty identifying which sound of a whispered minimal pair such as 'see' and 'zee' is in which word; when the voiceless [s] is whispered, 'see' is much louder than the devoiced [z̥] in whispered 'zee.'

Table 30.1 presents etic tendencies for fortis and lenis consonants proposed by Eunice Pike (1963:131) together with material from more recent studies.

Table 30.1. Etic tendencies for fortis–lenis consonants

	Fortis	Lenis
Stops[a]	aspirated voiceless long affricated affricated with palatalized or labialized release	unaspirated/weakly aspirated fluctuation between voiced and weak voicing fluctuation between weak closure and continuant affricated without a palatalized or labialized release or without length on the fricative portion of the affricate
Fricatives	voiceless long	fluctuation between voiced and voiceless short
Affricates	longer release of the fricative part of the affricate	short nonaffricate, affricate without length on the fricative portion of the release
Laterals, nasals, approximants	long	short

[a]A fortis–lenis contrast in double stops and double nasals is uncommon, but attested.

Fortis/lenis notation

IPA does not provide a diacritic for the fortis characteristic of a consonant. However, an Extension to the IPA (ExtIPA), prepared by the International Clinical Phonetics and Linguistics Association includes the double quote mark ["] which indicates 'stronger articulation.'

The notations given here for fortis and lenis segments come from the Americanist tradition of phonetic transcription which uses a double quotation mark below the consonant symbol to indicate that the consonant is fortis. For example, in Jju of Nigeria, /ga̎/ [gɣːɑ] 'hurry', the first consonant is fortis /g̎/. To symbolize lenis, the Americanist tradition uses a "squiggle" under the consonant symbol, e.g., in Jju, /g̰ɑ/ [g̰ɑ], a verb prefix meaning 'in order that' or 'may'. (The slanted lines enclosing these segments indicate that the enclosed transcription is not a phonetic transcription but a phonological one.) Phonetically, the first sound in /ga̎/[gɣːɑ] 'hurry' is an affricate, while the first sound in the verb prefix /g̰ɑ/ is not affricated. An Extended IPA notation to indicate lenis is the "weak articulation" diacritic " ̞ ", e.g., /t̞/.

Jju fortis and lenis consonants

While some linguistic descriptions attribute the difference between fortis and lenis consonants to a difference between two values of a single phonetic feature (e.g., voiced versus voiceless), in other languages linguists have reported that the contrast is due to differences in multiple features. That is, either one or more phonetic features differentiate a single pair of fortis and lenis minimal pair of sounds, or else the set of contrastive features is different for one set of consonants than for another. For example, the contrast between velar fortis and lenis stops in Jju includes both length and fricative release whereas with the postalveolar pair, it is only length.

All consonants in Jju, with the exception of the double stops [k͡p] and [g͡b], have fortis-lenis counterparts. The fortis consonant is longer, (more) labialized, (more) palatalized, (more) affricated, or some combination thereof than its lenis counterpart (N. McKinney 1984, 1990). The word list in table 30.2 illustrates this contrast.

30: Fortis and Lenis Consonants; Controlled and Ballistic Syllables

Table 30.2. Phonetic contrasts of Jju fortis and lenis consonants

Phonological transcription	Phonetic transcription	English gloss
/ga̰/	[gá]	'in order that, may (verb prefix)'
/ga/	[gɣːá]	'to hurry, to be quick'
/d͡ʑḭ/	[d͡ʑì]	'concord particle'
/d͡ʑi/	[d͡ʑːì]	'winged female flying termites'
/jḭ/	[jí]	'second person plural subject pronoun'
/ji/	[jːí]	'to steal'
/ɾa̰k/	[ɾák]	'to refuse'
/ɾak/	[ɾʲák]	'to lick'
/b̰o/	[bvó]	'again'
/bo/	[bvːò]	'to know, to understand'
/c̰í/	[t͡ʃí]	'to cut, to make ridges when farming'
/cí/	[t͡ʃːí]	'to perform sorcery, to conjure'

Table 30.3 summarizes the phonetic features that distinguish Jju fortis and lenis consonants.

Table 30.3. Summary of lenis-fortis consonants in Jju

Length		Consonants with affrication or length on release of the affricate		Secondary articulation added to fortis consonant	
Lenis	Fortis	Lenis	Fortis	Lenis	Fortis
s	sː	pʲ	ps	ɾ	ɾʲ
z	zː	bv	bvː	ɥ	ɥːʷ
ʃ	ʃː	f	pf	ɥ̥	ɥ̥ːʷ
m	mː	ts	tsː		
n	nː	tʃ	tʃː		
ŋ	ŋː	dz	dzː		
w	wː	dʒ	dʒː		
w̥	w̥ː	k	kx		
j	jː	g	gɣ		
Consonants without a lenis-fortis consonant contrast					
k͡p		g͡b			

Given these data, the concept of a fortis-lenis consonant contrast in Jju is best treated as a phonological contrast, manifested phonetically by a bundle of phonetic features. In addition to the basic fortis-lenis contrast, many of these consonants can be labialized or palatalized. One consonant has both palatalization and labialization, labial-palatization: [tᶣʰ].

Korean consonants

In Korean, the fortis-lenis contrast has been reported for word-initial voiceless stops and affricates. In addition, there is a third feature, aspiration, which may occur on voiceless stops and affricates, giving an apparent three-way contrast of fortis, lenis, and aspirated. For example, /pʰ/ is strongly aspirated, while /p/ (fortis) is produced with tight lip closure and no aspiration. /p/ (lenis) is produced with looser lip closure and may or may not be slightly aspirated. Many linguists have attempted to identify the exact feature or features which distinguish these lenis consonants from both the aspirated and the unaspirated (fortis) consonants. However, while there do appear to be some unique features of the lenis consonants (e.g. slightly longer VOT, some breathiness on release), the most noticeable feature of the syllables which begin with lenis consonants is a lower pitch on the following vowel.[1] This is a case of what is sometimes referred to as *displaced contrast*. For example,

aspirated	/pʰɑdɑ/	(much aspiration)	'digging'
fortis	/pɑdɑ/	(no aspiration)	'grind'
lenis	/pàdɑ/	(slight aspiration)	'ocean, sea'

In the description of Korean phonetics in the *Handbook of the International Phonetic Association* (1999), the orthographic symbols for this three-way contrast are written as follows. Heavily aspirated consonants are written with a superscript 'h', e.g., [pʰɑ]. The weak slightly aspirated consonants are written with a voiced consonant symbol, e.g., [bɑ]. And the strongly articulated unaspirated consonants are written with a voiceless consonant symbol, e.g., [pɑ]. Table 30.4 gives illustrative examples.

Table 30.4. Examples of three-way Korean consonant contrast

p	pɑldɑ	'sucking'	t	tɑl	'daughter'	k	kɑldɑ	'spreading'
pʰ	pʰɑl	'arm'	tʰ	tʰɑl	'face mask'	kʰ	kʰɑl	'knife'
b	bɑl	'foot'	d	dɑl	'moon'	g	gɑl	'to grind'
			c	cɑdɑ	'squeeze'			
			cʰ	cʰɑdɑ	'kick'			
			ɟ	ɟɑl	'well'			

Controlled and ballistic syllables

Linguists working with some dialects of the Chinantec language in central Mexico use the term BALLISTIC syllable to contrast the perceived unusual dynamics of some syllables with the normal dynamics that they call CONTROLLED syllables. In an older writing system a "decrescendo" symbol borrowed from musical notation was placed over the vowel. More recently Merrifield and Edmondson (1999:319) have used a high pitch diacritic over the vowel, e.g., [kíᴹ] 'the rain' and [kíᴸ] 'I paid' to indicate that a syllable is ballistic. (They indicate mid and low tone with [ᴹ] and [ᴸ], respectively, following the syllable.)

This contrast may be analyzed as a difference between plain vowels (controlled) and a vowel-*h* (ballistic) sequence. Merrifield and Edmondson found that the rate of airflow rises sharply and then falls sharply in the latter part of a ballistic syllable in Palantla Chinantec, lending support to the use of [h] in the transcription. Further, they found that the most distinctive characteristic of ballistic syllables is their relatively short duration and the relative speed of the pitch changes before and after they reach their apexes. Mugele (1982) reported that the ballistic feature on syllables in Lalana Chinantec occurs only on syllables with falling contour tones.

---

[1] This pitch contrast is thought to derive originally from voicing on these consonants, which has apparently been lost in initial position (Kim and Duanmu 2004:66).

While it is important to know about the possibility of controlled and ballistic syllables, this is a phenomenon that has been reported for only a few languages, notably in Chinantec dialects in Mexico. If you plan to work in one of the many Chinantec dialects, learn about these interesting phonetic phenomena by reading the literature and eliciting data on it from Chinantec speakers. To the best of our knowledge, it has not been found in other languages of the world.

Key terms

fortis consonants, lenis consonants
controlled syllables, ballistic syllables

Exercises

Practice the Jju and Korean data displayed in tables 30.2, 30.3, and 30.4.

31

Speech Variants, Accents, Dialects, and Sociophonetics

Probably at some time you have noticed a person speaking in your mother tongue or a language you are very familiar with but in a manner that is different from what you are used to hearing. That person is using a SPEECH VARIANT that is different from your own. You might say the person has an accent. Social *speech variants* or *speech styles* refer to varieties of speech within one language used by one or more speakers. There are also speech variants between speakers, often due to socioeconomic factors, including social class, economic status, the dialect of the geographic location where they live, and education. If a society has a high degree of social stratification, especially if it is highly urbanized, you will likely find that there are speech variants among different social groupings and strata. Often one of the variants of a language is more generally accepted than the others, thus making it the standard speech style, and there are usually a number of non-standard speech variants. In the United States standard English is the form spoken in the north central plains. Often a person aspiring to be a news reporter on radio or television, but who habitually speaks a non-standard variety of English, must attend classes to learn to speak the standard variety. For example, in non-standard English a person may say 'I ain't never gonna do it' for 'I'm not going to do it.' In the first sentence certain vocabulary words as well as the use of a double negative mark this as non-standard.

DIALECTS are speech variants within a single language, often based on regional differences. Gillian Hansford writes,

> Concerning [British] English pronunciation, there are two main varieties of dialect. The country was divided by a line going roughly from NW to SE when the Vikings invaded. One area retains 'northern' pronunciation, and the other is 'southern' or so-called Received Pronunciation [RP]. You can tell a Northerner by the way s/he says 'brush'. If with a back rounded...vowel, they are northern. If the vowel would be written with a phonetic symbol of a hat, they are southern. Similarly northerners pronounce the *g* as well as the *eng* at the end of sing and singer, whereas 'we' don't. This is, of course, a gross exaggeration of the true facts of dialect in the United Kingdom. (Personal e-mail, April, 2003. Used with permission)

A noticeable feature of RP is that it drops the 'r' sounds that come at the end of syllables. Cockney, a less prestigious dialect of English, substitutes glottal stops for other stops in certain positions. Also Cockney and RP sometimes use completely different words to mean the same thing. The play *My Fair Lady* dramatizes these dialect differences very well. (For more on English dialects see Cassidy 1985, 1991, 1996; Hall 2002; Labov 1970; McDavid 1980; and Wolfram and Schilling-Estes 1998.)[1]

---
[1] RP itself has been changing in recent years, leading to "old RP" and "new RP," but still marked as upper class, while southern British English is somewhat different, being similar to RP, but more commonly used.

Accents are characteristic ways of pronouncing words. Non-native speakers of a language often have a pronunciation influenced significantly by their mother tongues. In distinguishing between dialects and accents, *accents* refers to pronunciation only, while *dialects* refers to all linguistic differences, including lexical and grammatical differences. An example of an accent is that many non-native English speakers have difficulty pronouncing English interdental fricatives [θ, ð].[2] These non-native speakers are likely to substitute [d] or [t] (or dental stops) for interdental fricatives. The reason for this substitution is that their mother tongue does not have interdental fricatives, so they substitute the closest sounds present in their mother tongue.

Dialect differences include changes in pitch patterns, vocabulary, pronunciation, grammatical changes and so on. Some vocabulary differences for automobile parts in British and American English are listed in table 31.1.

Table 31.1. Dialect differences in automobile vocabulary for British and American English

British English	American English
bonnet	hood
boot	trunk
windscreen	windshield
wing	fender
petrol	gas
headlamp	headlight

Dialect differences include English spoken in the Philippines, Hong Kong, Nigeria, Ghana, Kenya, South Africa, Zimbabwe, India, America, and elsewhere around the world. Each dialect is influenced by other languages spoken in the area as well as by other sociolinguistic factors. In India, for example, people tend to substitute retroflex 'r' for [ɹ]. In the Boston area of the United States the [ɹ] in syllable-final position is dropped. In Boston and some varieties of British English, [ɹ] is inserted between some words. Both are exhibited in the phrase "law and order" [lɔːɹændɔːdə].

There are variations in the sounds of speech that occur over time within speech communities, and in the speech variants of an individual who is a member of a social network. These variations are studied under the rubric of SOCIOPHONETICS which deals with phonetic variations that relate to the use of language in its social context. Included under this general topic are the study of regional and geographical variants (diatopical varieties), social differences of speech (diastratic), and individual (diaphasic) phonetic variations that appear as a result of speaking in different communicative situations.

Several significant phonetic features which contribute to speech variants are introduced in this chapter. These phonetic features may be used in certain contexts to mark a person as a native or non-native speaker of a language. This chapter points to areas for ethnographic and sociolinguistic study in order to discover when a particular speech variant is used and by whom. The information derived from such a study will help you know when to use features appropriately, thus improving your accent when speaking that language.

People have an amazing ability to switch speech variants and styles within one language when in

> When we lived in the village of Ungwar Rimi in Nigeria and were inside the house and heard people speaking outside, without seeing who had come to the house, we could tell whether our children were talking with a Nigerian or with an expatriate because they would fluently switch between Nigerian English and American English when appropriate!

---

[2] A carpenter working at our house routinely pronounced [t, d] for interdental fricatives; otherwise he spoke standard English. Curious about this difference, we inquired where he was from. Though born in Germany, he was of Hungarian descent. It was one minor phonetic difference which gave us the clue that he was not a native speaker of English.

different contexts. For example, when we apply for a job, we are more apt to speak as close to the standard variant as we are able, while, with our friends, we tend to relax and speak with less attention paid to the standard form. What is amazing is that native speakers of a language tend to recognize and accommodate to the variety of their own language with little difficulty. In fact, without some speech variation we would sound rather like speakers of automated speech or "Special English," as is heard on the Voice of America radio, where sentences have been changed to an abnormally slow speech pattern.

Interaction between adjacent language groups or with speakers of the dominant trade language and national language may also lead to speech variants, and potentially to sound change and the emergence of a new dialect. In historical and comparative linguistics the focus of study is on sound change in language over time from a common parent language, often by collecting the same word list from different related dialects and tracking specific sound changes. Comparative linguistics focuses on comparisons of different languages, dialects, and variations of languages. A genetic relationship between languages exists if they are related to a common parent language. Sometimes migration routes can be traced by use of the study of the historical relationship between different dialects and daughter languages of the same PROTO-LANGUAGE.

Another interesting area to study is the development of pidgins and creoles. Pidgins develop when speakers of several mutually unintelligible languages find themselves together and need some language to communicate with. A PIDGIN is a language with a reduced grammatical structure, simplified phonological structure, limited lexicon, and few stylistic features. It is not the native language of any of its speakers. Over time a pidgin language may develop into a CREOLE, a pidgin language that has become the mother tongue of speakers of a language community. By this time additional grammatical and stylistic features have been added.

The IPA provides diacritics with which to write some, though not all, of these modifications to vowels and consonants occurring in speech variants. (Speech pathologists have supplemented the IPA to represent a large number of modifications of what we consider to be normal speech production.) Suppose, however, you find that a certain language is consistently spoken using a particular variant, and that there is no contrast between the meaning of an utterance spoken in that variant and another utterance just like the first except that it is not spoken in that variant. In that case you may want to stop transcribing the specific phonetic detail that represents the variant and include in your notes on the language a careful prose description of the variant; however, if your focus is on that variant, then phonetic details are important.

In rapid speech, inertia takes over with a speaker paying less attention to the precise pronunciation of specific segments. Lass (1984:298) writes that in casual speech, there is increased frequency of assimilation, suppression of boundaries between words, vowel reduction with vowels shortened and moving towards a central position on the vowel chart and even vowel loss, shortening of long segments, and reduction of clusters of sounds.

Some of these speech variants occur regularly, such as American intervocalic [t, d] becoming [ɾ], voiced stops becoming voiceless before silence, or in some cases, even deleted or replaced with a glottal stop, as occurs in some dialects of British English. In some dialects of English final velar nasals are replaced with alveolar ones, such as 'watchin' for 'watching,' and 'happenin' for 'happening' (Hawkins 1984:228).

Speech variants are often the result of some of the following phonetic features: differences in vowel quality; position or range of movement of the tongue, lips or jaw; and use of the nasal cavity; as well as rhythm, speed, pitch register, pitch modulation, volume, and phonation. This list is not exhaustive.

Citation form

To identify an example of a speech variant, consider how you say something in isolation as a *citation form* compared to how you would say it in context. In context pitch, timing, intonation, and other factors emerge as significant in how a particular word is spoken. A citation form differs from how that word is spoken in casual speech, in rapid speech where elisions are present, in formal speech contexts, in fast speech rather than slow speech, in angry speech, in sermons and song, and so forth. Sapir recognized this difference between the citation form and its use in connected speech: "In watching my Nootka interpreter write his language, I often had the curious feeling that he was transcribing an ideal flow of phonetic elements which he heard, inadequately from a purely objective standpoint, as the intention of the actual rumble of speech" (Sapir 1921, as quoted in Lass 1984:297).

Systemic differences

As you study speech variants between two speech communities or within one speech community, you may find that there are systemic differences. For example, between different dialects the entire vowel system may have changed. This is illustrated by the differences between the vowel systems of Scottish English versus RP. In Scottish English there are nine basic vowels with four vowel glides: [i ɪ e ɛ a ɔ o u ʌ ʌi ae ʌu ɔe], and in RP there are ten vowels with five vowel glides [i ɪ ɛ æ ɑ ɒ ɔ ʉ u ʌ eɪ oʉ aɪ aʊ ɒɪ] (Hawkins 1984:239).

Systemic dialectal differences exist between Tyap and Jju, two closely related sister languages of the same proto-Plateau language in Nigeria. In Jju there are far more fortis-lenis consonant contrasts and two contrastive tones, while in Tyap there are fewer fortis-lenis consonants and three contrastive tones. That difference is sufficient to make these two dialects mutually unintelligible, even though on the Benue-Congo comparative word list the number of COGNATES between these two languages is very high. A further systemic difference between these two closely related languages is that the noun class system has been simplified in Tyap while in Jju the noun class system is more complex.

When there are systemic differences in the phonetic system, it tends to affect only part of the system, with other aspects remaining the same (Hawkins 1984:240). The differences between dialects and speech variants may be very selective between how different phones are realized. For example, there may be a phonetic difference between two vowels in one context that is neutralized in another context.

Vowels

A very common distinction between speech variants is in the pronunciation of vowels, i.e., a difference in vowel quality. For example, a Bostonian is likely to use the open front vowel [a], where speakers of standard American English would use the open back vowel [ɑ]. Speakers of southern American English will likely not glide vowels that are glided in standard English, e.g., 'I' may be pronounced as [ɐ] rather than as [ɐⁱ]. Vowel pronunciation differences are evident in the distinctions between Australian, British, New Zealand, and American English.

In order for you to discover pronunciation differences, ask people from different parts of the country how they pronounce certain words such as 'cot' and 'caught,' and 'tot' and 'taught.' You will likely find that those from the West coast of the United States pronounce the first one of each pair with a vowel very close to the vowel in the second set, while those from the East coast are more apt to make a greater distinction. Minnesotan is also a well-defined regional variant that is evident in the pronunciation of these pairs of words. (For an example of dialect differences see the sidebox.)

Y'all please come

One of our friends, originally from Arkansas, had also lived in Louisiana and Texas, then moved to San Diego, California. She got a job working at K-Mart where there are routine "blue light specials," sales of short duration, announced over the store's public address system. On one occasion she was asked to announce the blue light special. She began by saying, "Would y'all please come to the sweater rack where we're having a blue light special." Someone very quickly came and took the microphone out of her hand, as her Southern dialect was not considered acceptable and was jarring on local ears. 'Y'all' is not recognized as the correct second person plural subject form of 'you.'

Sound distribution between variants

Some variants of languages and dialects have differences in distribution of the same sound. In other words, both have the same phones, but where they occur differs. For example, both RP and most dialects of American English have the sound [ɹ], but the distribution of that phone differs. In RP it occurs only word initially, whereas in standard American English it occurs in word initial and word final positions. For example, 'car' is [kʰɑː] in British English, but [kʰɑɹ] in American English. Usually these distributional differences are quite regular.

Rate of speech

Phoneticians often distinguish between the RATE OF SPEECH, with SLOW casual speech contrasting with FAST speech, and other rates in between these two. In fast speech, assimilation of two sounds at the same place of articulation or even deletion of one of the sounds may occur. For example, in slow casual speech one might say 'Did you enjoy it?' while in fast speech it may come out as 'Djin joy it?' Sometimes, as in this example, a vowel may be deleted. Some of the constraints in syllable patterns may be violated, yet there is sufficient redundancy present in the speech wave and the context that people usually still understand what was spoken.

The rate of speech, especially fast speech, may result in de-stressing function words and even their reduction. According to Dogil, this destressing and reduction in the form of function words also applies to determiners, complementizers, and conjunctions (1984:94).

Stylistic differences

The remainder of this chapter describes contrasting speech styles.[3] These include styles varying due to lip, tongue, and jaw positions, faucalization, nasalization, rhythm, pitch register and modulation, volume, and different types of phonation.

Lip position

Lip position may be used in certain social situations to signify emotions or moods. For example, Spanish speakers may use LIP ROUNDING to show pity, e.g., *pobrecito,* 'you poor little one'. English speakers may do something similar, as in 'oh, don't pout.' Lip rounding is apt to be used when speaking "baby talk" in American English. In contrast to lip rounding, there can be protruding lips, or SPREAD LIPS.

Tongue position

In some speech variants people speak with the tongue positioned further forward. For example, in English when people speak to a baby, they may use this speech style, e.g., 'coochi coochi coo.' This occurs together with lip rounding. Different tongue positions, FRONTED or BACKED, cause interesting differences in speech, as seen in cartoon and other media characters, e.g., Bugs Bunny, Fred Flintstone, Elmer Fudd, Yogi Bear, and Kermit the Frog.

Jaw position

For pronunciation of some languages, the jaw is held in a fairly set position and moves little (SET JAW). For others, the jaw may move more freely, involving a great deal of motion (FREE JAW). These jaw positions affect the tongue height of vowels more than anything else. Languages with a set jaw speech variant, such as Seminole, tend to have vowels in a narrower, closer area of the vowel space, while languages with a free jaw will vary their vowels over a wider range of vertical tongue positions (West 1962). How freely the jaw moves can sometimes indicate the speaker's mood, formality, or some other extra-linguistic factor. For example, when Seminole speakers become excited or when they are speaking carefully for the benefit of a stranger, they are likely to deviate from this set jaw position. People sometimes exaggerate the amount of jaw motion when speaking to foreigners, thus seeking to be clear and understandable.

---

[3] Some styles included here have been taught traditionally in SIL phonetics courses. Some should be re-evaluated based on what we know about phonetics and phonology today, even though you may find them useful in the fieldwork context. Other styles described in literature from the field have been added to the traditional ones.

Faucalization

The FAUCAL PILLARS, two pairs of muscles that run vertically at the back of the oral cavity, are used to move the velum up and down. One pair is in front of the uvula, and the other is behind the uvula. Tensing one or both pairs of these muscles, thereby narrowing the vocal tract in that region, faucalizes speech sounds. Speech by the cartoon character, Bugs Bunny, "What's up, doc?," is an example of FAUCALIZATION.

Nasalization

Speech sounds may be nasalized by having the nasal port open wider for longer intervals than for the standard variant, giving them a quality of HYPERNASALITY. Alternatively, modifying speech sounds by having the nasal port open less widely and for shorter intervals than for the standard variant gives them a quality of HYPONASALITY. There is also a singing style among some religious groups that is nasalized.

These descriptions most accurately characterize nasalization phenomena when the nasal passageway is clear. Nasal congestion complicates the phenomena. However, nasal congestion does not prevent sounds from being nasalized at all; since nasal congestion usually does not fill the nasal cavity, opening the nasal port still adds another chamber to the oral acoustical configuration of vowels and semivowels, giving them a nasalized quality.

Rhythm

Using STRESS TIMING instead of SYLLABLE TIMING will produce a radical variant of a language. For example, a person whose native language is Spanish may speak English with syllable timing, resulting in a variant of English that may not be very intelligible to a mother tongue speaker of English.

Pitch register

Differences in PITCH REGISTER may be used as a speech variant. For example, a person gossiping in Jju speaks in a lower pitch register than for other social situations. The drop in pitch register indicates to the hearers that what they are about to hear is gossip or information that is disapproved of. Note the comparable English expression, 'He lowered his voice.'

It is interesting to note that Fulani women of Nigeria tend to speak with a much higher pitch register than Fulani men, higher than would be expected based on the usual fundamental frequency differences between men's and women's voices. (See chapter 33 for more on fundamental frequency.)

A high-pitched voice is used to show respect and honor as well as politeness to those of a higher social status than the speaker among the Zapotec speakers of Santa María Lachixío in Mexico. Persons (1997:59–60) writes,

> Actual speaking in high voice varies from individual to individual. While some speakers raise their pitch an octave, others seem to raise it as high as their larynxes will allow. Speaking in a higher pitch is the important thing; how much so is immaterial. When speaking in high voice, no voice quality changes occur, such as laryngealization or breathiness.

Santa María Lachixío speakers begin teaching their children to use this voice quality from age four on. They assert that it is easier to teach their girls than their boys. It is obligatory for children to address their godparents and their godparents' children who are older than fifteen with a high-pitched voice in order to show respect and honor.

In certain situations, people switch to a falsetto voice. This higher pitch register is often heard in song.

Pitch modulation

PITCH MODULATION is used to reflect our moods and emotions, or sometimes the socioeconomic class we belong to. Speakers of some languages use a WIDE RANGE of pitches, varying from very high to very low within one sentence. Other speech variants use a NARROW PITCH RANGE. Some people even speak in a MONOTONE. This is especially true when an individual has suffered injury to a certain part of the brain.

Commonly, speaking in a monotone would mean that there is no pitch variation. In speech situations, however, it does not mean that there is no variation of the pitch frequency, nor even that a listener cannot discern any rise or fall in the pitch of the speaker's voice. Ordinary human ability to identify very tiny changes in pitch exceeds human ability to maintain a constant pitch when speaking.

Volume

Loudness or softness of speech may indicate social class, mood, or a specific situation. When we call someone, we tend to raise the VOLUME of our voices. For example, a Bajju person uses a high rising tone and louder volume when calling another Bajju. And when a Jju speaker is drunk, the volume tends to increase. It is interesting that non-Yoruba (Nigeria) speakers often mistakenly think that the Yoruba are angry because they speak loudly in many situations. Rather, the non-Yoruba are hearing a Yoruba speech variant that uses a loud volume.

Among the Hausa (Nigeria) an emir or paramount chief will speak quietly to his spokesman who in turn will shout out to the audience what the emir has said. By speaking quietly the emir is maintaining his dignity and high position within the culture.

Contrast these speech patterns with the pattern a person might use when talking softly to their neighbor at a concert or in a church service. In that case the volume may shift so low that the person may even whisper.

Different types of phonation

Breathy or creaky voice may be used in different speech variants. J. Crawford found that Mixe speakers used breathy voice when they were excited or when they wanted to emphasize something, and creaky voice when asking to borrow money (Bickford and Floyd 2003:126).

Mikasuki, a case study

Now that we have discussed various phonetic features which contribute to speech variants, it is instructive to see how these various phonetic features combine in one language, namely Mikasuki, also called Seminole, spoken in Florida primarily on the Big Cypress, Hollywood and Miccosukee reservations, as well as by smaller groups in the Everglades in Dade and Collier counties.[4] This section is based on the work of David West (1962), who studied the language extensively.

Mikasuki speakers tend to speak with their lips spread and the pitch lower than is typical in English. West noted that in nervous or excited speech the pitch registers are far apart and stress is prominent. He pointed out that in sermons preachers use a speech variant that builds up to a climax. In building up the degrees of stress, the levels of tone are minimized. Gradually at the climax the volume becomes very loud and "the whole pause group may appear to be spoken almost on a monotone with syllable-timed rhythm rather than stress-timed rhythm. In these conditions, there is no perceptible step-down of pitch between rhythm groups. However, the end of a pause group is marked by a pause and a sharp drop in pitch" (1962:90).

---

[4] The word *Seminole* seems not to have been widely used prior to 1750. Rather, there were the Yamassee Native Americans who originated in the Carolinas and who moved to Florida in 1715, and the Hitchiti-speaking Oconee who migrated along the Apalachicola River. The word *Seminole* translates as 'wild' or 'undomesticated'. The word *Mikasuki* used here derives from the name of the dialect the Hitchiti speakers used (Garbarino 1972:1).

West also noted a difference in speech variants between slow and fast speech. In slow, very precise speech, consonants and consonant clusters are lengthened, additional allophones of consonants occur, a voiced lateral may become a lateral flap, and short transition vowels do not occur. By contrast, in fast speech "syllables with high tone and those with glide tone seem to become more stressed, while those with mid tone become less so" (1962:91). West stated, "In slow, deliberate speech, transition [vowels]…do not occur. Instead, the first member of the cluster may be lengthened, or, if it is a stop, it may be slightly aspirated" (1962:90–91).

This case study demonstrates that the phonetic features of stress, pitch, syllable timing versus stress timing, a voiced lateral versus a lateral flap, and consonant lengthening contribute to produce speech variants. The particular speech variants mentioned include sermon variant preaching, and fast and slow speech. It is an interesting case study because many linguists fail to write about different speech variants in field languages, but West took careful note of these stylistic phonetic features in Mikasuki.

How to acquire a good accent

In order to acquire a good accent in another language, it is important for a language learner to pay attention to and mimic the speech variants that native speakers use. Kenneth L. Pike captures the essence of this in the following paragraphs (italics added, 1942:1–3).

> A person who wishes to learn to speak any language with an accent like that of its native speakers must constantly focus his attention on three things:
>
> *He must listen attentively.* In every conversation he must listen to individual sounds and to the sentence melodies of the language. He must compare these sounds and melodies with [those of] his own [language]. He can then use features native to the language he is learning rather than foreign sounds from his own language.
>
> *He must learn to be a mimic.* If we mimic our friends in our own language, we may insult them. They won't like it. But in a foreign language the opposite is true. The more we can mimic the people whose language we wish to learn, and the closer we can come to their pronunciation, the better. If we sound exactly like them, they are pleased, never offended. They don't like to have us sound different and 'weird'. So do not be afraid to mimic the native speakers you listen to. Repeat utterances after them, [do simultaneous tracking of tapes], and try to sound exactly the same. People will not mind but will be [honored].
>
> *Learn how sounds are made.* We need to know how the sounds of our own language are made. We can then make a transfer from our own sounds to those of the language we are learning. Further, we must know the patterns in which the voice seems to 'sing' as it talks, so we can learn the intonation of the native speakers.
>
> Above all, *we must listen, listen carefully, and mimic well*. If we wish to have a good accent, we must not be afraid to mimic people.
>
> *Readjustment of habits.* The intricate movements used to make the sounds of one's own language form themselves into ironclad patterns, nearly unbreakable habits. It is very difficult to change them. In order to turn from one language to another and have a good accent in each, one must be able to make rapid changes both in the basic, sweeping articulatory placements, and in the detailed differences. To prepare for this change, one needs articulatory calisthenics to weaken old muscular habits. Oral gymnastics facilitate the readjustment of old methods of forming sounds, so as to produce new habits.

Pike's advice given above is well worth the effort to implement when learning a language. When you do so you may well learn more about the language that will help your language learning and analysis.

31: Speech Variants, Accents, Dialects, and Sociophonetics

Key terms

accent
dialect
speech variants, speech style
standard speech style
sociophonetics
proto-language
pidgin, creole
cognates
rate of speech: rapid, normal, slow
tongue position: fronted, backed

lip position: rounded, spread
jaw position: set, free
faucalization, faucal pillars
hypernasality, hyponasality
rhythm: stress-timed, syllable-timed
pitch register: ranges from high to low
pitch modulation: wide range, narrow range, monotone
volume: ranges from loud to soft
state of vocal folds: breathiness, creakiness

Exercises

1. Practice the following limericks in British and standard American dialects. After doing so, try some of the other speech styles discussed in this chapter (rapid speech, slow speech, breathy voice, creaky voice, faucalized voice, syllable timed, nasalized voice, and a wide pitch register) with these limericks (authors unknown):

   There was a pious young priest
     who lived almost solely on yeast.
   For he said, "It is plain
     we must all rise again,
     and I plan to get started at least."

   There was an old man of Peru
     who dreamt he was eating his shoe.
   He woke in the night
     in a terrible fright
     and found it was perfectly true.

   There was a young lad of Quebec
     who was buried in snow to his neck.
   When asked "Are you friz?"
     He replied, "Yes, I is,
     but we don't call this cold in Quebec."

   A tutor who tooted a flute
     once taught two young tooters to toot.
   Said the two to the tutor,
     "Which is harder – to toot, or to
     tutor two tooters to toot?"

2. Define the following:

   a. speech variants or speech styles _____

   b. dialects _____

   c. accents _____

   d. sociophonetics _____

   e. pidgin _____

   f. creole _____

32

Palatography

PALATOGRAPHY is a procedure used to determine the active and passive articulators for a particular consonant. Knowing the precise articulatory details of the production of a specific consonant helps identify the place of articulation for a sound you may have found puzzling. It may also help describe accurately what you have discovered about the phonetic detail of a sound.

Ladefoged (1957) pioneered the type of palatography discussed here. He called it *direct palatography,* because in this procedure the researcher views directly the places on the tongue and the palate that touch each other during a given articulation.

Palatography is best used when studying in detail the pronunciation of a single speaker for sounds made with the tongue. When doing palatography the fieldworker studies the speaker's pronunciation of one sound in several different contexts, such as looking at the place of articulation of the consonant when it is adjacent to different vowels. For example, a researcher may investigate the different places of the articulation for English /k/, as [c] in 'key', [k] in 'coo' and in some dialects, [q] in 'caw'.

A PALATOGRAM is a two-dimensional display. As such, it fails to indicate the shape of the tongue, i.e., whether it is grooved or flat in the production of sibilants.[1]

It is much more difficult to use palatograms to study different speakers' pronunciation of the same consonant. While trained listeners may agree that the pronunciations of two speakers making the same consonant are auditory equivalents, they may produce that same sound quite differently. In English there is a good deal of variation in the pronunciation of the same sound. This is true in other languages as well.

Researchers have used many different instrumental procedures in studying the articulation of consonants. Direct palatography is one that is relatively simple to learn and easy to perform, and the results are often informative. The supplies and equipment required for direct palatography are easily portable and the procedure requires no power except for batteries for a flashlight and an optional camera. Thus the procedure is well suited for use in remote field locations.

Human subjects research

Palatography involves invasive research into a human subject's mouth. As such a fieldworker must follow appropriate protocol concerning human subjects research. (See chapter 34 in which human subjects research and informed consent are described more fully.) These procedures require obtaining

---

[1] There are two ways to deal with this. One is to make a cast of the palate, and then draw contour lines on it that correspond to the cast of the palate you made. Second, you could paint barium sulfate on the tongue, and then have an x-ray taken of it. This will help particularly when you are puzzled about how the speaker is pronouncing a particular consonant. Even if you do not make a cast of the palate or use barium sulfate painted on the tongue, you can still use palatography profitably.

approval from the institution you work for, and their Institutional Review Board (IRB), prior to conducting field research. You will explain the procedure very carefully to the individuals who are to serve as subjects of the research. The positive and possible negative consequences of the research must be included in your explanation. The subjects must sign an appropriate informed consent form that states that they agree to the procedure, and that they may discontinue participation in this procedure at any time without prejudice to themselves.[2]

Materials and equipment

The equipment and supplies for palatography are inexpensive and relatively easy to acquire. In order to do direct palatography, the following materials and equipment are needed:

- A few teaspoons of charcoal powder, available from a pharmacy, hopefully as a powder. Capsules of powdered charcoal can be opened and the powder poured out. If only charcoal tablets are available, they can be crushed into a fine powder by using a coffee grinder, food processor, blender, food chopper, or even a hammer or rolling pin. When using a hammer or rolling pin, put the tablets in a plastic bag so that the powder is contained.
- Olive oil.
- A small paintbrush to apply the charcoal and olive oil mixture to the palate or the tongue.[3]
- Two mirrors, one about 4 cm x 10 cm, to serve as a "mouth mirror." Such mirrors are sold as pocket mirrors. Preferably the edges should be covered with something to protect the mouth when the mirror is inserted into the speaker's mouth—a narrow plastic frame around the edges, tape, or a coating of epoxy are all workable alternatives. A coating of epoxy or some other means for protecting the reflective coating is also needed on the back of the mirror. A second, larger, hand-held mirror can be used for the speaker to check the mixture application for himself.
- A digital camera with a close-up lens, mounted on a fixed tripod with a flash unit underneath it. This is needed only if you want a permanent record of the palatogram, a record of where the articulation occurred on the speaker's palate. A ring flash, which encircles the lens, would be better than the usual kind of flash unit, if available. Make sure that what you rent will work with the particular camera and lens length you are using.
- A flashlight to see the palate.
- A removable artificial palate to fit into the mouth of the language speaker (optional).

Procedure for palatography

The basic procedure of direct palatography begins with coating either the palate (or false palate) or the tongue with some dark mixture of charcoal and olive oil. Then the speaker says a word with the focused consonant in it; the word you choose for the speaker to pronounce will be one where the tongue touches the palate with only the articulation being investigated. The basic principle of palatography is that when the tongue touches the palate, either the upper articulator transfers the coating to the lower articulator or vice versa. Then, by looking into the mouth to view where the coating has been rubbed off and where it has been rubbed onto, you can identify the active and passive articulators and thus determine the place of articulation. These procedures are explained in more detail in Ladefoged 1997.

The following are steps in making a palatogram:

1. Submit your research protocol involving palatography to have it approved by a Human Subjects Review Board of the institution sponsoring your research, and receive their approval. Your research proposal should include a human subject's informed consent form. This form should list the procedures to be performed and any possible risks and benefits involved with

---

[2] In some cases, it is culturally inappropriate or otherwise impractical to have a signed statement. In such cases, a digital oral recording of informed consent may be made.

[3] In the past phoneticians have used a powder insufflator to puff a mixture of powdered charcoal and chocolate onto the roof of the mouth. Today insufflators are difficult to obtain, so that procedure is largely obsolete.

this experimental procedure. Further, it should specify that the language speaker(s) may discontinue involvement in the research at any time without prejudice to himself.[4]

2. Choose a language speaker who agrees to take part in this procedure, preferably someone who has a sense of humor.
3. Go over the informed consent form with him and ask him to sign it.
4. Review the steps together before you begin the procedure, so that he feels comfortable, knowing in advance what will happen. It may be helpful to demonstrate by making a palatogram on yourself before proceeding with your helper. By experimenting on yourself, you demonstrate to the native speaker what is involved in the procedure.
5. Assemble all the materials for this experiment. If you are going to do palatography with more than one speaker in a given session, you should have some means for sterilizing the mouth mirror between sessions. Have more than one small brush so that you do not use the same brush on different subjects. Have separate containers for each subject's powdered charcoal and olive oil mixture.
6. Have your camera positioned on a tripod, ready to photograph the palate.
7. Decide before beginning this procedure what one consonant articulation you want to make a palatogram of. The sound should be one where the tongue touches the roof of the mouth, because palatography is helpful when looking at places of articulation for consonants, from dental to velar or possibly even uvular. The segment in focus is then placed in a word, for example, [sæpʰ] 'sap' in English. The word should not contain any other consonants that involve the tongue touching the front teeth or the roof of the mouth, e.g. English [stɪl] 'still' would not be a good choice because the tongue touches the palate for all three consonants. You may also place vowels on each side of the target sound, for example, Jju [aʃʲaː] 'Did you find it?'.
8. Mix the powdered charcoal and olive oil. Tell the speaker what the black powder is, and that it is not harmful. He might want to taste it before you paint it on his tongue or the roof of his mouth. If he does, have him rinse his mouth thoroughly afterwards, before continuing with the rest of the procedure.
9. Have the speaker practice the test word several times before proceeding with the experiment.
10. Ask the speaker to moisten his upper teeth and his hard and soft palate. Next paint the mixture onto his palate or the tongue. If the tongue is painted, be sure that the tip of the tongue is coated with the mixture. From this time on he should not swallow until the procedure is over.
11. Have the speaker say the test word three times. He should not say anything else besides the test word; if he does, the palatogram will need to be redone. After producing the test word, the language speaker should leave his mouth open so that the passive and active articulators can be identified.
12. Insert the small mirror into the speaker's mouth to the velum in order to see where the mixture has been removed from the palate or the roof of his mouth; this will be the place of articulation showing on the passive articulator. When you insert the mirror, place it far enough in to see the passive articulator, but not so far as to cause a gag reflex. If the palate was painted, use the flashlight to see exactly where the mixture has been removed from the roof of the mouth during the production of the test word. The mixture removed from the palate will be on the tongue, showing the precise location of the active articulator. The procedure can also be done by painting the mixture on the tongue and, after saying the test word as above, observing where the mixture has been removed from the tongue and transferred to the palate. The speaker may also want to see his tongue and palate with the larger mirror or both mirrors together.
13. For a record of this palatogram, photograph the speaker's palate either directly or photograph its reflection in the mirror. You may want to photograph his tongue so that the active articulator can be identified. Have him put his tongue as far out as is comfortable, then photograph it. Since the speaker will likely be salivating by this point, have your camera positioned directly in front of the speaker's mouth and focused so that you can take the picture(s) quickly. Some phoneticians use a video camera for this purpose. Two advantages of a video camera—or a

---

[4] We refer to the speaker as 'he' here for simplicity, but the speaker could also be a woman.

digital camera—are that 1) a zoom lens can be used so that the camera does not have to be too close for comfort to the subject and 2) the input can be fed directly into a computer for further processing.⁵

14. The speaker may now rinse his mouth, swallow, and talk again. Repeat this process for any other consonants you want to focus on.
15. Repeat this procedure with other speakers so that you are able to make statements about how the places of articulation of specific speakers reasonably correlate with how speakers in that speech community say particular words.
16. If you plan to publish your results, develop a diagram that shows the shape of the particular speaker's mouth in the form of a sagittal section. There are various ways to do so. One is to make an impression of the oral cavity using alginate impression material such as dentists use. Mix an adequate quantity of this material and place it on the back of the mirror used in viewing the roof of the subject's mouth. Have the subject lean forward slightly, and insert the mirror with the alginate material on it into the mouth. The mirror should be placed firmly against the upper teeth. The goal is to obtain an impression of the shape of the upper lip, and the curvature of the palate. When you find that the material around the lip is firm, then remove the impression from the mouth. You may find that you have to move it slightly back and forth and raise and lower it slightly so that the seal to the roof of the mouth is broken. If you plan to keep this impression for an indefinite length of time, immerse it in water so that it does not dry and shrink. Cut the impression in half at the midsagittal plane, thus giving you a diagram of the upper shape of the lips and the soft palate. From that you can make a sagittal diagram that reflects that of the subject's mouth.

> *An interesting evening's work*
>
> "Part of the joy of palatography is that it is possible to improvise and get some data without being too elaborate. At a party I once met a speaker of Basque who said that he distinguished a dental [s̪] from an alveolar [s], a distinction I wanted to observe.
>
> "I borrowed a small hand mirror, and made some charcoal by burning a piece of toast and scraping the black parts onto a flat surface. I ground them into a fine powder using a beer bottle as a rolling pin. There was some olive oil in the kitchen to mix with the powder, and a cotton swab served as a paintbrush. Lacking a camera, I looked into his mouth and sketched what I could see. An interesting evening's work." (Ladefoged 2003:38)

The use of palatography may be undertaken quite easily when doing phonetic research in a field situation. Powdered charcoal can usually be obtained from any pharmacy or chemist, as it is used to treat diarrhea. So obtaining the materials for palatography should not be a problem; however, you may want to bring the mirror with you because it may be difficult to find a properly shaped mirror. At the same time we recognize that people can be incredibly creative in field situations where some fieldworkers may use a glass-cutter to cut a mirror to the right size.

Palatography is an easy and painless way to find the place of articulation of oral consonants. We commend it to you.

Key terms

palatography, palatogram   test word

Exercises

1. Decide which of the following would make a good test word for use in palatography. Check either yes or no. Explain why it would make a good test word or why it would not.

---

⁵ The zoom feature on digital cameras also helps in positioning the camera.

32: Palatography

	Yes	No	If not, then why not? If it would make a good test word, why would it?
[zifɑ]			
[bañɪ]			
[ʒ]			
[meɫo]			
[izi]			

2. Look up *palatography* on the Internet. Describe various techniques phoneticians have used and applications they have made of palatography.

33

Acoustic Phonetics

In the previous chapters sounds have been presented according to how they are produced within the vocal tract, in terms of their articulation. Speech sounds may also be described according to their acoustic structure, that is, how our ears hear them. This chapter gives a brief introduction to the basic concepts of acoustic phonetics, at least sufficient for a field linguist to know when it would be helpful to study particular sounds and pitch patterns acoustically. Then we explore some of the ways in which a linguistic fieldworker can use computer programs, such as sound editors and speech analysis programs, to analyze speech sound waves.

ACOUSTIC PHONETICS is the study of the physical characteristics of the speech sound wave as it is produced in one person's vocal apparatus and radiates outward to another person's ears. This area of phonetics studies instrumental and computer representations of speech sounds. It is a part of the study of acoustics, the branch of physics that studies sound.

When studying a specific set of sounds in a language, a field linguist wants to know exactly what is happening. Is one sound longer than another? Does the pitch rise, fall, or remain level? What is the acoustic difference between two utterances? Is there a short vowel present or is there a syllabic lateral or nasal? What acoustic features are present when we perceive that one syllable is more stressed than another? All these questions and many more may be answered by acoustic analysis.

It is useful for a field linguist to understand some fundamentals of the relationships between how a speech sound is produced, and its physical and acoustic characteristics. For example, if you have difficulty *hearing* the exact difference between two words, you may be able to *see* the difference on a sound SPECTROGRAM. The spectrogram will be described later in this chapter. Also, if you understand how different articulations produce similar sounds, you can give plausible explanations for your phonological analysis.

Four important ways in which you may perceive speech sounds as being different from one another are these: one speech sound may be perceived as being longer than another; it may have a different pitch than another sound; it may be louder than the other; or it may have a different quality. Each of these differences may be studied acoustically.

Vibration and speech sounds

SOUND is a vibration of particles, and a speech sound is vibration of air particles. Sound vibration consists of longitudinal or compression waves in which air particles are displaced; it is started by some source of energy. For example, in a voiced sound, the source of energy is a pulse of air coming up through the glottis. This GLOTTAL PULSE gives the air just above the glottis a sudden shove upward, which in turn shoves the air above it upward, and so on. It is not a steady shove. The displacement of the air just above the glottis propagates through the vocal tract as a SOUND WAVE.

It is similar to when you clap your hands, in which most of the sound energy released into the air is produced at the moment when your hands make contact with each other. Similarly, most of the energy in a voiced speech sound is injected into the vocal tract at the glottis at the moment that the vocal folds come together, closing the glottis.

Each glottal pulse causes the air in the vocal tract to vibrate for a small fraction of a second. In normal voicing, very similar glottal pulses follow, one after another, at fairly regular intervals. Before the vibration caused by one pulse fades away completely, the next pulse sets the air in vibration again with renewed energy. Thus the vibrations continually repeat so long as voicing continues. Figure 33.1 illustrates the repetitive shape of the speech wave of a voiced vowel.

When glottal pulses enter the vocal tract, they cause the air in the vocal tract to echo back and forth briefly due to RESONANCES. Resonances are secondary vibrations of a sound at particular frequencies according to the rate of vibration of the vocal folds and the size and shape of the resonator; in speech the resonator is the vocal tract. Thus, when the sound emerges from the mouth, it has ripples whose intervals in time and space depend on the shape and size of the various parts of the vocal tract at that moment, as well as on the shape of the glottal pulse. The relative size of the ripples in the sound wave directly affects our perception of how loud the sound is. The shape of the speech wave emanating from the speaker's vocal tract and impinging on a listener's eardrums determines the PHONETIC QUALITY of the sound perceived by the listener. The rates at which the air particles vibrate back and forth allow us to perceive the sound as being a particular vowel or consonant.

The speech wave

As a person speaks, he produces an acoustic speech wave of energy which radiates outward from his vocal tract and quickly fades away. The shape of this speech sound wave depends upon what that person did with his vocal apparatus to produce the sound. By examining various characteristics of a speech wave you may find out more about what he did to produce that sound than you can by merely listening with your ears, fine instruments though they are.

When sound emanates from the lip opening, it radiates outward in a fading spherical ripple pattern, much like the circular ripples on the surface of water when a pebble is tossed into it. (Reverberation which is in the speaker's environment, e.g., echoes from hard surfaces such as walls of a room, may be significant, causing blurring of speech sounds.)

Formants

It is helpful to think of the vocal tract as an air-filled tube which acts as a resonator. It has certain natural frequencies of vibration which respond to the sound wave produced by the glottis. A resonance of the vocal tract is called a FORMANT, and the rate at which the air vibrates due to that resonance is called its FORMANT FREQUENCY. The vocal tract has several formants. Each formant resonance contributes to the shape of the speech sound WAVEFORM. The first three formants with the lowest frequencies are the most important in determining our perception of vowel quality and the place of articulation of a consonant.

Speech waveform

A speech waveform is readily seen on a computer as an output of a speech analyzer computer program as in figure 33.1.[1] In the following waveforms, the vertical axis represents amplitude, measured in decibels (dB), and the horizontal axis represents time, measured in milliseconds (msec).

---

[1] Recordings for figures 33.1, 33.2, 33.3 are of Norris McKinney in 1965–1970.

33: Acoustic Phonetics

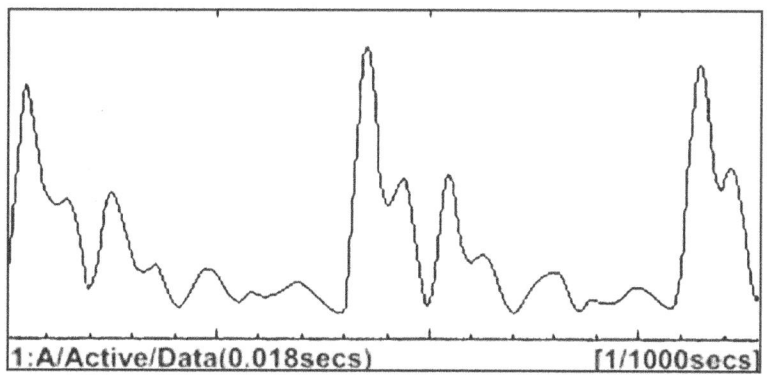

Figure 33.1. The waveform during a brief interval in N. McKinney's pronunciation of the vowel [ɔ] in [ɔɹ̯eɪntʃɨs] 'oranges'.

In figure 33.1 you can see the variations in air pressure during a little more than two repetitions of the waveform, corresponding to two glottal pulses. In this display the air pressure variations were transformed into an electrical signal by a microphone, and captured and displayed by speech analysis software. The air pressure variations are directly related to the movement of the air particles.

The waveform repetitions here are not exact replicas of one another; there are always measurable differences between speech sounds, even from one glottal pulse to the next. However, the repetitions or CYCLES, are very similar, so we can identify and measure the PERIOD, i.e., the duration of one cycle of the waveform. In this case a single cycle spans about eight divisions along the horizontal scale or eight milliseconds (8 msec = 0.008 sec). Dividing the period into the integer one (because we measured the duration of exactly one cycle) will give us the rate of repetition of the waveform (i.e., the rate at which the vocal folds vibrate), namely its FUNDAMENTAL FREQUENCY, symbolized as F_0. Thus the fundamental frequency of the wave in figure 33.1 is F_0 = 1 cycle / 0.008 sec = 125 cycles per second. The term for *cycles per second* is HERTZ, abbreviated *Hz*, thus in this example, F_0 = 125 Hz.

The differences in pitch of the voices of men, women, and children correlate with the average fundamental frequencies of their voices. The median fundamental frequency for men ranges from 134 to 146 Hz; for women, 199 to 295 Hz; and for children, usually higher (Lehiste 1970:58). These differences in fundamental frequency relate to the length of, and tension on, the vocal folds. In addition, fundamental frequency increases when the subglottal pressure is increased due to air built up below the vocal folds. Greater subglottal pressure release is the primary determinant of loudness.

Figure 33.2 illustrates the random shape of the speech wave of a voiceless sibilant. It shows the random air turbulence of noise.

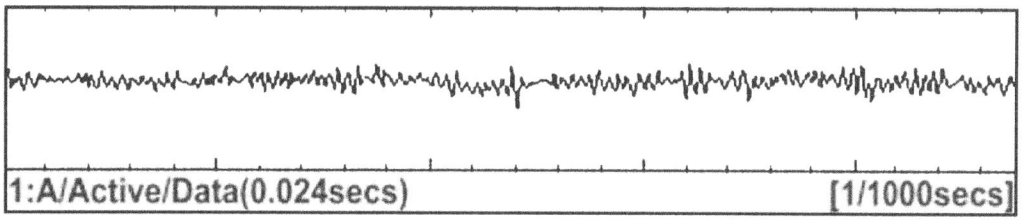

Figure 33.2. The waveform during a brief interval in N. McKinney's pronunciation of the voiceless sibilant [s] in [ɔɹ̯eɪntʃɨs] 'oranges'.

If we wish to examine the acoustic waveform for a longer period of time, e.g., for the duration of a complete utterance, we can compress the horizontal time scale and get a display such as that in figure 33.3.

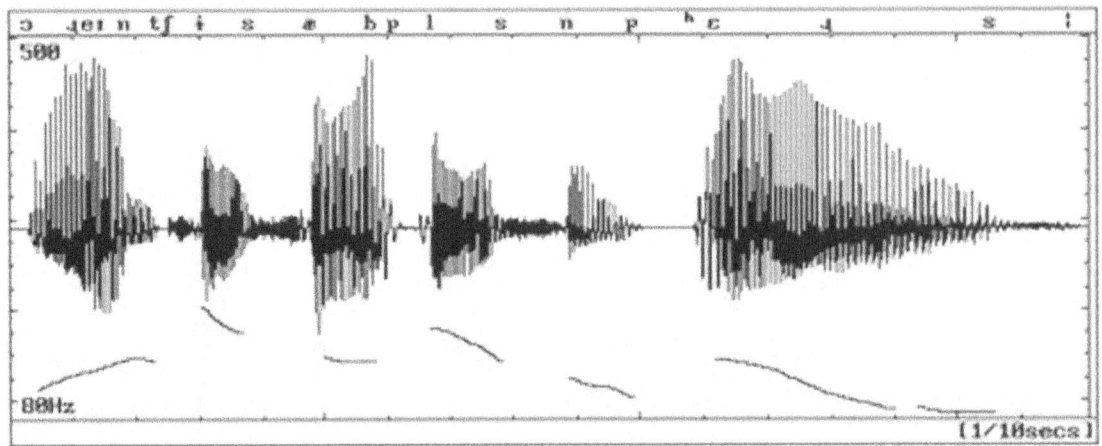

Figure 33.3. The waveform of the phrase 'oranges, apples, and pears'.

In figure 33.3 each character in the phonetic transcription along the top is aligned along the horizontal axis from the beginning of the waveform. The discontinuous curve in the lower part of the figure shows the fundamental frequency (pitch frequency) of the sound wave which corresponds to the rate at which the vocal folds vibrate; this is perceived as tone or intonation. The horizontal scale is 0.1 sec per division, and the vertical scale for the frequency curve is 25 Hz per division. Notice that the pitches are moving either upward or in a falling pattern. Even when we perceive that a pitch is level, we may see that it is actually glided because of the acoustic signal shown.

In figure 33.3 the [p] in 'apples' was partially voiced as seen by the continuation of the waveform. It also becomes clear, by looking at short portions of the waveform and listening to the corresponding sounds, that the pluralizing [s] at the end of each noun was voiceless.

In most cases, each small vertical line along the top or bottom of the waveform corresponds to a single glottal pulse, or one repetition of the waveform of the speech sound. Thus in the middle of 'orange' there are about eight cycles in an interval of about 0.06 sec or 0.07 sec. Dividing the number of cycles by the time interval during which they occurred gives us a fundamental frequency of about 125 Hz. Similarly, in the [æ] of 'apples' there are about thirteen pulses in an interval of about 0.09 sec, giving a fundamental frequency of about 145 Hz. While it may be possible to determine fundamental frequency in this way, it is not nearly as convenient as reading the fundamental frequency from calculations made by the computer software program, such as the ones represented by the curves below the waveform in figure 33.3.

By examining speech waveforms we can also often identify segment boundaries and measure segment duration, distinguish voiced from voiceless sounds, measure voice onset time, and sometimes identify the manner of articulation of a sound, i.e., whether it is a fricative, stop, affricate, lateral, approximant, nasal, or vowel. It is very difficult to identify the quality of a sound from the waveform. For example, compare the words 'apples' and 'pears.' It would be very difficult to describe the difference between the waveforms of [æ] and of [ɛ] in a way that would enable us to recognize these two sounds in other words. The same is probably true of [ɨ] in 'apples' and [ɹ] in 'pears.'

Noise

NOISE is sound that is APERIODIC (not periodic), i.e., sound passing through a narrow constriction such as the vocal tract or the glottis; this produces a sound with audible air turbulence. Noise may also be defined as a sound or a component of a sound which has irregular vibrations of the sound wave, e.g., fricatives or sounds produced with breathy voice. This contrasts with the repetitive waveform of voiced non-fricative sounds. Noise is produced by random movement of air particles. The quality of the noise heard by the listener is determined largely by the size and shape of the vocal tract, especially the part in front of the constriction producing the turbulence.

Sound spectrograms and the cavity just behind the constriction

Spectrograms were initially produced by a sound SPECTROGRAPH which analyzed approximately 2.5 seconds of speech. Sound spectrographs were developed at Bell Telephone Laboratories during World War II. When they became available to speech scientists soon after the war, there was a surge of interest and research into the nature of speech sounds. Currently, computer programs such as Speech Analyzer produce digital displays of the sound SPECTRUM and have replaced the older sound spectrograph machines.

In order to see the contrasts between vowels, we use spectrograms that show the speech wave spectrum and its variations over time. The speech wave spectrum refers to "the frequency and intensity of the sinusoidal components of the speech wave" (Denes and Pinson 1993:141). Sound spectrograms give a quantitative analytical picture of speech sounds. They include a lot of detail about the speech wave, length and intensity of a sound, and the resonances (formant frequencies) within the vocal tract. A sound spectrogram allows us to recognize visually the pattern of the transition from a vowel to a consonant or from a consonant to a vowel, indicating the place of articulation of the consonant.

Figure 33.4 and figure 33.5 together display spectrograms of the sequence of words "he, hay, high, how" and "ha!, hoe, who" spoken fairly carefully and a bit rapidly. Time is measured along the horizontal axis of the spectrogram from left to right in milliseconds, as was the case with the OSCILLOGRAMS in figure 33.1, figure 33.2, and particularly in figure 33.3; the oscillogram is at a time scale similar to that of the spectrogram.

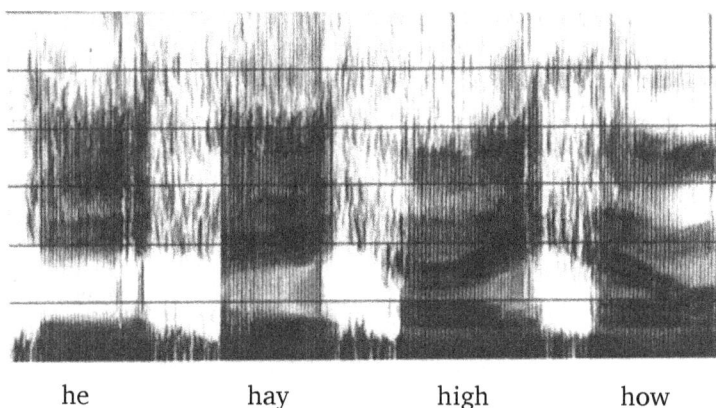

Figure 33.4. Sound spectrogram of 'he, hay, high, how'.

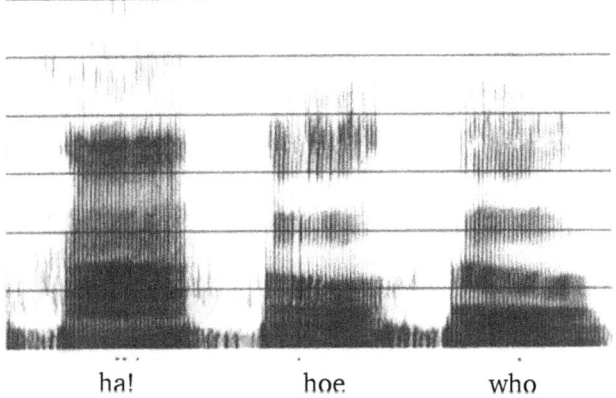

Figure 33.5. Sound spectrogram of 'ha!, hoe, who'.

A key difference between the two portrayals of speech sound is that the vertical position of a point on the waveform in an oscillogram represents AIR PRESSURE at that moment, whereas the vertical position of a point on a spectrogram represents FREQUENCY measured in Hertz. The darkness of the spectrogram at that point represents the INTENSITY or energy densities of the sound at that time and frequency. It is indicative of stress on a particular segment. The horizontal lines straight across the spectrograms provide a frequency scale along a time line. The bottom of the spectrogram is at zero frequency, the first grid line from the bottom is at 1000 Hz, the second at 2000 Hz, and so on.

Readings along the vertical axis are used to measure the frequencies of formants and other concentrations of energy, such as the range of frequency of the noise component of sibilants, distinguishing, for example, alveolar sibilants from postalveolar ones. The wave from each glottal pulse causes a vertical spike on the spectrogram. Whenever you observe regularly spaced spikes on the spectrogram, the sound is voiced. By counting the number of spikes per second, you can obtain the FUNDAMENTAL FREQUENCY of a sound from a spectrogram in the same way that you can from an oscillogram.

Progressing from left to right in the spectrograms of 'he, hay, high, how' and 'ha!, hoe, who', there is a sequence of lighter areas alternating with darker areas. The lighter areas are the [h] in each word, and the darker areas are the vowels (whether the vowel is glided, diphthongized, or unglided). Look first at the spectrogram of 'high.' There is a dark band just under the 1000 Hz grid line that represents the first formant, i.e., the vocal tract resonance with the lowest frequency. Below it, running along the baseline, is another dark band that is sometimes called the VOICE BAR which is present whenever there is voicing; it does not represent a formant. The center of the first formant band (or formant bar) appears to be at about 750 Hz; it is a reasonable estimate of the frequency of the first formant for the first portion of the word. Toward the end of the word, the first formant band drops lower, and it reaches a frequency of about 400 Hz at the end.

The second formant band for 'high' starts about midway between 1000 Hz and 2000 Hz; it is at around 1450 Hz. (A shorthand notation for summarizing the formant frequencies at the first of the voiced portion of 'high' is: F_1 = 750 Hz and F_2 = 1450 Hz.) By the end of the word the second formant has risen to around 2300 Hz. A third formant band starts at something over 2000 Hz and rises toward the end. A fourth formant band remains between 3000 Hz and 4000 Hz throughout the word. Since the first three formants are the most important in determining our perception of vowel quality and consonant place of articulation for most sounds, we focus our attention primarily on them.

The frequency of F_1 (often written as F1) is inversely related to tongue height (i.e., high vowels have a low F_1). The frequency of F_2 is related to tongue advancement (i.e., F_2 increases as the tongue moves forward). The effect of lip rounding is generally to lower the formant frequencies of F_1, F_2, F_3, and F_4. The fourth formant, F_4, is nearly constant in frequency for any one speaker.

Vowel formant frequencies

Many researchers have measured the formant frequencies of vowels in various languages. Table 33.1 summarizes some results of a study of midwestern American English vowels.[2] Since women on the average have a shorter vocal tract than men, the average formant frequencies are higher for women than for men. The frequencies in this table are the average of men's and women's formant frequencies.

Table 33.1. Formant frequencies of midwestern American English vowels

	i	ɪ	ɛ	æ	ɑ	ɔ	u	ʊ
F_1	290	410	570	760	790	580	335	455
F_2	2540	2230	2080	1880	1150	880	910	1090
F_2-F_1	2250	1820	1510	1120	360	300	575	635

The formant frequency grid in table 33.2 is specially oriented with low numbers at the top and to the right in order to display vowels in their traditional orientation. For the same reason, we plot F1 along the vertical scale. The horizontal and vertical scales are specially proportioned to correspond to

---

[2] A more recent study published in *The Journal of the Acoustical Society of America* by Hillenbrand, et al. (1995) supersedes the classical study by G. E. Peterson and H. L. Barney (1952), "Control Methods Used in a Study of the Vowels," *JASA* 24(2):175–184.

the way we hear differences in frequency as differences in pitch. Following Ladefoged 1993, we plot F_2-F_1, the difference between the second formant frequency and the first formant frequency, along the horizontal scale.

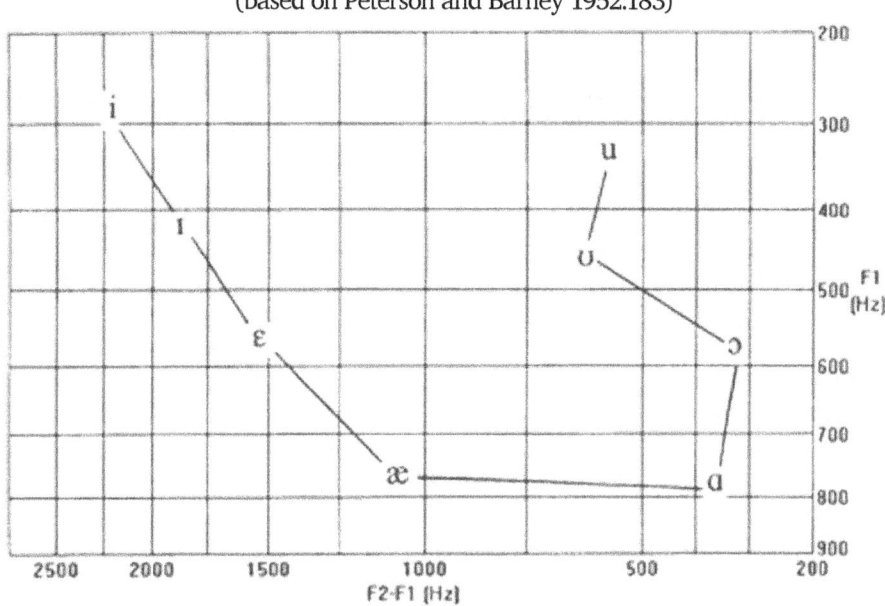

Table 33.2. Vowel formant chart, with formant frequencies F_1 versus F_2-F_1 plotted for averages of American English vowel data (based on Peterson and Barney 1952:183)

As an exercise, you may wish to measure the formant frequencies of the vowels in figures 33.4 and 33.5 and plot them in table 33.2 for comparison. You will notice that the vowels in figure 33.6 are distributed in a pattern similar to that of the traditional vowel diagram. By various experiments, research has shown that the frequencies of the first two or three formants determine the vowel quality that we perceive. Thus, measuring vowel formant frequencies provides a quantitative method to observe and describe vowels.

Measuring vowel formant frequencies can be fraught with certain difficulties. For example, it is often difficult to decide where the center of a formant band is on a spectrogram. Some programs have built-in algorithms to identify the center of a formant.

Vowel-consonant formant transitions

The analysis of vowels considered up to this point has been static. The recorded vowels were said in isolation, or else in a context such as [h] which has little effect on their articulation and thus on their quality. In the normal flow of speech, however, each speech sound typically has considerable effect on the articulation and the quality of the sound preceding or following it, or both. For example, during the articulation of [b] in 'bee' /bi/, the tongue moves into the [i] position, whereas, during the articulation of [b] in 'boo' /bu/, the tongue, and to some extent the lips, move into the [u] position.

Transitions of formant frequencies during the movement of the articulators from a vowel to a consonant and from a consonant to a vowel are perceptibly different for different places of articulation of consonants. In fact, these transitions influence our perception of a consonant's place of articulation.

On spectrograms researchers began to notice that the formant bars at the onset and coda of consonants seemed to point toward a single place on the frequency-versus-time scale. A formant bar on a spectrogram has sometimes been said to point toward a particular point somewhere in the consonant gap. This point has been called the LOCUS for that place of articulation. Many researchers thought that each place of articulation had a single *locus* for each formant, a point on the spectrogram toward which the formant bar pointed. Eventually they realized that the frequency toward which a formant points depends not only on the place of articulation of the consonant, but also on the ever present coarticulation with adjacent vowels.

While the locus is not a very accurate description, because of the influence of neighboring sounds on the articulation of the consonant, still it is a useful approximation, and we use it in describing sounds. In the remainder of this chapter we look briefly at the loci for different places of articulation. We also address ways in which sounds made with different manners of articulation are distinguishable on a spectrogram.

The sound at the beginning of English 'hay' functions as the consonant /h/ in the language. It is the speech sound indicated in figure 33.4 by the consonant *gap* between the vowel [i] of 'he' and the vowel [eⁱ] of 'hay'. The random vertical spikes above about 2000 Hz in this gap are evidence of noise during the /h/, showing that the sound is a glottal *fricative*. (The 2000 Hz level is marked by the second horizontal line from the bottom.) While an analyst might be tempted to transcribe this sound phonetically as [h], it is not voiceless. Each of the regularly spaced vertical spikes rising from the baseline up to about 500 Hz is caused by a glottal pulse. These pulses are evidence that there was some kind of voicing throughout the production of the /h/ sound. The appropriate phonetic transcription is [ɦ], symbolizing what IPA calls a voiced glottal fricative, and is produced with a murmur state of the glottis. The /h/ has the same vocalic quality as the beginning of the vowel; it has a negligible effect on the quality of the vowel.

The vowel in 'hay' is a glide, ending with a somewhat low first formant frequency (F1) and a fairly high second formant frequency (F2) of about 2100 Hz, indicating a close front [i] vocalic sound. Thus the word 'hay' can be transcribed ending with [eⁱ] or [ei̯].

In figure 33.6 the word 'way' starts with very low F_1 and F_2, the formant structure of a very close back [u]. However, both formant frequencies rise rapidly, indicating that the initial sound in this word is an approximant rather than a syllabic vowel. F_2 continues to rise rapidly throughout the word, and the word ends with high F_2 and low F_1 of [i], indicating a postvocalic glide in 'way' [weⁱ], just as in 'hay'. However, the rapidity of the rise in F_2 in glide [weⁱ] 'way' shows that the sound quality traverses a path through [e] much more rapidly than in figure 33.4 'hay'.

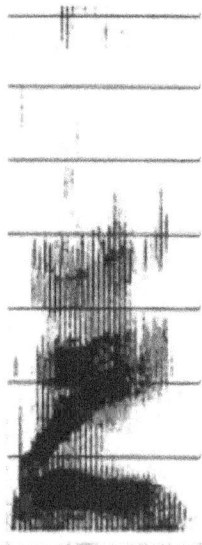

Figure 33.6. Sound spectrogram of 'way'.

The gap at the beginning of figure 33.7 'bay' represents the lack of any resonances or formants preceding the onset of 'ay', thus indicating that, acoustically, the first consonant is (voiceless) [p]. The regularly spaced vertical spikes following the gap indicate that 'ay' is voiced. The lack of any markings in the gap above about 5000 Hz indicates that there is little or no significant sound intensity at the higher frequencies. The voiceless stop has no intensity visible on the spectrogram. This is because there is no air passageway for the sound to escape from the vocal tract, and the pathway through the flesh greatly attenuates or dampens all the higher frequency components of the sound. The vowel formant bars begin sharply at the moment of the release of the stop closure. The F_1, F_2, and F_3 formant bars all bend downward near the gap, pointing toward some lower frequency locus within the gap, typical of bilabial consonants.

Figure 33.7. Sound spectrogram of 'bay'.

In figure 33.8 the nasal gap of [m] in 'may' has a voice bar similar to that of the stop [b] in 'bay', figure 33.7. The nasal has an additional weak second formant at about 2000 Hz not found in the spectral pattern of the voiced stop [b].

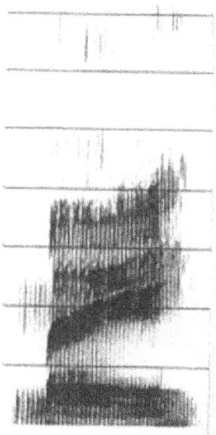

Figure 33.8. Sound spectrogram of 'may'.

Neither formant bar is changing much in amplitude or frequency during the closure. The vowel formant bars begin sharply at the moment of release of the nasal. There is a tendency for the formant bars to point downward near the consonant gap of the bilabial consonant, but this tendency is barely visible because of the rapid transition from nasal sound to vowel sound. This is characteristic of the typical nasal sound. Nasals at the various places of articulation look very similar during the closure gap because the mouth cavity is not in the direct path of the sound waves, and therefore its shape and size have only secondary effects on the sound. You can demonstrate the similarity of nasals at different places of articulation by pronouncing a sequence such as [mŋn] and having a friend listen. For each of the nasals, have them try to identify which place of articulation you have used.

In figure 33.9, prior to the closure of [k] in 'rack', the second formant bar bends upward and the third formant bar bends downward, so that they seem to point to the same locus. This pattern is typical for velars, especially for postvocalic velars.

Figure 33.9. Sound spectrogram of 'rack'.

Word-initial /r/ realized as [ɹ] in 'rack' (figure 33.9) and in 'ray' (figure 33.10) is another articulation for which the first three formants point to a lower frequency.

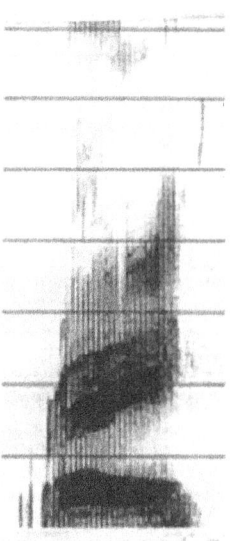

Figure 33.10. Sound spectrogram of 'ray'.

You will recall that the first three formants in bilabial consonants were lowered, but in this typical pronunciation of [ɹ], F_2 and F_3 go lower than for any other sounds. In fact, the F_3 band seems to merge with the F_2 band. You can tell, however, that two formants are represented by the band centered at about 1900 Hz in these words because the band is considerably wider than for a single formant. If you wish to measure the frequencies of formants with overlapping bands (F_2 and F_3 in this case), first measure the width of a single formant band, and then read off the frequencies half the width of a single band in from each edge of the merged band.

Absence of a voice bar on the baseline of the figure 33.9 spectrogram of [kʰ] in 'rack' confirms that the stop was voiceless. There was complete silence for the space of several milliseconds. When the [k] was released, there was a brief strong burst of sound concentrated at about 1900 Hz, followed by the noise of aspiration spread from the top of the spectrogram nearly to the bottom. The energy of both the burst and the aspiration was strongest at about the same frequencies as those of the formants at the moment of the closure that produced the stop.

The utterance 'say sea' (figure 33.11) introduces the spectrographic pattern of fricatives in general, and sibilants in particular. The pattern of voiceless fricatives is one of short straight vertical spikes randomly scattered in certain parts of the frequency spectrum. Of all the fricatives, sibilants have the greatest intensity, seen as the darkest overall fricative pattern on a spectrogram.

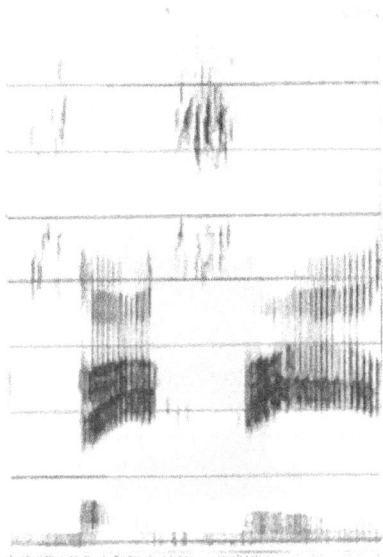

Figure 33.11. Sound spectrogram of 'say sea'.

The first sibilant [ʃ] in 'she's where?!' (figure 33.12), has a spectrum similar to that of [s] except that the relatively dense markings indicating high intensity extend downward to somewhere around 2000 Hz. They extend down only to about 3500 Hz or more for [s], as seen in 'say sea' (figure 33.11), and in 'say gnaw' (figure 33.13). Usually voiceless sibilants are readily identified by their strong random sound and readily distinguished from one another by the lowest frequency to which the strong intensity extends.

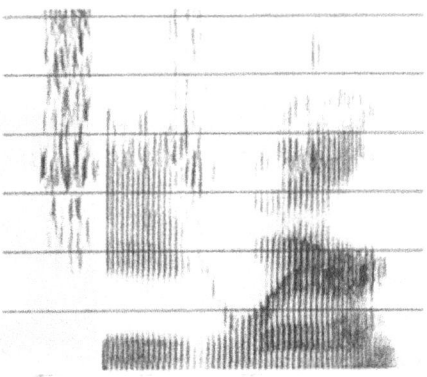

Figure 33.12. Sound spectrogram of 'she's where?!'.

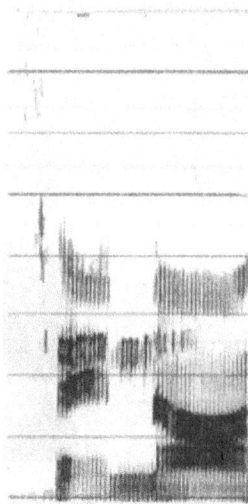

Figure 33.13. Sound spectrogram of 'say gnaw'.

The voiced alveolar sibilant [z], like its voiceless counterpart [s], has random energy down to about 3500 Hz. This is seen in figure 33.12 as random vertical spikes above about 4300 Hz and random marks mixed with the spikes of voicing from there down to about 3500 Hz. Notice that the random marks are lighter (indicating less intensity) on the spectrogram of the voiced fricative [z] (figure 33.12) than they are for the voiceless fricative [s] (figure 33.11, figure 33.13). The fairly uniform spikes of voiced sounds are lighter below 3000 Hz and are lighter than those of the vowel [i] just before the [z]. Presumably this is because the SUBGLOTTAL PRESSURE must be divided between the production of voicing and the production of noise in a voiced fricative. In some spectrographic displays it is also possible to see that the fricative noise is produced in short bursts, each the result of a glottal pulse.

In figure 33.12 notice that F2 and F3 do not reach as low in frequency in the word final [ɹ] of 'where', as in the word initial [ɹ] of 'rack' and 'ray'. This is probably the result of rounding the initial [ɹ] but not the final [ɹ], due to preparation for forming the following vowels. Try watching and listening for this difference in your speech and that of others.

Notice, too, in figure 33.12 the difference in spacing of the spikes at the beginning and the end of 'where', indicating that the end pitch is higher than at the beginning. In figure 33.14 the [l] in 'lease' has a lighter first formant bar than the neighboring [i]. The second formant bar is weak but visible at about 1200 Hz; this difference is important for distinguishing the spectrographic appearance of [l] from that of a nasal, whose second formant is higher than 2000 Hz. Notice, too, that over half of the duration of the vowel [i] between the [l] and the [s] is taken up by the CV transition from [l]. This is typical of vowels; they are usually on the move, first accommodating one consonant articulation and then another. It has been said that a consonant is just one way to end (or begin) a vowel.

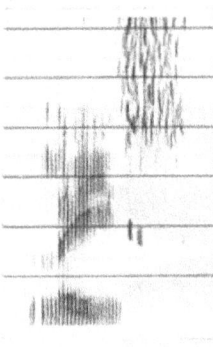

Figure 33.14. Sound spectrogram of 'lease'.

By now you have probably realized that reading spectrograms is an art as well as a science. Because of this, we present some guidelines about identifying sounds on a spectrogram. Some of the simpler ones have been set forth by Ladefoged (1993). Table 33.2 is adapted from Ladefoged's table 8.1 (1993:203), and includes a few of our own additions, as well. Happy spectrogram reading!

The descriptions in table 33.3 should be regarded only as rough guides. The actual acoustic correlates depend to a great extent on the particular combination of articulatory features in a sound. All frequencies, durations, and amplitudes are relative. They depend on speaker (size and shape of larynx and vocal tract), mood, context, and other circumstances.

Table 33.3. Acoustic correlates of consonantal features

State of Vocal Folds	
Voiced	Regularly spaced vertical spikes corresponding to the glottal pulses caused by vibration of the vocal folds.
Place of Articulation	
Bilabial	Locus of both second and third formants comparatively low.
Alveolar	Locus of second formant about 1700–1800 Hz.
Velar	Usually high locus of the second formant. Common origin (locus) of second and third formant transitions.
Retroflex	Second formant low, third formant very low.
Manner of Articulation (Note: obstruents have a low first formant locus)	
Stop	Gap in pattern, followed by momentary burst, then perhaps the fricative noise (aspiration) for voiceless stops. Gap, followed by sharp beginning of formant structure, for voiced stops.
Fricative	Random noise pattern, often especially in the higher frequency regions, but this is dependent on the place of articulation plus coarticulation with contiguous sounds.
Nasal	Formant structure similar to that of vowels, but with nasal formants at about 250, 2500, and 3250 Hz. Most of the formants have considerably less intensity than vowel formants.
Lateral	Formant structure similar to that of vowels, but with formants in the neighborhood of 250, 1200, and 2400 Hz. Most of the formants have considerably less intensity than vowel formants.
Approximant	Formant structure similar to that in vowels, usually changing rapidly. Lower intensity when vowel quality of approximant is very close.

Table 33.4 gives a summary of some basic concepts for acoustic analysis of speech. While it could be expanded to include more of the detail necessary for analyzing spectrograms, vocal waveforms, etc., it nevertheless is a useful beginning for understanding some fundamentals about the acoustics of speech.

Table 33.4. Summary of concepts and methods for acoustic analysis of speech

Partially Correlated Phenomena			Observation of Physical Attributes		
Phonological Function	Primary Psychophysical Percept	Physical Attribute of Speech Sound (and Units)	See or measure on an oscillogram?	See or measure on a spectrogram?	Notes
Boundary between segments	Change in sound quality	Change in sound spectrum	Often see, as a change in wave shape	Quite often see, as a change in spectral pattern	Segment boundaries often are vague and ill-defined as a result of coarticulation
Length difference as phonemic contrast or as allophonic variation	Length or duration	Length or duration (msec)	Yes, if and to the extent that segment boundaries can be seen (see above)	Yes, if and to the extent that segment boundaries can be seen (see above)	
Voicing	Presence of musical pitch	Presence of a periodic (i.e., repetitive) component	Often, as repetition of waveshape	Yes, as regular spacing of vertical striations	
Tone, intonation, and/or stress	Musical pitch	Fundamental frequency F_0 (Hz)	Yes, as density of cycles (repetitions) in waveshape	Yes, as density of spacing of vertical striations on broad band spectrogram	F_0 = number of cycles divided by time lapse; method is tedious and inaccurate
			Yes, as height of output curve from "pitch analysis" program	Yes, as $1/n$ times the frequency of the nth harmonic trace on a narrow band spectrogram	Method is easy and fairly accurate, but sometimes fails
Stress	Loudness	Amplitude or intensity (dB)	Yes, can see amplitude as height of sound pressure wave or amplitude curve	Vaguely, as darkness of pattern, or as area under "spectral section" curve	Amplitude of intensity can be very different for two sounds made with same stress or having similar loudness
Vowel phonemic contrast or allophonic variation	Vowel quality	Formant frequencies F_1, F_2. or less importantly, F_3, F_4. (Hz)	No	Usually, as center frequencies of formant bands for F_1, F_2, and sometimes F_3, F_4	
Consonant contrast or variation in place of articulation		Pattern of formant frequencies and formant frequency transitions	No	Usually, as locus frequencies of formant transitions, frequency of aspiration burst or fricative noise, etc.	
Consonant contrast or variation in manner of articulation		Amplitude and frequency pattern of formants; presence of noise	Can see to some extent as differences in wave shape and size	Usually, as one or a combination of patterns of regular or random striations	

Key terms

sound
spectrogram
spectrograph
decibel
duration
milliseconds
formant, formant frequency
fundamental frequency
intensity
voice bar

noise
locus
subglottal pressure
glottal pulse
waveform
Hertz, cycles per second
resonances
sound wave spectrum
speech wave

Exercises

1. After your instructor teaches you how to use a speech-analyzer computer program, pronounce each of your vowels and plot them on a vowel formant chart, with formant frequencies F1 versus F2-F1 (see table 33.2). Use the speech analyzer computer program in order to obtain the formant frequencies for F1 and F2. Then do the calculations for F2-F1. Plot F1 versus F2-F1 on a vowel formant chart. How closely does your vowel chart match that presented in table 33.2? Compare your vowel formant frequencies diagram with it. Write about any differences you have found that reflect your speech dialect.

34

Phonetic Fieldwork

This book began by introducing the anatomical structures and the physiological functions of each part of the speech apparatus for speech production. We introduced the various categories of speech sounds, including their identification, pronunciation, and transcription. It is this information which forms the core knowledge for this text. The topics covered are those taught in a traditional articulatory phonetics course, with the possible exceptions of palatography and acoustic phonetics. This final chapter focuses on phonetic fieldwork.

Phonetic fieldwork involves linguistic research on your own language, research with speakers of another language, such as may occur with an ENDANGERED LANGUAGE, and research on languages in a cross-cultural linguistic situation, such as described by Everett.

> Fieldwork describes the activity of a researcher systematically analyzing parts of a language other than one's native language (usually one the researcher did not speak prior to beginning fieldwork), within a community of speakers of that language, prototypically in their native land, living out their existence in the milieu and mental currency of their native culture. (Everett 2001:168)

The goals of your phonetic field research will inform how you use the phonetic knowledge that you gain in studying phonetics. These goals may include a careful description of the sounds of a particular language; a broader written linguistic description of a language, with phonetics as one component of that description; an aid to language learning; description and analysis of an interesting sound or group of sounds, e.g., clicks, double stops; language learning and analysis as part of a larger language development project; the discovery and analysis of regular sound variations across a number of languages; the historical reconstruction of a proto-language through analysis of sound correspondences in related dialects; and a deeper understanding and appreciation of all the sounds used in the world's languages. Any phonological analysis of a language rests upon accurate phonetic data collected during fieldwork.

The following statement by Ladefoged summarizes the importance of phonetic field research: "Fieldwork is like heart surgery: you can learn to do it well only by practicing on someone" (2003:x). Having a good understanding of what is involved in phonetic field research comes from actively doing it.

Maddieson speaks of LINGUISTIC PHONETICS which he defines as "the phonetic properties and parameters underlying linguistically-relevant contrasts at segmental, prosodic, or other levels of analysis" (2001:212). He further states that there may be no boundary between phonetics and phonology. It is through doing phonetic fieldwork that a researcher finds the ALLOPHONES or variants of a particular phoneme, the prosodic patterns, and the contrasts and variations of sound units.

Selecting a fieldwork topic

An important part of initial planning for fieldwork is to decide what research topic to pursue. If you decide to study a particular language, what specific phonetic feature(s) of that language will be the focus of your research? A literature review will give some guidance about what is interesting and unknown about sounds in a specific language or language family.

Some linguists conduct *surveys* of the languages in the geographic area of interest before deciding which phonetic feature(s) to study in detail. A *linguistic survey* utilizes a list of words, usually based on some standard list that has been compiled for that area; for example, the Swadesh word list has been used extensively for languages of the Americas, the Benue-Congo comparative word list has been used for languages in the Benue-Congo language family in Africa, and more recently the SIL Comparative African Word List has been proposed for use across various language families in Africa (Snider and Roberts 2004:73–122). Such word lists usually consist of basic concepts for which terms are not likely to have been borrowed from another language.

Surveyors study phonetic features, phonological features, grammatical features, semantics, and, in general, all aspects of languages and dialects, to ascertain how closely related they are. Through linguistic surveys some linguists have discovered previously unknown dialects of languages. For example, Arensen thought there were two Murle dialects in Sudan when he began work there. However, linguistic surveys revealed that there are ten Murle dialects, not just two (Jon Arensen, personal communication).

Preparation for phonetic fieldwork

A literature search for relevant information on the language in focus and related languages in the area is vitally important in preparation for phonetic fieldwork. This literature review will make you aware of sounds, pitch patterns, and other prosodic features that you are likely to encounter. Once you become aware of some of the possible sounds that are present in the language you are studying, read the phonetics literature to help you understand those specific sounds, especially about how they are produced and any acoustic correlates of those sounds. When you arrive in the language area, elicit and practice the relevant sounds that you read about. You can then confirm, modify, or refute what others have written, based on your own field data. Good research builds on what others have done. However, if the language you plan to study is a little-known language and you are unable to find relevant literature, read on related dialects or languages. Once you arrive, listen, record, transcribe, and practice the sounds you hear. The lack of adequate literature provides you with an opportunity to report on the phonetics of a little-known language.

Be sure to read about the culture of those who speak the language and related languages. The knowledge gained from a literature review will likely make you aware of social norms that you will be expected to follow. This kind of preparation helps you to be aware of how to adapt to cross-cultural situations and saves you from embarrassment in situations that arise.

An internet search of the language and people in question is also important. This search may make you aware of other researchers currently working on the language or who have done so in the past. With e-mail you can get in touch with them and profit from their insights on the sounds and other linguistic features, as well as the culture. It may also lead to collaborative research. Look for websites of language communities related to your project. These will help you to understand the language and culture before you enter the community.

If there are language learning materials available, as is true for many of the world's major languages, use them to become acquainted with the language and to begin to learn it. Being able to communicate, even with a few phrases, is helpful when you first arrive in a field location. In our personal linguistic fieldwork we worked with a speaker of the language a few afternoons a week for several months while Norris also worked at the local university in the city. Through working with this speaker we learned how to greet, and how to begin to relate to the Bajju people in Jju. When we moved to the village, that knowledge helped ease our culture and language stress and enabled us to build on the language knowledge we had already acquired.

Prior to going to the field, you will need to obtain the necessary funding for your field research. This usually involves writing a research proposal and submitting it to various funding agencies. Some universities have seed money for graduate students to help with initial expenses, though usually the amount of money available is insufficient for the length of time most linguists spend conducting their field research. A larger research grant is usually necessary.

In addition to obtaining funding, you will need to establish a research affiliation in the country where you plan to work. Many fieldworkers obtain a research associateship with a local university. To obtain this associateship, send them your proposal, fill out any forms they require, and wait for the appropriate university officials to give their approval. It is helpful to have an alternate project in mind if you do not receive permission for your first choice. Having a research affiliation is then the basis upon which you can obtain a visa to enter the country. Once in the country, you will need to obtain permission from the appropriate agencies to carry out the research and to live there (e.g., obtain a residence permit from the Ministry of Internal Affairs and work with the ministry or university to obtain permission to conduct your field research).

Human subjects research

A biomedical model for HUMAN SUBJECTS RESEARCH has now become part of any number of areas of research, including linguistic and ethnographic research. While one can argue about the applicability of this model to social science and linguistic research, particularly when dealing with a preliterate population, it is an important area with which those who do phonetics field research must deal. Prior to leaving for a field location, have the *Institutional Review Board* (IRB) of the institution sponsoring your research approve your research proposal so that it is in compliance with accepted guidelines for working with human subjects. If you are working with a preliterate population, ask the IRB if it is acceptable to have those who work with you record or video their verbal consent. Some IRBs accept this in place of a signature or thumbprint.

Reasons for going through the approval process with an IRB are as follows: 1) it ensures that people understand what is involved in working with you on your research, 2) it protects their privacy, 3) it reduces the possibility of litigation and risk for yourself and those with whom you work, and 4) it protects the institution sponsoring your research. Any university or other institution which sponsors your field research and which receives government funding requires informed consent. If you plan to do graduate work at a university which receives government funding, any research that you undertook prior to moving there must have gone through the informed consent process.

In order to obtain INFORMED CONSENT, ask each individual who is to work with you to sign a form that states the goals of the research, gives each person's permission for involvement in the research, specifies what is expected, and states that these individuals may discontinue working with you without prejudice at any time. If you are recording oral informed consent with nonliterate people, make sure that the recording includes your explanation to the people of the specifics of your research and the statement that they may stop working with you at any time. It also states the possible risks and benefits of the research.

Informed consent is an essential component of any linguistic research, particularly if it is intrusive, such as palatography, fiber-optic research on phonation, or use of the ROTHENBERG MASK for airflow measurements.

Ethics in (phonetic) fieldwork

The most basic ethical principle of fieldwork is that you respect those with whom you work. There are a variety of ways to show respect.

When you begin fieldwork, communicate the goals of your work with those you plan to work with. They want to know why you have come, what you plan to do, whether others will come to work with you, who is funding you, what benefit if any they will receive from your fieldwork; they will want a copy of your research write-up. Further, they may want to know if you work for your government, for some intelligence-gathering organization such as the CIA, or for some subversive group. Your response to their questions must be honest, concise, and consistent for all who ask you. When your grasp of the local language increases, answer their questions more fully.

Another way of showing respect is to acknowledge those who have provided data in all of your write-ups of the data. Some may prefer to remain anonymous while others prefer to have their names included. Be sure to check with them about their preference. If you work extensively with one local person, it may be appropriate to co-author an article or book with him or her.

When you are doing fieldwork, it is important not to exploit individuals or groups for your personal gain. Rather, people should receive fair remuneration for their help and service. While you are in the field, discuss payment of local assistants with other scholars who have worked there, with the community leaders, and with the individuals involved. Payment is usually in accordance with the local salary scale. In some instances hospitality, gift giving and reciprocal service may be more important than money. Nancy Dorian discusses the situation she encountered in her work on Gaelic with the Highland people:

> Payment was out of the question, since the very mention of it proved offensive, and the small hostess gifts that I learned were acceptable at each of my visits seemed completely inadequate thanks to people who were giving up whole afternoons and evenings to answer my questions and were regularly pressing great quantities of tea and baked goods on me besides. Even after I left that first year, five of my sources carried on answering my questions, putting long lists of phonologically relevant lexical items and short sentences onto tape for me so that I could consult this material during the ten months that I had spectrographic equipment at my disposal. (Dorian 2001:140)

People may make multiple requests of you. It is important not to make promises that you cannot or do not intend to keep. They will remember your promises, and their opinion of you will be based partially on the extent to which you keep your word to them. As Batchelor states, "When you leave… you won't be remembered for what you achieved, but for how you fitted in" (1997:20).

Beginning fieldwork

Once you have decided on a research project, obtained funding, received permission through the IRB for your research, collected your equipment, obtained a research affiliation, done literature and internet research on the language, and arrived in the country, you need to decide on a place to live while doing your field research. Set criteria for selecting a research site to live and work. While there, you will need to deal with culture shock and stress, engage in participant observation, learn the language, and engage in many other aspects of cross-cultural fieldwork. For assistance with these activities, see C. McKinney 2000. This helpful reference covers topics relevant for anyone doing cultural and linguistic field research.

The next task is to find a speaker to work with for initial transcription of the language. This person will work with you day by day as you elicit language data. Your language assistant also provides a window on the local culture. Note that in an egalitarian society, such as most hunter-gatherer groups, you may need to have a different language speaker each week so that all have an opportunity to work with you. By doing so, you do not disrupt their egalitarian social structure.

In many societies you are their guest, and they will likely feel a responsibility to take care of you. This will likely be their assumption, though not necessarily yours. However, remember that if anything were to happen to you while you are living among them, they are the ones who will likely be held responsible for you. As their guest you may be shown warm hospitality, including their giving you gifts, being with you when you are ill, and making sure that you are not lonely. This fits well with the communal cultures where much fieldwork is carried out, though it tends to contradict our individualism which is so much a part of western culture. It is best to graciously receive their hospitality.

While your proposal likely sets a timetable for accomplishing your various research goals, be aware that the difficulties of living in many field situations may mean that you modify your goals, or even abandon some of them (Newman and Ratliffe 2001:2). One aspect of a field situation that may hinder you from reaching your goals is your physical health. Many who have lived in malarial areas have spent time in bed with malaria. Given possible health problems and other hazards of living in a developing country, you need to hold loosely to your timetable for research goals, and be willing to change your schedule as necessary.

Language of wider communication vs. the local language

While it is possible to do phonetic research using a LANGUAGE OF WIDER COMMUNICATION (LWC) and employing a translator to aid in eliciting language data, this is far from ideal. In some instances fieldworkers work with a speaker of a LWC who then serves as an interpreter for work with a local language. This is most often the case when you begin your fieldwork, but as your fluency in the language increases, you can rely more and more on your own speaking ability.

Good linguistic fieldwork involves language learning so that you can communicate with speakers in their language and so that you can concentrate on the sounds in question. On occasion field linguists have learned the language using a MONOLINGUAL APPROACH. This is difficult, but the advantage is that it may result in your thinking in the local language categories, perhaps more quickly than you would if you work bilingually. Field linguists may find that they have to work monolingually in isolated language communities that have had little contact with outsiders.

For you to progress in learning the language and doing phonetic fieldwork, direct observation and listening to speakers pronounce sounds are essential. Other techniques supplement these, but certainly do not replace visual observation and careful listening to speech sounds, including tones, intonation, and other prosodic features.

One important goal of fieldwork is to obtain data representative of speakers within a specific speech community. In general, representative data are more readily obtained when you are living in the community where the language is spoken. However, some have found that they cannot live in the language community for a host of reasons, and that they have only a single speaker from whom to elicit data. The problem is knowing to what extent the language spoken by that individual is representative of the speech community and to what extent that speech is idiosyncratic.

Some field phoneticians have found that they must check the sounds they encounter with speakers in other villages. Dialectal differences impact the data field phoneticians collect. For example, if a phonetician is interested in studying the acoustic correlates of fortis consonants in daughter languages of the same parent language, that fieldworker would need to consult with speakers of the various dialects that descended from the same proto-language. Are the same acoustic correlates present for fortis sounds in each daughter language, or are there different ones in the various daughter languages?

Language assistants

For any linguistic fieldwork project to succeed, linguists work with local speakers of the target language. Language assistants have been called informants, language speakers, language teachers, sources, subjects, language assistants, language colleagues, and language consultants. Although the term *informant* has traditionally been used in linguistics and anthropological fieldwork, it has often been considered a pejorative term. Because there is an increased sensitivity to the rights of local language speakers, fieldworkers need to use terminology that shows respect to those who work with them. As the list of possible terms given here indicates, there is not unanimity on one term to use. If you are working with local linguists, they are your colleagues and consultants for your field research.

Because, in the initial stages of your project, it is not possible to know which people will make good language assistants, try to work with several different people on a trial basis before employing someone for regular work.

Ladefoged suggests that good language assistants for phonetics research are those who use the language in their daily life, have all their teeth, and are not hard of hearing (2003:13). Stutterers or those with other speech impediments usually do not make good language assistants. Sometimes you can find a

---

A stuttering language assistant

At one summer school for a Linguistics Field Methods class, the instructor inadvertently hired a stutterer as a language assistant for the students. He would say a word, and the students dutifully mimicked his pronunciation. The language assistant laughed as he heard his students stutter words! They had no idea that reduplication of sounds and syllables was not part of the language they were studying.

good language assistant by asking who is the best speaker of the language. It helps to find someone who is capable and eager to work with you on the language.

Some people qualify as language assistants by virtue of speaking the local language no matter their level of education. Other people have university degrees in linguistics or related subjects and understand your goals in phonetic research, a qualification many will not have. Consider both those who are literate and those who are preliterate, though being literate is a plus.

You and your language assistant will gather language data. A language assistant may help by providing linguistic data, collecting data from other speakers, and assisting in the analysis of the data. Some of the tasks that a language assistant may perform include the following:

1. Assist you in language learning
2. Assist you in learning the sounds of the language
3. Serve as a speaker and subject for instrumental and acoustic analysis
4. Assist you in organizing your data into groups of like sounds
5. Go over data to ensure its correctness
6. Suggest speakers to collect further data from
7. Work cooperatively with you on phonetic analysis
8. Co-author linguistic articles. This is especially important when you are working with a competent local scholar.

Working with a language assistant is essential in language learning. Together you can set up language learning word, phrase, and sentence drills, scenarios, and greetings, then record, mimic, and go out into the community to practice that material. For progress in language learning, immerse yourself in the community. As you do so, your knowledge of the language will increase rapidly. Language assistants teach you their language, correct your mistakes (sometimes over and over), and help with all aspects of the language project. One language assistant we had would repeat a word over and over until he was almost going to sleep or until we produced it to his satisfaction.

Equipment and documentation

You will need a laptop computer together with the necessary software programs you plan to use in your project; these may include Speech Analyzer® software, and the FieldWorks® program. This software is available through SIL. In addition you will need word processing software. A digital camera and a video camera are important for phonetic fieldwork. You will also want to have a good digital voice recorder to aid with your language learning and phonetics field research. Some computer software has the capacity to record and reproduce good quality recordings for phonetic fieldwork. Learn how to use each piece of equipment and each computer program prior to going to the field. Find out what will be necessary to protect your equipment on the field, e.g., in areas that are quite moist such as rain forest environments, or areas where dust is a problem, as in harmattan areas. Take heavy plastic ziplock bags to protect your equipment.

Making good quality audio recordings is essential for language learning and speech sound analysis. Whereas some sound analysis may not be possible in many field situations, making good data sound recordings is essential for phonetic field research. Recordings can be brought to a phonetics laboratory for acoustic analysis, whether your focus is on length, pitch patterns, individual segments, co-articulations, or formant frequencies. In these days, acoustic analysis computer software programs are available for use on laptop computers including programs such as the Speech Analyzer®, PRAAT®, Audacity®, or Macquirer®.

Use good-quality recording equipment. Recorders vary widely in quality. If you are using one, select one with a good frequency response so that it will reproduce the range of frequencies the speaker uses. A frequency range of up to 12,000 Hz is adequate for recording speech. The recorder should have a good signal-to-noise ratio (at least 46 db). Any recorder that you take with you to the field should be tough and reliable. Taking a recorder to a village over a rough, potholed, and bumpy road can result in damaged equipment. Some good quality recorders have been fished out of rivers, dried out, and found to work. This is the type needed in a field situation!

The first thing to observe in making a good recording is the amount of ambient noise present. Most people unconsciously filter out much of the noise in their environments. In order to be aware of this background noise, sit and listen to all the noises present. Train yourself to be aware of noise. It is the enemy of good recordings.

Choose a quiet place to do the audio recording. You may need to be outside for light purposes, but then the wind in the microphone can ruin the recording—so check the quality. Eliminate or at least minimize the ambient noise. In a room sparsely furnished with flat walls, sounds reverberate, giving the recording a "hollow" echo sound. If possible, record in a smaller room with heavily padded furniture, especially in rooms constructed from cinder block. Propping up mattresses against walls also helps to deaden an otherwise "live" room. Do whatever is necessary to dampen the noise, e.g., turn off the electric refrigerator, shoo away household animals, feed the children so that they are not crying, get away from noise of automobiles, the market place, and other urban noise. Some electric lights, especially fluorescents, give a hum. Avoid recording during rain, particularly when you are in a room with a corrugated metal roof. The noise from the rain will likely make it difficult to distinguish rain sounds from the speaker's voice. Always record in a room with a ceiling; recording directly under a metal roof causes considerable reverberation. If you find a good recording studio, that is ideal. Often open-air settings in rural environments work well. Maddieson describes his setting for audio recordings in northern Australia as follows.

> When recording speakers of the Australian language Tiwi on Bathurst Island, north of Darwin, walking a half mile away from the village got us away from engine noise and out of a reverberating classroom. The trade-off was some wind noise in the eucalyptus trees and the occasional loud cries of kookaburras. Since both were intermittent, I tried to monitor when wind gusts or bird calls coincided with a speaker's voice and asked for the word to be repeated an extra time. Recording more repetitions than you plan to analyze is one way to try to protect against the likelihood of being obliged to discard some tokens due to overlying sounds. (2001:221)

Ivan Lowe (personal communication) was able to make good audio recordings among the Nambikwara in Brazil. The main noise problem was the village rooster which he put in a box and took to the far end of the airstrip in order to avoid having cockcrows on the audio recording. In looking at sound spectrograms from audio recordings made in rural settings, we have occasionally seen cockcrows on sound spectrograms!

Begin the session by recording pertinent information including the speaker's name, language, location of recording, place where the person is from to aid in dialect identification, and date. As you do the recording, be aware of extraneous sounds that may make acoustic analysis difficult.

When making an audio recording, you can also use a video camera to record what the speaker says. This is helpful when you plan to use the material for language learning. You can mimic the audio and video recordings, paying particular attention to the intonation and tone patterns, and other suprasegmental features. Transcribe your recordings as soon as possible after making them. These transcriptions form the basis for accurate phonetic analysis.

What material should you record? Record language learning material, such as greetings, leave-takings, citation words, phrases and sentences, texts—for hearing sounds in context and for future analysis, conversations, and just about anything that will further your phonetic research. In recording citation words, line up your data with similar sounds in the same list. For example, if you are recording English words to investigate the vowel schwa [ə], the following list would be helpful:

some/sum	rum
plum	hum
come	

When you are preparing a wordlist, place words with the same tone patterns together in one list. It is helpful to put words in a phrase with unvarying words preceding and following. For example, the phrase "Say _____ again" could be used. If this turns out to be too abstract for the speaker, and he or she pauses before the target word, often "I saw a _____ yesterday" can be used. When you line up words and listen to the list, it quickly becomes evident when a word does not fit the pattern and should be put in a different list. Ask the language assistant to say each word three times, with a brief pause between each utterance. If you become aware of some problem with one of the utterances, e.g., if a plane flies overhead, have the language assistant repeat it a fourth time.

Prepare wordlists to substitute in other contexts, e.g., preceding or following different consonants. For example, /N/, representing any nasal, may be realized as [m] before a bilabial sound, as [n] preceding an alveolar sound, and as [ŋ] in the context of a velar sound. By placing sounds in differing contexts, the variants become evident.

Instrumentation for phonetic research

As we mentioned previously, have informed consent forms signed by those who will serve as subjects for phonetic experimentation before using various types of instrumentation in your field research.

Palatography procedures are described in some detail in chapter 31. If you want to understand more accurately the place of articulation for a particular oral consonant, consider doing palatography. The materials needed are usually available in most urban settings.

Some phoneticians use a LARYNGOSCOPE to examine the larynx. It consists of a mirror placed at an angle inside the mouth. Some researchers use more complex fiber-optic laryngoscopic technology which allows more direct examination of the vocal folds. Fibers are inserted through the nose, interfering less with normal phonation, and allowing direct observation of phonation during speech. Field conditions must be such that you have access to electricity to make use of this technology. This procedure is usually conducted in a phonetics laboratory or medical facility.

Another piece of equipment is a Rothenberg mask used to measure airflow; this uses pressure transducers. A Rothenberg mask consists of a "hard plastic mask with a protruding handle, a soft rubber gasket around the base that prevents air from leaking out when the mask is pressed tightly against the face. The mask has two chambers separated by a piece of plastic and a gasket that runs across the upper lip to divide the space into an oral chamber and a nasal chamber. In each of the two chambers is a pneumotachograph that measures air pressure" (Merrifield and Edmonson 1999:305). This mask can be used for studying aspirated stops to measure the amount of airflow following the release of the stop; also it can help in studying the airflow level when voicing starts, and how long it takes for the airflow to build up. Merrifield and Edmondson used it to study controlled versus ballistic syllables in Chinantec. It would be helpful in studying Korean stops; two of the three have no aspiration.[1] This technology could also be used for the study of voiceless vowels, as found in some Native American Athabaskan languages.

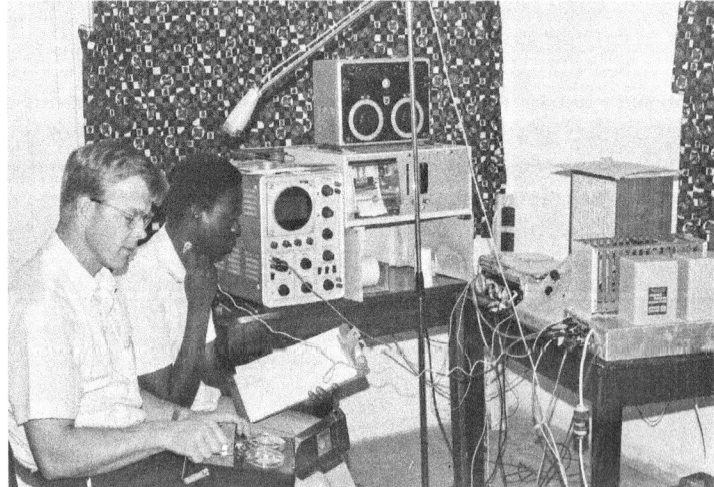

Figure 34.1. Karl Grebe working on tone with a Nso speaker from Cameroon by use of a throat microphone in the Institute of Linguistics phonetics laboratory, Jos, Nigeria.
© 1973, Norris P. McKinney. Used by permission.

---

[1] The Korean stop series with no aspiration has very low air pressure with not much of a burst at the stop release. The second series has high pressure and a big burst at the release of the stops. The third series has heavy aspiration. See discussion in chapter 30.

By transforming the acoustic speech wave into graphs and spectral displays, acoustic phonetics helps the phonetician identify sound patterns of speech sounds being investigated. As mentioned earlier, increasingly these days speech wave computer programs are available for use on laptop computers in programs such as PRAAT© and Speech Analyzer©. Because these programs run on small laptop computers, they can be used in field contexts. Fieldworkers can also conduct acoustic analysis on their data once they have access to a phonetics laboratory.

Practical considerations for field research

There are many practical considerations ranging from what equipment to take, how to have a source of clean water, how to work with the speech community, and where to obtain medical care when you get sick. Basically, you can expect the unexpected. Think of fieldwork as an adventure that has lots of challenges. Occasionally you may ask yourself, "Why did I ever come here?" or "How did I get into this predicament?"

Computers and printers may encounter problems in some areas due to constant dust, the natural enemy of computers. In West Africa, during the dry season, the harmattan winds blow in off the Sahara Desert bringing fine red sand and dust particles harmful to electronic equipment with moving parts. Having adequate plastic dust covers for the computer and printer is a start for protecting your equipment.

Ideally when you take equipment to the field, bring two of each item. Ladefoged writes,

> I use…a checklist before I go out into the field, but in this respect it is incomplete in that it does not stress the necessity of backup. Ideally one wants two of everything, certainly of small things like flashlights, and even if possible of major things like computers. On our last trip in the Kalahari Desert we accidentally poured a jug of water over my laptop computer. Fortunately my wife had hers with her, so all was not lost. There are some other small items that you should remember, as things always go wrong, and you need to be able to deal with them. In addition to some multipurpose tool or Swiss army knife, I have a supply of chewing gum (very useful for holding two wires together, as I found when repairing part of the ignition system that had caught fire), modeling clay (holds mirrors in place when photographing side views of the face), and duct tape (straps things together when the screws have fallen out). (2003:190)

Mosquitoes bring diseases such as malaria, filaria, meningitis, dengue fever, and West Nile virus. Waterborne diseases are a serious problem in many areas of the world. To deal with this problem bring a Katadyn silver nitrate (or other current technology) water filter, boil your drinking water, or use chlorine that can be put into the water supply (e.g., a water barrel or cistern) to purify the water. Some fortunate fieldworkers conduct fieldwork where there is a good source of clean water.

If you will be in an area where malaria is a problem, bring a treated mosquito net to protect yourself from mosquitoes at night. Begin taking your malaria prophylaxis medicine before going into a malarial area. Bring a sufficient supply of malaria medicine to last until you are able to find where to purchase medicine locally. In malarial areas medicine for malaria is usually readily available.

As you work with a speech community, the people will begin to expect things from you, including practical help with everyday problems. We have served as the ambulance service to the village when we took seriously ill people to the hospital, adjusted glasses, provided a bucket and rope to help a farmer pull his goat out of a well, and the list goes on and on. It is naïve to think that a fieldworker can live in an area without being neighborly and helpful to those around.

Many fieldworkers have difficulty dealing with requests for money (e.g., for school fees). Read Maranz 2001, who discusses money matters in an African context. His material is relevant to other areas as well as Africa.

Working with the speech community

As a field phonetician you will find it best to work cooperatively in partnership with local native speakers, linguists, and academicians. Their goals may be those that you should focus on rather than goals that you as an outside researcher come with. Insiders have an emic perspective, and they might want to study some interesting feature of a language. This often leads to practical applications of your linguistic fieldwork. Having said this, note that local linguists, who are speakers of majority languages, may not see any use for minority language study. Further, if local scholars do study minority languages, they may want to maintain political, social, and financial control of the minority language society, a possibly disadvantageous situation for the minority language speakers. Language issues can be politically charged. It often takes outside researchers time to tune into the local political scene before they can conduct research that does not bring disadvantage to the people whose language they study.

A potential problem in working with local linguists is that they may not want competition from you on any level, particularly if you are working on the same language. It may be advisable to work on another language and to try to win the local linguist's friendship, if not collaborating in working on the same language.

Practical applications of field phonetics include doing careful phonetic analysis to prepare for phonological analysis of a language and the subsequent development of a system for writing the language. An oral language with a good orthographic system enables a speech community to begin to 1) become literate, 2) write letters to each other and read them, 3) teach their children first in their mother tongue before having to study in a second language, and 4) develop a literature in their own language. All of these accomplishments contribute to the self-esteem of the minority language community. These reasons, among many others, help motivate careful research that will benefit the speakers of the language.

Working with the speech community on researching its own language is called PARTICIPATORY RESEARCH. This is research in which the people themselves are involved in the decisions about what research to conduct; they assist in developing the research design, participate in language data collecting, and they decide on the use of the knowledge of their sound system for the benefit of their people. In our field research we held a number of meetings among the Bajju leaders on the Jju orthography, and one with Atyap leaders. The goal of these meetings was to work with the people to decide how they would like their language written. At some point in each meeting they sounded like a large phonetics class as the people present began to recognize the sound distinctions present in their language.

Research results

As you proceed with phonetic fieldwork, develop hypotheses about the phonetic and phonological system of the language. Begin writing down the material, lining up utterances with similar sounds or pitch patterns. Check these lists with speakers of the language. Write up your tentative results as the research progresses.

In writing up your data, it may help to select one or a few other linguists' write-ups to serve as models to help you. Begin writing up your results early, preferably while still in the field. Your doing so will show you what data still need to be collected. Even if you find that you must rewrite what you initially wrote, it helps to write early because of the benefit of finding the holes in your data, including sounds, tones, and other prosodic features that you may not have thought to ask about.

Once you have completed your field research, before returning to your home country, recognize that you have a responsibility to make the results of your research available to the local university and to the local speech community that you worked with. You can do this, initially, before you leave the country through giving a lecture, and by leaving a paper to be published locally. It is acceptable to indicate that these are preliminary findings and that you plan to do further analysis of the linguistic data. Once you have completed your final write-up, send at least one copy back to the university that granted you permission to conduct the linguistic research project. Your final write-up should go into the university library so that other researchers have access to it. It is also important to give copies to those who have helped you within the language community.

Also, part of normal procedure for fieldwork should be archiving the data you obtain. It should not reside only on your personal laptop computer! Your university or organization probably has some procedure and site for archiving, and archiving is often a requirement for obtaining funding. Whether it is required for funding or not, archiving your data is now the norm in field research.

Many fieldworkers thank those who worked with them by having a party and/or giving gifts to them. Remember that your research would not have been possible without their assistance.

Key terms

endangered language
human subjects research
informed consent
Institutional Review Board (IRB)
language of wider communication (LWC)
laryngoscope
linguistic survey
participatory research
phone chart
Rothenberg mask

Appendix A
International Phonetic Alphabet (IPA)

THE INTERNATIONAL PHONETIC ALPHABET (revised to 2015)

CONSONANTS (PULMONIC)

© 2015 IPA

	Bilabial	Labiodental	Dental	Alveolar	Postalveolar	Retroflex	Palatal	Velar	Uvular	Pharyngeal	Glottal
Plosive	p b			t d		ʈ ɖ	c ɟ	k ɡ	q ɢ		ʔ
Nasal	m	ɱ		n		ɳ	ɲ	ŋ	ɴ		
Trill	ʙ			r					ʀ		
Tap or Flap		ⱱ		ɾ		ɽ					
Fricative	ɸ β	f v	θ ð	s z	ʃ ʒ	ʂ ʐ	ç ʝ	x ɣ	χ ʁ	ħ ʕ	h ɦ
Lateral fricative				ɬ ɮ							
Approximant		ʋ		ɹ		ɻ	j	ɰ			
Lateral approximant				l		ɭ	ʎ	ʟ			

Symbols to the right in a cell are voiced, to the left are voiceless. Shaded areas denote articulations judged impossible.

CONSONANTS (NON-PULMONIC)

Clicks	Voiced implosives	Ejectives
ʘ Bilabial	ɓ Bilabial	ʼ Examples:
ǀ Dental	ɗ Dental/alveolar	pʼ Bilabial
ǃ (Post)alveolar	ʄ Palatal	tʼ Dental/alveolar
ǂ Palatoalveolar	ɠ Velar	kʼ Velar
ǁ Alveolar lateral	ʛ Uvular	sʼ Alveolar fricative

OTHER SYMBOLS

ʍ Voiceless labial-velar fricative   ɕ ʑ Alveolo-palatal fricatives
w Voiced labial-velar approximant   ɺ Voiced alveolar lateral flap
ɥ Voiced labial-palatal approximant   ɧ Simultaneous ʃ and x
H Voiceless epiglottal fricative
ʢ Voiced epiglottal fricative   Affricates and double articulations can be represented by two symbols joined by a tie bar if necessary. t͡s k͡p
ʡ Epiglottal plosive

VOWELS

```
         Front        Central        Back
Close    i•y——————ɨ•ʉ——————ɯ•u
           ɪ  ʏ              ʊ
Close-mid  e•ø——————ɘ•ɵ——————ɤ•o
                        ə
Open-mid     ɛ•œ———ɜ•ɞ———ʌ•ɔ
              æ       ɐ
Open            a•ɶ——————ɑ•ɒ
```

Where symbols appear in pairs, the one to the right represents a rounded vowel.

SUPRASEGMENTALS

ˈ Primary stress   ˌfoʊnəˈtɪʃən
ˌ Secondary stress
ː Long   e ː
ˑ Half-long   eˑ
˘ Extra-short   ĕ
| Minor (foot) group
‖ Major (intonation) group
. Syllable break   ɹi.ækt
‿ Linking (absence of a break)

TONES AND WORD ACCENTS

LEVEL		CONTOUR	
e̋ or ˥ Extra high	ě or ˩˥ Rising
é ˦ High	ê ˥˩ Falling
ē ˧ Mid	e᷄ ˩˧ High rising
è ˨ Low	e᷅ ˧˩ Low rising
ȅ ˩ Extra low	e᷈ ˧˦˨ Rising-falling
↓ Downstep	↗ Global rise
↑ Upstep	↘ Global fall

DIACRITICS Some diacritics may be placed above a symbol with a descender, e.g. ŋ̊

̥ Voiceless	n̥ d̥	̤ Breathy voiced	b̤ a̤	̪ Dental	t̪ d̪
̬ Voiced	s̬ t̬	̰ Creaky voiced	b̰ a̰	̺ Apical	t̺ d̺
ʰ Aspirated	tʰ dʰ	̼ Linguolabial	t̼ d̼	̻ Laminal	t̻ d̻
̹ More rounded	ɔ̹	ʷ Labialized	tʷ dʷ	̃ Nasalized	ẽ
̜ Less rounded	ɔ̜	ʲ Palatalized	tʲ dʲ	ⁿ Nasal release	dⁿ
̟ Advanced	u̟	ˠ Velarized	tˠ dˠ	ˡ Lateral release	dˡ
̠ Retracted	e̠	ˤ Pharyngealized	tˤ dˤ	̚ No audible release	d̚
̈ Centralized	ë	̴ Velarized or pharyngealized	ɫ		
̽ Mid-centralized	ẽ	̝ Raised	e̝ (ɹ̝ = voiced alveolar fricative)
̩ Syllabic	n̩	̞ Lowered	e̞ (β̞ = voiced bilabial approximant)
̯ Non-syllabic	e̯	̘ Advanced Tongue Root	e̘
˞ Rhoticity	ɚ a˞	̙ Retracted Tongue Root	e̙

IPA Chart, http://www.internationalphoneticassociation.org/content/ipa-chart
© 2015 International Phonetic Association, CC BY-SA 3.0.

Appendix B

Americanist Phonetic Alphabet (APA)

Chart 1: Nonmodified contoids

	Bilabial	Labiodental	Interdental	Dental	Alveolar	Retroflexed alveolar	Fronted alveopalatal	Alveopalatal	Retroflexed alveopalatal	Palatal	Velar	Back-velar	Labio-velar	Uvular	Glottal	Manner of articulation
Vl.	p			t̪	t	ṭ		t,			k̯	k	ḳ	ᵏp		ʔ	Stop
Vl. A	pʰ				tʰ						k̯ʰ	kʰ	ḳʰ				Aspirated stop
Vl.	pʔ				tʔ						k̯ʔ	kʔ	ḳʔ				Glottalizd stop
Vl.	pˤ				tˤ							kˤ	ḳˤ				Vl. Implosive
Vd.	b			ḏ	d	ḍ		d,			g̯	g	g̣	ᵍb			Stop
Vd.	bʱ				dʰ							gʰ					Aspirated stop
Vd.	ɓ/bˤ				ɗ/dˤ							ɠ/gˤ					Implosive
Vl.	pƥ	pf	tθ								k̯x̯	kx	ḳx̣				Affricate
Vl.		pfʔ	tθʔ									kxʔ					Glottalized affricate
Vd.	bƀ	bv	dđ								g̯ǥ	gǥ	g̣ǥ				Affricate
Vl.					ts		tš	ṭṣ̌									Grooved affricate
Vl.					tsʰ		tšʰ										Aspirated grooved affricate
Vl.					tsʔ		tšʔ										Glottalized grooved affricate

223

	Bilabial	Labiodental	Interdental	Dental	Alveolar	Retroflexed alveolar	Fronted alveopalatal	Alveopalatal	Retroflexed alveopalatal	Palatal	Velar	Back-velar	Labio-velar	Uvular	Glottal	Manner of articulation
Vd.					dz			dž	dẓ̌							Grooved affricate
Vd.								džʱ								Aspirated grooved affricate
Vl.					tł											Lateral affricate
Vl.					tłʰ											Aspirated lateral affricate
Vl.					tłʔ											Glottalized lateral affricate
Vd.					dl											Lateral affricate
Vd.	ɸ	f	θ							x̣	x	x̱				Fricative
Vl.		fʔ	θʔ								xʔ					Glottalized fricative
Vd.	β	v	ð							g̣	g	g̱				Fricative
Vl.				s̱	s	ṣ	š̱	š	ṣ̌							Grooved fricative/sibilant
Vl.					sʔ			šʔ								Glottalized grooved fricative/sibilant
Vd.				ẕ	z	ẓ	ẕ̌	ž	ẓ̌							Grooved fricative/sibilant
Vl.					ł											Lateral
Vl.					łʔ											Glottalized lateral
Vd.					l			l,								Lateral
Vd.					ḷ											Fricative lateral
Vl.	M				N			Ñ			N̂					Nasal
Vd.	m			ṇ	n	ṇ		ñ			ŋ̣	ŋ	ŋ̱			Nasal
Vl.		f̌			ṟ̌											Flap
Vd.		v̌			ř	ṛ̌										Flap

Appendix B: Americanist Phonetic Alphabet (APA)

	Bilabial	Labiodental	Interdental	Dental	Alveolar	Retroflexed alveolar	Fronted alveopalatal	Alveopalatal	Retroflexed alveopalatal	Palatal	Velar	Back-velar	Labio-velar	Uvular	Glottal	Manner of articulation
Vd.					ľ											Lateral flap
Vd.					ň											Nasal flap
Vl.	p̃				r̃									R		Trill
Vd.	b̃				r̃									ʀ		Trill
Vl.	p<			t̪<	t<	ṭ<										Click
Vl.					ł<											Lateral click
Vd.	b<			d̪<	d<											Click
Vd.					l<											Lateral click
Vd.	m<			ṇ<	n<	ṇ<										Nasal click

Chart 2: Voiced vocoids

Tongue height	Front		Central		Back	
	Unrounded	Rounded	Unrounded	Rounded	Unrounded	Rounded
High close	i	ü	ɨ	ʉ	ï	u
High open	ɪ	Ü	ɪ̵		ï̞	ʊ
Mid close	e	ö	ə		ë	o
Mid open	ɛ		ʌ			
Low close	æ					ɔ
Low open	a		ɑ			

Chart 3: Voiceless vocoids

Tongue height	Front		Central		Back	
	Unrounded	Rounded	Unrounded	Rounded	Unrounded	Rounded
High close	I	Û	ɨ	ʉ	Ï	Ŭ
High open	ɪ	Ü			ï̞	ʊ
Mid close	E	Ö	Ə		Ɔ	O
Mid open	Ɛ		Ɔ			
Low close	Æ					Ɔ̆
Low open			A			

Chart 4: Non-syllabic vocoids

Voicing	Palatal	Indeterminate	Labio-velar	Accompanying distinguishing feature
Voiced	y		w	
Voiceless	Y	h	W	
Voiced		ɦ		Breathy
Voiceless		ḥ		Whispered
Voiced		r		Retroflexed
Voiceless		r̥		Retroflexed

Chart 5: Releases and transitions

	Rhythm Wave Final		Rhythm Wave Medial	
	Released	Unreleased	Released	Unreleased
Voiceless	at^h	a^t (or at)	at^{h}ta, at^{h}ka	at·a, atka
Voiced	ad^ə	a^d (or ad)	ad^{ə}da, ad^{ə}ga	ad·a, adga
Voiceless glottalized	at^ʔ	a^{ʔt}	at^{ʔ}t^{ʔ}a, a^{ʔ}k^{ʔ}a	at·^{ʔ}a

"Rhythm wave medial transitions, released and unreleased, are traditionally known as open transition and close transition" (E. V. Pike 1963:179).

Chart 6: Modifications

Modification	Example
Retroflexed	ạ
Nasalized	ą
Whispered	A̬
Breathy	a̤
Laryngealized	å
Raised	aˆ
Lowered	aˇ
Fronted	a<
Backed	a>
Syllabic	ṇ
Fortis	t̡
Lenis	t̢
Faucalized	t,
Labialized	tʷ
Palatalized	tʸ
Velarized	tⁱᵘ̂
Pharyngealized	tᵅ

Chart 7: Air mechanisms and direction of the airstream

Air mechanism	Direction of the airstream	
	Ingressive	Egressive
Pulmonic	ɫ←	ɫ
Oral	ɫ<	ɫ>
Pharyngeal	tˤ	tˀ

Chart 8: Stress

No stress	tata
Stress	ˈtata (or táta, or tàta)
Heavier stress	ˈˈtata

Chart 9: Length

Short	a, t
Half long	aˑ, tˑ
Long	aː, tː

Appendix C

Review Exercises for Chapters 1–20

1. In the following list, what characteristics differentiate phonetics from phonics? For your answer, write "phonetics" or "phonics" in the blank below.

    _____ It describes the sound system of one language.

    _____ It describes the sounds of any language.

    _____ A method of teaching reading, writing, and spelling using a system of simple phonetic symbols and rules.

    _____ A method of studying speech sounds including their production, transcription, acoustics, and physiology.

2. Identify the following concepts:

    a. idiophone
    b. idiolect
    c. language interference
    d. International Phonetic Alphabet
    e. Americanist Phonetic Alphabet
    f. sound-symbol concept
    g. tone
    h. stress
    i. intonation
    j. cardinal vowels
    k. egressive
    l. ingressive
    m. active articulator
    n. passive articulator

3. What are the three airstream mechanisms, and what is the initiator of each?

Airstream mechanism	Initiator

4. What type of sound is produced with each of the following:

   a. Complete closure in the oral cavity and the nasal port is closed.
   b. Intermittent closure in the oral cavity.
   c. A constriction in the oral cavity sufficient to produce audible air turbulence, with the nasal port closed.
   d. Complete closure in the oral cavity with the nasal port open.
   e. Slight closure in the oral cavity with insufficient constriction to produce audible air turbulence.
   f. Closure in the oral cavity, nasal port closed, and the airstream escapes over the sides of the tongue.

5. Fill in the places of articulation described in the following chart:

	Place of articulation	Active articulator	Passive articulator
1.		lower lip	upper lip
2.		lower lip	upper teeth
3.		tongue tip	teeth
4.		tongue tip	behind upper teeth
5.		tongue tip	alveolar ridge
6.		tongue blade	behind alveolar ridge
7.		tongue front	hard palate
8.		tongue back	front of velum
9.		tongue back	back of velum
10.		tongue root	back wall of pharynx
11.		epiglottis	back wall of pharynx
12.		vocal folds	—

6. List the four possible phases of articulation of sounds in an utterance.

   a.
   b.
   c.
   d.

7. Which of the symbols are sounds made with velic closure?

   [m] [tʰ] [θ] [ã] [z] [m̥] [ñ] [v] [pʰ] [kx] [y] [ɾ̥] [ʔ]

8. Circle the symbols that represent sounds made with vocal folds not vibrating:

   [s] [θ] [g̊] [ɛ̥] [gɣ] [ʟ] [kʰ] [ɔ] [i̥] [n̥] [β] [w̥] [ɸ]

Appendix C: Review Exercises for Chapters 1–20 231

9. Identify the state of the nasal port in the following sagittal sections:

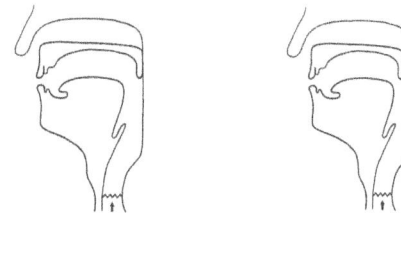

_____   _____

10. Identify the sounds represented in the following sagittal sections:

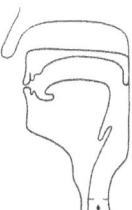

[ ]   [ ]

11. Fill in the fricative phonetic symbols in the following chart:

	Bilabial	Labiodental	Interdental	Velar	
Voiceless					Fricative with egressive pulmonic air (wepa)
Voiced					
Passive articulator	upper lip	upper teeth	teeth	front of velum	
Active articulator	lower lip	lower lip	tongue tip	tongue back	

12. Write the name for each of these sounds:

   a. [s] _____
   b. [i] _____
   c. [ʤ] _____
   d. [kʰ] _____
   e. [pɸ] _____
   f. [w] _____
   g. [g] _____
   h. [ʒ] _____
   i. [o] _____
   j. [ʔ] _____
   k. [m] _____

l. [tʃ] _____

m. [θ] _____

13. Complete the following table concerning vowels and their counterparts if a particular phonetic feature were not present:

Feature	Description of feature	What the sound would be if this feature were not true of that sound?
Central	Airstream flows over the center of the tongue on a midsagittal plane	
Resonant/ Sonorant	No audible noise	
Continuant	Could be continued indefinitely	
Oral	Nasal port closed	

14. Write the symbols for the following sounds:

   [ ]   glottal stop

   [ ]   voiced bilabial nasal

   [ ]   voiced labial-velar approximant

   [ ]   voiceless alveolar lateral fricative

   [ ]   voiced velar affricate

   [ ]   close-mid central unrounded vowel

15. Give the symbol for the corresponding fricative of the following stops:

   [p]   [ ]

   [t]   [ ]

   [k]   [ ]

   [b]   [ ]

   [d]   [ ]

   [g]   [ ]

Appendix D

Review Exercises for Chapters 21–34

1. Name the four states of the glottis in order, from least glottal airflow to greatest airflow. Write the symbol of a sound made with each state.

   _____ [ ]
   _____ [ ]
   _____ [ ]
   _____ [ ]

2. True or False:

   _____ The fortis/lenis contrast applies to consonants.

   _____ The ballistic/controlled contrast applies to vowels.

   _____ Ballistic syllables are sometimes symbolized by placing a "decrescendo" symbol above the vowel character.

   _____ There is no such thing as a lateral click.

   _____ The term *click* implies "ingressive velaric airstream."

   _____ An egressive pulmonic airstream is implied by the term *voiced click*.

3. Sounds made with advanced tongue root are characterized by

   _____ a "choked" quality.

   _____ relatively lower pitch.

   _____ "muffled" or "non-faucalized" sound.

4. Sounds made with retracted tongue root

   _____ may have a relatively higher pitch.

   _____ are produced with the tongue root in the "normal" or default position.

   _____ are articulated by moving the tongue root toward the back of the throat.

   _____ are articulated by making the pharyngeal cavity smaller.

234 An Introduction to Field Phonetics

5. Define the following concepts:

   a. fundamental frequency

   b. resonant frequency

   c. palatography

   d. pitch

   e. spectrogram

   f. juncture

   g. speech variant

   h. dialect

   i. formant

   j. natural classes

6. Give the phonetic names for the following IPA symbols:

   a. [n] _____
   b. [m̥] _____
   c. [ŋ] _____
   d. [ʒ] _____
   e. [pɸ] _____
   f. [j̰] _____
   g. [w̥] _____
   h. [qʰ] _____
   i. [ʟ] _____
   j. [ɑː] _____
   k. [ɠ] _____
   l. [g͡ɓ] _____
   m. [c'] _____
   n. [ʃ'] _____
   o. [qχ'] _____
   p. [ɻ̥] _____
   q. [l̪] _____
   r. [ʒ̰] _____
   s. [ð] _____
   t. [ʕ] _____
   u. [ŋ͡ʘ] _____
   v. [g͡ɟ] _____
   w. [ǁ] _____
   x. [ŋ͡!] _____

y. [œ] ______________________________

z. [g͡!] ______________________________

7. Give the phonetic symbol for the following sagittal diagrams:

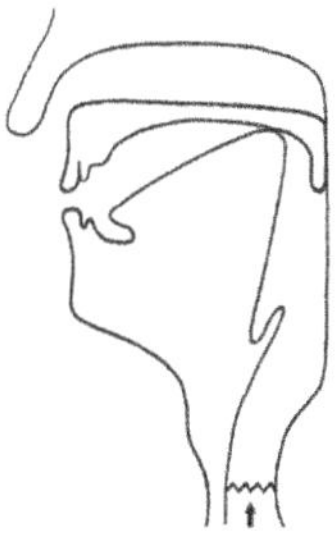

[ ]

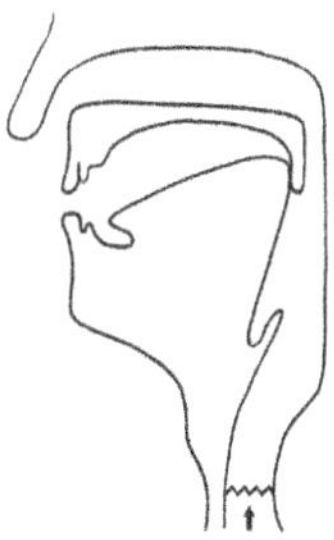

[ ]

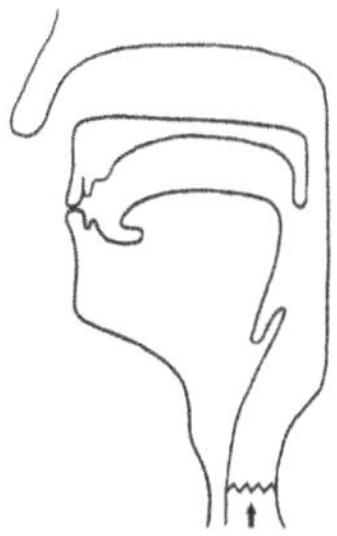

[ ]

8. Give the name and complete the sagittal diagram for the following symbols:

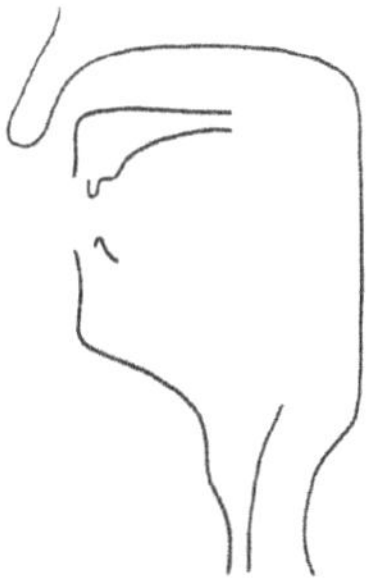

[t’]

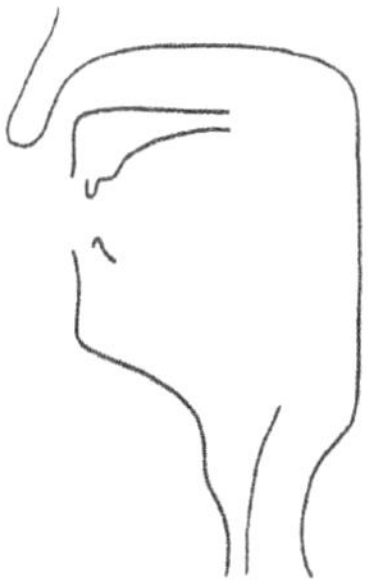

[ŋ͡!]

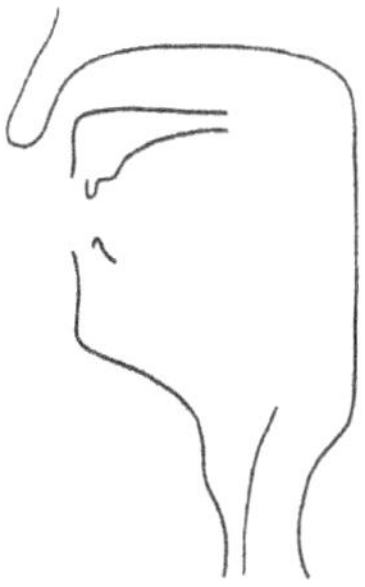

[ɓ]

____

____

____

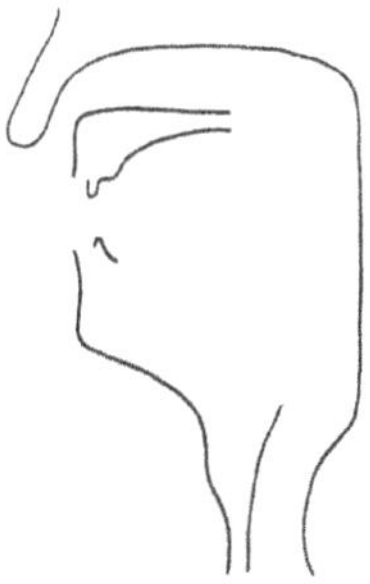

[n̺]

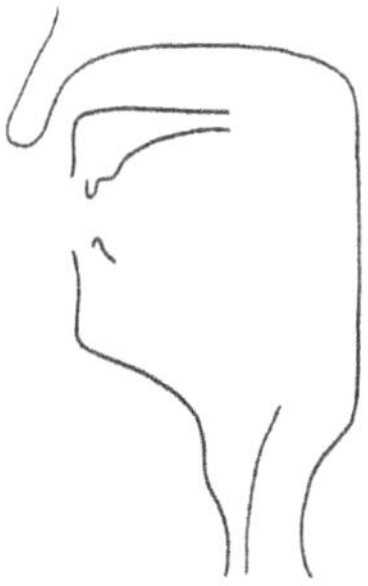

[t̻]

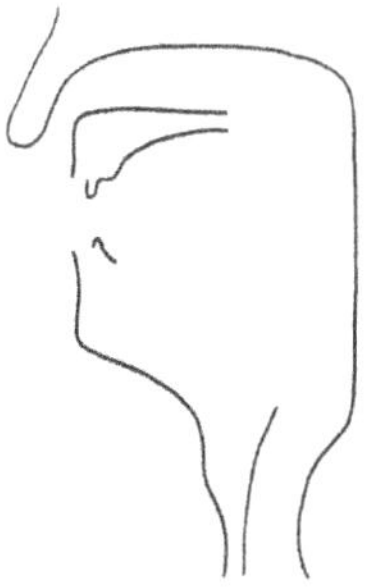

[ɖ]

____

____

____

9. Match the following terms with their definitions:
   _____ open transition
   _____ close transition
   _____ juncture
   _____ vowel glide
   _____ semivowels
   _____ geminate segments

   a. no audible release on the first consonant
   b. audible release of first consonant before starting the second consonant
   c. sequence of identical segments
   d. central approximants
   e. movement from one vowel to another
   f. phonetic feature marking existence of a grammatical boundary

10. Match the following terms with their definitions:
    _____ approximant
    _____ central approximants
    _____ central oral sonorants
    _____ labial-velar
    _____ retroflexion
    _____ rhotacized speech sounds
    _____ labial-palatal
    _____ labial-velar
    _____ labiodental
    _____ labial-alveolar
    _____ alveolar-velar
    _____ coarticulation
    _____ double articulation

    a. have an "r" sound quality
    b. curling tongue tip upward and backward
    c. speech sound produced by two articulators coming close without audible turbulence
    d. non-syllabic vowels
    e. semivowel
    f. central approximant articulators: lips, hard palate, tongue front
    g. central approximant articulators: lips, front of velum, tongue back
    h. central approximant articulators: upper teeth, lower lip
    i. double articulation: lips, front of velum, tongue back
    j. double articulation: tongue tip to alveolar ridge, tongue back to front of velum
    k. double articulation: lips, alveolar ridge, tongue tip
    l. two constrictions with same degree of closure at two different places of articulation at the same time
    m. complete constriction at two places at the same time; first articulation is released well before the second

Appendix D: Review Exercises for Chapters 21–34   237

11. Identify the following IPA diacritics and tell what each indicates:

Symbol	Diacritic name	What it indicates
Ex.: [d̚]	Corner	No audible release on a consonant
[dᵊ] or [də̯]		
[kʰ]		
[ʃʷ]		
[t̪]		
[z̪]		
[ɑː]		
[ɑˑ]		
[ă]		
[a.ɑ]		
[a̰]		
[ḁ]		

12. The following data comes from the Kamasau language (Papua New Guinea, data from Joy Sanders, personal communication). With these limited data, what hypothesis would you want to check out?

[ˈa.bo nand]	'he scolds someone'	[ˈa.mbo]	'red'
[ˈba.di]	'we come'	[ˈma.ndi]	'they come'
[ˈbo.bo]	'my father's sister'	[mbo]	'to, toward'
[gɾoʔ nand]	'he pours out'	[ŋgɾok ŋgɾok wund]	'frog croaks'

_____
_____
_____

Glossary

absolute pitch
See *pitch*.

accent
A variety of pronunciation of a given language, including the use of rhythm, tone, intonation, stress, duration, and consonant and vowel qualities, which differs from other varieties of the same language. Speaking with a good accent requires pronouncing the strings of vowels, semivowels, and consonants with appropriate patterns of syllable rhythm and syllable stress, pitch, intonation, and duration of syllables, all in a manner that is typical of a mother-tongue speaker's pronunciation. The term *accent* refers to pronunciation only. See *dialect,* a broader term that includes grammatical features and vocabulary as well as pronunciation.

acoustic phonetics
The study of the physical properties of the speech sound wave as it is produced in one person's vocal apparatus and radiates outward to another person's ears. It is the study of instrumental representation of speech sounds, a part of the study of acoustics, the branch of physics that studies sound. For contrast, see *auditory phonetics*.

acoustic spectrum (spectra, pl.)
A graphic representation of a sound with amplitude plotted against frequency. See *spectrum*.

active articulator
A part of the vocal apparatus that blocks, constricts, or directs the airstream by coming close to or touching a relatively fixed part of the vocal apparatus which is the passive articulator. The lower lip, tongue tip, tongue front, tongue blade, tongue back, tongue root, epiglottis, and sometimes the vocal folds may serve as active articulators. The active articulator is also called the *lower articulator;* the passive articulator is the *upper articulator.*

advanced tongue root [+ATR]
An [+ATR] vowel sound is produced with the tongue root pulled forward and/or the larynx lowered, thus enlarging and elongating the pharyngeal cavity. Vowels that are [+ATR] tend to have lower formant frequencies and lower pitch frequencies. The features [+ATR] and [−ATR] are often used to describe languages with vowel harmony.

affricate, heterorganic
An affricate is heterorganic if the place of articulation of the fricative is different from that of the stop, e.g., [ps, bz]. If the stop and fricative, though produced at different places of articulation, function as one sound unit in a language, they form a heterorganic affricate.

affricate, homorganic
A sequence of a stop released into a fricative. An affricate is *homorganic* if the place of articulation of the fricative is the same as that of the stop or very close to it, e.g., [pf, bv], [ts, tʃ], [dz, dʒ], [kx, gɣ]. The stop and the fricative in an affricate have the same phonation, though devoicing may occur throughout a

voiced affricate. Voiceless affricates may be aspirated or unaspirated. An affricate functions as a single unit in language, with no syllable boundary between the stop and the fricative. Some phoneticians consider a stop released into a fricative to be an affricate only if the stop and fricative are homorganic. Other phoneticians include heterorganic stop and fricative combinations as affricates, e.g., [ps], [bz]. In a phonological transcription, if an affricate functions as one sound unit, a tie bar [⁀] may be used to join the two segments, e.g., /t͡ʃ/.

air pressure

The force of air against a flat surface, as the diaphragm of a microphone or the force of air necessary to produce voicing. Some speech scientists have measured subglottal air pressure during speech.

airstream mechanism

A cavity in the vocal tract that changes size due to muscular contraction which thereby initiates the motion of air used in speaking. The airstream mechanism of a speech sound is pulmonic if the air comes from the lungs, glottalic if the air comes from the pharynx, and velaric if the motion is initiated by the back of the tongue against the velum. The airstream is ingressive if the air flows inward, and egressive if the air flows outward. Most speech sounds are made with an egressive pulmonic airstream.

allophone

One or more variants of a single phoneme or phonological unit. Because sounds are conditioned by their environments, a nasal consonant will likely be realized as bilabial before a bilabial stop, as alveolar before an alveolar stop, and as velar before a velar stop. If bilabial, alveolar, and velar nasals occur in contrast in other contexts in the language, they are analyzed as separate phonemes, but if they do not, they are likely part of a single nasal phoneme with three allophones. For two sounds to be recognized as allophones they must be phonetically similar, and they must not be in contrast in any environment.

alveolar place of articulation, apico-alveolar place of articulation

The place of articulation produced by a closure between the tongue tip and the alveolar ridge. The tongue tip is the active articulator, with the alveolar ridge as the passive articulator.

alveolar ridge, alveolus, gum ridge, upper gums

The bony ridge located on the roof of the mouth behind the upper teeth. It is important in the production of alveolar consonants.

alveolar-velar place of articulation

Sounds produced with the alveolar ridge and the front of the velum as the passive articulators and the tongue tip and the tongue back as the active articulators, e.g., [k͡tʰ, k͡t, g͡d, ŋ͡n].

alveolus

See *alveolar ridge*.

alveopalatal place of articulation

See *postalveolar* place of articulation.

Americanist Phonetic Alphabet (APA)

A phonetic alphabet designed to be practical for typing phonetic transcriptions on a typewriter, the primary tool early phoneticians used for their data. For example, in the Americanist Phonetic Alphabet the sound at the beginning of the word 'shoe' is written as [š]; in IPA it is written as [ʃ]. The Americanist Phonetic Alphabet has been used in transcribing languages worldwide.

anticipatory coarticulation

During the production of one sound the articulators begin to move toward the target position of the following sound. For example, in pronouncing the word [bvon] 'goat' in Jju, the lips are fully rounded at the beginning of the vowel and fully unrounded by the end of the vowel [o], anticipating the unrounded quality of [n]. This anticipatory coarticulation in Jju occurs with most rounded vowel sounds preceding unrounded consonants.

aperiodic wave

A waveform without regular repetitions, e.g., noise. Fricatives and sibilants have aperiodic waves. See *periodic wave*.

apical

An articulation made with the tongue tip.

apical postalveolar

A retroflex sound. See *sub-apical retroflexed sound*.

apical vowel

A vowel produced with the tongue blade so close to the roof of the mouth that audible friction occurs. It may alternate with a syllabic fricative. Apical or fricative vowels occur in a number of languages and language families.

approximant
See *central approximant* and *lateral approximant*.

articulation
The process that includes movements and positions of those parts of the vocal tract that produce speech sounds. Sounds are classified according to their manner and place of articulation. For example, for [tʰ] in 'to', the tongue tip touches the alveolar ridge.

articulator
The parts of the vocal apparatus that obstruct or direct the airstream. There are two types, the active articulator and the passive articulator. See *active articulator* and *passive articulator*.

articulatory gestures
Somewhat independent units into which the articulation of a segment may be decomposed; for example, abstracting a laryngeal gesture and a supralaryngeal gesture to describe what occurs in the oral and nasal cavities.

articulatory phonetics, physiological phonetics
The branch of phonetics that studies the ways in which sounds are produced by movements and positions (articulations) of various parts of the vocal apparatus (in the chest, larynx, pharynx, mouth, and nose), all of which work together to produce the sequences of vowels and consonants, syllables and stress, tones and intonation, in a stream of speech.

aryepiglottic folds
Fleshy folds located above the vocal folds and the ventricular folds. They are active in speech production, particularly in some vowels that have traditionally been described as [+ATR]. They are sphinctered nearly closed in the production of harsh voice and may also contribute to other types of phonation.

arytenoid cartilages
A pair of triangularly shaped cartilages in the larynx that the vocal folds attach to at their posterior ends. These cartilages slide sideways and also swivel around a vertical axis. The arytenoid cartilages are located just above the cricoid cartilage.

aspiration, stop release
The release of air pressure that has built up behind a voiceless stop closure. It occurs immediately after the release of the stop, resulting in aspirated stops, e.g., [pʰ, tʰ, kʰ, ʔʰ]. There are also unaspirated stops—voiceless stops produced without any audible noise release. Aspiration on stops results in a delay of voice onset time (VOT).

audible release
See *released stop*.

auditory phonetics, perceptual phonetics
The study of speech perception through the human auditory system (ear, auditory nerve, and brain). It includes language processing and interpretation in the human brain. For contrast, see *acoustic phonetics*.

back
Sounds produced with the tongue back as the active articulator including velar, uvular, and pharyngeal. The term *back* applies to both consonants and vowels.

backed tongue position
In some speech variants people speak with the tongue positioned further back.

ballistic syllable
A syllable with a crescendo, a sharp increase in the rate of airflow and volume. It contrasts with a *controlled syllable,* a syllable without the ballistic element. The rate of the airflow rises sharply in the latter part of a ballistic syllable, lending support to the use of [h] in its transcription. This description has been applied to contrastive syllables in Chinantec dialects in Mexico. Ballistic syllables occur on falling tones in Chinantec. They have sometimes been symbolized by placing a *crescendo* symbol, borrowed from musical notation, above the vowel.

base character
A minimum sound unit without any modification; a phonetic character that can have one or more diacritics added to it.

Bernoulli effect
Trask (1996:50–51) defines the Bernoulli effect as "the physical phenomenon by which the air pressure on a solid body is reduced when the air is flowing past the body; the faster the air moves, the lower the pressure...the principle

is chiefly important in phonetics in causing the vibration of the vocal folds: air flowing upwards forces the vocal folds apart, but as it flows past them, the pressure drops, and the folds spring back together; the rapid repetition of this sequence constitutes voicing. The effect is also crucial in the production of trills." This effect was named for Daniel Bernoulli (1700–1782), a Swiss mathematician.

bilabial place of articulation

Sounds articulated by the two lips completely closing or coming close to each other, e.g., [m, m̥, b, p, β, β̥].

brackets

See *phonetic transcription*.

bracketing

A technique similar to slurring, except that in bracketing, the speaker concentrates on the extremes of the tongue position, moving fairly quickly from one to the other, e.g., [i] to [ɯ]. The speaker may choose to consciously place his or her tongue at a point intermediate between the extremes, e.g., [ɨ]. This is a good way to locate in-between vowels that may be difficult to pronounce. See also *slurring*.

breath group, tone group

The utterance, whether word, phrase, or sentence, produced between two intakes of air.

breath phonation

A turbulent noisy voiceless flow of air passing through the glottis. For contrast, see *nil phonation*.

breathy glottal fricative

A glottal fricative produced with breathy voice, e.g., [ɦ]. See *breathy phonation*.

breathy phonation, breathy voice, murmur

A type of phonation in which there is low muscular tension on the vocal folds such that they vibrate, but they are not so close as to touch. This produces audible air turbulence as the vocal folds vibrate with a high rate of airflow through the glottis. It results in a breathy or sighing sound at the vocal folds. Acoustically, a dominant first harmonic is highly correlated with breathy phonation. An umlaut under the symbol indicates that the sound is breathy, e.g., [a̤]. Sounds like [bɦ], as in Hindi, are breathy. The symbol [ɦ] may be used for a breathy vowel if its quality is predictable from that of an adjacent voiced vowel.

breve, wedge

A diacritic [˘] placed over a vowel to indicate that it is extra short, e.g., [ă]. An alternate symbol is a wedge [ˇ]; a subscript wedge is used to indicate voicing on an otherwise voiceless consonant, e.g., [s̬].

broad phonetic transcription

A transcription of phonetic data that leaves out much of the fine phonetic detail. See *narrow phonetic transcription*.

buccal

A term used in place of the term *oral* (e.g., the buccal cavity); however, most often this term refers to sounds produced in the cheek cavity, e.g., like the buccal voice of Donald Duck.

cardinal vowels

A system of vowels proposed by Daniel Jones (1881–1967) which phoneticians use as reference points in vowel space when analyzing vowels they encounter in languages. Each vowel is theoretically equidistant from every other vowel between the extremes [i] and [ɑ]. There is also a set of secondary cardinal vowels.

carrier

The frame that remains constant in a frame drill. See also *substitution item*.

carrier phrase

In tonal analysis, a phrase whose tone is known that serves as the context to discover the tone pattern of another phrase, the citation phrase.

cavities in the vocal tract

Spaces or chambers in the vocal tract within which sounds resonate; they change shape due to muscular contractions during speech. These are the pulmonic, pharyngeal, and oral cavities. The nasal cavity, including the sinuses, also serves as a chamber where sounds resonate.

central approximant

A speech sound produced by one articulator coming close to another, but not so close that constriction of the airstream causes audible turbulence, with the passageway for the airstream centered along the midline of the tongue, e.g., [j, w, ʋ, ɥ]. See *semivowel*.

citation form
The form of a word pronounced in isolation. When put into context the citation form may be altered as it is influenced by its surrounding environment, including changes in pitch pattern, or tone sandhi.

clear l
The voiced alveolar lateral at the beginning of English words. For contrast, see *dark l*.

click
A speech sound made with an ingressive velaric airstream and with two closures in the mouth which trap a small volume of air in the space between. The back of the tongue forms one of the closures by pressing against the velum; it serves as the initiator of the ingressive velaric airstream. The lips press together or the tongue presses against the roof of the mouth, forming the other closure at the place of articulation. While the closures are maintained, the tongue pulls downward and toward the rear, forming a partial vacuum between the two closures. When one of the two closures is released, air bursts through the opening into the cavity between the two closures, producing a sharp sound. Clicks are found in Khoisan languages in southern Africa and in some neighboring Bantu languages (e.g., Zulu and Xhosa), and elsewhere. See also *voiced click* and *voiced nasal click*.

close
A parameter in the vertical tongue position classification for vowels. In IPA [i, ɨ, ʉ, ɯ, u] are all described as close vowels. For contrast, see *open*. See also *tense*.

close juncture
See *juncture*.

close transition
A transition between two consonants when there is no audible release of the first consonant before the second one is articulated.

closed syllable
A syllable that ends with a consonant, e.g., [kʰɑp] 'cop'.

closure, complete closure
Complete blockage of the airstream in the vocal cavities, producing a maximum degree of stricture.

cluster
A sequence of two or more segments, whether two or more vowels or two or more consonants.

coarticulation
Sounds produced with two places of articulation simultaneously or overlapping at some point in their articulation, e.g., [g͡b, k͡p]. If both places of articulation have the same degree of closure it is "coordinate coarticulation." If there are differing degrees of closure, as for [kʷ], it is "secondary coarticulation" (Catford 1988:103).

coda
The consonant(s) that follow the syllable nucleus within a syllable, e.g., [d] in English [meʲd] 'made/maid'.

coda phase
See *offset phase*.

cognate
1. A word or form in two or more daughter languages that derives from the same proto-language form.
2. Two or more daughter languages are cognates if they descend from the same proto-language. For example, Spanish, Italian, Portuguese, and French are cognate languages.

complete closure
See *closure*.

consonant
A general category of speech sounds made with closure or constriction of the vocal tract such that either the airflow is completely blocked or restricted with audible air turbulence. They are described by place and manner of articulation. For contrast, see *contoid*.

consonant cluster
A sequence of two or more consonants.

consonant gap
See *gap*.

consonant with no audible release
See *unreleased stop*.

constriction, degree of
Stricture or contraction of the vocal tract muscles such that the airflow may be stopped with complete closure, narrowed sufficiently to produce audible

turbulence, thus producing fricatives, or partially narrowed with little audible turbulence. merely shaping the wave form to create characteristic formants for vowels, etc.

continuant
A sound that could be continued indefinitely if the volume of air flowing up from the lungs were unlimited; vowels or consonants produced with incomplete closure of the vocal tract, e.g., fricatives, liquids, semivowels and vowels. For contrast, see *non-continuant*.

contoid
A phonetic term coined by Kenneth L. Pike (1943) to refer to all sounds that are not central resonant oral sounds. For contrast, see *consonant* and *vocoid*.

contour tone
Moving pitch glides, for example, high-low, high-low-mid, low-high, within the voice range of a speaker. The critical feature is often the direction of tone movement, rather than relative level of the tone.

contour tone language
A tone language which has contour tones (often in addition to level tones). *Contour tone languages* contrast with *register tone languages*.

controlled syllable
See *ballistic syllable*.

coordinate coarticulation
See *coarticulation*.

creaky phonation, creaky voice, glottal fry, vocal fry, tense voice
Phonation with variation in the mode of vibration of the vocal folds, in which the arytenoid cartilages keep the posterior end of the vocal folds together so that they vibrate only in the front. The sound is somewhat creaky, hence the term *creaky voice*. *Creaky phonation* can be produced with laryngeal settings (adjustments) such that a slight change in the setting causes the phonation to "creak" between one mode of phonation and another. This enables the speaker to "break" between modal and creaky phonation, a feature of significance in some languages. The terms *vocal fry, laryngealization,* and *glottal fry* are also used for creaky phonation. It may also be a component in harsh voice. Acoustically, a relatively strong second harmonic is correlated with creaky phonation. In IPA a symbol with a tilde written below represents a sound with creaky voice, e.g., [g̰].

creole
A pidgin language which has become the mother tongue of speakers of a language community.

cricoid cartilage
A signet ring-shaped cartilage located at the base of the larynx. The arytenoid cartilages which are important in phonation are located just above the cricoid cartilage.

cricothyroid muscle
A muscle that runs along the outer front surfaces of the thyroid cartilage and attaches to the cricoid cartilage.

cycles
The number of repetitions, as of the waveform.

dark l
The velar or velarized lateral found after a vowel in English words. For contrast, see *clear l*.

decibel, dB
A measure of the relative intensity of a sound; it refers to an intensity ratio (exactly 10 times the logarithm to the base 10 of that ratio). If one sound has 20 dB intensity difference from another sound, there is a one hundred-fold intensity change (10 times 10, or 10^2).

declination
The tendency of the pitch to fall throughout an utterance as the supply of air in the lungs decreases. This tends to occur both with tone and intonational languages.

degree of constriction
See *stricture, degree of constriction*.

dental place of articulation
The place of articulation of a sound produced between the tongue tip and the upper teeth. The tongue tip is the active articulator.

descender
The part of a phonetic symbol that extends below the base line. Descenders are present in the phonetic symbols [g, j, p, q, ɠ, ɖ, ʄ]. The underring

[̥] indicating voicelessness is written above a symbol with a descender.

devoicing
A phonetic process by which a voiced segment becomes voiceless contiguous to a voiceless environment.

diacritic
In IPA a small mark or notation that is added to a base phonetic symbol, whether consonant or vowel, to indicate some feature, such as tone, nasalization, voicelessness, position (as of a vowel, whether further front, or further back, or lower, or higher than the vowel is normally pronounced), breathiness, laryngealization. Stress is marked by use of the diacritic [ˈ] before a syllable.

dialect
A regional or socially distinct variety of speech spoken within a single language family, often with local pronunciation, grammatical, and vocabulary differences present between dialects. Social or class dialects indicate a social scale people fall into, e.g., an individual may speak an upper class, a middle class, or lower class dialect. When there are a number of dialects spoken, one of them may be selected as the official form of the language for use in the media and in written form.

dialect chain, dialect continuum
A series of mutually related dialects, with those spoken in areas adjacent to each other more likely to be mutually intelligible than those at each end of the continuum. Dialects within a continuum descend from the same proto-language. Dialect continua form over time through speakers' migration from one area to another, often with some physical barrier separating groups, or through settling adjacent to people who speak another language.

dialectology
The systematic study of speech dialects. Dialectology is divided into two areas of the study of language usage: geographic and social (e.g., age, status, gender).

diaphragm
A dome-shaped muscle that is attached to the pelvis and separates the thoracic cavity from the abdominal cavity.

differentiation drill, frame drill
A constant context into which new sounds or words are put. The new sounds or words are called *substitution items*. A carrier or frame provides context into which the phonetician inserts a substitution item, e.g., "it's a _____," or "say _____ again." Use of differentiation drills is especially helpful in studying similarities and contrasts, whether segmental or tonal.

diphthong
A vowel glide or audible change in vowel quality within a single syllable, e.g., [oᵘ]. See *glided vowel*.

direction of the airstream
The course along which the airstream moves, whether it is outward, termed *egressive,* or inward, termed *ingressive*.

dorsal
Sounds produced with the tongue body or back (the dorsum). Dorsal sounds include those with palatal and velar places of articulation.

dorsum
The tongue back.

double articulation
A sound produced at two places of articulation. Most common are stops, e.g., [k͡p, g͡b]; nasals, e.g., [ŋ͡m], and approximants, e.g., [w] and [ɥ].

double nasal
A sound produced with the nasal port open and two complete closures in the oral cavity, e.g., [n͡m, ŋ͡n].

double stop
A sound produced with the nasal port closed and two closures in the oral cavity, e.g., [k͡p, g͡b]. There is coarticulation at some point during the articulation.

downstep
In some tone languages a high (H) tone or a mid (M) tone is lowered after a similar high or mid tone. Sometimes this is due to loss of an intervening tone. Downstep is marked with a [ˌ].

duration, phonetic length
The physical length of time of a phonetic segment, word, or phrase. Duration of a sound in a speech wave is measured in milliseconds. See *length, phonetic*.

egressive

A sound produced when the airstream flows outward, e.g., an egressive pulmonic airstream. For contrast, see *ingressive*.

ejective, glottalized sound

A sound produced with an egressive glottalic airstream. The larynx is raised and the glottis is closed while the sound is articulated in the oral cavity. The nasal port is also closed. Examples include ejective stops, fricatives, and affricates. The diacritic ['] is added to the consonant symbol to indicate an ejective, e.g., [p', ʃ', kx'].

ejective affricate

An ejective stop released into a fricative.

ejective fricative

An ejective formed while there is partial articulatory closure in the mouth.

ejective stop

An ejective formed while the tongue or lips completely block the passage of air through the mouth.

emic perspective

That which is significant to a native speaker of a language. It is an insider's perspective. *Emic* is a term coined by Kenneth Pike from the word "phonemic." For contrast, see *etic perpective*.

endangered language

A language at risk of becoming extinct within the foreseeable future. The result of the extinction of an endangered language is language death. A language that is not being passed on to the next generation of speakers is endangered. It may be revitalized through specific programs.

epiglottal place of articulation

The constriction for a speech sound produced between the epiglottis and the back wall of the pharynx. The epiglottal fricatives are [ʕ] (voiced) and [H] (voiceless) and the epiglottal stop is [ʔ].

epiglottis

A spoon-shaped flap of cartilage in the larynx that extends up behind the tongue root. Its base attaches to the thyroid cartilage. The aryepiglottic folds drape it; it moves down to cover the passageway to the larynx when there is danger that anything except air is entering the lungs, thus causing choking or pneumonia. The epiglottis is used in speech for a number of sounds, including epiglottal stops and epiglottal fricatives in some dialects of Arabic.

ethnolinguistics

A field of linguistics that studies language and its relationship to culture. This overlaps with sociolinguistics, anthropological linguistics, cultural linguistics, and the ethnology of communication or the ethnology of speaking. Those who study ethnolinguistics often focus on ethnosemantics, the study of meaning in different cultural settings.

etic perspective

That which is significant to an analyst, the unanalyzed phonetic data. *Etic* is a term coined by Kenneth Pike from "phonetic." For contrast, see *emic perpective*.

external intercostal muscles

See *intercostal muscles*.

external open juncture

See *juncture*.

extra short, short, half-long, long

Varying physical durations of speech sounds. See *length, phonetic*.

face diagram

See *sagittal diagram*.

false vocal folds

See *ventricular folds*.

falsetto voice

A type of phonation in which the vocal folds are stretched longitudinally, leaving the glottis slightly open, resulting in a very high-pitched voice due to the high tension placed on the vocal folds. While falsetto voice is not known to be contrastive in language, it is used as a speech style over an entire utterance or is used in some styles of singing, e.g., some country music.

faucal pillars

The part of the pharynx just behind the oral cavity. The faucal pillars consist of two pairs of muscles that run vertically at the back of the oral cavity on each side of the pharynx. One pair is in front of the uvula and one pair is behind it. The tonsils are located between each pair of the faucal pillars.

faucalization

A phonation type or voice quality produced by tensing the faucal pillars and moving them inward, often accompanied by raising the larynx. Faucalization may be involved in the production of [–ATR] vowels.

feature

A component of a sound. For example, the nasal port being open is a feature of a nasalized vowel, [ã)]. See *phonetic feature*.

flap

A sound produced in which the active and passive articulators come into contact with each other only once and the movement of the active articulator is ballistic and less controlled than are otherwise similarly articulated stops, e.g., [ⱱ, ɾ]. See *tap, trill*.

flat fricative

A speech sound made by forming a constriction in the oral cavity in which the airstream flows over the surface of the tongue that is either grooved less than for a sibilant, or is not grooved at all, e.g., [ç, x].

formant

A resonance of the vocal tract. Formants are a group of overtones that correspond to the resonating frequencies in the vocal tract. The vocal tract has several formants; the most important formants in determining our perception of vowel quality or consonant place of articulation are the three formants with the lowest frequencies. A resonant frequency may be graphically displayed on a spectrogram by thick dark formant bands, also called *formant bars*.

formant bar, formant band

Thick dark bands on a sound spectrogram indicating resonant frequencies within the vocal tract. Average bandwidths for F_1, F_2, and F_3 are as follows: F_1: 54 Hz, F_2: 65 Hz, and F_3: 70 Hz (House and Stevens 1958). Acoustic phoneticians who study formant bandwidth have found that for synthetic speech, if the formant bandwidths are too narrow, a vowel sounds artificial, but is still recognizable.

formant chart

A plot of the first formant against the first formant minus the second formant, e.g., F_1, F_1–F_2.

formant frequency

The rate at which the air vibrates due to a resonance in the vocal tract.

fortis consonant

A consonant produced with greater effort and energy (i.e., muscular tension), sometimes realized as length, greater frication or affrication, a longer release, or a combination of features. Fortisness and its contrastive counterpart, lenisness, are both phonetic and phonological features of consonants in some languages. The *Extension to the IPA* (ExtIPA), prepared by the International Clinical Phonetics and Phonetic Association, uses a IPA fortis diacritic (͈) to indicate "stronger articulation" for a fortis consonant, e.g., [g͈]. See also *tense*. For contrast, see *lenis consonant*.

frame drill

See *differentiation drill*.

frame

The part that remains constant in a frame drill. See also *carrier*.

free jaw

See *set jaw*.

frequency

The rate of occurrence of some phenomenon. In speech it is the rate of vibration of completed cycles of speech sound waves. Frequency is usually measured in Hz. The higher the frequency of a sound wave, the higher the pitch, and conversely, the lower the frequency, the lower the pitch.

fricative, grooved

See *sibilant*.

fricative, spirant

A speech sound articulated with a constriction in a vocal cavity (oral or pharyngeal) between the active and passive articulators with the airstream forced through that constriction, thereby producing audible air turbulence or friction noise, e.g., [ɸ, β, θ, ð, f, v]. A fricative may be voiced or voiceless, and can also be produced with other types of phonation.

fricative release
A stop followed by a fricative release, e.g., [t͡ʃ].

fricative vowel
See *apical vowel*.

front vowel
A vowel produced in the front part of the oral cavity, e.g., [i, ɪ, e, ɛ, a].

fronted postalveolar
See *laminal alveolar*.

fronted sound
A sound produced with a place of articulation further forward than a certain reference, either alveolar or postalveolar. A dental sound is classified as fronted because it is articulated by the tongue tip touching forward of the alveolar ridge. The active articulator for a dental sound is the tongue tip, and the passive articulator the back of the teeth just forward of the alveolar ridge. Postalveolar sounds can also be fronted; they are articulated by the tongue blade at the alveolar ridge, which is forward of the passive articulator for non-fronted postalveolar sounds. Fronted postalveolar sounds are also classified as laminal alveolar.

fronted tongue position
In some speech variants people speak with the tongue positioned further forward. For example, in English when people speak to a baby, they may use this speech style, e.g., 'coochi coochi coo.'

fundamental frequency
In speech, the rate at which the vocal folds vibrate—the first harmonic. The fundamental frequency is represented as F_0 or F0. It is measured in Hertz (Hz), that is, cycles per second. Fundamental frequency relates closely to the movement of pitch as used in tone and intonation.

gap, consonant gap
1. The absence of a linguistic unit that one might expect to occur based on the patterns of relationships between phonetic units present in a specific language. A consonant gap is one example of such an absence. It represents a hole or missing consonant in the sound system in a language.
2. On a spectrogram the absence of resonances or formants.

gemination, geminate
Two identical sounds occurring in sequence coalescing into one long sound. This may occur across a syllable boundary.

glide
1. Movement from one full vowel to a very brief vowel, e.g., [ɑⁱ] or [ɑj].
2. Movement of the formants within a sound, e.g., [j, w].
3. Change of pitch, as in contour tone languages, e.g., a low-high, high-low, high-low-mid glide.
4. A transitional sound in which the speech apparatus moves from one sound to another, e.g., an on-glide or an off-glide.

glided vowel, unglided vowel
In a glided vowel the tongue position changes, thus changing the vowel quality, e.g., [eⁱ] or [ei̯]. Glided vowels are also called *diphthongs* or *triphthongs*. An unglided vowel is one in which the quality of the vowel sound is nearly constant because the articulators are held relatively motionless throughout the articulation.

glottal fricative
An [h] sound articulated at the glottis. The vocal folds are open and there is only a little air turbulence. Because of this, some phoneticians state that [h] is not a fricative (Ladefoged 2001:254). See *voiceless vowel*.

glottal fry
See *creaky phonation*.

glottal place of articulation
Consonant sounds made in the larynx with the glottis as the place of articulation. The glottis may be completely closed producing a glottal stop [ʔ, ʔʰ], or there may be a narrowing of the glottis such that audible friction occurs, producing a glottal fricative [h, ɦ].

glottal pulse
A pulse of air coming up through the glottis that gives the air just above it a sudden shove upward, which in turn shoves the air above it, and so on. Thus the tiny displacement of the air just above the glottis propagates through the vocal tract as a sound

wave. It provides the energy to the vocal tract by a rapid sequence of short bursts of air.

glottal stop
A glottal stop is produced by pressing the vocal folds tightly together and thus closing the glottis completely, as in the English expression [ʔoʔo] 'oh oh'.

glottalic airstream mechanism
The airstream produced by movement of air in the pharyngeal cavity. The air is set into motion by the glottis; the air may be either an ingressive or an egressive airstream. Ejectives and implosives are produced with the glottalic air mechanism.

glottalized sound
See *ejective*.

glottis
The V-shaped opening between the vocal folds. The glottis is opened and closed by action of the arytenoid cartilages.

grammatical tone
The use of pitch to indicate a difference in grammatical function in a language. For example, a language may use low pitch to indicate present tense on a verb and high pitch to indicate future tense.

grapheme
A symbol or letter in a writing system, e.g., 'a, e, i, o, u, p, t, k'.

grooved fricative
See *sibilant*.

gum ridge
See *alveolar ridge*.

guttural
A term referring to sounds that are produced in some languages (e.g., Semitic languages and Welsh) produced in the pharynx.

half-length mark
See *length*.

half-long, long, short, extra short
Varying physical durations of speech sounds. See *length, phonetic*.

hard palate
The bony structure of the roof of the mouth.

harmonic, overtone
Any frequency that is a whole number multiple of the fundamental frequency. For example, if the fundamental frequency is 180 Hz, the next harmonic is 360 Hz (the first overtone), the following harmonic is 540 Hz (the second overtone).

harmonic singing, harmonic changing
See *throat singing*.

harsh voice, tense voice
A type of phonation in which there is hypertension in the larynx resulting in approximation and irregular vibrations of the vocal folds and sometimes vibration also of the ventricular folds and the aryepiglottal folds. The type of sound produced is deep and hoarse-sounding. Harsh voice may be combined with creaky voice or falsetto.

heavy syllable
See *mora-timed language*.

heterorganic affricate
See *affricate, heterorganic*.

Hertz, Hz
A unit of frequency indicating cycles-per-second (cps). The common abbreviation is Hz.

heterorganic
Two adjacent consonant sounds produced at different places of articulation, e.g., [ps, mk]. See *homorganic*.

high
Sounds, whether consonants or vowels, produced with the tongue body raised higher than its normal resting position. These include postalveolar, palatal, and velar consonants and also high vowels.

homorganic
Two adjacent sounds produced at the same or very similar places of articulation, e.g., [ts], [gɣ], and [nd]. In phonetics this term is usually applied to affricates and prenasalized stops.

homorganic affricate
See *affricate, homorganic*.

human subjects research
A means of showing respect for and obtaining permission from those who work with a researcher on a particular research project. It

involves obtaining informed consent. Most sponsoring universities have an Institutional Review Board (IRB) which must approve any work with human subjects. See *informed consent.*

hyoid bone
The bone located at the top of the larynx. Its shape is similar to that of a stirrup.

hypernasality
Sounds modified by having the nasal port open more widely and for longer intervals than for the standard variant.

hyponasality
Sounds modified by having the nasal port open less widely and for shorter intervals than for the standard variant.

ideophone
A word which gives a vivid sound representation of an idea. Ideophones describe sounds, smells, colors, shapes, and manner. They are often interjections, picture words or are onomatopoeic.

idiolect
The linguistic system of a single individual; a person's unique dialect.

idiophone
1. A speech sound of an individual speaker, part of one's own idiolect.
2. A speech sound that is not part of the regular sound system.

implosive
A sound made with an ingressive glottalic airstream. The larynx is lowered with the glottis closed except for any voicing that occurs with the sound. The nasal port is also closed. A raised hook bending to the right is added to the consonant symbol, e.g., [ɓ, ɗ, ʛ, ʄ].

inaudible release
See *released stop.*

informed consent
A document signed by a research subject and the researcher that informs the subject of the nature of the research, outlines the research goals, research procedures, possible risks and benefits of the research, and states that subjects may discontinue participation in a research project at any time without prejudice to themselves. It enables people to understand what is involved in working on a specific research project, protects their privacy, avoids possible litigation, saves the researcher and the research subject from possible risks, and protects the institution that is sponsoring the research.

ingressive
A term applied to a sound made by the airstream flowing inward, e.g., an ingressive glottalic airstream.

ingressive velaric airstream
The airstream used in producing clicks involving two closures in the mouth that trap a small volume of air in the space between them. For contrast, see *egressive.*

initiating action
Muscular action that initiates the movement of the airflow. In speech production it is that which causes the stream of air to move through the vocal tract. See *airstream mechanism* and *initiator.*

initiator
That part of the speech apparatus which causes the airstream to move. The respiratory system is the initiator for the pulmonic airstream, the glottis for the glottalic airstream, and the back of the tongue for velaric airstream.

Institutional Review Board
A committee with a minimum of five persons, set up at universities, colleges, or medical institutions, to oversee all research that deals with people. It ensures that people are aware of the procedures to be performed and possible outcomes of those procedures; it protects their privacy; and it insists that all people who engage in human subjects' research sign an informed consent form. See *human subjects research* and *informed consent.*

instrumental phonetics
The use of various instruments to study speech sound: airflow measurement devices, pressure transducers, materials for doing palatography, sound spectrograph, fiber-optic laryngoscope, and speech analysis computer programs, among others.

intensity
The amount of acoustical energy of a speech sound. This often correlates with stress. On a spectrogram the darkness represents the intensity of the sound at that time and frequency.

intercostal muscles

Two sets of muscles that connect adjacent ribs to each other. The external intercostal muscles are used in inhalation, and the internal intercostal muscles in exhalation. In speech production both sets of muscles are involved in the movement of the airflow to the cavities involved in sound production and resonance.

interdental place of articulation

Consonant sounds produced by the tongue tip placed between the upper and lower teeth, e.g., [θ, ð].

intermittent closure

Closure in which the articulators contact each other more than once in rapid succession. See *flap, trills*.

internal intercostal muscles

See *intercostal muscles*.

internal open juncture

See *juncture*.

International Phonetic Alphabet (IPA)

A phonetic writing system developed by the International Phonetic Association, used in transcribing speech sounds in any language.

International Phonetic Association

A society set up in France in 1886 to promote the use of the phonetic script, particularly for modern European languages. Since 1897 it has been known as the International Phonetic Association. The two leading figures in its history are Paul Passy and his pupil Daniel Jones. It produced *Le Maître Phonétique*. In 1970 the *Journal of the International Phonetic Association* replaced the earlier journal. This association has worked to refine the IPA as the need to do so arises due to new sounds encountered in languages around the world.

intonation

The use of pitch over an entire utterance, whether a word, phrase, clause, or sentence, to indicate emotions, moods, or attitudes. For example, intonation may mark sarcasm, puzzlement, anger, or joy of the speaker. This use of pitch does not make a lexical difference between words. Study of intonation focuses on the distinctive pitch patterns of the voice over an utterance. Pitch levels over an utterance are described as pitch contours. Intonation may be indicative of grammatical and syntactic features, such as in phrases, sentences, or paragraphs. In some languages intonation distinguishes declarative and interrogative sentences, and commands. When a language is predominately a tone language, intonation may also be present.

intonational phrase

The section of an utterance covered by a particular intonational pitch contour.

juncture

1. Any phonetic feature that marks the existence of a grammatical boundary, whether by tone, intonation, pause, or lengthened segment(s).

2. Close juncture refers to the normal transitions between words.

3. Internal open juncture occurs within word boundaries.

4. External open juncture occurs at utterance boundaries.

labial

Sounds made with one or both lips as articulators, e.g., bilabial, labiodental, or linguolabial place of articulation. Rounded vowels and labialized consonants are labial sounds.

labial-alveolar place of articulation

Sounds produced with the upper lip and the alveolar ridge as the passive articulators and the lower lip and the tongue tip as the active articulators, e.g., [t͡pʰ, t͡p, d͡b, n͡m].

labial flap

Sounds including both bilabial and labiodental flaps. In producing a labiodental flap the lower lip is retracted behind the upper teeth, then brought forward rapidly to strike the upper teeth in passing. While the basic flap is labiodental, a bilabial variant has also been found in some languages, with the lower lip flapping against the upper lip. Up to this time a contrast between labiodental and bilabial flaps has not been found in language, rather, one is usually a variant of the other. These two flaps are often referred to as *labial flaps*, a generic term that covers both places of articulation.

labialization, labial-velarization

A secondary articulation in which lip rounding and sometimes lip protrusion is added to a primary consonant articulation. In addition, the tongue back is raised toward the palate. [ʷ] is added to the primary symbol to indicate labialization. Any consonant, including labial consonants, may be labialized, e.g., [bʷ, bw]. [bʷ] represents the primary articulation with a secondary off-glide, and [bʷ] represents simultaneous articulation of the primary and secondary articulations. Note that voiceless labialized stops may also be aspirated, e.g., [kʷʰ].

labial-palatal place of articulation

Sounds produced with the upper lip and the palate as the passive articulators and the lower lip and the tongue as the active articulators, e.g., [ɥ, ɥ̊].

labial-palatalization

A secondary articulation in which there is a combination of palatalization and labialization, i.e., the lips are rounded and the blade or center portion of the tongue is humped up towards the hard palate, simultaneously with a primary articulation, e.g., [tᶣ, tᵤ]. [tᶣ] represents the primary articulation with a secondary offglide; [tᵤ] represents simultaneous articulation of palatalization and labialization added to the primary consonant.

labial-velar place of articulation

Consonant sounds produced with the upper lip and the velum as the passive articulator and the lower lip as the active articulators, e.g., [w, ẘ] and [k͡p, ɡ͡b].

labial-velarization

See *labialization*.

labiodental place of articulation

Consonant sounds produced with the upper teeth as the passive articulator and the lower lip as the active articulator, e.g., [f, v, ɱ].

labiodentalization

A secondary articulation in which the lower lip is brought close to the upper front teeth at the same time as a primary articulation occurs. This occurs in some languages in the Caucasus. The symbol [ᶹ] is added to the primary consonant symbol to indicate labiodentalization.

laminal

Sounds made with the tongue blade as the active articulator. The underbox diacritic, [̬], is used with the primary symbol to indicate that the sound is laminal.

laminal alveolar, fronted postalveolar

The fronted postalveolar place of articulation. It indicates that the tongue blade is the active articulator and the alveolar ridge is the passive articulator.

language family

A group of languages or dialects that are historical descendants of the same proto-parent language. Linguists collect basic vocabulary (e.g., the Swadesh word list and the Benue-Congo comparative word list) from a large number of languages in order to understand the development of languages and dialects within language families. From these data they propose proto-phonological units in the parent proto-language. They also use these basic word lists to compute percentages of cognates between dialects, thus giving some indication of how closely related daughter languages are. Grammatical factors are also taken into account when studying language families (e.g., comparison of noun class affixes in Bantu languages).

language interference

When the sound patterns of one language hamper hearing and producing sounds of another language, particularly sounds that differ from those in one's own language.

language of wider communication (LWC), trade language

A pidgin, creole, or other language that has become the lingua franca used by speakers of other mutually unintelligible languages. A LWC allows communication across language boundaries. It is often used in market, religious, and business contexts as a means to communicate with speakers of mutually unintelligible languages. Many local language speakers have limited understanding of the LWC, and communicate best in their mother tongues.

laryngeal

The place of articulation with the glottis as the articulator, e.g., [h, ʔ].

laryngealization, creaky voice, vocal fry, glottal fry

See *creaky phonation*.

laryngopharynx

The area of the pharynx that extends from the oropharynx down to, but not including, the larynx. Although there are no sharply defined divisions in the pharynx, it is helpful to divide it into three parts, the oropharynx, the laryngopharynx, and the nasopharynx.

laryngoscope

An instrument used to examine the larynx. It consists of a mirror positioned at an angle so that it can be placed inside the mouth. Some use complex fiber-optic technology that allows direct examination of the larynx. Fibers are inserted through the nose, interfering minimally with normal phonation and allowing observation of phonation during speech.

larynx, voice box, supralaryngeal cavity

The muscular structure of the upper part of the trachea where the vocal folds are located. It consists primarily of cartilages and soft tissue. The hyoid bone is at the top of the larynx; it fastens to the thyroid cartilage at the back. The thyroid cartilage is hinged to the cricoid cartilage at the back. At the top part of the cricoid cartilage is a pair of tiny cartilages, the arytenoid cartilages, which move in two important ways. They slide sideways and swivel around a vertical axis under the control of various muscles. The vocal folds are located within the larynx. The front ends of the vocal folds attach to the inside surface of the thyroid cartilage and to the arytenoid cartilages at the back.

lateral, lateral approximant

A sound in which the airstream flows over one or both sides of the tongue, and there is complete closure some place along the midline of the tongue preventing the airstream from passing over the midline of the tongue, e.g., [l, l̥, ʟ, ɭ]. See *liquid*.

lateral affricate

A sound consisting of a stop released into a lateral approximant or fricative, in which the airflow is over one or both sides of the tongue, e.g., [tɬʰ, tɬ, dl].

lateral approximant

See *lateral*.

lateral fricative

A sound produced with audible noisy air turbulence of the airstream as it passes over the sides of the tongue due to complete closure of the vocal tract midline by the tongue and constriction of the airflow.

lateral release, lateral plosion

A plosive/stop articulation released into a lateral, in which one or both sides of the tongue drop while maintaining the medial closure. In IPA this is symbolized as [ˡ] e.g., [tˡ].

lax

1. Sounds thought to be produced with less muscular effort and movement than those described as "tense". Lax consonants are also called *lenis* with spread glottis.

2. Lax vowels are also called *open vowels,* and those with [–ATR]. They occur in closed syllables in American English, e.g., [ɪ, ɛ, ɑ, ɔ, ʊ].

length, phonetic; length marks

A vowel or consonant is said to be long when it lasts perceptibly longer than the same speech sound (or a similar one) in a different environment. Duration of the sound is measured in milliseconds. A pair of small triangles [ː] following a vowel or consonant character indicates length. A long sound may contrast with a short sound in a specific language. Sometimes more than one degree of length is contrastive. IPA provides three symbols for marking degrees of length, with a fourth degree of length left unmarked: [ː] long, [ˑ] half long, unmarked for short, and [˘] extra short, marked with a breve. Koasati and Finnish are languages in which both vowel length and consonant length are contrastive.

length in phonics

In phonics, *long* vs. *short* refers to a contrast in vowel quality, not a difference in length. In English phonics, a short vowel occurs in the middle of a word spelled with a consonant-vowel-consonant sequence such as in 'mat', and a long vowel occurs in the middle of a word spelled with a consonant-vowel-consonant-silent [e] sequence, such as 'mate'.

lenis consonant

A consonant produced with less effort and tending to be shorter than its fortis counterpart. An Extended IPA notation which can be used to indicate lenis is the "weak articulation" diacritic [̣], e.g. /ḅ/. The APA diacritic is a "squiggle" [̰], e.g., /b̰/.

lexical tone

The use of pitch to distinguish meanings of words. Pitch is intrinsic to the word, just as consonants and vowels are. Lexical tone occurs in tone languages, as in Mandarin Chinese [má] 'hemp', [mǎ] 'horse', [mà] 'scold'. (Data from J. D. McCawley as cited in Fromkin 1978:120.)

light syllable
See *mora-timed language*.

Linear Predictive Coding (LPC)
A mathematical technique that encodes the waveform of speech that has been digitized. It uses a small number of coefficients (10 to 12) to calculate successive short segments of the speech wave. LPC is used as the basic principle in analysis-speech synthesis systems.

linguistic phonetics
According to Maddieson, linguistic phonetics focuses "on the phonetic properties and parameters underlying linguistically-relevant contrasts at segmental, prosodic, or other levels of analysis" (2001:212).

linguistic survey
Study of the linguistic relationships of different languages and dialects through collection of linguistic data. These data include phonetic, phonological, lexical, grammatical, and sociolinguistic material. Language surveyors often collect data based on a comparative wordlist for part of their linguistic survey, as well as using listening tests, to ascertain mutual intelligibility among related dialects.

linguolabial place of articulation
Labial sounds produced with the tongue tip as the active articulator and the upper lip as the passive articulator. Linguolabial consonants, whether nasals, stops, or fricatives, are found in some Austronesian languages spoken in Vanuatu.

lip position
The lips may be round or spread. This may indicate a speech variant, as when lip rounding is used to show pity.

lip rounding
See *round*.

lip spreading
See *spread*.

liquid
An alternate term for lateral and various [r] sounds. See *lateral* and *central approximant*.

locus
In acoustic phonetics, the apparent place of origin of a formant of a particular sound for a given place of articulation.

long, half-long, short, extra short
Varying physical durations of speech sounds. See *length, phonetic*.

loudness
An auditory property of a speech sound as perceived by a listener who can place that sound on a scale from soft to loud; volume.

low
Sounds made with the tongue body in lower than its normal resting position. These include low (open) vowels, and pharyngeal consonants.

lower articulators
The active articulators, for example, the lower lip, various parts of the tongue, and the epiglottis.

manner of articulation
The degree of constriction of the airstream and the type of modification of the airstream, whether there is no constriction, slight, intermittent, partial, or complete constriction.

medial phase
See *steady state phase*.

midsagittal section
See *sagittal diagram*.

milliseconds
Time is measured along the horizontal axis of the spectrogram from left to right in milliseconds. Thus, 8 milliseconds is 0.008 seconds.

modal phonation, modal voice, voiced
Speech sounds made with the air flowing through the glottis and the vocal folds vibrating without audible air turbulence. Modal voice is used for many consonants and most vowels and semivowels. These are voiced speech sounds.

monolingual approach to language learning
A method of learning a language where the researcher and speakers of that language do not share a common language. It often involves pointing to objects, acting out actions to find verbs, building up an understanding of adverbs and adjectives, and, in general, working solely in the target language.

monophthong
The phonetic classification of a vowel in which there is no audible change in quality within a syllable. For contrast, see *diphthong*.

monosyllabic
A word with one syllable.

monotone
Very little or no perceptible pitch variation in the voice over a string of speech. However, ordinary human hearing ability allows an individual to identify very tiny changes in pitch; this ability exceeds the human ability to maintain a constant pitch when speaking.

mora, morae/moras (pl.)
A timing unit longer than a single segment, but typically shorter than a syllable. A light syllable has one mora, and contrasts with a heavy syllable. A syllable that ends in a short vowel has one mora, and a syllable that ends in a long vowel or consonant has two morae. Morae are an important part of the rhythm pattern in some languages, such as Japanese.

mora-timed language
A type of rhythm in a language which recurs at regular intervals. It is the syllable weight, whether a light or heavy syllable, that is significant in the rhythm.

mother tongue, native language
The language a person is most comfortable speaking; the first language a person acquires as a child.

mouth air mechanism
See *velaric airstream mechanism*.

mouth cavity
See *oral cavity*.

murmur
See *breathy phonation*.

name of a sound, technical name
A phrase that summarizes the values of the phonetic features of a sound in a standard order. This order is phonation (voiced, voiceless, whispered, etc.), place of articulation, any modification of the sound (e.g., aspiration, palatalization), manner of articulation, direction of the airstream, and airstream mechanism. For example, the technical name for [β] is 'voiced bilabial fricative with egressive pulmonic air'.

narrow phonetic transcription, systematic phonetic transcription
A phonetic transcription that includes fine phonetic detail. For contrast, see *broad phonetic transcription*.

nasal cavity
The area extending from the pharynx to the nostrils, including the nose and sinus cavities. The nasal cavity may be closed by raising the velum for oral sounds, or open by lowering the velum for nasals and nasalized sounds.

nasal click, voiced
See *voiced nasal click*.

nasal plosion
A stop released into a nasal articulated at the same place of articulation, e.g., [dn] as in 'sudden.'

nasal port
The passageway between the oral and nasal cavities. See more at *velic closure* and *velic opening*.

nasal release of clicks
A click in which the velar closure is released first, allowing air to escape via the nasal passage.

nasal sound, nasal stop
A sound produced with the nasal port open (i.e., the velum is lowered), allowing sound to resonate in the nasal cavity, while closure between articulators in the mouth prevents the airstream from passing out through the mouth. This configuration forces air coming up through the larynx and the pharynx to flow through the nasal cavities and out through the nose. Sound waves going through these passages and cavities resonate in each one, including the oral cavity, behind the place of closure of the articulation, and the nasal cavity, e.g., [m, ɱ, n, ɲ, ɳ, ŋ].

nasal vowel
See *nasalized vowel*.

nasalization
A sound produced with the nasal port open, e.g., [n]. See also *hypernasality* and *hyponasality*.

nasalized vowel, nasal vowel
A vowel is nasalized when the soft palate is lowered. Nasalization of vowels is symbolized by a tilde above the vowel symbol, e.g., [ã].

Because a nasalized sound is one in which the airflow is through both the oral and nasal cavities, a nasalized vowel is considered oral even though it also has some airflow through the nasal cavity.

nasopharynx

The part at the back of the nasal cavity, above the velum, which divides it from the oropharynx. Although there are no sharply defined divisions in the pharynx, it is helpful to divide it into three parts, the oropharynx, the laryngopharynx, and the nasopharynx.

native language

See *mother tongue*.

natural class

A group of sounds having some property in common that distinguishes them from other sounds. For example, nasals form a natural class.

neutral tongue root position

The default position intermediate between [+ATR] and [–ATR]. Most languages with a contrast in the tongue root position have a two-way contrast, e.g., [+ATR] vs. [–ATR].

nil phonation

Phonation occurring in any of three ways:

1. the glottis may be tightly closed, producing a glottal stop [ʔ];

2. the glottis may be open wide enough so that air flowing through produces neither vibration of the vocal folds nor audible air turbulence in the larynx (as with voiceless vowels and voiceless fricatives; and

3. the airstream is completely blocked in both the oral and nasal tracts, resulting in the voiceless stops, e.g., [p, t, c, k]. Nil phonation is symbolized by an underring diacritic written beneath a symbol which is otherwise voiced, e.g., [w̥].

no audible release

See *unreleased stop*.

noise

1. Sound that is aperiodic (not periodic), i.e., sound produced by air passing through a narrow constriction such as the vocal tract or glottis.

2. Sound with audible air turbulence.

3. Sound that has irregular vibrations of the sound wave, i.e., a fricative or a sound produced with breathy voice.

4. Undesirable or extraneous sounds that interfere with, or obscure, the sound in focus, e.g., any sound that interferes with a good audio recording of speech.

non-continuant

A sound produced with closure of the vocal tract, for example, a stop. Non-continuants contrast with continuants such as vowels and fricatives. For contrast, see *continuant*.

non-nasalized

See *nasalization*.

non-predictable quality

A voiceless vowel which cannot be predicted from the environment in which it occurs and thus must be represented with a vowel symbol. This contrasts with a predictable quality [h] as in English.

non-rounded

See *spread*.

non-sibilant

See *flat fricative*.

non-sonorant

A sound produced with the airstream modified sufficiently to produce audible friction, e.g., a fricative, or completely constricted, e.g., a stop. See *obstruent*.

non-syllabic vowel

See *semivowel*.

nucleus

The center of a syllable that usually consists of a vowel or a diphthong; the most prominent part of a syllable.

obstruent

A class of sounds made with articulation that constricts or completely obstructs the airstream in the oral cavity, e.g., fricatives, affricates, and stops. For contrast, see *sonorant*.

offset phase, release phase, coda phase

The period in which the vocal organs are moving away from the steady state phase of the syllable nucleus.

onset phase, onset

The period when an active articulator is approaching the place in the vocal tract at which the maximum degree of closure will occur. The onset phase consists of the consonant(s) that occur before the syllable nucleus. These are followed by the medial or steady state phase and the offset or release phase.

open
In the IPA system, open vowels [ɛ, ɜ, ɔ, æ, a, ɑ] are those made with the tongue position lower than its resting place. In the Americanist system open refers to various points along a vertical tongue position scale, e.g., [ɪ, ʊ, ɛ, ʌ, a, ɑ, ɒ] are all described as open vowels, as opposed to their close counterparts: [i, u, e, ə, o, æ, ɔ].

open syllable
A syllable that ends with a vowel, e.g., [kɑ]. See *closed syllable*.

open transition
A transition occuring between two consonants if there is an audible release of the first consonant before the second consonant is fully pronounced.

oral cavity, mouth cavity
The resonating chamber formed by the mouth. See *nasal cavity* and *pharyngeal cavity*.

oral sound
A sound in which the sound waves resonate in the mouth, the oral cavity.

oral stop
See *stop*.

oropharynx
The part of the pharynx behind the mouth, or oral cavity. Although there are no sharply defined divisions in the pharynx, it is helpful to divide it into three parts, the oropharynx, the laryngopharynx, and the nasopharynx.

orthography, practical orthography
A system of writing or spelling of a particular language for the general public.

oscillogram
A plot of some function of time, typically with time plotted along the horizontal axis and the function plotted along the vertical axis. In acoustic phonetics typically the function graphed on an oscillogram is the sound waveform on the vertical axis against time on the horizontal axis. It is the output of an oscilloscope.

overlapping phase, transition
When two sounds are adjacent to each other, the offset phase for the first sound is the same as the onset phase of the second sound, resulting in an overlapping phase.

overtone
See *harmonic*.

overtone singing
See *throat singing*.

palatal place of articulation
Sounds articulated by the tongue front coming close to or contacting the hard palate, forward of the velum, e.g., [c, ɟ, ç, j, ɲ].

palatalization
A secondary articulation in which the tongue is raised toward the hard palate; it is in position to articulate an [i] or [j] during a primary articulation, e.g., [tʲ, tj]. [tʲ] represents the primary articulation with a palatal off-glide, and [tj] represents simultaneous release of primary and secondary articulations.

palate
The roof of the mouth consisting of the hard bony front with the fleshy soft palate further back in the mouth.

palatogram
A two-dimensional record of the place of an articulation on a speaker's palate; phoneticians photograph the palate to make a record for documenting the place of articulation for a particular sound.

palatography
An instrumental procedure used to determine the place of articulation for the active articulator's contact on the palate, in the production of a particular consonant.

partial closure
A constriction in a vocal cavity (oral or pharyngeal) between the active and passive articulators through which the air is forced. See *fricative, lateral fricative*.

participatory research
Research in which the community in focus is involved in decisions about what topics of research to conduct, how they will assist in developing the research design, data collection and analysis, and how the results may benefit their community.

passive articulator, upper articulator

The relatively fixed parts of the vocal apparatus located on the upper surface of the oral cavity. For contrast, see *active articulator*.

period

A term used in acoustic phonetics for the amount of time that it takes for the cycle of air pressure vibration of a sound wave to repeat itself. The period is 1/f, where f represents the frequency. When the period is long, the frequency is low; when the period is short, the frequency of the sound wave is high.

periodic wave

A waveform with regular repetitions. Most speech sound waves are treated as though they are periodic. See *aperiodic wave*.

perseverative coarticulation

A feature from one sound that carries over onto the following sound, e.g., the voicelessness of one sound continues through the following sound.

pharyngeal cavity

The throat area located immediately above the larynx. It includes the epiglottis, (used in the production of a few speech sounds and for closing off the trachea so that food does not enter the lungs). The pharynx also includes the thyroid cartilage and the tongue root. The shape of the pharynx may be constricted or enlarged by movement of the tongue root and by lowering or raising the larynx during speech production.

pharyngeal place of articulation

An articulation with the constriction between the tongue root and the back wall of the pharynx, e.g., a pharyngeal fricative, such as [ħ] or [ʕ]. See *guttural*.

pharyngealization

A secondary articulation in which the tongue root is retracted toward the back wall of the pharynx thus narrowing the pharynx, during the primary articulation of another consonant sound. The place of articulation of the base consonant is fairly far forward in the mouth, e.g., [tˤ]. Pharyngealization is a feature of emphatic consonants in Arabic.

pharynx

The cavity that connects the oral and nasal passages with the esophagus. The nasal pharynx is the part of the pharynx above the velum. The oral pharynx is the part of the pharynx from the larynx to the velum. The laryngopharynx is the cavity that extends from the larynx to the oral pharynx.

phase of articulation

A stage in the production of a speech sound. There are three distinct phases of articulation in context: the onset phase in which the articulator approaches the place where the maximum degree of closure occurs, the medial or steady state phase, and the offset or release of the vocal organs as they move to make the following sound. The offset phase of one sound may be the onset of the following sound, resulting in overlapping phases; this is called *the transition*.

phonation, phonation types

Any vocal activity at the larynx; the acoustic energy produced by vibrations of the vocal folds resulting in the production of sound at the larynx, and the acoustic energy produced by the vibrations of the vocal folds (including zero energy for voiceless sounds). Different types of phonation may be distinguished: voiced or modal phonation, breathy, whisper, laryngealization, or creaky voice. There are also different voice registers caused by the length, thickness, and tension of the vocal folds, resulting in various pitches.

phone

The smallest speech unit that is perceptible within a steam of speech; a single phonetic segment.

phone chart

A table showing symbols for the sounds that a fieldworker finds in a particular language. A phone chart has two parts, one for consonants and one for vowels. This chart is organized for place and manner of articulation.

phoneme

The smallest contrastive sound unit in a given language. Phonemes are abstract units derived through phonological analysis. Phonemes make a difference in meaning; for example, the phonemes /p, b/ contrast in the words 'pat' and 'bat' in English. /p/ is composed of the phones [pʰ] and [p]. Slant marks / / indicate a phoneme or phonological unit, while brackets [ ] indicate phones (phonetic sounds).

phonetic feature

"Any independently controllable component of speech" (Trask 1996:269). Five main phonetic features are the airstream mechanism and direction of the airstream, the state of the vocal folds and the vocal cavities, the velic opening or closure, the manner of articulation, the place of articulation, and the articulators (including both the active and passive articulators).

phonetic length

See *length*.

phonetic quality of a sound

The shape of the speech wave emanating from the speaker's vocal tract and impinging on a listener's eardrums, resulting in how the sound is perceived by the listener. For Example, [s] has a different phonetic quality from [ʃ].

phonetic transcription, phonetic representation

The phonetic symbols (often IPA) used by a phonetician to represent the perceived sounds of a language. Brackets [ ] indicate that the symbols are phonetic.

phonetician

A scientist who specializes in the study of speech sounds. Phoneticians study articulatory phonetics (how sounds are produced physiologically), auditory phonetics (how sounds are perceived), acoustic phonetics, and instrumental phonetics.

phonetics

The science which studies the characteristics of speech sounds from natural languages. This includes production, transcription, and classification of speech sounds. In addition, physiology of speech production, perception, and the acoustic parameters of speech are studied. Four important fields of study are:

1. articulatory phonetics, which addresses the way sounds are produced by the human vocal apparatus;

2. acoustic phonetics, which studies the sound wave as it moves from one person's vocal apparatus to another person's ears;

3. instrumental phonetics, which uses various instruments such as airflow measurement devices, pressure transducers, palatography, etc., to study speech sounds; and

4. auditory phonetics, the study of speech perception.

phonics

A way of teaching reading and writing based on a system of phonetic symbols, usually limited to one language.

phonological system, sound system

The analyzed group of sounds of a particular language as a whole.

phonological transcription

Use of speech symbols for contrastive sound units of a language, set off by diagonal lines / /.

phonology

The study of significant sound patterns within a language. This study results in a description of the sound system of a language.

physiological phonetics

See *articulatory phonetics*.

pidgin

A language formed by speakers of different languages, with a reduced grammatical structure, simplified phonological structure, limited lexicon, and few stylistic features. It is not the native language of any of its speakers. Over time it may develop into a creole language. See *creole*.

pitch, relative pitch, absolute pitch

Our auditory perception of a sound in terms of where it is on a scale from low to high. This corresponds to the rate at which the vocal folds complete each vibration cycle—the fundamental frequency of the voice. Relative pitch is important in speech production and perception; it refers to the pitch range or register of a person depending on his or her vocal apparatus. Absolute pitch refers to an unchanging pitch pattern, such as on a piano scale.

pitch accent

A type of word accent that occurs in some languages, such as Japanese. In a pitch accent language the syllables or morae have one of a particular permitted sequence of pitches. A pitch accent language contrasts with a tone language in that in a pitch accent language only the pitches on accented syllables are contrastive, with other pitches being predictable by phonological rule. On the other hand, in a tone language all of the pitches in words are significant and must be specified.

pitch modulation
Pitch changes used to reflect moods and emotions, or sometimes a person's socioeconomic class. Speakers of some languages use a wide range of pitches, varying from very high to very low within one sentence. Other speech variants use a narrow pitch range. Monotone speech may be indicative of brain injury.

pitch range
The upper and lower limits of the fundamental frequency in a person's voice.

pitch register
The specific range a person uses in speaking. Differences in pitch register may be used as a speech variant. A high pitched voice shows respect in some cultures.

place of articulation, point of articulation
The location in the vocal tract where a constriction between active and passive articulators occurs, forming a sound. Places of articulation include bilabial, labiodental, interdental, dental, alveolar, postalveolar, palatal, velar, uvular, pharyngeal, epiglottal, glottal, and some combinations of these.

plosive, stop
See *stop*.

polysyllabic
A word with more than one syllable.

postalveolar place of articulation
Sounds articulated by the tongue blade which moves to the posterior slope of the alveolar ridge, e.g., the place of articulation for [ʃ] and [ʒ].

postvocalic
A consonant which follows a vowel in the same syllable.

practical orthography
See *orthography*.

predictable quality [h]
In English an [h] is used to represent a voiceless vowel when the quality of the vowel is predictable from the environment, that is from the voiced vowel that occurs next to it. Both the voiced and the voiceless vowel will have the same articulation and vowel quality.

prenasalized stop
A stop with a short nasal onset articulated at the same place of articulation, e.g., [ᵐb] and [ⁿd].

preplosion of a nasal
A nasal with a short stop onset articulated at the same place of articulation, e.g., [ᵇm] and [ᵈn].

prevocalic
A consonant sound which precedes a vowel in the same syllable.

primary articulation, primary articulator
An articulation that blocks or constricts the airstream. The terms *primary articulation* and *primary articulator* are used when there is a secondary articulation present. The primary has a greater degree of closure than the secondary articulation added to it.

profile diagram
See *sagittal diagram*.

prominence
The degree to which a particular sound or syllable stands out from surrounding sounds or syllables, based on pitch (whether higher or lower), greater loudness, longer duration, and stress.

proprioception
A speaker's awareness or feeling of his/her own articulations by nerve receptors.

prosody
The pitch, loudness, tempo, and rhythm variations over an utterance. The term *prosody* is sometimes used interchangeably with *suprasegmental*. See *suprasegmental*.

proto-language
The parent or ancestor language of two or more linguistically related dialects. A proto-language is derived through analysis of the attested dialects by historical and comparative linguistic techniques.

pulmonic airstream mechanism
The movement of the air in the lungs set into motion by the respiratory mechanism including the diaphragm and the intercostal muscles. The pulmonic airstream is used in the vast majority of speech sounds of the world's languages.

pulmonic cavity
The abdominal cavity behind the ribs. It includes the respiratory system and the diaphragm to produce egressive pulmonic airstream.

quality of a speech sound
The combination of the perceptual characteristics of a speech sound, causing the hearer to perceive a certain sound as a particular consonant or vowel. The quality comes from its acoustic spectrum or resonance frequencies. See *vowel quality*.

radical
Sounds produced with the tongue root or the epiglottis as the active articulator. Such sounds involve partial or almost complete constriction of the pharynx. Some of the sounds characterized as radical are those with advanced or retracted tongue, and epiglottal stops and fricatives.

rate of speech
The rate of speech refers to whether the speech is rapid, normal, or slow. In rapid speech, certain words may be distressed or reduced in form.

Received Pronunciation (RP)
A British English accent spoken in the southeastern area of England. According to Trask (1996:301–302) RP includes a group of closely related accents. While only approximately 3% of the British population speak it, RP is the prestige standard in England. It is the dialect of broadcast media, of royalty, the aristocracy, academics, senior politicians, and the upper class. Daniel Jones, a well-known British phonetician, called it "public school pronunciation." Just as most accents and dialects change, so RP is changing because it is in contact with regional varieties of British English, particularly in the direction of glottaling, not previously present.

reduced vowel
A vowel pronounced with a noncontrasting centralized vowel quality, such as schwa [ə]. Often the underlying form is the full form of the vowel. In some languages a reduced vowel occurs in unstressed positions of the word.

register tone
A pitch system that is perceived to stay relatively level on individual syllables.

register tone language
A tone language with register or level tones. For contrast, see *contour tone language*.

relative pitch
See *pitch*.

release phase
See *offset phase*.

released consonant; released stop
The stage of an articulation immediately following a stop. A voiceless stop may have an audible release with either light or heavy aspiration, or an inaudible release without aspiration. A voiced stop may be released into an epenthetic vowel from the mid central region of the vowel space. For contrast, see *unreleased stop*.

resonance
Secondary vibrations of a sound at particular frequencies according to the size and shape of the resonator; in speech this is the vocal tract. By changing the configuration of the vocal tract the resonance frequencies change. Formants are resonant frequencies of the vocal tract. See *formant*.

resonant
A sound in which any constrictions in the path of the airstream are insufficient to produce audible noise or friction; thus the sound is not a fricative. Examples of central resonant continuants are vowels, laterals, nasals, and frictionless continuants. A nonobstruant. For contrast, see *obstruent*.

retracted tongue root, [-ATR]
A vowel is [–ATR] when the tongue root is pulled back and the larynx is raised. There may also be a change in phonation. The pharyngeal cavity is narrowed. The features [+ATR] and [–ATR] are often used to describe languages with vowel harmony. For contrast, see *advanced tongue root [+ATR]*.

retroflex flap
A sound produced with the underside of the tongue tip contacting the back of the alveolar ridge, in a back-to-front movement.

retroflexed postalveolar sound
See *sub-apical retroflexed sound*.

retroflex sound, retroflexion
A sound produced with the tip of the tongue curled upward, and sometimes back, the active articulator being some part of the tongue tip. The passive articulator is located behind the alveolar

ridge. These sounds usually have rhoticity, an 'r' sound quality that often extends onto adjacent vowels.

rhotacized approximant, rhoticity

A sound with an /r/ [ɚ] quality. These sounds may be produced by curling the tongue tip upward and back toward the back of the alveolar ridge or by humping up the center of the tongue with the acoustic outcome being a lowered third formant.

rhotic

A form of English in which an 'r' sound occurs following a vowel within a syllable, e.g., 'car,' 'far,' 'bar.' While midwestern English is rhotic, some southern English dialects are nonrhotic.

rhoticity

See *rhotacized approximant*.

rhyme, rime

The part of a syllable that consists of its nucleus and any following consonants.

rhythm

The perceived regular occurrence of prominent elements in a stream of speech. These elements may be stresses, syllables (heavy or light), or morae. When the rhythm is caused by stresses, it is a stress-timed language. When the regular occurrence is that of syllables, it is a syllable-timed language.

rime

See *rhyme*.

Rothenberg mask

A "hard plastic mask with a protruding handle, a soft rubber gasket around the base that prevents air from leaking out when the mask is pressed tightly against the face. The mask has two chambers separated by a piece of plastic and a gasket that runs across the upper lip to divide the space into an oral chamber and a nasal chamber. In each of the two chambers is a pneumotachograph that measures air pressure" (Merrifield and Edmondson 1999:305).

round, rounded, lip rounding

The lips being in a protruded position that reduces the lip opening during the production of a sound, e.g., [o, u]. For lip rounding on consonants see *labialization*.

sagittal diagram, sagittal section, midsagittal section, face diagram, profile diagram

A static schematic picture of the side view of the head used to indicate positions of the vocal apparatus in the production of a speech sound. This diagram indicates what articulators are involved, the position of the velum, the airstream mechanism and its direction of flow, and the action of the vocal folds. Since speech involves a continuum of sounds, and, since a sagittal diagram represents a static picture of one sound, there are limitations to what a sagittal section can tell about a sound.

secondary articulation, secondary articulator

An articulation added to a primary articulation though with a lesser degree of stricture. There are seven types of secondary articulation: labialization, palatalization, velarization, pharyngealization, labiodentalization, labial-palatalization, and labial-velarization. See also *coarticulation*.

segment, segmental

A discrete unit such as one consonant or one vowel within a stream of speech. This unit may be defined based on articulatory, auditory, or acoustic criteria.

semivowel, central approximant, non-syllabic vowel

1. A sound in which there is no audible friction, with the air flowing unrestricted through the oral cavity as it does for a vowel, but with a narrower constriction than that for the vowel.
2. A central approximant, such as [j, ȷ̊, w, w̥, ʋ, ʋ̥].
3. A sound functioning as a consonant in language though without many of the features usually associated with consonants in which the partially constricted airstream has audible friction or is completely obstructed.
4. Acoustically, a sound in which the formants move throughout production without a steady state portion.

set jaw

Languages with a set jaw speech variant tend to have vowels in a narrower, closer area of the vowel space, while languages with a free jaw will vary their vowels over a wider range of vertical tongue positions. How freely the jaw moves can sometimes indicate the speaker's mood, formality, or some other extra-linguistic factor.

short, extra short, half-long, long

Varying physical durations of speech sounds. See *length, phonetic*.

sibilant, grooved fricative

A fricative made with the airstream flowing between the narrow groove shape of the tongue as it is in contact with the alveolar ridge, e.g., [s, z, ʃ, ʒ]. In the production of a sibilant there is a narrower passageway for the airstream than is for other fricative sounds. This results in a high frequency hush or hiss sound. Acoustically, there is a concentration of noise in the higher frequencies largely due to the noise from the airstream passing through the groove in the tongue.

slight closure

A movement of articulators that is not close enough to cause audible noise. See *vowel, central approximant, lateral approximant*.

slurring

Sliding one's tongue back and forth or up and down through the whole range of vowel qualities while maintaining a constant lip position. This is an articulatory method to aid in pronouncing vowel qualities which a speaker may have difficulty saying. By use of slurring the speaker can stop at any vowel quality along a continuum. See also *bracketing*.

sociolect

A dialect that is defined by social factors such as a particular social class or occupational group, rather than on regional grounds.

sociolinguistics, sociology of language

The study of all aspects of the relationship of language and society. It involves analysis of communicative events, conversations, and the use of language in all contexts, including the media, the Internet, the relationship between language and power, language and ideology, language and social groups (subcultures), language and gender, and standard and non-standard variations of speech usage. Sociolinguists may specialize in particular areas such as sociophonetics, sociophonology, and sociosemantics. There is overlap between sociolinguistics, ethnosemantics and anthropological linguistics. Some view dialectology, the study of regional dialects, as a branch of sociolinguistics. Sociolinguistics is often divided into two areas, micro (the variations in the use of a particular language) and macro. Macro sociolinguistics is often called the sociology of language; it focuses on the relationships between languages (e.g., multilingualism, language choice).

sociophonetics

The study of phonetic variations relating to the use of language in its social context, such as the study of the phonetics of different accents.

soft palate

See *velum*.

sonorant

A speech sound in which the airstream, though modified, flows relatively freely. Sonorants include vowels, semivowels, nasals, and laterals. For contrast, see *obstruent*.

sonority

A term used in auditory phonetics referring to the inherent loudness of a sound; for example, the vowel [ɑ] has greater inherent loudness than the vowel [u] when both are produced with the same pitch, stress, and duration. The nucleus is more sonorous than other sounds in a syllable.

sound

In speech, a vibration of air particles started by some source of energy.

sound spectrograph

A machine for analyzing speech acoustically, developed in the 1940s by Bell Laboratories. It displays 2.5 seconds of speech on paper specifically developed for use on the sound spectrograph. It produces a spectrogram which indicates the sound spectrum and formant frequencies of sounds within the vocal tract.

sound-symbol concept

The use of one symbol or a symbol together with one or more diacritics to represent one sound. This is often considered the ideal for a practical orthography, though it is not always possible. Digraphs and trigraphs may be necessary to represent one sound, e.g., use of 'sh' for [ʃ].

sound wave

A three-dimensional radiation of sound energy that fades away into the distance. In speech it is caused by vibration of the glottis which displaces air above itself; it continues to displace air through the vocal tract. The speech sound wave then quickly fades away in air. It is received by a listener's ear, resulting in the hearer's interpretation into meaning.

spectral tilt

Any deviation from a normal spectral slope. Such a deviation has been correlated with different types of phonation. For example, a dominant first harmonic correlates with breathy voice, while a relatively strong second harmonic correlates with tense or creaky voice. See *spectrum*.

spectrogram

A two-dimensional graphic display that indicates time, frequency, and intensity of a speech sound. Time is represented on the horizontal axis and frequency on the vertical axis. Dark bands of acoustic energy indicate formants, the resonant frequencies of the vocal tract. Intensity of a sound is indicated by the darkness of the formants. Voicing, formant frequencies, length, intensity, and harmonics of the speech wave are all displayed on a spectrogram. A sound spectrogram allows a phonetician to visually recognize the steady state of a sound, and the pattern in the transition from a vowel to a consonant or from a consonant to a vowel, helping to identify the place of articulation of a consonant.

spectrograph

A machine developed during World War II that produces a spectrogram showing an analysis of approximately 2.5 seconds of speech. Now replaced by computer programs such as Speech Analyzer.

spectrum, spectral slope

"The frequency and intensity of the sinusoidal components of the speech wave" (Denes and Pinson 1993:141). This can be graphed with amplitude of each harmonic of a sound plotted against the frequency of each harmonic. The resultant graph shows the contribution of each component frequency. A spectral slope is a display of the spectrum in which the frequency of the harmonics gradually decreases in amplitude. As the sound is modified in the oral cavity, the speech output spectrum has peaks and valleys in its harmonics.

speech style, speech variant

A way of speaking that is different from that used by other speakers of the same language.

speech wave

See *sound wave*.

speed

See *rate of speech*.

spirant

An older term for fricative. See *fricative*.

spread, lip spreading, unrounded [vowels], non-rounded

Lip position during the production of vowels, such as [i] and [e] where the lips are stretched sideways, as in a smile.

standard speech style, standard speech variant

One of the variants of a language which is considered to be more prestigious than others, thus making it the standard. There are frequently a number of non-standard variants.

state of the vocal folds, state of the glottis

The condition or action of the vocal folds, whether vibrating, thus producing pitch, apart and not vibrating, closed, partially open and vibrating, partially open but not vibrating, and so on. This may be used to indicate a speech variant.

steady state phase, medial phase

A sound produced during which the articulators briefly remain in one position. On a sound spectrogram the formants are shown not changing frequencies during the steady state phase.

sternum

The flat bone that extends down the chest front and connects to the ribs.

stiff voice

A type of phonation in which the vocal folds are held more tightly or stiffly than for modal phonation, with a slightly lower flow of air. This results in voicing with a slight degree of phonation. Ladefoged and Maddieson (1996:55) state that the term *stiff voice* can be used to describe a slight degree of laryngealization.

stop, plosive, oral stop, occlusive

A consonant produced with the airstream completely blocked, that is, closed both in the oral cavity and the nasal cavity, e.g., [p, b, t, d, c, ɟ, k, g, q, ɢ, ʔ]. While both nasal and oral sounds may be classified as *stops,* the term usually refers to oral sounds. For contrast, see *continuant*.

stop burst, stop release

1. A small audible explosion accompanying the release of a stop.

2. On a sound spectrogram a stop burst is indicated by a sudden peak of energy at the release of a stop. See *aspiration*.

stress, stressed syllable, stress mark

A syllable produced with greater effort of the respiratory system giving it greater prominence. A stressed syllable has one or more of the following features: extra length, loudness, pitch change (often it is higher in pitch), and vowel quality difference from that of an unstressed syllable. Primary stress is symbolized with the stress mark [ˈ] before the stressed syllable, and secondary stress by the diacritic [ˌ] before the syllable.

stress-timed language

A language in which stressed syllables tend to recur at regular intervals, regardless of the number of unstressed syllables between stresses. Examples include English, Thai, Arabic, and Russian. For contrast, see *syllable-timed language*.

stricture, degree of constriction

Complete or partial closure of the vocal tract resulting in sounds made with a constricted airflow such as stops and fricatives.

strident

Sounds produced with a considerable amount of noise (e.g., a loud or harsh sound), particularly in the higher frequencies. These include sibilants and fricatives, e.g., [s, ʃ].

strong form

The form of a word or syllable when stressed. This term describes words or syllables that are normally unstressed, particularly function words such as the English indefinite article 'a' [eɪ̯] vs. the unstressed form, [ə], and definite article 'the' [ði] vs. the unstressed form, [ðə].

sub-apical retroflexed sound, retroflexed postalveolar sound

A sound made with the underside of the tongue tip behind the alveolar ridge.

subglottal pressure

Pressure that builds up under the vocal folds forcing them apart so that they vibrate. Subglottal pressure is a primary determinant of loudness.

substitution item

A sound or word placed into a frame word, phrase or sentence drill in order to study contrasts between substitution items. This technique aids in language learning and linguistic analysis. See also *carrier*.

supralaryngeal vocal tract, supralaryngeal cavity

That part of the vocal tract above the larynx. See *larynx*.

suprasegmental, suprasegmental feature

A term used both in phonetics and phonology to refer to a feature that extends over more than one segment, for example, pitch used as tone or intonation, rhythm, stress, and nasalization. See *prosody*.

survey

See *linguistic survey*.

syllabic

1. Sounds that occur at the syllable nucleus. In general, vowels are syllabic and consonants are not. However, nasals and liquids may be syllabic in some languages.

2. Syllabic writing systems or syllabaries are based on one symbol for each syllable, e.g., the Amharic writing system.

syllabic consonant, syllabicity mark

A syllabic consonant serves as a syllable nucleus, e.g., [l̩, n̩, ɹ̩, ɣ̩]. A stroke *(syllabicity mark)* [̩] is written below a consonant to indicate that the consonant is the syllable nucleus. For example, a syllabic nasal occurs in the English word [bətn̩] 'button'.

syllabic fricative

See *syllabic consonant*.

syllabic lateral

See *syllabic consonant*.

syllabic nasal

See *syllabic consonant*.

syllable

A fundamental phonological unit consisting of one or more sounds, with an obligatory nucleus and an optional onset and coda. The nucleus may be a single vowel, diphthong, or syllabic consonant, and the onset and coda may have one or more consonants. Typical syllable patterns include V, VC, CV, CVC, CCV, CCVC, CCVCC, with C representing any consonant, and V representing any vowel. Syllables may carry both stress and tone. Boundaries between syllables are marked with a period [.] placed between the two syllables.

syllable break
　The boundary between two syllables, marked by a period: [ba.ba].

syllable coda
　One or more consonants which follow the nucleus; they occur at the end of a syllable, e.g., the second consonant in a CVC syllable.

syllable nucleus, syllable peak
　The central position of a syllable which is usually occupied by a vowel, though a syllabic consonant may also function as a syllable nucleus.

syllable onset
　One or more consonants preceding the nucleus of a syllable, as the first C in a CVC syllable.

syllable-timed language
　A language in which every syllable tends to have approximately the same duration. Examples of syllable-timed languages are Spanish, French, Greek, Swedish, Hindi, and Yoruba. See *stress-timed language*.

systematic phonetic transcription
　See *narrow phonetic transcription*.

tap
　A sound made with a burst of muscular tension, throwing the active articulator—the tongue tip—against the passive articulator. The muscular tension does not continue long, and the active articulator promptly falls back to its resting position, again propelled by some combination of the elasticity of the tongue and the air pressure that builds during the time that the airstream is completely blocked. Taps are probably simply the limiting case of shortening certain stops, nasals, or laterals. See *flap*.

target position
　An idealized articulatory position for the production of a particular speech sound. The target position serves as a reference point for comparison with the produced sound. Sagittal diagrams represent target positions for articulation of specific speech sounds.

technical name
　See *name of a sound*.

tense
　1. Sounds produced with greater muscular tension, more extreme movements of the vocal apparatus, longer duration, and greater subglottal air pressure than for lax sounds. Tense consonants are also called *fortis* consonants.
　2. Tense vowels are also called *close vowels, narrow vowels, those with a constricted glottis,* and *those with* [+ATR]. They occur in open syllables in American English, e.g., [i, ei, ɑ, ɔ, u, ɑi, oi].

tense voice
　See *creaky phonation, harsh voice*.

test word
　A word used in palatography studies containing the consonant in focus in which the tongue touches the roof of the mouth.

throat singing, overtone singing, harmonic singing, harmonic changing
　A type of singing that involves regular vibrations by the vocal folds in which the focal folds stay open for shorter lengths of time and closed longer, thus giving greater amplitude to the harmonics. In addition, vibrations often include the ventricular folds and/or aryepiglottic folds. The root of the epiglottis and the arytenoid cartilages are also involved in phonation by throat singers. It is a form of overtone singing. The use of these structures allows throat singers to produce one, two, three, or even four tones simultaneously. High-pitched throat singing sounds like whistling, which occurs in the larynx with modifications by the tongue in the vocal cavity. In making the whistling sound singers focus on strengthening of a single harmonic through placement of the tongue. When singing the lower harmonics, a throat singer places the base of his tongue near the rear of his throat.

thyroid cartilage
　Cartilage between the hyoid and cricoid cartilages, shaped like a shield or a pair of wings. The vocal folds attach in the front; this cartilage protects the vocal folds. It is hinged to the cricoid cartilage at the back. The 'Adam's apple' is the upper front corner of the thyroid cartilage. It is the largest of the cartilages in the larynx.

tilde
　1. In IPA the tilde diacritic [˜] is placed over a base character indicating nasalization, as of a vowel.

Glossary

2. A tilde [˷] may also be placed beneath a base character to indicate that the sound is produced with laryngealization or creaky voice, e.g., [b̰a̰].

3. In some transcription systems, a tilde is also used in combination with the symbol n to represent a postalveolar nasal [ñ].

token
An incidence of a particular sound within an utterance, e.g., there are two tokens of [m] within the word *movement*.

tone
The use of pitch on a word or syllable to indicate lexical or grammatical meaning distinctions. Register tone languages predominately have level pitches, whereas contour tone languages consist mainly of gliding tones. See *lexical tone* and *grammatical tone*.

tone contour
In intonation the sequence of pitches over a phrase or sentence.

tone glide
Pitch that is perceived to rise or fall or both, within a single syllable. See *glide*.

tone group
See *breath group*.

tone sandhi
The modification of tones due to influence of adjacent tone patterns.

toneme
A unit of pitch which contrasts with one or more other pitches, making a difference in meaning. See *phoneme*.

tongue
The fleshy moveable organ in the mouth used for eating and speaking. It is the main organ of articulation in speech, for producing consonants and vowels.

tongue position
The tongue may be positioned fronted or backed compared to the normal position for a certain speech variant, as in baby talk in American English.

tongue root
The active articulator for pharyngeal consonants and pharyngealization of consonants, the passive articulator being the back wall of the pharynx.

tonic syllable
A syllable which stands out in an intonation pattern over an utterance, usually due to a major pitch change.

trachea, windpipe
A stack of ring-shaped cartilages, open toward the back and joined by soft tissue. The top of the trachea attaches to the larynx and the cricoid cartilage, and the bottom extends to the lungs.

transglottal pressure
The difference in air pressure across the glottis.

transition
1. The movement of the articulators from the position of one sound to that of another.

2. A rapid change in formant frequencies from one sound to another sound, which may be seen on a spectrogram; this formant transition is often the primary clue to the place of articulation of a sound. The transition consists of an offset phase of one sound and an onset phase of the following sound, which may result in overlapping phases.

trill
A speech sound in which the articulators contact each other more than once in rapid succession. The airstream is intermittently closed by the vibration of part of the vocal tract, e.g., lips, the tongue tip, or the uvula.

true vocal folds
See *vocal folds*.

umlaut
1. In traditional linguistics an umlaut above a vowel represents a change in which a sound is influenced by a vowel in the following syllable, particularly in Germanic languages, e.g., [ö].

2. The umlaut symbol can be placed underneath a sound to indicate breathy voice, e.g., [b̈].

unaspirated stop
A consonant produced with complete obstruction in the oral cavity and released without any audible airflow from behind the closure. It is released directly into the following sound. Voicing begins immediately on the following sound with no delay of *voice onset time*.

underring diacritic
In IPA the diacritic [˳] which indicates that an otherwise voiced sound is voiceless, e.g., [q̥].

unglided vowel
See *glided vowel*.

unreleased consonant; unreleased stop
When in final position in a word, usually preceding silence, a stop may lack an audible release. An unreleased stop is symbolized by a small corner diacritic following the consonant, e.g., [p̚, t̚, k̚]. See *released consonant*.

unrounded
See *spread*.

upper articulators
The passive articulators located on the upper surface of the oral cavity.

upper gums
See *alveolar ridge*.

upstep
The raising of a high tone following a high, or the upgliding of a high tone, symbolized in IPA with [↑].

uvula
A small fleshy mass of tissue hanging down from the center of the soft palate above the back of the tongue.

uvular place of articulation
Sounds articulated by the tongue back coming close to or contacting the back part of the velum, including the uvula, resulting in a uvular place of articulation, e.g., [q, ɢ, χ, ʁ, ɴ].

velar place of articulation, dorso-velar place of articulation
Sounds produced between the palatal and uvular places of articulation, in which the tongue back moves towards the front of the velum, e.g., [k, g, x, ɣ, ŋ].

velaric airstream mechanism, mouth air mechanism
Movement of mouth air with the tongue back against the velum as the initiator of the ingressive airstream. Clicks are sounds made with the velaric airstream mechanism.

velarization
A secondary articulation in which the tongue back rises towards the velum as for the close back unrounded vowel [ɯ] with the primary articulation occurring towards the front part of the mouth, e.g., [tˠ, t̴]. The first symbol represents a primary articulation with a secondary velar off-glide, and the second represents simultaneous articulation and release of the primary and secondary articulations. The second [l̴] in the English word 'little' is velarized.

velic closure
The velum is raised against the pharyngeal wall, closing the passageway to the nasal cavity, the nasal port.

velic opening
The velum is lowered away from the pharyngeal wall, thus opening the passageway to the nasal cavity.

velum, soft palate
The soft or fleshy moveable part of the palate located at the back of the roof of the mouth.

ventricular folds, false vocal folds
A pair of folds or tissue located just above and parallel to the true vocal folds. They attach to the thyroid cartilage at the front and to the arytenoid cartilages at the back. They may remain open while the vocal folds close. Concerning their relevance to speech, Trask states, "They can...be approximated to produce ventricular whisper; they can be set in vibration to produce ventricular voice; and they can be completely closed to produce a ventricular stop. Catford (1977:104) reports that ventricular fricatives, trills and stops have phonemic status in several Caucasian languages" (1996:375).

vibration
A back-and-forth movement of air particles started by some source of energy. See *sounds*.

video fluoroscope
A motion x-ray that can be used to study speech instrumentally.

vocal cavities
The chambers that are involved in speech production, namely the lungs and their musculature, the pharyngeal cavity, the oral cavity, and the nasal cavity, including the sinus cavities.

vocal folds, vocal cords, true vocal folds
Two thin muscular membranes in the larynx which can vibrate to produce pitch. At the front they attach to the inside of the thyroid cartilage and at the back to the arytenoid cartilages. The

arytenoid cartilages rotate to bring the vocal folds together or to move them apart. The space between the vocal folds is called the *glottis*.

vocal fry
See *creaky phonation*.

vocal tract, vocal apparatus
1. A general term that describes the parts of the body involved in speech production, including the diaphragm, the lungs and its musculature, the trachea with the vocal folds, the pharyngeal cavity, the oral cavity, and the nasal cavity. Sagittal diagrams represent schematically some of what is included in the vocal tract as speech is produced.

2. Some phoneticians restrict the use of the term *vocal tract* to the parts that lie above the larynx, e.g., the pharyngeal tract, the oral tract, and the nasal tract. It is basically a tube through which sounds travel that modifies those sounds according to the resonance frequencies (formants) of the vocal tract.

vocoid
A phonetic term coined by Kenneth L. Pike (1943) to refer to a central oral resonant continuant. See *vowel* and *semivowel*. It contrasts with *contoid*, a parallel term for consonant. These are intended to be etic terms to describe sounds that would later be placed by phonological analysis into the emic terms *vowel* and *consonant*.

voice bar
The lowest band on a sound spectrogram, representing the fundamental frequency at which the vocal folds vibrate. If it is present, it indicates that the sound is voiced; if the bar is absent, it indicates that the sound is voiceless.

voice box
See *larynx*.

voice onset time (VOT)
The length of time between the release of a stop and the vibration of the vocal folds.

voice register
The voice quality of an individual based on the physiology of his/her larynx. There are various voice qualities based on the length, thickness, and tension of the vocal cords. To have a high or low voice register refers to the particular range of pitches used by a single person. Women tend to have higher voice registers than men, and children tend to have higher voice registers than both men and women.

voiced click
A click in which in addition to the velaric airstream mechanism, egressive pulmonic airstream is causing the vocal folds to vibrate, and the nasal port is closed.

voiced implosives
An implosive sound made simultaneously with ingressive glottalic airstream mechanism as well as egressive pulmonic aistream. The vocal folds are not held as tightly together as for a voiceless implosive with the result that air leaks upward through the glottis, causing the vocal folds to vibrate.

voiced nasal click
A click in which in addition to the velaric airstream mechanism, egressive pulmonic airstream is causing the vocal folds to vibrate, and the nasal port is open.

voiced sound, voiced phonation
A speech sound produced with the vocal folds vibrating. Voiced sounds can be made with modal voice, breathy voice, creaky voice, harsh voice, or stiff voice. Falsetto sounds may also be voiced.

voiceless glottal fricative
A sound made with the vocal folds slightly apart with the air flowing through them, producing the fricative [h].

voiceless implosives
A voiceless sound made with ingressive glottalic airstream. The glottis remains closed.

voiceless sound, voiceless phonation
A speech sound produced without the vocal folds vibrating.

voiceless vowel
A vowel articulated with the rate of airflow through the glottis and the degree of constriction at the glottis sufficient to produce audible air turbulence. A vowel is also voiceless when there is nil phonation or breath phonation. The underring diacritic placed below the vowel indicates voicelessness, e.g., [i̥, e̥, ḁ, o̥, u̥].

volume
The degree of loudness of speech. This may indicate social class, mood, or a specific situation and thus mark a speech variant.

vowel

1. A general category of speech sounds that are central oral resonant continuants. A vowel is central because the airstream goes over the center of the tongue. It is oral because it is produced in the oral cavity, the mouth. It is resonant in that any constriction in the path of the airstream is insufficient to produce audible noise and friction. It is a continuant because the sound could be continued indefinitely, were it not that the lungs have a limited airflow capacity. Vowels are best described acoustically rather than articulatorily because of the different shapes of individuals' vocal tracts, yet we can still recognize auditorily what vowel we hear.

2. In phonology a vowel is usually the syllable nucleus. See *apical vowel, vocoid.*

vowel cluster

A sequence of two or more vowels.

vowel glide

A vowel sound beginning in one vowel position and gliding to another. The shorter of the two is usually the second vowel. Vowel glides are symbolized by a superscript symbol following the first vowel, e.g., [ɑⁱ] or the non-syllabic diacritic [̯], e.g., [eɪ̯].

vowel harmony

In some languages only certain combinations of vowels are permitted in words; there is agreement among vowels with respect to some phonetic feature, e.g., backness, rounding, advanced tongue root, such that only vowels sharing some feature may occur within a word, "harmonizing" with each other. In some languages there may be a neutral vowel which does not participate in the vowel harmony.

vowel quality

All of the distinguishing phonetic features of a particular vowel resulting from the positions of the tongue and the lips; this term does not include pitch, loudness, or duration. There is some discussion among phoneticians as to whether nasalization is a feature of vowel quality. IPA considers it an independent feature, while acoustically it is part of the vowel quality.

vowel reduction

In causal speech, when a vowel shortens and moves towards a central position (on the vowel chart). There may even be vowel loss, and shortening of long vowels.

vowel space

The area in the oral cavity in which vowel sounds are produced.

wave, waveform

In the physics of sound, a wave refers to the cycles of air pressure variations of a sound over time. Some waveforms are periodic, indicating that there are regular repeating patterns of the speech sound wave (e.g., modal voice). Others are aperiodic, e.g., sibilants.

weak form

The unstressed form of a word, such as occurs when a word is said in context, not in isolation. Vowels in function words frequently occur in weak form, e.g., the articles 'a,' and 'the.'

wedge

See *breve.*

wepa, wela

Abbreviation for *with egressive pulmonic/lung air.*

whisper phonation

A type of phonation in which the vocal folds are pressed tightly against each other, closing the main part of the glottis; the arytenoid cartilages are rotated beyond the position necessary for complete glottal closure, leaving a small glottal opening between the arytenoid cartilages in the back of the vocal folds. Air is forced through the small opening producing considerable noisy air turbulence. The sound produced is louder than that for breath phonation.

whispered vowel

A vowel produced with the high-pitched quality of air rushing through the narrow glottis under high pressure. See *whisper phonation.*

whistle

A high-pitched shrill sound produced by air passing through a narrow constriction, e.g., the lips.

windpipe

See *trachea.*

References

Armstrong, Robert G. 1989. Idomoid. In Bendor-Samuel and Hartell (eds.), 323–336.
Atkins, Beryl, Alain Duval, Rosemary C. Milne, Pierre-Henri Cousin, Helene M.A. Lewis, Lorna A. Sinclair, Renee O. Birks, and Marie-Noelle Lamy. 1987. *Collins Robert French~English, English~French dictionary.* 2nd ed. Paris: Harper Collins.
Backstrom, Peter C., and Carla F. Radloff. 1992. *Languages of northern areas: Sociolinguistic survey of Northern Pakistan,* Vol. 2. Islamabad: National Institute of Pakistan Studies Quaid-i-Azam University and Summer Institute of Linguistics.
Bargery, G. P., compiler. 1934. *A Hausa-English dictionary and English-Hausa vocabulary.* London: Oxford University Press.
Barley, Nigel. 1986. *Ceremony: An anthropologist's misadventures in the African bush.* New York: Henry Holt and Co.
Batchelor, Peter. 1997. *People in rural development.* Rev. and enlarged ed. Carlisle, UK: Paternoster Press.
Bendor-Samuel, John, and Rhonda L. Hartell, eds. 1989. *The Niger-Congo languages: A classification and description of Africa's largest family.* Lanham, MD.: University Press of America.
Bickford, Anita C., and Rick Floyd. 2003. *Articulatory phonetics: Tools for analyzing the world's languages.* 3rd ed. Dallas: SIL International.
Bickford, Anita C., and Rick Floyd. 2006. *Articulatory phonetics: Tools for analyzing the world's languages.* 4th ed. Dallas: SIL International.
Blench, R. M. 1993. An outline classification of the Mambiloid languages. *Journal of West African Languages* 23:105–118.
Breeze, Mary. 1988. Phonological features of Gimira and Dizi. In Marianne Bechhaus-Gerst and Fritz Serzisko (eds.), *Cushitic-Omotic: Papers from the International Symposium on Cushitic and Omotic languages,* Cologne, January 6–9, 1986, 473–487. Hamburg: Helmut Buske Verlag.
Burquest, Donald A. 1998. *Phonological analysis: A functional approach.* 2nd ed. Dallas: SIL.
Canonge, Elliott D. 1957. Voiceless vowels in Comanche. *International Journal of American Linguistics* 23(2):63–67.
Cassidy, Frederic Gomes, and Joan Houston Hall, eds. 1985. *Dictionary of American regional English.* Vol. I: Intro. and A–C. Cambridge, Mass.: Harvard University Press.
Cassidy, Frederic Gomes, and Joan Houston Hall, eds. 1991. *Dictionary of American regional English.* Vol. II: D–H. Cambridge, Mass.: Harvard University Press.
Cassidy, Frederic Gomes, and Joan Houston Hall, eds. 1996. *Dictionary of American regional English.* Vol. III: I–O. Cambridge, Mass.: Harvard University Press.
Catford, John C. 1977. *Fundamental problems in phonetics.* Edinburgh: Edinburgh University Press.

Catford, John C. 1983. Pharyngeal and laryngeal sounds in Caucasian languages. In D. M. Bless and J. H. Abbs (eds.), *Vocal fold physiology: Contemporary research and clinical issues,* 344–350. San Diego: College Hill Press.

Catford, John C. 1988. *A practical introduction to phonetics.* New York: Oxford University Press.

Coleman, J. 1996. Syllabicity and syllabification in Tashlhiyt Berber. In J. Durand and B. Laks (eds.), *Current trends in phonology: Models and methods,* 1:175–216. Manchester: European Studies Research Unit, University of Salford.

Crystal, David. 2003. *A dictionary of linguistics and phonetics.* 5th ed. Oxford: Blackwell Publishers.

Denes, Peter B., and Elliot N. Pinson. 1993. *The speech chain: The physics and biology of spoken language.* 2nd ed. New York: W. H. Freeman and Company.

Dent, G. R., and C. L. S. Nyembezi. 1969. *Scholar's Zulu dictionary.* Pietermaritzburg: Shuter and Shooter.

Dixon, R. M. W. 1980. *The languages of Australia.* Cambridge: Cambridge University Press.

Dogil, Grzegorz. 1984. Grammatical prerequisites to the analysis of speech style: Fast/casual speech. In Dafydd Gibbon and Helmut Richter (eds.), *Intonation, accent and rhythm: Studies in discourse phonology,* 91–119. Berlin: Walter de Gruyter.

Dorian, Nancy C. 2001. Surprises in Sutherland: Linguistic variability amidst social uniformity. In Newman and Ratliff (eds.), 133–151.

Dubert, Raymond, and Marjorie Dubert. 1973. Biangai phonemes. In A. Healey (ed.), Phonologies of three languages of Papua New Guinea. *Workpapers in Papua New Guinea Languages* 2:5–35. Ukarumpa: Summer Institute of Linguistics.

Everett, Daniel L. 1982. Phonetic rarities in Piraha. *Journal of the International Phonetics Association* 12:94–96.

Everett, Daniel L. 2001. Monolingual field research. In Newman and Ratliff (eds.), 166–188.

Floyd, Rick, comp. 1981. *A manual for articulatory phonetics.* Dallas: Summer Institute of Linguistics.

Floyd, Rick, comp. 1986. *A manual for articulatory phonetics.* Revised ed. Dallas: Summer Institute of Linguistics.

Fromkin, Victoria A., ed. 1978 *Tone: A linguistic survey.* New York: Academic Press.

Gallman, Andrew Franklin. 1974. A reconstruction of Proto-Mansakan. M.A. thesis. University of Texas at Arlington.

Garbarino, Merwyn S. 1972. *Big Cypress: A changing Seminole community.* New York: Holt, Rinehart, and Winston.

Gieser, C. Richard. 1958. The phonemes of Kalinga. In A. Capell and S. Wurm (eds.), *Studies in Philippine linguistics.* Oceanic Linguistic Monographs 3:10–23. Sydney: University of Sydney.

Gopnik, Alison, Andrew N. Meltzoff, and Patricia K. Kuhl. 1999. *The scientist in the crib: What early learning tells us about the mind.* New York: Perennial.

Hall, Joan Houston, ed. 2002. *Dictionary of American regional English.* Vol. IV P–Sk. Cambridge, Mass.: Harvard University Press.

Harmon, Carol W. 1979. Proto-Manobo pronouns and case marking particles. In Andrew F. Gallman, E. Joe Allison, Carol W. Harmon, and Jeannette Witucki (eds.), *Papers in Philippine Linguistics* 10. Pacific Linguistics A55:113–133.

Hawkins, Peter. 1984. *Introducing phonology.* London: Hutchinson.

Hillenbrand, James, Larua A. Getty, Michael J. Clark, and Kimberlee Wheeler. 1995. Acoustic characteristics of American English vowels. *Journal of the Acoustical Society of America* 97:3099–3111.

Hoard, J. E. 1978. Syllabification in Northwest Indian languages, with remarks on the nature of syllabic stops and affricates. In Alan Bell and Joan B. Hooper (eds.), *Syllables and segments,* 59–72. Amsterdam: North-Holland.

Hombert, Jean-Marie. 1978. Consonant types, vowel quality, and tone. In Fromkin (ed.), 77–111.

House, Arthur S., and Kenneth N. Stevens. 1958. Estimation of formant band widths from measurements of transient response of the vocal tract. *Journal of Speech and Hearing Research* 1(4):309–315.

International Phonetic Association. 1999. *Handbook of the International Phonetic Association: A guide to the use of the International Phonetic Alphabet.* Cambridge: Cambridge University Press.

Jenewari, Charles E. W. 1989. Ijoid. In Bendor-Samuel and R. Hartell, 106–118.

Jones, Daniel. 1940. *An outline of English phonetics.* 6th ed. New York: E. P. Dutton & Co., Inc.

Kim, Mi-Ryoung, and San Duanmu. 2004. Tense and lax stops in Korean. *Journal of East Asian Linguistics* 13:59–104.

Kinkade, M. Dale. 1967. Uvular-pharyngeal resonants in Interior Salish. *International Journal of American Linguistics* 33:228–234.

Kotapish, Carl, and Sharon Kotapish. 1973. *Darai phonemic summary.* Kathmandu: Summer Institute of Linguistics and Institute of Nepal and Asian Studies.

Kutsch Lojenga, Constance. 1989. The secret behind vowelless syllables in Lendu. *Journal of African Languages and Linguistics* 11(2):115–126.

Kutsch Lojenga, Constance. 1994. *Ngiti: A Central-Sudanic language of Zaire.* Köln: Rüdiger Köppe Verlag.

Labov, William. 1970. *The study of non-standard English.* Champaign, Ill.: National Council of Teachers of English.

Ladefoged, Peter. 1957. Use of palatography. *Journal of Speech and Hearing Disorders* 22:764–774.

Ladefoged, Peter. 1993. *A course in phonetics.* 3rd ed. Fort Worth, TX: Harcourt Brace Jovanovich.

Ladefoged, Peter. 1997. Instrumental techniques for linguistic phonetic fieldwork. In W. Hardcastle and J. Laver, eds., The handbook of phonetic sciences, 137–166. Oxford: Blackwell Publishing.

Ladefoged, Peter. 2001. *A course in phonetics.* 4th ed. Fort Worth, TX: Harcourt Brace Jovanovich.

Ladefoged, Peter. 2003. *Phonetic data analysis: An introduction to fieldwork and instrumental techniques.* Malden. MA: Blackwell Publishing.

Ladefoged, Peter, and Ian Maddieson. 1996. *The sounds of the world's languages.* Oxford: Blackwell Publishing.

Lass, Roger. 1984. *Phonology: An introduction to basic concepts.* Cambridge: Cambridge University Press.

Laufer, Asher, and Iovanna D. Condax. 1979. The epiglottis as an articulator. *Journal of the International Phonetic Association* 9:50–56.

Laufer, Asher, and Iovanna D. Condax. 1981. The function of the epiglottis in speech. *Language and Speech* 24:39–61.

Laughlin, Robert M. 1975. *The great Tzotzil dictionary of San Lorenzo Zinacantan.* Washington, DC: Smithsonian Institution Press.

Laver, John. 1994. *Principles of phonetics.* Cambridge: Cambridge University Press.

Lee, Ernest Wilson. 1966. Proto-Chamic phonological word and vocabulary. Ph.D. dissertation, Indiana University.

Lehiste, Ilsa. 1959. *An acoustic-phonetic study of internal open juncture.* Ann Arbor: Speech Research Laboratory, University of Michigan.

Lehiste, Ilsa. 1970. *Suprasegmentals.* Cambridge, Mass.: The M.I.T. Press.

Levin, Theodore C., and Michael E. Edgerton. 1999. The throat singers of Tuva. *Scientific American* 281(3):80–87.

Lindau, Mona. 1979. The feature expanded. *Journal of Phonetics* 7(2):163–176.

Maddieson, Ian. 2001. *Phonetic fieldwork.* In Newman and Ratliff (eds.), 211–229.

Maranz, David. 2001. *African friends and money matters.* Dallas: SIL International.

McDavid, Raven, ed. 1980. *Linguistic atlas of the Middle and South Atlantic states.* Chicago: University of Chicago Press.

McKinney, Carol V. 2000. *Globe trotting in sandals: A field guide to cultural research.* Dallas: SIL International.

McKinney, Norris P. 1984. The fortis feature in Jju (Kaje): An initial study. *Studies in African Linguistics* 15:177–188.

McKinney, Norris P. 1990. Temporal characteristics of fortis stops and affricates in Tyap and Jju. *Journal of Phonetics* 18:255–266.

Merrifield, William R. 1963. Palantla Chinantec syllable types. *Anthropological Linguistics* 5(5):1–16.

Merrifield, William R., and Jerold A. Edmondson. 1999. Palantla Chinantec: Phonetic experiments on nasalization, stress, and tone. *International Journal of American Linguistics* 65:303–323.

Mugele, Robert L. 1982. Tone and ballistic syllables in Lalana Chinantec. Ph.D. dissertation, University of Texas at Austin.

Newman, Paul, and Martha Ratliff, eds. 2001. *Linguistic fieldwork.* Cambridge: Cambridge University Press.

Olson, Kenneth S., and Brian Schrag. 1997. An overview of Mono phonology. Paper presented at the Second Congress on African Linguistics, Leipzig, Germany, July 27 through August 3, 1997.

Olson, Kenneth S., and John Hajek. 1999. The phonetic status of the labial flap. *Journal of the International Phonetic Association* 29(2):101–114.

Olson, Kenneth S., and John Hajek. 2001. The geographic and genetic distribution of the labial flap. *Electronic Working Papers.* Dallas: SIL.

Olson, Kenneth S., and J. V. Mbomate. 2006. Ngbugu digital wordlist: Archival form. SIL-LCA-47050, SIL Language and Culture Archives, Dallas.

Persons, Jan A. 1997. High pitch as a mark of respect in Lachixío Zapotec. In Stephen A. Marlett (ed.), *Work Papers of the Summer Institute of Linguistics,* University of North Dakota Session 41.59–60.

Peterson, Gordon E., and H. L. Barney. 1952. Control methods used in a study of the vowels. *Journal of the Acoustical Society of America* 24(2):175–184.

Pike, Eunice V. 1963. *Dictation exercises in phonetics.* Santa Ana, Cal.: Summer Institute of Linguistics.

Pike, Eunice V. 1974. A multiple stress system versus a tone system. *International Journal of American Linguistics* 40:169–175.

Pike, Eunice V. 1981. *Ken Pike: Scholar and Christian.* Dallas: Summer Institute of Linguistics.

Pike, Kenneth L. 1942. *Pronunciation.* Vol. 1. An intensive course in English for Latin-American students. Ann Arbor: English Language Institute.

Pike, Kenneth L. 1943. *Phonetics: A critical analysis of phonetic theory and a technic for the practical description of sounds.* Ann Arbor: University of Michigan Press.

Pike, Kenneth L. 1948. *Tone languages.* Ann Arbor: University of Michigan Press.

Pike, Kenneth L., Gary F. Simons, Carol V. McKinney, and Donald A. Burquest. 1996. *The mystery of culture contacts, historical reconstruction, and text analysis: An emic approach.* Washington, DC; Georgetown University Press.

Sapir, Edward. 1921. *Language.* New York: Harcourt, Brace.

Schuh, Russell G. 1978. Tone rules. In Fromkin, 221–256.

Smalley, William A. 1989. *Manual of articulatory phonetics.* Rev. ed. South Pasadena, Cal.: William Carey Library.

Snider, Keith, and James Roberts. 2004. SIL Comparative African Word List (SILCAWL). *Journal of West African Languages* 31:73–122.

Stein, Jess, and P.Y. Su, eds. 1978. *The Random House dictionary.* New York: Ballantine Books.

Stucky, Alfred and Dellene Stucky. 1973. Nii phonology. In Alan Healey (ed.), *Phonologies of three languages of Papua New Guinea,* 37–78. Workpapers in Papua New Guinea Languages 2. Ukarumpa: SIL.

Tranel, Bernard. 1987. *The sounds of French: An introduction.* Cambridge: Cambridge University Press.

Trask, R. L. 1996. *A dictionary of phonetics and phonology.* London: Routledge.

Tucker, A. N. 1940. *The Eastern Sudanic languages,* 1. London: Oxford University Press.

Tucker, A. N., and M. A. Bryan. 1966. *Linguistic analyses: The non-Bantu languages of northeastern Africa.* Handbook of African languages series. London: International African Institute, Oxford University Press.

Urua, Eno. 1995. The status of contour tones in Ibibio. In Akınbıyı Akınlabı (ed.), *Theoretical approaches to African linguistics,* 329–343. Trenton, NY: Africa World Press, Inc.

Welmers, William E. 1973. *African language structures.* Berkeley: University of California Press.

West, John David. 1962. The phonology of Mikasuki. *Studies in Linguistics* 16:77–91.

Westermann, D., and I. C. Ward. 1933. *Practical phonetics for students of African languages.* London: Oxford University Press.

Wiens, Hartmut. 1976. Phonological features of Limos Kalinga, with comments on affected speech. *Philippine Journal of Linguistics.* 7:38–47.

Williamson, Kay. 1989. Niger-Congo overview. In Bendor-Samuel and Hartell (eds.), 3–45.

Wolfram, Walt, and Natalie Schilling-Estes. 1998. *American English: Dialects and variation.* Cambridge: Basil Blackwell.

Subject Index

A

accent, 42, 177, 184, 239
    how to aquire a good one, 53
accent mark
    acute, 24
accents, 178
acoustic parameters of speech sounds, 1
acoustic phonetics, 2, 193, 217, 239, 258, 259
active articulator, 13, 18, 19, 22, 47, 239, 241
advanced tongue root, 161, 162, 239, 270
affricate(s), 89, 91, 196
    breathy, 126
    central, 91
    ejective, 133, 246
    heterorganic, 91, 239, 249
    homorganic, 91, 239, 249
    lateral, 92, 253
air pressure, 7, 8, 47, 125, 137, 195, 216, 240, 262
air turbulence, 21, 195, 256
airflow, 8, 129, 174
    direction of, 17
airflow measurements, 211, 216
airstream, 7, 9
    direction of, 9, 10, 17, 227, 245
    egressive glottalic, 11, 133
    ingressive glottalic, 11, 133, 135
airstream mechanism, 9–11, 17, 22, 240
Ajami script, 4
allophones, 209, 240
alphabet,
    Greek, 4
alveolar, 13
alveolar click, 166
alveolar place of articulation, 14, 240
alveolar ridge, 12, 14, 240
Americanist Phonetic Alphabet (APA), 4, 223, 240
Americanist phonetic transcription, 172
Amharic script, 117, 265
anatomy
    laryngeal, 121
    of speech production, 7, 11
    of the vocal tract, 7
anticipatory coarticulation, 79, 240
aperiodic, 196
apical vowels, 117, 118, 240
approximant(s), 13, 83, 99, 158, 205
    central, 99, 100, 143, 242, 262
    epiglottal, 157
    interdental, 100, 101
    labial-palatal, 100
    labial-velar, 100
    lateral, 13, 83, 99, 253
    near open front unrounded, 101
    palatal, 100
    pharyngeal, 157
    rhotacized, 100, 262
    velar, 100
    velarized lateral, 113
articulation, xiii 2, 241
    manner of, xv, 9, 12, 17, 19, 196, 200, 254
    place of, xv 9, 13, 14, 18, 260
articulator(s), 13, 14, 241
    active, 13, 18, 19, 239
    active and passive, 13
    lower 13
    passive, 13, 18, 19, 241

tongue tip, 14
upper 13
articulatory gestures, 153, 241
articulatory phonetics, xiii, 2, 241, 259
aryepiglottic folds, 124, 125, 129, 161, 241
    trill, 124
arytenoid cartilages, 123, 241
aspirated
    glottal stops, 27, 29
    stops, 27, 28
    voiced, 27, 126
aspiration, 27, 203, 241
audible release, 141, 142
audio recordings, 214, 215

B

baby talk, 181
ballistic syllable, 174, 241
Benue-Congo comparative word list, 180, 210, 252
Bernoulli effect, 47, 125, 241
bilabial, 13
bilabial click, 166, 167
bone
    hyoid, 121, 250
bracketing, 43, 242
brackets, 22
breath phonation, 95, 124, 128, 242
breathy affricates, 126
breathy glottal fricative, 96, 242
breathy stops, 126
breathy voice, 96, 124–127, 130, 183, 242
breve, 88, 242
broad transcription, 91
burst, 30, 202–204

C

cardinal vowel system, 39
cardinal vowels
    secondary, 39, 242
carrier drills, 23
cartilage(s)
    arytenoid, 123, 241
    cricoid, 121, 122, 124, 244
    thyroid, 121, 123, 124, 266
cavity, 10
    nasal, 11, 12, 65, 70, 71, 255
    oral, 10–12, 65, 70, 257
    oropharyngeal, 70
    pharyngeal, 10, 11, 70, 258
central, 36, 37
central affricate, 91
central approximant, 99, 100, 143, 242, 262

citation form, 62, 179, 243
citation phrase, sentence, 60
classification of speech sounds, 1
clear l, 85, 113, 243
click, 165, 243
    alveolar, 166
    bilabial, 166, 167
    dental, 166
    lateral, 166
    nasal, 166
    palatal, 166
    voiced, 166, 269
    voiced nasal, 166, 269
    voiceless, 166
close juncture, 144, 251
close transition, 142, 243
closure, 8, 29, 243
    complete, 12
    incomplete, 12
    intermittent, 12, 251
    oral, 27
    slight, 13, 263
    velic, 11, 27, 268
closure phase
    stop, 30
cluster, 141, 142, 243
    consonant, 142, 143, 243
    vowel, 142, 143, 270
coarticulation, 79, 106, 152, 200, 243
coda, 243
    of consonants, 199
    phase, 14, 243, 256
cognates, 180, 243
colon, 87, 88
communicate goals
    of phonetic fieldwork, 211
complete closure, 12, 243
consonant, 12, 13, 197, 243
    bilabial, 201, 202
    cluster, 142, 143, 243
    coda, 199
    epiglottal, 157, 158
    fortis, 171, 172, 247
    fronted, 149, 152
    fronted postalveolar, 149, 150
    interdental, 100, 101, 152
    lenis, 171, 172, 253
    onset, 199
    retroflex, 149, 150, 151, 152
    unreleased, 141, 142, 268
constriction, 8
    complete, 12, 106
    slight, 12
continuant, 244

Subject Index

central resonant, 35
contoids, 35
controlled syllables, 174
creaky voice, 11, 124, 125, 127, 130, 183, 244, 252
creole, 179, 244
cricoid cartilage, 121, 122, 124, 244
cricothyroid muscle, 124, 244
cuneiform writing, 4
cycles, 195, 244
Cyrillic script, 4

D

Daniel Jones, 39
dark l, 85, 113, 244
declination, 56, 244
degrees of phonetic duration, 88
dental click, 165, 166
dental place of articulation, 14, 244
dental sounds 149
descender, 65, 244
de-stressing
    function words, 181
Devanagari script, 4
devoiced, 91
diacritic(s), 245
    aspiration, 27
    audible release of consonant, 142
    corner for no audible release of consonant, 142, 268
    extra short, 88, 242
    for fortis consonant, 172
    for postalveolar stops, 150
    for rhoticity, 118, 152
    stress, 24
    tie bar, 91, 106, 166
    tilde, 65, 125, 266
    tone, 61
    umlaut, 126
    underring, 128
    unreleased stop, 30
    voiceless vowel, 95, 101
    vowels, 42
    wedge, 125
diagrams (see *sagittal diagrams*)
dialects, 177–180, 213, 245
    differences, 177, 178, 180, 213
diaphragm, 7
differentiation drills, 23, 245
diphthongs, 40, 41, 143, 198
direct observation, 213, 216
direct palatography, 187, 188
double articulations, 105, 106, 245
double nasal, 105, 106, 245

double stop, 105, 106, 245
downstep, 61, 245
duration, 87, 89, 195, 245

E

egressive airstream, 11, 246
egressive glottalic airstream, 133
egressive pulmonic airstream, 133, 166
ejective(s), 133, 134, 136, 246
    affricate, 133, 246
    fricative, 133, 246
    stop, 133, 246
emic perspective, 218, 246
emic tone pattern, 60
endangered language, 209, 246
epiglottal, 157, 158
    fricative, 157, 158
    stop, 124, 158
epiglottis, 124, 125, 246
ethics in phonetic fieldwork, 211
ethnographic study, 178
etic tone pattern, 60
external intercostal muscles, 7
external open juncture, 144, 251

F

face diagrams, 17
false vocal folds, 121, 124, 125, 268
falsetto, 11, 127, 182
    whispery, 11, 130
falsetto voice, 11, 124, 127, 182, 246
faucal pillars, 70, 182, 246
faucalization, 182, 247
fiber-optic research, 211
fieldwork
    selecting a topic, 210
flap(s), 47, 48, 49, 101, 247
flat fricatives, 73, 83
formant(s), 36, 109, 194, 200, 247
    bar, 199, 201, 202, 247
    first, second, third, forth 198
    frequency, 194, 197, 198, 200, 247
fortis consonant(s), 171–175, 213, 247
    fortis-lenis consonant contrasts, 173, 180
    multiple phonetic features, 172
frame drills, 23
free jaw, 181
frequency, 11, 198, 247
fricative(s), xiii, 12, 21–24, 92, 93, 151, 196, 200, 203
    ejective, 133, 246
    epiglottal, 157, 158

flat, 73, 247
glottal, 96, 200, 248
grooved, 73, 247, 263
interdental, 22, 152, 178
lateral, 83, 253
palatal, 77–80, 158
pharyngeal, 157, 158
uvular, 77, 158
velar, 77, 158
voiced, 21, 23, 24
voiced glottal, 200
voiceless, 21, 77, 158, 203
voiceless epiglottal, 158
fricative vowels, 118
fronted consonants, 149, 150
fundamental frequency, 55, 182, 195, 196, 198, 248
funding, obtain the necessary, 211

G

gemination, 141, 144, 248
glide, 141, 143, 144, 248
vowel, 40, 143, 198, 248, 270
glottal consonants, 95, 96, 97
fricative, 96, 200, 248
stop, 4, 29, 31, 96, 97, 134, 135, 249
glottal fry, 125, 244
glottal pulse(s), 124, 125, 127, 193–196, 198, 200, 204, 248
glottalic airstream mechanism, 10, 249
glottalized sounds, 133
glottis, 8, 17, 96, 123, 133, 249
closed, 8, 133
open, 8
goals of phonetic field research, 209
grammatical tone, 59, 249
grooved fricatives, 73

H

habits, readjustment of, 184
half-long, 88, 89, 246, 249, 254, 262
handwritten script, 4
harsh voice, 11, 124, 127, 131, 249
heavy syllable, 53
heterorganic affricate, 91, 239
higher musical pitch 193
Hiragana script, 117
homorganic affricate, 91, 239
human subjects research, 187, 211, 249
palatography, 187
hyoid bone, 121, 250
hypernasality, 182, 250

hyponasality, 182, 250

I

ideophone, 3, 250
idiolect, 3, 250
idiophone, 3, 250
implosive(s), 133, 135–137, 250
voiced, 135, 136, 269
voiceless, 135, 137, 269
incomplete closure, 12
informed consent form, 188, 189, 216
ingressive airstream, 11, 250
glottalic airstream, 11, 133, 135, 136
velaric airstream, 11, 165–167, 250
initiator(s), 10, 15, 250
Institutional Review Board, 188, 211, 250
instrumental phonetics, 2, 250, 259
instrumentation
phonetic research, 216
insufflators 188
intensity, 197, 198, 250
interdental place of articulation, 14, 100, 251
sounds, 149
intermittent closure, 12
internal intercostal muscles, 7, 251
internal open juncture, 144, 251
International Phonetic Alphabet (IPA), 1, 4, 222, 251
Internet search of language and culture, 210
intonation, xiii, 55–58, 251

J

jaw position, 181
free jaw, 181
set jaw, 181
juncture
close, 144, 251
external open, 144, 251
internal open, 144, 251

L

labial flaps, 101, 251
labial-palatal approximants, 100
labial-palatalization, 109, 112, 252
labial-velar approximantes, 100
labial-velar stop, 106, 167
labial-velarization, 109, 112, 113, 251
labialization, 109, 110, 251
labiodental approximants, 100
labiodentalization, 112, 252
laminal, 65, 150, 252

Subject Index

language assistant, 212–216
language interference, 2, 3, 252
language learning, 1, 184, 209, 213, 214
    materials, 210, 215
language of wider communication, 1, 213, 252
languages, 1, 9
    of Indian subcontinent, 126
laptop computer, 214, 217, 218
laryngeal anatomy, 121
laryngealization, 125
laryngealized voice, 11
laryngoscope, 2, 121, 216, 253
    fiber-optic technology, 2, 121, 216
larynx, 7, 8, 9, 121, 123, 136, 137, 253
lateral(s), 12, 37, 83, 196, 253
    affricate, 92, 253
    approximant(s), 13, 83, 99, 253
    clear l, 85, 113, 243
    clicks, 166
    dark l, 85, 113, 244
    fricative, 83, 253
    handwritten, 84
    interdental, 152
    Spanish, 114
    velarized, 113
lax vowels, 162, 253
length, 87, 253
    extra short, 89, 246, 249, 254, 262
    half-long, 89, 246, 249, 254, 262
    long, 87, 89, 246, 249, 254, 262
length mark, 87, 88, 253
lenis consonants, 171–174, 253
lexical tone, 59, 253
light syllable, 53
limericks, 185
linguistic phonetics, 209, 254
linguistic research, 209, 211, 218
linguolabial place of articulation, 14, 254
lip position, 181, 254
lips, 19, 109, 110
listening, 184, 213
literature search, 210
locus for place of articulation, 199
lower articulators, 13, 254
lung cavity, 7, 8

M

Macquirer, 214
major languages, 210
manner(s) of articulation, 9, 12, 17, 19, 69–70, 196, 200, 205, 254
medial phase, 14, 141, 264
midsagittal section diagram, 17

mimic, 1, 184
mimicry, 4
modal phonation, 121, 124, 125, 254
modal voice, 124–127, 254
monolingual approach, 213, 254
monotone, 183, 255
mora, 52, 255
mora-timed language, 53, 255
mother tongue, 1, 255
multiple phonetic features, 172
murmur, 96, 126, 200, 242
muscle
    cricothyroid, 124, 244

N

name, technical, 22, 255
    affricates, 91, 92
    approximants, 100
    laterals, 84
    nasalized vowels, 69, 71
    nasals, 65
    phonation types, 124–130
    sibilants, 73
    stops, 28
    vowels, 36
        voiceless, 95
narrow pitch range, 183
narrow transcription, 91
nasal(s), 12, 65, 69, 196, 201
    click, 166
    interdental, 152
    plosion, 66, 255
    port, 11, 18, 65, 69, 166, 255
    stops, 12, 65, 255
nasalization, 69, 255
    hypernasality, 182, 250
    hyponasality, 182, 250
    vowels, 69–71, 255
near-open front unrounded approximants, 101
nil phonation, 95, 124, 128, 256
no audible release, 141, 142
noise, 8, 21, 196, 256
    ambient, 215
    aperiodic, 196
    fricative, 204
non-standard speech variant, 177
non-syllabic vowels, 99
nucleus, 14, 52, 256

O

obstruent, 37, 157, 256
offset phase, 14, 141, 256

one consonant articulation, 189, 204
onset
　of consonants, 199
　　phase of articulation, 14, 256
　　stops, 29
open syllable, 88, 257
open transition, 106, 142, 257
opening
　velic, 9, 11, 12, 69, 268
oral cavity, 10–12, 37, 257
oral sounds, 11
orthographic system, 218
orthography
　Jju, 218
　practical, 4, 22, 257
oscillograms, 197
overlapping phase of articulation, 14

P

palatal place of articulation, 77–79, 257
　approximates, 100
　click, 166
　fricative, 158
palatalization, 109, 110, 257
palatogram, 187–190, 257
palatography, xiv, 187, 190, 211, 216, 257
　direct, 187
　equipment and supplies, 188
　procedure, 188–190
partially obstructed, 12
participatory research, 218, 257
passive articulator, 13, 18, 19, 22, 258
perception of speech sounds, 1
pharyngeal place of articulation, 157, 158, 258
　fricative, 158
pharyngeal wall, 11, 18
pharyngealization, 109, 111, 157, 161, 258
pharynx, 8, 121, 157, 161, 258
phases of articulation, 14, 258
　coda, 14
　medial, 14
　nucleus, 14
　offset/release, 14
　overlapping, 14
　steady state, 14
phonation, 11, 121, 124–131, 211, 216, 258
　breath, 95, 124, 128, 242
　co-occurence of different types, 130
　nil, 95, 124, 128, 256
　types of, 11, 127–129, 183, 258
　voiced/modal, 121, 124, 125, 254, 269
　voiceless, 121, 124, 128, 269
　whisper, 124, 128, 270

phoneme(s), 22, 209, 258
phonetic feature(s), 7, 9, 15, 17, 35, 36, 251, 259
　single and multiple, 172
phonetic fieldwork, 1, 209, 210, 213, 214, 218
phonetic length, 87–89, 245
phonetic quality, 194
phonetic science, 1
phonetic transcription, 22, 60, 89, 113, 119, 142, 172, 196, 259
phonetics, 1, 259
　acoustic, xiii, xiv, 2, 193, 239
phonics, 1, 2, 89, 259
phonological transcriptions, 22
phonologically contrastive, 42
physiology of speech production, 1
pictographs, 4
pidgin, 179, 259
Pike, Eunice V. 62, 171
Pike, Kenneth, 2, 184
pitch, xiii, xiv, 11, 21, 55, 124, 143, 199, 259
　absolute, 55, 259
　accent, 63, 239, 259
　higher musical, 193
　modulation, 183, 260
　patterns, 178
　range, narrow and wide, 183
　register, 182, 260
　relative, 55, 259
place(s) of articulation, 9, 13, 18, 197, 201, 205, 260
　alveolar, 13, 14, 240
　bilabial, 13, 242
　dental, 14, 244
　epiglottal, 157, 158, 246
　interdental, 14, 251
　labiodental, 13, 252
　linguolabial, 14, 254
　palatal, 77, 79, 257
　pharyngeal, 157, 158, 258
　postalveolar, 13, 260
　retroflex, 48, 49, 118, 149–152, 205
　uvular, 77, 79, 268
　velar, 13, 77, 79, 268
plosives, 12, 30
point of articulation, 13, 260
PRAAT software, 214, 217
practical considerations for phonetic fieldwork, 217
practical orthography, 4, 22, 257
prenasalized stops, 119, 260
preparation for phonetic fieldwork, 210
preplosion of nasals, 117, 119
pressure transducers, 216
prevocalic and postvocalic laterals, 85
primary articulation, 109, 260

Subject Index

primary stress, 52
profile diagrams, 17
prominence, 51, 52, 117, 260
prosodic patterns, 209
proto-language, 179, 209, 213, 260
pulmonic air, 11, 17
pulmonic airstream mechanism, 10, 260
    egressive, 22, 133, 135, 166

Q

quality of a sound, 196
quality of a speech sound, 11, 261

R

rate of speech, 181, 261
regional differences in dialects, 177
release of consonants, 141, 142
    audible, 141, 142
    fricative, 91
release phase of articulation, 14
    stops, 29
remuneration, 212
repetitions of waveform, 195
representative data of speakers, 213
research
    affiliation, 211, 212
    associateship, 211
    goals, 209, 211, 212, 214, 218
    proposal, 211
    quantitative, xiii
    site for phonetic fieldwork, 212
resonances, 11, 194, 261
resonant, 37, 261
resonate, 11
respiratory muscles, 7
retracted advanced tongue root, 161, 162, 163
retroflex consonants, 149, 150, 151, 152
    alveolar, 149, 150
    postalveolar, 149, 150
retroflex sounds, 149–152, 261
retroflexion, 100, 152
    affect on vowels, 152, 261
rhotacized approximants, 100
rhotacized vowel, 118
rhoticity, 100, 149, 152, 262
rhyme, 52, 262
rhythm, 52, 53, 182, 262
    experiment in, 52
rhythm of stress placement, 52
ribs, 7
rime, 52, 262
Roman alphabet, 4

Rothenberg mask, 211, 216, 262

S

sagittal diagram, 17, 262
    airstream mechanism, 17
    alveolar consonants, 150
    clicks, 167
    dental consonants, 149, 150
    difference between stop and nasal, 66
    direction of the airstream, 17
    fricatives, 22, 28, 78
    fronted, 150, 151
    glottalic sounds, 134
    glottal stop, 29, 134
    implosives, 136
    limitations of, 19
    manner of articulation, 19
    nasal port, 11, 18
    pharyngeal, 112, 157
    placement of velum, 18
    place of articulation, 14, 18
    postalveolar consonants, 150, 151
    stops, 28, 29, 107, 111, 112, 134
    tongue positions, 35, 37
    vocal folds, 17
script
    Ajami, 4
    Amharic, 4, 117
    Devanagari, 4
    Hiragana, 117
secondary articulation, 109, 262
    labialization, 109, 110, 251
    labial-palatalization 109, 112, 252
    labial-velarization 109, 112, 251
    labiodentalization, 109, 112, 252
    palatalization, 109, 110, 257
    pharyngealization, 109, 111, 258
    velarization, 109, 111, 268
secondary stress, 52
segments, phonetic, 141
Seminole, 181, 183
semivowels, 99–101, 143
set jaw, 181, 262
sibilant(s), 73, 74, 83, 84, 151, 198, 203, 204, 263
    postalveolar, 74, 109
    voiced alveolar, 74, 204
    voiceless, 74, 195, 203
signal analysis, xiii
SIL phonetics curriculum, xiii
single phonetic feature, 172
slight constriction, 12
slurring, 43, 263
social norms, 210

sociolinguistic factors, 178
sociolinguistic study, 178
sociophonetics, 177, 178, 263
soft palate, 9, 11, 268
sonorants, 65, 125, 263
    voiced, 118
sonority, 117, 263
sound distribution, 180
sounds,
    dental, 149
    fronted, 149, 248
    interdental, 149
    nasal, 12
    nasalized, 12
    oral, 11, 257
    retroflex, 149, 150, 261
sound-symbol concept, 4, 263
sound units, 22
sound waveform, 194
sound waves, 7, 11, 12, 193, 194, 263
southern American English, 41, 66, 180
spectrogram(s), 193, 195–198, 199–205, 215, 264
speech analyzer program, 194, 197, 214, 217
speech styles, 177, 181
speech variant(s), 177–184, 264
    non-standard, 177
    standard, 177, 264
speech wave, 127, 194
    spectrum, 197, 264
spinal column, 7
spirants, 21, 247, 264
steady state phase, 14, 29, 264
sternum, 7, 264
stiff voice, 125, 264
stop, xiii, 12, 27, 78, 79, 196, 202, 203, 264
    aspirated, 27, 28, 216
    breathy, 126
    double articulation, 99, 106, 107, 245
    ejective, 133, 246
    English, 27, 28
    glottal, 27, 29, 249
    labial-velar, 167
    prenasalized, 119, 260
    release, 29, 30, 241, 261, 264
    retroflex, 150
    Spanish, 27
    unaspirated, 27, 28, 267
    unreleased, 30
    voiced, 27, 126, 135
    voiceless, 27, 135
stress, 51, 52, 265
    primary, 52
    secondary, 52
    tertiary, 52

stress diacritic, 24
stressed syllables, 24, 51, 52, 265
stress mark, 32, 51, 265
stress-timed language, 52, 265
subglottal pressure, 204, 265
supralaryngeal cavity, 11, 130, 253, 265
Swadesh word list, 210
syllabic, 35, 85, 265
    consonants, 117, 118, 265
    fricatives, 118
    nasals, 66, 118
    sonorants, 118
    writing systems, 4
syllabicity mark, 117, 265
syllable(s), 117, 118, 265
    ballistic, 171, 174, 175, 241
    coda, 40, 117, 243, 266
    controlled, 171, 174, 175
    nucleus, 35, 40, 117, 256, 266
    onset, 40, 117, 266
    open, 88
syllable break, 143, 266
syllable-timed language, 52, 266
syllable timing, 182

T

tap(s), 47, 48, 266
target language, 213
tense vowels, 162, 266
tertiary stress, 52
test word for palatography, 189
throat, 11
thyroid cartilage, 121, 123, 124, 266
tie bar, 91, 106, 166
tilde, 65, 125, 266
timetable for research goals, 212
timing in languages, 52, 53
    mora-timed, 53
    stress-timed, 52, 182
    syllable-timed, 52, 182
tone, xiii, 55, 59, 267
    contour, 58, 60, 244, 267
    downstep, 61, 245
    glide, 60, 144, 248, 267
    level, 58, 60
    lexical, 59, 60, 253
    notation, 61
    register, 60, 261
    sandhi, 60, 267
    upstep, 61, 268
tongue, 9, 267
    position, 181, 267
    root, 124, 161, 267

tip, 12, 13, 14
trachea, 8, 121, 122, 267
trade language, 1, 252
transcription of sounds, 1, 2, 4
    broad, 91
    narrow, 91
transglottal pressure, 124, 267
transition, 14, 141, 197, 199, 204, 257, 267
    close, 142, 243
    open, 142, 257
trill(s), 12, 47, 267
true vocal folds, 121, 125, 268

U

unaspirated stops, 27, 28
underring diacritic, 128, 267
unglided vowel, 40, 143, 198, 248
unreleased consonant, 142, 268
unreleased stop, 30
upper articulators, 13, 268
upstep, 61, 268
uvula, 182, 268
uvular place of articulation, 77, 268
    fricative, 158

V

velar, 13
velar approximants, 100
velar fricative, 158
velar place of articulation, 77, 268
velaric airstream, 10
    ingressive, 165, 167, 250
velaric airstream mechanism, 10, 268
velarization, 109, 111, 268
    lateral approximant, 113
velic closure and opening, 11, 268
velum, 9, 11, 17, 18, 268
ventricular folds, 121, 124, 125, 127, 268
verbal consent, 211
vibration(s), 9, 11, 268
    air particles, 193
    audible, 9
vocal cords (see *vocal folds*)
vocal folds, 8, 11, 123, 268
    false, 121, 124, 125, 268
    rate of vibration, 124
    state of, 9, 11, 17, 264
    true, 121, 125, 268
vocal fry, 125, 244
vocal tract, 7, 10, 11, 21, 193, 194, 269
vocal tract shapes, 36
vocoids, 35

voice
    breathy, 96, 124–127, 130, 183, 242
    creaky, 11, 124, 125, 127, 130, 183, 244
    falsetto, 11, 124, 127, 182, 246
    harsh, 11, 124, 127, 131, 249
    laryngealized, 11
    modal, 124–127, 254
    tense, 124, 125, 244, 249
    whispery creaky, 130
    whispery creaky falsetto, 11, 130
voice bar, 198, 269
voice onset time, 196, 269
voice qualities, contrastive, 124, 130
voice register, 56, 269
voiced sound(s), 8, 11, 124, 269
    aspirated, 126
    click, 166, 269
    epiglottal fricative, 158
    implosives, 135, 269
    nasal click, 166, 269
    pharyngeal fricative, 157
    stop, 27, 28, 30, 31, 78, 79, 126, 135
voiceless sounds, 11, 269
    implosives, 135, 269
    pharyngeal fricative, 157
    stops, 27, 28, 31, 128, 135, 150
    vowel, 95, 269
volume, 183, 269
vowel(s), 12, 35–43, 270
    apical, 117, 118, 240
    articulatory features, 35
    back, 36
    central, 36
    central, oral, resonant, 37
    cluster, 142, 143, 243, 270
    formant frequencies, 198
    front, 36, 248
    function in syllables, 40
    glide, 40, 198, 248, 270
    harmony, 163, 270
    most common, 40
    nasalized, 69, 255
    non-syllabic, 99, 262
    quality, 35, 36, 40, 180, 270
    reduction, 179, 270
    rounded, 36, 42
    space, 36, 270
    system, 180
    unglided, 40, 198, 248
    unrounded, 36, 42, 264
    voiceless, 95, 269
    whispered, 95, 270

W

waveform, 194, 196, 270
wedge, 48, 87, 125, 242
wepa, 22, 270
whisper, 158, 183
whisper phonation, 11, 124, 128, 270
whispered vowel, 95, 270
whispery creaky falsetto, 11, 130
whispery creaky voice, 130
whispery falsetto, 130
word list
    Benue-Congo comparative, 180, 210
    Swadesh, 210
writing system, 1, 4, 22, 174

Language Index

A

Afro-Asiatic languages, 118
Aguacatec, 138
Akan, 163
Akyem, 163
Amharic, 4, 50, 90, 114, 117, 139, 265
Arabic, 4, 124, 157, 159, 163, 246, 258, 265
Athabaskan, 36, 216
Atyap, 218
Australian, 67, 180, 215

B

Bai, 130
Bajju, 2, 166, 183, 210, 218
Balti, 86
Bantu, 101, 118, 166, 243, 252
Benue-Congo comparative word list, 180, 210, 252
Biangai, 75
Bongii, 120
Bor Dinka, 130
British, 177–180, 185, 261

C

Cantonese, 62
Chatino, 62
Cheyenne, 96, 128
Chinantec, 174, 175, 216, 241
    Lalana, 174
Chinook, 142, 146
Cockney English, 177

Columbian, 157, 159
Comanche, 89, 96, 98
Cuicatec, 97

D

Dahalo, 154
Darai, 154
Dinka, 127, 130, 162, 163
    Bor, 130
Dowayo, 3
Dutch, Rotterdam dialect, 80

E

Ejagham, 63
English, 3, 12, 21, 23, 27, 28, 114, 265
    American, 41, 100, 178, 180, 181, 199, 253, 266
    American dialects of, 178, 180
    Australian, 180
    British, 177–180, 185
    Cockney, 177
    midwestern American, 36, 198
    New Zealand, 180
    Scottish, 180
    southern American, 41, 66, 180
    Special, 179
Estonian, 88
Ewe, 67, 70, 154

F

Fasu, 62

Finnish, 253
Foi, 25, 103
French, 12, 27, 44, 45, 52, 74, 103, 149, 243, 266
    Belgian, 90
Fulani, 127, 182

G

Gaelic, 212
German, 44
Germanic languages, 52, 267
Gimira, 150, 154
Gogodala, 145
Gumuz, Southern, 114
Gunwinggu, 67

H

Hausa, 125, 139, 144, 183
Highland Mazatec, 63
Hyam, 127

I

Ibibio, 63, 120
Igbo, 60, 139, 163
Ijaw, 163
Isoko, 154
Italian, 144, 243

J

Japanese, 4, 53, 63, 118, 255, 259
Jju, 2, 40, 49, 60, 74, 87–89, 91, 93, 100, 103, 105, 108, 114, 119, 120, 143, 172, 173, 175, 180, 182, 183, 210, 218, 240

K

Kagayanen, 104
Kalinga, 104
Kamasau, 25, 115, 237
Kashinawa, 72
Kele, 119
Khoisan languages, 3, 166, 243
Kickapoo, 145
Kikiyu, 67
Kiowa, 28, 93, 138
Koasati, 88, 89, 253
Komo, 136
Korean, 4, 174, 175, 216
Kru, 164
Kwa languages, 163
Kwanyama, 67

L

Lalana Chinantec, 174
Lango, 131
Lao, 44, 146
Lendu, 119

M

Maasai, 127
Majang, 67, 139
Malayalam, 154
Mandarin Chinese, 60, 253
Mazatec, 130
Mende, 25, 67
midwestern American English, 36
Mikasuki, 183, 184
Mixe, 183
Mixtec, 2, 3, 49
Mixteco, 71, 72
Mono, 103

N

Nambikwara, 215
Nangere, 139
Native American Athabaskan languages, 216
Navajo, 90
New Zealand English, 180
Ngiti, 119, 120
Niger-Congo languages, 163
Nigerian English, 178
Nii, 114
Nilotic languages, 127
Nootka, 157, 179
Northern Totonac, 93
Norwegian, 45, 90
Nuer, 127

O

Oaxaca Chontal, 145

P

Paez, 98
Palantla Chinantec, 70, 174
Pame, 97, 124
Pashto, 25, 32
Pitjantjatjara, 68
Popoluca, 62

Language Index

Q

Quiche, 80

R

Roglai, 136, 143
Rumanian, 57, 62
Russian, 4, 113, 114, 265

S

Salish languages, 118
Scottish English, 180
Seminole, 181, 183
Shilluk, 131
Shipibo, 45
Shona
    Zezuru dialect of, 101, 106
Shoshone, 98
Sino-Tibetan languages, 118
Somali, 124, 130
southern American English, 41, 66, 180
Spanish, 23, 25, 27, 28, 31, 49, 52, 57, 85, 114, 149, 181, 182, 243, 266
Special English, 179
Sudanese languages, 124
Sudanic languages, 118

T

Tabasco Chontal, 138

Thai, 59, 60, 62, 265
Tlingit, 138
Tojolobal, 138
Totonac,
    Northern, 93
Trique, 60, 64
Tsonga, 68
Twi, 163
Tyap, 86, 90, 94, 180
Tzotzil, 29, 103

V

Vietnamese, 105, 106

X

Xhosa, 129, 166, 168, 243
Xiŋkuna, 68

Y

Yala, 163
Yi, 124
Yoruba, 183, 266

Z

Zambali, 145
Zapotec, 130, 182
Zulu, 86, 166, 168, 169, 243
Zuñi, 88

www.ingramcontent.com/pod-product-compliance
Lightning Source LLC
Chambersburg PA
CBHW081801300426
44116CB00014B/2202